Ritual Voices of Revelation

THE ORIGIN NARRATIVES OF THE ROTENESE OF EASTERN INDONESIA

Ritual Voices of Revelation

THE ORIGIN NARRATIVES OF THE ROTENESE OF EASTERN INDONESIA

James J. Fox

Australian
National
University

ANU PRESS

Australian
National
University

ANU PRESS

Published by ANU Press
The Australian National University
Canberra ACT 2600, Australia
Email: anupress@anu.edu.au

Available to download for free at press.anu.edu.au

ISBN (print): 9781760466572
ISBN (online): 9781760466589

WorldCat (print): 1452127770
WorldCat (online): 1452124638

DOI: 10.22459/RVR.2024

Cover design and layout by ANU Press. Cover photograph: 'The Poet, Esau Pono (2013)'.

This book is published under the aegis of the Summations editorial board of ANU Press.

Contents

1. Introduction   1

2. The metaphoric creation of a complementary world   29

3. Background and exegesis of the origin narratives of Termanu   63

4. The origin narratives of Termanu   75

Recitation 1. The origin of fire, of cooking and of the implements for living
Petrus Malesi

Recitation 2. The origin of fire, of cooking and of the implements for living
Lisbeth Adulilo

Recitation 3. The origin of cooking and of the marriage with the Sea
Eli Pellondou

Recitation 4. The origin of fire, of cooking and of the implements for living
Esau Markus Pono

Recitation 5. The origin of fire, of cooking and of the implements for living,
and the sadness of the axe and adze
Ayub Amalo and Stefanus Adulanu (Old Meno)

Recitation 6. The origin of red millet
Ayub Amalo

Recitation 7. The origin and spread of rice and millet
Stefanus Adulanu and Petrus Malesi

Recitation 8. The origin of weaving and dyeing and the spread of cloth patterns
Stefanus Adulanu

Recitation 9. The origin of the nautilus shell for indigo dye and the baler shell
for resting the spindle
Stefanus Adulanu

5. Background and exegesis on the origin narratives of Thie   169

6. The origin narratives of Thie   181

Recitation 1. The origin of fire, of cooking and of the implements for living
N.D. Pah and Samuel Ndun

Recitation 2. The origin of the house and its roofing
N.D. Pah

Recitation 3. The origin of the first ancestral house, at Do Lasi and Ledo Mbena
N.D. Pah and Samuel Ndun

Recitation 4. The war between the Heavens and the Sea and its consequences
N.D. Pah and Samuel Ndun

Recitation 5. The origin of rice and millet and of their celebration
N.D. Pah

Recitation 6. The origin of the grains and seeds and of their celebration
Jonas Mooy

Recitation 7. The origin of the celebration at Nasi Dano
N.D. Pah

7. Christian narratives of origin   247
Genesis: Dae Ina Dadadi
Yulius Iu

Dae Ina a Dadadi Masosana
Anderias Ruy

Appendix I: A portrait gallery of poets   297

Appendix II: The idea of topogeny and its use in the origin
narratives of the Rotenese   321

Bibliography   333

Index   343

1

Introduction

Introductory comments

Among the Rotenese of eastern Indonesia, certain recitations were of profound spiritual significance. The most important of these recitations were origin narratives that recounted primeval relations between the realm of the Sun and Moon and the realm of the Sea. Until recently, these chants were restricted and could only be recounted in a ritual setting.

The origin narratives in this volume come from two long-established domains on the island of Rote in eastern Indonesia: the domain of Termanu and the domain of Thie[1]—both small communities whose populations shared related ideas about a spiritual world concerned with primeval relations between the Heavens and of the Sea. Presenting these narratives here in an ordered fashion with commentary provides a glimpse of that world of ancestral ideas that were once celebrated but have now passed away. This volume is intended as a tribute to that world, preserving for future generations the possibilities for consideration and contemplation of a sphere of once powerful spiritual significance.

Preserving the oral narratives of a tiny island of marginal significance may appear to be an effort of little value. Viewed, however, within the context in which I wish to present these tales, they are of major significance. The forms of composition used by the poets of Rote go back to the origins of oral

---

1   I have chosen to use the historical name for the domain of 'Thie'—the name originally recorded in Dutch records in the mid-seventeenth century and retained for most of the domain's history. Thie, along with Termanu, was recognised by the Dutch East India Company between 1653 and 1662 as one of an original group of 12 domains on the island of Rote. For historical background and comparison of these two domains, see Fox (1971a, 1979a).

poetry. They speak to the first poetry recorded from Sumer and to an enormous array of oral poetry from around the world. Understanding the composition of the oral narratives from Rote sheds light on the creativity of compositions that underlie some of the greatest works of world literature. As expressions of creative imagination, they can take their place within this canon of the world's poetry.

***

I gathered many of these oral narratives—especially those in their most extended form—during my first fieldwork on the island in 1965–66. Gathering the full array of these recitations, transcribing, translating and then trying to understand them, has been an effort of more than 50 years.

The oral poets who recited these chants for me intended that they be transmitted to subsequent generations but in a ritually restricted and respectful manner. For this reason, I have hesitated for decades to make them widely available. At a gathering with some eight master poets from Rote in October 2011, I discussed the issue of how I might best make these sacred recitations public. It was the unanimous opinion of all the poet-chanters that now was the time to do so. Hence, I set to work to prepare this collection for publication.

***

This study records several ritual voices whose collective import constitutes the equivalent for the Rotenese of an 'oral scripture'. Whereas the idea of a scripture emphasises the preservation of spiritual ideas through a written text, this volume can be considered as a rendering of ideas of the sacred through recognised recitation, the authority, stability and continuing coherence of which are preserved by fixed linguistic conventions. Many of the world's scriptures began, similarly, as oral revelations and many of these were couched in a form like those of the Rotenese. It is this form of oral preservation and presentation that I examine in this book. The language of many such similar recitations has served as the oral prelude to the scripting of spiritual ideas.

All the Rotenese oral recitations in this book are composed in a strict canonical parallelism that requires the pairing of terms: all nouns, verbs, adjectives and adverbial elements. Originally, these chants were restricted and could only be spoken in a ritual setting. Improper recitation—mistakes in the wording of a chant, deviations or misrepresentations in the narrative—was believed to provoke serious consequences.

Although I recorded these chants as separate recitations, these narratives are related to one another and together hint at an ancestral epic—an epic that recounts relations between the Sun and the Moon and their heavenly descendants and the rulers of the Ocean and Sea, identified as Shark and Crocodile. The common meeting place for these great lords was the flat Earth with its pointed rocks. Their primal deeds set the pattern for the humans who came to dwell there.

Each of these narratives explains how a vital feature of Rotenese life came into being. These narratives include several recitations that recount the Sun and Moon's discovery of the wealth of the Sea. These initial recitations focus on the origin of cooking and the origin of the house and its construction, but they also recount the establishment of relations between the realms of the Sun and Moon and the Lords of the Sea. Subsequent narratives from Termanu relate the origins of rice and millet, the origin of the process of weaving and dyeing, including the patterning of traditional cloth, the origin of the container for indigo and the base used for spinning cloth— all ultimately gifts from the Sea.

The origin narratives of Thie, like those of Termanu, recount a related array of events linking the realm of the Sun and the Moon with the realm of the Sea. This includes the origins of planting but also other narratives that were of celebratory significance in Thie.

None of these ritual narratives is entirely intelligible without appropriate commentary and exegesis. In some of these narratives, their most important element is hinted at but purposely unstated. It is essential, therefore, to present more than just the texts themselves.

Underlying all these narratives is the fundamental idea that the knowledge of origins is empowering. This knowledge was once celebrated as an essential guide to action in the present.

The idea of an 'oral scripture' and of a 'scriptural voice'

The pairing of words and the composition of phrasing that occur in Rotenese-origin narratives are a means of expression common to oral traditions among diverse populations around the world. This pairing is consistent and systematic, and compositions tend to be formulaic. This 'ritual voice' is a form of heightened speech intended to enhance the significance of the message it conveys. This ritual voice in its highest register can also be referred to as a 'scriptural voice' and as such is a feature of numerous and varied religious traditions. This scriptural voice is many-faceted; its liturgical scope may encompass a diverse range of utterances. It can be revelatory, admonitory, directive, performative or extensively narrative but its utterances are intentionally elevated for spiritual effect. A key vehicle for this scriptural voice across a great variety of religious traditions is a pervasive semantic parallelism. It is the dominant feature of the Rotenese narratives in this volume.

The term 'parallelism' was originally used to describe the compositional structures of parts of the Old Testament. Thus, in 1753, in lectures delivered at the University of Oxford, the esteemed Professor of Hebrew Poetry Bishop Robert Lowth noted that

> the poetic conformation of the sentences, which has been so often alluded to as characteristic of the Hebrew poetry, consists chiefly in a certain equality, resemblance, or parallelism between the members of each period; so that in two lines (or members of the same period) things for the most part shall answer to things, and words, to words, as if fitted to each other by a kind of rule or measure.

> (1829: 157)

Later in his 'Preliminary Dissertation' on a new translation of *Isaiah*, he described this arrangement of sacred compositions as *parallelismus membrorum*:

> The correspondence of one verse or line with another, I call parallelism. When a proposition is delivered, and a second is subjoined to it, or drawn under it, equivalent, or contrasted with it in sense, or similar to it in the form of grammatical construction, these I call parallel lines; and the words or phrases, answering one to another in the corresponding lines, parallel terms.

> (Lowth 1834: IX)

Lowth described the voice conveyed by the parallelism that he had identified as a 'prophetic' one. Since Lowth's time, similar usages have been identified in numerous contexts in a great variety of writings as well as among an even greater variety of oral traditions. Far more than simple correspondences are involved in such compositions. Where the ordering of words and phrases becomes stricter and such compulsory strictures are elevated to a canon, these forms of parallelism, as the Russian linguist Roman Jakobson (1966: 399) has argued, can be considered as 'canonical parallelism' or, more aptly, as 'semantic parallelism'. Based on the rigorous culturally defined pairings of specific terms, all Rotenese origin narratives constitute a form of semantic parallelism.

Traditions of composition in parallelism have been developed and elaborated across a range of diverse cultures: from the earliest ritual poetry of Sumer through a scribal continuity of transmission over centuries across other languages in the Middle East, but just as distinctively in the Chinese and Mongolian traditions as well those of the Uralic languages, in numerous diverse South-East Asian languages including the Austronesian traditions of island South-East Asia and extensively, as well, in the Americas, most notably among the Incas, Aztecs and Mayan languages. *Explorations in Semantic Parallelism* (Fox 2014: 19–90) provides an extensive survey of the now substantial literature on the varieties of these forms of parallelism, particularly the use of elevated forms of canonical parallelism, in both the oral and the written traditions around the world.[2]

---

2   Because parallelism occurs in so many diverse oral traditions and has repeatedly been 'rediscovered' and often separately studied in different 'literary' traditions, its comparative study is beset with a plethora of terminology that can be confusing, contradictory or ambiguous. Depending on the analyst, pairs in parallel expressions may be designated as 'couplets', 'doublets', 'binaries', 'binominals', 'polarities', 'polar extremes', 'complementary pairs' or 'formal oppositions'. To take one example, however, a 'couplet' may refer to a pair of words and thus constitute a 'semantic couplet' or it may refer to the pairing of successive parallel verses. The pairing of terms may be regarded as evidence of 'semantic' or 'lexical' parallelism, yet when such pairs occur in a particular morphological context, these pairs may as often be taken as evidence of syntactic parallelism. My focus is on semantic parallelism. Lowth initiated a certain train of analysis that distinguished between 'synonymous parallelism', 'antithetic parallelism' and 'synthetic or constructive parallelism'. Many subsequent analysts have followed Lowth in sorting pairs in a similar vein but precisely what is achieved by this sorting process is not clear. In an early and important study of Nahuatl parallelism, Ángela Maria Garibay (1953) coined the term *difrasismos* for what Lowth would have classified as 'synthetic' or 'constructive' parallelism: pairs whose combined terms have a wider metaphorical meaning. This expression and, more importantly, the focus on such pairings as emblematic of the traditions of Aztec and Maya parallelism have tended to overshadow other forms of parallelism, which form part of the poet's compositional repertoire. It is, in my view, misleading to concentrate attention on specific sorts of pairings instead of considering the full repertoire of all such pairings. For my analysis of Rotenese parallelism, I have used the label 'dyadic set' to refer to all pairs that can be formally represented by the notation (a, b). This use of this designation and notation allows the possibility of a formal representation of all Rotenese parallel compositions. It also allows the possibility of 'triadic sets', which occur in some traditions of parallelism, as is the case among the Maya. The key to understanding the processes of oral composition is a recognition that any semantic term or element 'a' can form a set not just with 'b' but also with 'c' and possibly other elements, 'd', 'e' and so forth. This opens the study of any tradition of parallelism to a formal network analysis in which certain semantic elements possess wider crucial linkages than others, many of which may have only a single linkage. In Fox (2014), I have discussed this theoretical approach (pp. 149 ff.) and illustrated this partial network for Rotenese (pp. 381–83).

Mesopotamian sources of parallelism

The Hebrew traditions for which Lowth coined the term parallelism were part of an older and more widespread Mesopotamian tradition that can be traced back to the earliest period of written records: those of Sumer, which date back some 5,000 years.

Samuel Noah Kramer, in his *From the Poetry of Sumer* (1979), has provided a glimpse of this extraordinary poetry—some of the world's earliest poetic compositions. A creation passage of great beauty occurs as a prologue to the myth of the hero Gilgamesh, which Kramer translates as follows:

> In primeval days, in distant primeval days.
> In primeval nights, in far-off primeval nights,
> In primeval years, in distant primeval years—
> In ancient days, when everything vital had been brought into existence,
> In ancient days, when everything vital had been nurtured,
> When bread had been tasted in the shires of the land
> When bread had been baked in the ovens of the land—
> When heaven had been moved away from the earth,
> When earth had been separated from heaven,
> When the name of man had been fixed—
> When An had carried off heaven,
> When Enlil had carried off earth …
>
> (Kramer 1979: 23)

This prologue, which goes on to recount the deeds of the gods and the planting of the *huluppu* tree on the banks of the Euphrates River, is composed in a strict and balanced parallelism. Although Kramer makes no mention in this work of the parallelism that he so carefully translates, he and other researchers have commented on and examined this pervasive use of parallelism in many other studies.

In his book *Reading Sumerian Poetry*, Jeremy Black discusses the 'technical features' of this Sumerian poetry in a way that paraphrases Lowth:

> This includes parallelism of word patterning within the individual line of verse or between pairs of lines; grouping of lines into pairs, or groups of three or four on the basis of meaning, structure or sound; assonance and alliteration; and rhyme.
>
> (1998: 8)

A short selection of illustrative lines from a cuneiform text (from the *Electronic Corpus of Sumerian Literature*) in praise of the god Enlil in his shrine in the settlement of Nibru gives a further illustration of the rich forms of parallelism in this poetry.[3]

In this text, Enlil is Father and Great Mountain; E-kur is his shining temple and lofty shrine; it is a dais of abundance and a mountain of abundance; it rises from the soil and grows on pure land; its festivals are celebrated with fat and cream; its presence brings joy and abundance:

> In the city, the holy settlement of Enlil,
> In Nibru, the beloved shrine of Father Great Mountain,
> He has made the dais of abundance,
> The E-kur, the shining temple, rise from the soil.
> He has made it grow on pure land as high as a towering mountain.
> Its prince, the Great Mountain,
> Father Enlil has taken his seat on the dais of the E-kur, the lofty shrine ...
> In the festivals, there is plenty of fat and cream.
> They are full of abundance.
> Its divine plans bring joy and rejoicing ...
>
> (Dahl 1997–2006: t.4.05.1)

Even in translation, this Sumerian fragment pours forth a profusion of recognisable pairs including godly names and titles identified in named locations. Pairing in these verses is as specific as it is general. It is in the detailed examination of extended poetic lines that the full extent of composition based on pervasive parallelism becomes apparent.

Rotenese comparisons

For comparison, it is instructive to consider the initial 10 lines of the first version of the Rotenese origin narrative to gain an idea of the semantic pairing features of this parallelism. This passage reads as follows:

1.	*Boe ma ala soku Mandeti Ledo*	They set off, Mandeti Ledo
2.	*Ma lali Patola Bulan.*	And they go forth, Patola Bulan.
3.	*De ala fu-toleu asu*	They whistle for their dog

---

3   This text, like most such texts, has gaps. For this reason, I have selected passages from different stanzas to highlight the recurrence of pairing.

4.	*Ma ala kati-kofio busa*	And they call for their hound
5.	*Busa nade Pia Dola*	The hound named Pia Dola
6.	*Ma asu nade Hua Lae.*	And the dog named Hua Lae.
7.	*Ala sopu lai basa dae*	They hunt through all the land
8.	*Ala fule [lai] basa oe.*	They stalk through all the water.
9.	*Leu Ledo lasi nana-papadak*	They go to the Sun's forbidden forest
10.	*Ma Bulan nula nana-babatak.*	And the Moon's restricted wood.

This passage introduces the sons of the Sun and Moon, whose paired double names are Mandeti Ledo//Patola Bulan. These names highlight a fundamental feature of Rotenese parallel expression and one of the challenging aspects of the translation of Rotenese parallel verse. The doubling of names, particularly of persons, can render these chant characters as either singular or plural persons. In this passage, as indicated by the pronoun *ala* ('they'), the sons of the Sun and Moon are presented in the plural. In other recitations of this same origin narrative and often in Rotenese exegesis on these narratives, Mandeti Ledo//Patola Bulan can be treated as the single son of the Sun and Moon. This feature is pervasive, and some poets purposely play on this potential difference by pairing singular and plural pronouns in contrastive lines. To maintain sense in English, consistency is essential. Hence the plural form, which is used most frequently in these origin narratives, has been adopted for the sake of translation.

In this passage, the first lexical elements, Mandeti//Patola, of these paired double names form personal identifiers while the second elements, Ledo// Bulan, are genealogical identifiers indicating direct ancestry from the Sun (*Ledo*) and the Moon (*Bulan*). All personal names and all placenames in this oral tradition are paired and, in the case of placenames, these names often have a complex duality. Trees, animals and most other living creatures are also paired. In this passage, for example, Mandeti Ledo//Patola Bulan's hunting dog has the double name Pia Dola//Hua Lae.

This passage of 10 lines is composed of 10 paired terms: 'dyadic sets'[4] whose required pairings accord with the culturally accepted rules of composition.

---

4   I use both 'pair' and 'dyadic set' in my discussion of Rotenese parallel verse. I use the expression 'dyadic set' as a more precise expression than 'pair'. I also use the term 'element' for each culturally recognised lexical term within such sets. Underlying the pairing expressed in parallel verse is a more complex semantic patterning because lexical elements may form multiple sets. The resulting interrelation of lexical elements produces a complex network of semantic relations (see Fox 2014: 379–83).

There are three paired verbs, one of which is a complex verb:

> *lali*//*soku*: 'go forth'//'set off'
> *fu-toleu*//*kati-kofio*: 'whistle'//'call'
> *fule*//*sopu*: 'stalk'//'hunt'

There are also three paired nouns:

> *asu*//*busa*: 'dog'//'hound'
> *dae*//*oe*: 'land'//'water'
> *lasi*//*nula*: 'forest'//'wood'

In addition, there is a dyadic set, which can be either a noun or a verb. In this passage, it functions in partially reduplicated form as a modifier:

> *bata*//*pada*: 'forbidden'//'restricted'

The remaining terms are invariant elements: sentence/statement makers *boe ma*, *de* and the connective *ma* ('and') plus the plural third-person pronoun *ala* ('they'). The term *nade* ('named') is here an invariant term, although in other contexts *nade* forms a dyadic set with *tamok* ('genealogical name'//'ancestral name').

The only recurrent set is Ledo//Bulan, which appears in lines 1 and 2 in the names of the two hunters and again in lines 9 and 10 in reference to the forbidden forest where they first hunt.

Given the ordered structure of these lines, it is possible—as it is possible with any such lines—to set out the formal arrangement of pairs. Most verse lines have either two or three lexical elements that pair with other such elements in another line. (This poetry also allows for internal pairing within lines.) Using a simple notation for sets but not for invariant elements, this formulaic ordering for the initial 10 lines of the first Rotenese oral narrative is as follows:

> a1 b1 c1
> a2 b2 c2
> d1 e1
> d2 e2
> e2 g1 f1
> e1 g2 f2
> h1i1
> h2i2
> c1j1k1
> c2j2k2

Comparison of the initial lines of the first version of the origin narratives with the initial lines of the second version offers an idea of the canonical similarity that characterises these recitations. The recitation of this second version was recorded from a different poet at a different time. Significantly, this passage follows a singular format.

The passage begins with a common formulaic opening and proceeds to introduce the son of the Sun and Moon, Patola Bulan//Mandeti Ledo, who is hunting pig and civet. It introduces his hunting dog but gives the dog a different double name to that in the first version. In the next two lines, it explains the meaning of these double names, which are a verb play on the Rotenese words for assistance (*doi*//*so'u*) and for carrying (*lepa*//*la'e*):[5]

1.	*Neu faik esa manunin*	On one certain day
2.	*Ma ledo dua mateben-na*	And at a particular time
3.	*Boe ma touk Patola Bulan*	The man Patola Bulan
4.	*Ma ta'ek Mandeti Ledo*	And the boy Mandeti Ledo
5.	*Neu sopu bafi ndondolo*	Wander about hunting pig
6.	*Ma ana fule kue lolota.*	And roam about stalking civet cat.
7.	*Asu nade Lepa La'e*	The dog named Lepa La'e
8.	*Ma busa nade Doi Sou,*	And the hound named Doi So'u,
9.	*Doi-la so'u ao*	Mutual aid in balancing a burden
10.	*Ma lepa-la la'e ao …*	And mutual support in carrying a load …

Although these 10 lines present a slightly different rendering from the 10 lines of the first version, the essential import is similar. Although the names of the hunting dogs in the two versions are not the same, this is not a significant difference. Names are often the subject of contention in the oral narratives. Since many persons and most places have multiple names, the citation of a different name for the 'same' hunting dog raises little concern.

There are four paired verbs in these lines, one of which is used adverbially in semi-reduplicated form:

---

5   Patola Bulan//Mandeti Ledo's dog's name, Lepa La'e//Doi So'u, is of special significance, which lines 9 and 10 make explicit. Both *lepa* and *doi* are carrying sticks: a *lepa* is used to support a balanced burden at both ends; a *doi* supports a burden at just one end. These words may be used as nouns that describe the object or verbs that describe the act of carrying (*la'e*) or lifting (*so'u*). Their pair is an illustrative instance of the specificity involved in the cultural pairing of terms.

fule//sopu: 'hunt'//'stalk'
lota//ndolo: 'wander'//'roam'
doi//lepa: 'aid'//'support'
la'e//so'u: 'lift'//'carry'

There are also five paired nouns:

esa//dua: 'one'//'two'
fai//ledo: 'day'//'sun'
ta'e//tou: 'boy'//'man'
kue//bafi: 'civet cat'//'pig'
asu//busa: 'dog'//'hound'

The invariant terms are the singular third-person pronoun *ana* ('he'), which appears only once, in line 6; the term *nade* ('name'), which functions as a verb; and the reflexive term *ao*.

In addition to the names Patola Bulan//Mandeti Ledo, this second set of 10 lines shares two dyadic sets—*fule//sopu* and *asu//busa*—with the set of 10 lines of the first version. As both versions of this narrative proceed, this sharing increases steadily, creating an elevated discourse of recurrent pairs.

This discourse lends these recitations a formal stability like that of a scriptural text. Although each recitation may differ, the constituent elements of its discourse—the canonical pairs of which it is composed—remain consistent and stable.

The continuity of canonical pairing

One of the characteristics of an 'oral' scripture is the continuity of its authoritative word—a continuity of stable pairing that extends over generations and marks traditions of canonical pairing. In the case of the succession of societies in the Middle East from Sumer onwards, this continuity was enhanced and perpetuated by scribal traditions of writing but was also firmly founded on a common poetic tradition of composition. While emphasis has been given to the similarity in the transmission of certain narratives, the historical continuity of this authority, based on the semantics of canonical pairing, has been given less attention.

One focus of scholarly attention has drawn on the comparison of 'parallels' between Hebrew and Ugaritic, both of which share a large repertoire of formal pairs. The discovery in 1928–29 at Ras Shamra in Syria of a hoard of cuneiform tablets opened the possibilities of comparison of the Ugaritic and Hebrew scriptural traditions (and, by extension, that of the older Akkadian tradition). This discovery led to an explosion of notable scholarship that carried forward the work of Lowth.[6]

Ginsberg (1935) was the first to call attention to what he described as 'certain fixed pairs of synonyms that recur repeatedly in the same order'. Following Ginsberg, Stanley Gevirtz, in his *Patterns in the Early Poetry of Israel* (1963: 8), examined these 'conventionally fixed pairs of words' to argue for 'a traditional poetic diction common to Syro-Palestinian literatures'. At the time, Gevirtz could point to just 'sixty-odd pairs of fixed parallels' shared between the two poetic traditions, but Michel Dahood's (1974, 1975, 1981) research over many years has extended this number to at least 450 such compositional pairs. This evidence would further indicate a continuity in formal poetic diction that extended, in some form, back to early Akkadian.

In *The Ugaritic Texts and the Origins of West-Semitic Literary Composition* (2012), Dennis Pardee has described this common shared tradition as one based on parallelism as 'the basic structural device for the poets working in those traditions'. Defining this poetry as 'the highest literary register in these two languages', he has examined in detail 'how parallelism functions to provide structure, meaning and a sense of compositional well-being' (Pardee 2012: 80). Although more narrative in its compositions than in the Hebrew tradition, Ugaritic possesses a similar authoritative scriptural voice. Pardee quotes, as one among numerous examples of this common poetic diction, the several lines of a Ugaritic parallel text that shares a similar idiom with Hebrew texts that emphasise the thunderous voice of Yahweh:

> He opens a window in the house
> A latticed window in the palace
> Ba'lu [himself] opens up the rift in the clouds
> His holy voice Ba'lu gives forth repeatedly
> Repeatedly utters, does Ba'lu, the outpouring of his lips
> His holy voice causes the earth to tremble,
> At the outpouring of his lips, the mountains take fright.

(Pardee 2012: 94)

---

6   References to a portion of this substantial scholarship—which includes the work of an array of Biblical scholars including Albright, Cross, Dahood, Driver, Gevirtz, Gordon and others—can be found in D.N. Freedman's (1972) 'Prolegomenon' to the reprinted edition of G.B. Gray's *The Forms of Hebrew Poetry*. References to later scholarship can be found in several studies devoted predominantly to an examination of parallelism (Gevirtz 1963; Geller 1979; Kugel 1981; Berlin 2008).

In Pardee's view, the scriptural voice expressed in Hebrew (as in Ugaritic) is fundamentally a poetic voice: '[T]he oldest Hebrew data on the prophets reveal these persons to have been poets in the fullest sense of the term, not so much prophets who knew something about poetry as poets who happened to be prophets' and whose literary production has been preserved in the Hebrew Bible (2012: 123).

Mesoamerican parallelism: The Maya

Shifting to another religious tradition provides a further perspective on the authority and continuity that canonical parallelism accords to the scriptural voice. The Mayan and Nahuatl languages of Mesoamerica possess traditions of parallelism as elaborate and as pervasive as those of Mesopotamia and these poetic traditions continue to the present. Extensive ethnographic documentation of the living traditions of this poetry combined with a renewed and concerted effort in translating texts of the colonial period and the notable achievement in the decipherment of ancient Maya glyphs have produced an enormous body of scholarship on the uses of this parallelism.[7]

As Kerry Hull, a researcher who has worked across the full range of Maya genres, has eloquently and amply argued:

> The preferred vehicle for literary expression among all Maya languages is paralleled discourse. Quite simply, parallelism defines poetic or ornate discourse in the minds of the Maya themselves. Within its seemly strict confines, the Maya are able to elaborate profoundly

---

7   The range of research on Mesoamerican parallelism is as copious and as various as that on Mesopotamian parallelism (for an extended discussion of these traditions of parallelism, see Fox 2014: 60–69). A useful starting point would be Miguel Leon-Portilla's *Pre-Columbian Literature of Mexico* (1969) or the more accessible anthology *In the Language of Kings* (2002) by Leon-Portilla and Earl Shorris. There exist various translations of colonial Maya texts: Munro Edmonson's translation in verse of *The Book of Counsel: The Popol Vuh of the Quiche Maya of Guatemala* (1971) and Dennis Tedlock's *Popol Vuh: The Mayan Book of the Dawn of Life* (1996); see also Tedlock's *Rabinal Achi: A Mayan Drama of War and Sacrifice* (2003) and Edmonson's *Heaven Born Merida and its Destiny: The Book of Chilam Balam of Chumayel* (2008). Gary Gossen's *Chamulas in the World of the Sun* (1974a) gives a glimpse of the range of Maya parallelism in a contemporary context, as do numerous ethnographies of modern-day Maya communities. Among these monographs, Evon Vogt's *Zinacantan: A Maya Community in the Highlands of Chiapas* (1969) is a classic of its kind, as is the earlier monograph by Robert Redfield and Alfonso Villa-Rojas, *Chan Kom: A Maya Village* (1934). The most valuable single compendium on Maya parallelism is *Parallel Worlds: Genre, Discourse, and Poetics in Contemporary, Colonial, and Classic Maya Literature* (2012), edited by Kerry M. Hull and Michael Carrasco, a collection of 18 papers devoted to some aspect and/or period of Maya parallelism. Michael Coe's *Breaking the Maya Code* (1992) is an engaging account of the long historical effort that eventually resulted in understanding and interpreting Maya glyphs.

complex cultural knowledge by means of associative connections …
[I]n modern Maya languages a general adage applies: the more formal
the discourse, the more parallel structures appear. In fact, in the case
of Maya there is an unequivocal link between the frequency and the
formality of the discourse … It is undoubtedly on ritual and other
formal speech occasions where the full flowering of parallel structures
can be found among the Maya … Both knowing which word
combinations are acceptable and understanding the metaphorical
extensions that often accompany such groupings are crucial elements
in one's communicative competence in many Maya societies.

(Hull and Carrasco 2012: 74–75)

A feature of this diversity of traditions of parallelism is the continuity of
its canonical pairings. The decipherment of Mayan glyphs has provided
a glimpse of a wide range of ancient pairs.[8] Hull, who has studied these
pairings across compositions of different periods, notes that 'many of
the lexical pairings we find in colonial and modern Maya literature can
be traced back to classical periods. In most cases such couplets represent
intimate cultural understandings, which explains their longevity' (Hull and
Carrasco 2012: 77). He refers to this use of canonical pairing as 'poetic
tenacity'—'a strong continuity and preservation of meaning over more than
a millennium' (Hull and Carrasco 2012: 7).

As evidence of this poetic tenacity, Hull has listed a range of shared pairs
that occur in the glyphic inscriptions, colonial manuscripts and numerous
contemporary ritual settings among different Mayan languages. For each of
these pairs, he illustrates its various usages including its glyph representations.
A list of the pairs that Hull has selected and labelled 'diaphrastic kennings'
are the following: 1) sky//earth, 2) sky//cave, 3) well//spring, 4) land//
well, 5) wind/air//water/rain, 6) male//female, 7) day//year, 8) day//night,
9) stone//wood, 10) flint//shield, 11) bread//water, 12) green//yellow,
13) god//lord, and 14) throne//mat.[9]

An illustration of the occurrence of the first of these pairs, sky//earth,
in different periods follows.

---

8   In fact, the linguist Floyd Lounsbury's (1980) recognition of couplet glyphs in the Temple of the
Cross at Palenque provided early critical insights into the process of decipherment.
9   While some of these pairs may be considered as semantically universal or general categories, others
are more particularistic (see Edmonson 1973). Significantly from my theoretical perspective, this small
selection contains pairs such as sky//earth and sky//cave whose elements form more than just one dyadic
set, making them likely major nodes clearly productive of a range of possible dyadic sets. This would
place this illustrative group at the core of a semantic network (see Fox 2014: 379 ff.).

Mayan glyphic occurrences

The following use of the pair sky//earth is inscribed on the Tikal Stela 3:

> 8,000 are the Gods of Sky
> Gods of Earth.

Similarly, this same pair is found on a bench in the southern subterranean building of the Palenque Palace:

> Passing in the sky
> Passing on the earth.

Colonial manuscript occurrences

This pair occurs in the two key colonial manuscripts of the Quiché (K'iche') Maya, the *Rabinal Achí* and the *Popol Vuh*.

In the *Rabinal Achí*, it is the single most frequent pair to occur. One such example is:

> On the face of the sky
> On the face of the earth.

In the *Popol Vuh*, an example of this pair is:

> The four corners of the sky
> The four corners of the earth.

Contemporary occurrences

Two Yucatecan Maya examples of the use of this pair in different contexts are:

> Burned was the sky
> Burned was the earth
> In the caves of the sky
> In the caves of the earth.

(Hull and Carrasco 2012: 80–81)

The *Rabinal Achí* ('Man of Rabinal') is a remarkable Mayan text that spans centuries. It is a dramatic enactment of events dating to an era of fierce struggle before the invasion of the Spanish, the Mayan-language 'script' of which was composed in the colonial period and eventually recorded by the notable parish priest of Rabinal, Charles Étienne Brasseur de Bourbourg, who also succeeded in preserving the *Popol Vuh*, another Mayan masterpiece. The Maya script has been transmitted to the local Quiché population of Rabinal in the highlands of Guatemala, who have rendered its dialogue into a costumed performance known as the *Xajoj Tun* ('Dance of the Trumpets'), which is performed each January before the feast of St Sebastian and in the following week in commemoration of St Paul, the patron saint of Rabinal. A superb English translation of the Mayan text of the *Rabinal Achí* has been done by Dennis Tedlock (2003).

An excerpt from this translation of the first speech of the Man of Rabinal, who addresses his prisoner, Cawek of the Forest People, highlights the strict parallelism of an altering discourse and the repeated invocation of Sky and Earth:

> Is that what your words say
> in the hearing of Sky
> in the hearing of Earth?
> You delivered them
> in range of my weapon
> in range of my shield
> and my upraised ax blade
> and my snail-shell bracelet
> my armband
> my white paint
> my gourd of tobacco
> and my strength
> and my manhood
> So whether you see it coming
> or it happens without warning
> I shall catch you
> with my henequen rope
> my henequen cord
> So say my words
> before Sky
> before Earth.
> May Sky and Earth be with you
> brave man
> prisoner, captive ...

(Tedlock 2003: 27–28)

Parallelism within the Chinese sphere: The Zhuang

Parallelism is a prominent feature in the earliest of Chinese recorded documents such as the *Book of Changes* (*I Ching*) and has a long history of subsequent elaboration within the Chinese tradition. In his 1830 disquisition, 'On the Poetry of the Chinese', John Francis Davis was one of the first literary scholars to draw on the insights of Robert Lowth and to point out the 'striking coincidence' of parallelism in the construction of Chinese verse. He argued that the key features of this verse—'the exact equality in the number of words, which form each line of a poetic couplet, and the almost total absence of recurring participles'—endow Chinese, like 'no other language', with a capacity for the elaboration of parallelism (Davis 1830: 417). Davis argued that, for the Chinese, this parallelism 'pervades their poetry universally, forms its chief characteristic feature, and is the source of a great deal of its artificial poetry' (1830: 415).[10] A host of subsequent scholars have extended Davis's observations.[11]

Complementary pairing, combined with the poetic juxtaposition of antithetic pairs, has been directed, to great effect, in the Daoist scriptures to highlight the paradoxes of being and, thus, create a powerful scriptural

---

10 Davis also called attention to the importance of parallelism as a form of decoration: 'The Chinese are so fond of their parallelisms, that the most common decorations of rooms, halls and temples, are ornamental labels hung opposite to each other, or side by side … These are sometimes inscribed on coloured paper, sometimes carved on wood, and distinguished by painting and gilding—but always in pairs' (1830: 418).

11 As with other major traditions of parallelism, the study of Chinese parallelism has produced an enormous and varied body of scholarship, the diversity of which is notable. Gustaaf Schlegel (1896) elevated parallelism to a 'law' of the syntax of Chinese poetry. Marcel Granet (1932) speculated that parallelism was a direct reflection of ancient Chinese society and its division of the world into the categories of yin and yang. Like Granet, Jabłoński (1935) emphasised the popular bases of this poetry. Similarly inspired by Granet, Tchang Tcheng-Ming (1937) wrote an extended treatise on parallelism in the *Book of Odes* (*Shih Ching*). In a series of short papers issued from the Berkeley Workshop on Asiatic Philology, Boodberg (1954–55a, 1954–55b, 1954–55c) commented on the 'stereoscopic' effect of Chinese parallelism. Following from Tchang Tcheng-Ming but relying on the work of Boodberg, Jakobson, Lowth and Schlegel, David Liu (1983) also examined both syntactic and semantic parallelism in the *Book of Odes*. Like Davis, he argued that 'a strict law of syntactical parallelism helps to define the grammatical function of the graphs' (Liu 1983: 640). Within this same tradition of commentary, Léon Vandermeersch (1989) has argued that parallelism is central to the origins of the ancient utterances based on turtle scapulary divination. More specifically, James R. Hightower (1959) has written on the *fu* style of the Han Dynasty that continued to the early T'ang as a form of erudite poetry with its multiple degrees of ornate elaboration. Roman Jakobson (1969) has also examined the 'modular' structure of such Chinese regulated verse. For a more detailed discussion of this commentary on Chinese parallelism and on the elaboration of parallelism in the Tibetan tradition, see Fox (2014: 22–24, 55–57).

voice. The opening lines of the *Yuandao*, the Chinese treatise on the Dao that forms a crucial component of the *Huainanzi*, an early Han Dynasty compendium of knowledge written in about 139 BCE, presents the Dao as the 'oneness of all things':

> It [the Dao] shelters the heavens and supports the earth
> Extends beyond the four points of the compass
> And opens up the eight points of the compass.
> It is high beyond reach
> And deep beyond reckoning
> It envelops the cosmos
> And gives to the yet formless.
> Flowing from its source it becomes a gushing spring
> What was empty slowly becomes full;
> First turbid and then surging forward,
> What was murky slowly becomes clear.

(Lau and Ames 1998: 1)

The antiquity of Chinese parallelism and its long history have had profound religious and intellectual influences on cultural traditions within China and among neighbouring populations. The Chinese script's detachment from any vernacular creates a separation of oral and writing forms of parallelism that is particularly pertinent to usages that continue to this day among the Zhuang of south-western China.

The Zhuang are a Tai-speaking population of some 16 million living in the western reaches of Guanxi province. They are an officially recognised minority (*minzu*), the largest such national minority in China. They are closely related linguistically to the Bouyei of Guizhou—a separately recognised minority with whom they share cultural traditions. They are also linguistically related to the Nùng, Thổ and Tày minorities of northern Vietnam. Given their long presence in the region and considerable cultural and linguistic diversity, their designation as Zhuang serves as an umbrella term for most of these Tai-speaking groups.

For centuries, the Zhuang have relied on a modified Chinese script to record their language and to preserve their traditions, including their own distinctive religious traditions. David Holm has been documenting these religious traditions by translating manuscripts used by vernacular priests in the performance of their rituals. These ancient manuscripts are passed down the generations through individual priestly lines.

The first of Holm's monumental studies,[12] *Killing a Buffalo for the Ancestors* (2003), which offers critical insights into the origins of Tai in southern China, examines an origin narrative used in rituals involving buffalo sacrifice. The narrative recounts a succession of creations and orderings of the world, leading to the first buffalo sacrifice to atone for primordial incest and to assure prosperity, culminating in the attainment of longevity rice. Notably the text of this narrative and its sung and chanted recitation, directed to an invited assembly of gods and spirits, are conducted in a pervasive parallelism. Following the invitation to attend, the recitation begins at the verge of creation and, after hundreds of lines, concludes with the prospect of longevity, progeny and plenty:

> In the beginning the world was suddenly dark and suddenly light
> All at once it was suddenly heaven and suddenly earth
> No one yet knew of night nor evening
> They knew not of short or long
> They knew neither crosswise nor straight ...
> Everyone eats this grain and will enjoy longevity
> Everyone eats this grain and will have many progeny
> At that time the folk had enough to eat everywhere
> Everyone under the sky had enough to eat everywhere
> This was the time of King Shennong of the time primordial
> Shennong of the time of yore.
>
> (Holm 2003: 108, 132)

Many of the ancient Zhuang manuscripts that record these recitations are of considerable, but uncertain, age and they often exist in tatters. The priests use them to guide their oral recitations and, as Holm notes, they can and do substitute their own terms for those of the written script. The tradition thus persists at two levels: as an oral tradition among priests and as a written tradition that dates back centuries. Holm's close, masterful examination of text and recitation illuminates this interrelation between script and performative.

As Holm has noted:

> Many of the scriptures recited by Zhuang vernacular priests also circulated as orally transmitted 'ancient songs' ... 'Ancient songs' were often many times the length of corresponding written texts,

---

12   Other major studies are *Recalling Lost Souls: The Baeu Rodo Scriptures, Tai Cosmogonic Texts from Guangxi in South China* (Holm 2004) and *Hanvueng: The Goose King and the Ancestral King—An Epic from Guangxi in Southern China* (Holm and Meng 2015).

and were regarded as sacred ... The words of the 'ancient song' were regarded as the 'words of the ancestors', in local parlance, and a premium was placed on accurate transmission of the entire song.

(Holm 2017: 377–78)

More importantly, Holm has highlighted how the oral and written transmission processes differ. Vernacular priests generally come from families with existing priestly traditions, and they begin their learning early. An aspiring priest, however, will apprentice himself to a master priest from whom he learns a set of performed oral recitations. On or before ordination, the apprentice is offered some of his master's ritual manuscripts to be carefully copied. This possession of manuscripts elevates the status of a vernacular priest in relation to Buddhist and Taoist priests, who rely on prestigious Chinese texts. These reference manuscripts, often obtained late in life, are not, however, the main basis of what a new priest has learned to recite. Oral transmission in the learning process takes precedence over the scripted word.

South-East Asian parallelism: Eastern Indonesian traditions

Holm's research offers a bridge to the traditions of South-East Asian parallel poetry. Many of these continue to this day as oral traditions. Taken together, they constitute by far the most diverse of the world's traditions of parallel poetry. The languages of four major families—Sino-Tibetan, Tai-Kadai, Austro-Asiatic and Austronesian—are found, often locally interspersed, in mainland South-East Asia while Austronesian languages extend into island South-East Asia and the Pacific. The Austronesian languages of eastern Indonesia in particular have some of the world's most elaborate oral traditions of pervasive parallelism.[13]

---

13   As a region of considerable linguistic and cultural diversity, South-East Asia, including island South-East Asia, has a remarkable diversity of traditions of parallelism. Summary discussions of some of the main references to these traditions can be found in Fox (2014: 23–24, 54, 92–94; 1988). Within the tradition of Tai parallelism, it is pertinent to cite *Hanvueng: The Goose King and the Ancestral King—An Epic from Guangxi in Southern China* (Holm and Meng 2015), which is a monument of critical scholarship directed to the detailed examination of a single long 'liturgical scripture' in pervasive parallelism (for a separate discussion of this work, see Holm 2017). In addition to an English translation, this study includes an interlinear transcription of the five-syllable verse structure of the text that sets out the modified Zhuang Chinese script of the text and matches it to the transcription of this script into standard Zhuangwen and its spoken priestly interpretation. This interlinear transcription is further provided with more than 1,500 textual and ethnographic notes. (Several Tai-Ahom texts, recorded in an Old Mon/Burmese script, that have been transcribed, edited and translated by B.J. Terwiel and Ranoo Wichasin [1992] provide a distant comparison. These texts from Assam are rich with pairs, but their parallel structure is not as consistent as those of the Zhuang.)

To Speak in Pairs (Fox 1988b) is a collection of 10 ethnographically focused studies of these living traditions from the islands of Sulawesi, Flores, Sumba, Rote and Timor. The scriptural voice in each of these traditions, expressed in oral compositions with strict pairing, is distinct and emphatic. This is a voice enunciated in a great variety of different ceremonial settings.

In an essay on 'Etiquette in Kodi Spirit Communication', Janet Hoskins cites a variety of ordered poetic forms required in addressing and inviting the participation of deities and spirits in divination ceremonies in the west Sumba domain of Kodi. The diviner directs a spear to the head pillar in the right corner of the house and begins his recitation with a general invitation to the spirit community and then to the double-gendered deity in the house pillar:

> So that you now—
> Great Mother, Great Father
> Who travels down the sacred corner,
> Who braces her/himself on the holy beam,
> Who gives girl children and boy children,
> Who gives thick rice sheaves and heavy ears of corn,
> Who gives us plentiful chicken and abundant pigs,
> Whose pillar reaches to the heavens
> And stretches down to the earth …

(Hoskins 1988: 36–37)

Another major deity to be addressed is the Elder Spirit (*Marapu Matuya*) resident in the rock and tree altar at the centre of the ancestral village:

> So that now, you
> Elder Mother, Ancient Father
> Who leads us out in the daytime,
> Who brings us out in the night-time,
> In the sewn-up circle of rocks,
> Among the heaped stone foundations,
> The sacred mat of pandanus leaves
> The holy ring of *mboro* leaves,
> Who oversees us from afar,
> Who watches over us from above …

(Hoskins 1988: 38)

The souls of dead founders of the clan village are also addressed in a long litany that begins as follows:

> Souls of grandparents, souls of forebears
> Souls of mothers, souls of fathers
> Who first dug the house foundation pillars
> Who formed the first even surface of stones ...

(Hoskins 1988: 39)

Another instance of this scriptural voice in strict parallelism comes from the creation myth of the Ata Tana 'Ai of central-eastern Flores. In a paper, 'A Quest for the Source', E. Douglas Lewis has provided the creation and origin chant of Sukun Ipir Wai Brama, the personal narrative of Mo'an Robertus Rapa Ipir Rai Brama, the Clan Lord of Ipir and Source Lord of the Domain of Tana Wai Brama. This 'earth-diver' creation myth involves multiple processes of creation after the first lump of earth is taken from the sea to form the land. A second descent requires the creation of a path from the centre of the Earth to the heavens above:

> Descend downward breaking the rock,
> Descend downward breaking the trees.
> The coral stone could be broken,
> The trees could be parted,
> Descend down to where dark[ness] is,
> Get to the place where blackness is found,
> Sit below on the protruding stone and the final reach,
> Lean at the cliff at the centre of the earth,
> Below the land was obstructed and dark,
> The earth below was tight and constricted
> Order the crab to open a path with its dorsal spines
> To chisel upward through the stone,
> Command the snail to show the path
> To bore upward through the earth ...
> Chisel, chisel upward
> Bore, bore upward
> Until the cord of heaven and earth is reached
> Until the hanging cord is reached ...

(Lewis 1988a: 265–66)

As different as these two recitations are, their expression reflects a common oral tradition that insists on the semantic pairing as its highest register of address and spiritual narration. As such, this similarity in pairing of elements creates metaphoric worlds that resemble each other.

Understanding Rotenese parallelism in its linguistic context

Eastern Indonesia is a large region with considerable linguistic and cultural diversity. Yet, comparisons among its traditions of parallelism are evident. In comparative perspective, Rotenese shares many of the same canonical pairs in its ritual language with other ritual languages in the region. This share of common canonical pairs increase considerably among the languages most closely related to Rotenese—those of the Meto-speaking and Tetun-speaking populations of Timor. A list of 20 such canonical pairs gives some idea of this sharing:

	Canonical pair	Rotenese	Tetun	Meto
1.	sun//moon	*ledo//bulan*	*loro//fulan*	*manse//ffunan*
2.	rock//tree	*batu//ai*	*fatu//ai*	*fatu//hau*
3.	trunk//root	*hu//oka*	*hun//abut*	*uf//baaf*
4.	areca//betel	*pua//manus*	*bua//fuik*	*puah//manus*
5.	seven//eight	*hitu//walu*	*hitu//walu*	*hitu//faon*
6.	eight//nine	*walu//sio*	*walu//sio*	*faon//siwi*
7.	pestle//mortar	*alu//nesu*	*alu//nesung*	*alu//esu*
8.	shame//fear	*mae//tau*	*moe//tauk*	*mae//mtaus*
9.	banana//sugar cane	*huni//tefu*	*hudi//tohu*	*uki//tefu*
10.	tuber//tales	*ufi//talas*	*fehuk//talas*	*laku//nali*
11.	lung//liver	*ba//ate*	*afak//aten*	*ansao//ate*
12.	thigh//navel	*pu//puse*	*kelen//hussar*	*pusun//usan*
13.	turtle//dugong	*kea//lui*	*kea//lenuk*	*ke//kunfui*
14.	friarbird//parrot	*koa//nggia*	*kawa//birus*	*kol ao//kit neno*
15.	orphan//widow	*ana-ma//* *falu-ing*	*oa kiak//balu*	*anmanat//* *ban-banu*
16.	*dedap//kelumpang*	*delas//nitas*	*dik//nitas*	*ensa//nitas*
17.	*waringin//*banyan	*keka//nunu*	*hali//hedan*	*nunuh//lete*
18.	spear//sword	*te//tafa*	*diman//surit*	*auni//suni*
19.	drum//gong	*labu//meko*	*bidu//tala*	*kee//sene*
20.	head//tail	*langa//iku*	*ulun//ikun*	*nakan//ikon*

This sharing of canonical pairs among major languages of Timor is evidence of a historical 'tenacity' similar to that noted by Dahood and others for the Syro-Palestinian traditions of parallelism and by Hull for Mayan traditions.

Some of these canonical pairs are general (sun//moon, rock//tree, head// tail), but others are specific (shame//fear, banana//sugar cane, lung//liver, *dedap//kelumpang* [two species of tree]) and, as such, these pairs create notable metaphoric linkages.

While many of these pairs share similar lexical terms, many do not. Those that do not are indicative of lexical changes that have occurred over centuries in these different but related languages.

The same dynamic is evident among the different 'dialects' on Rote that form a dialect chain across the length of the island. Neighbouring domains can understand one another's dialects but, for more distant domains, intelligibility diminishes. It is possible to distinguish at least six different 'dialect areas', each of which can be said to have its own language. The dyadic sets in Rotenese ritual language are composed of lexical terms from among these different dialects.[14]

This volume contains the origin narratives from two domains, Termanu and Thie, which belong to different, near-contiguous dialect areas. The majority of the dyadic sets in the ritual languages of these domains are the same, but there are several differences that distinguish them. A few examples may illustrate some of these differences. For example, the dyadic set for 'human' or 'person' in Termanu is *hataholi//daehena* (the lexical term *daehena* is drawn from an eastern dialect area), while in Thie this same dyadic set is *hatahori//andiana* (the lexical term *andiana* is shared with a dialect area to the west of Thie). The dyadic set for 'dryland fields' in Termanu is *tina// osi*, while in Thie it is *tine//lane* and, similarly, for 'field-markers', Termanu has *to batu//peu ai* while Thie has *to batu//lane ai*. Significantly, the dyadic set for 'origin ceremony' in Termanu is *hu//sio*—a set that links the term for 'trunk' or 'origin' with the term for the number 'nine', which signifies 'fullness' or 'completion'. In Thie, this set comprises two different specific lexical items: *limba//oli*.

Other examples are: in Termanu, 'to wake up' is *fafa'el//o'ofe*, while in Thie it is *fafa'el//titipa*; in Termanu, 'to divide and distribute' is *ba'el//tada*, while in Thie it is *ba'el//bati*. Another example is the dyadic set for 'full' or 'enough'.

---

14 This is a linguistic phenomenon that I have referred to as the 'semantics of dialect concatenation'— a creative process that I believe to be central to an understanding of parallelism (see Fox 2014: 374 ff.). To be understood in the Rotenese context, this dialect concatenation must be seen in relation to all the dialects on the island of Rote because there is no simple pattern to the creation of lexical pairs. My discussion here of Termanu and Thie is merely illustrative of more complex linguistic processes.

Here, the two domains share the other's dialect words. The dyadic set is *henu//sofe*. *Henu* is the everyday word for 'full' in Termanu, while *sofe* is the everyday word for 'full' in Thie. Another seemingly curious yet important dyadic set combines two kinds of bee, the smaller honeybee and the larger bumblebee: *fani//bupu*. This set in Thie combines the honeybee with a kind of wasp: *fani//nggunik*. The creatures are significant because they were once believed to represent the deceased's spirit that returns to partake of offerings set out after death.

Although differences among these various pairs may appear as part of the minutiae of cultural communication, they are indicative of the distinguishing subtlety of Rotenese parallelism. For a listener, each of these sets contains a familiar word with a less familiar word from another dialect. Ritual language thus utilises a rich array of dialect resources while at the same time preserving a tacit knowledge of different dialects. In this way, despite differences among spoken dialects, Rotenese ritual language is generally intelligible across the island. Its parallelism flourishes in a situation of linguistic diversity by drawing on the resources of different dialects to create its pairs. The remarkable feature of parallelism is that its pairings transcend linguistic diversity, remaining stable as its source languages change. This is probably the case in other areas of elaborate parallelism. It is this constituent stability of parallelism as a language of communication based on the rigorous organisation of hundreds, if not thousands, of canonical pairs that underlies its authority as a scriptural voice.

The significance of an underlying network of relationships in Rotenese parallelism

Parallelism in Rotenese ritual language is more than an organised accumulation of canonical pairs. An underlying network of relationships exists among these pairs. A critical number of lexical elements form multiple pairs while other elements form fewer pairs but still extend linkages within a wider network of relationships. The critical linking elements with multiple pairings constitute the symbolic core of Rotenese culture.[15] This symbolic core consists of basic terms such as 'earth', 'rock', 'water', 'tree' and

---

15 Tracing connections within this network and understanding its implications are a work in progress (for a discussion of this network and a representation based on the network program, *Pajek*, of one semantic cluster in Rotenese ritual language of 470 vertices, see Fox 2014: 381–84). This analysis derives from the ongoing compilation of a *Formal Dyadic Dictionary of Rotenese Ritual Language* (Termanu dialect).

'trunk, origin' along with key directional coordinates ('above', 'below', 'east', 'west'), key body coordinates ('head', 'tail', 'hand', 'leg', 'stomach', 'insides') and key plant designations ('fruit' and 'leaf'). All these key symbols have multiple meanings and connotations. They are linked to one another but also crucially linked to—paired with—other terms within ritual language.[16]

The ritual function of the oral narratives

All the oral narratives in this volume were once recited on specific ritual occasions. For Termanu, these occasions were directly related to the work processes whose origins they recount. These were for house-building, which once required multistage celebrations as construction proceeded; for marriages, which were conducted in stages; for the planting of rice and millet and, in relation to particular fields, for other crops; and for the initiation of both the weaving and the dyeing processes of cloth. The origin narratives from Thie include recitations intended to bless these same work processes but they also include the recitation for one of Thie's most significant origin ceremonies.

In Thie and Termanu today, these rituals are no longer performed. The recitations that once accompanied them are now preserved as memories of the ancestral past. That they are preserved reflects a continuing Rotenese concern with origins and the authority that this knowledge conveys.

Origin narratives represent only a portion of the Rotenese traditional liturgy. The more extensive portion of this liturgy consists of an array of mortuary chants that were once sung to honour the deceased on the nights before the burial ceremony and chanted, after burial, to lament the passing of the deceased's spirit.

Most Rotenese mortuary chants represent a substantial body of recitations. While many Austronesian societies in their mortuary rituals recount a precarious journey to an afterworld, the Rotenese at their funeral ceremonies select one chant from a repertoire of patterned life-course recitations intended symbolically to fit the life of the deceased. This life-course chant is then recited in celebration of the deceased. The narratives of

---

16   Understanding this network provides insights into how poets learn and eventually gain mastery in recitation; they begin by learning the basic multi-linked terms and use this base to expand their knowledge of more specific dyadic sets.

these life-course recitations with their imagined biographies are conceived of as particular paths that define a diversity of human possibilities of life on Rote (see Fox 2021).

Ritual language may be used to define all facets of life on Rote. It thus creates, for the Rotenese, a conception of life and its activities set forth in a complementary mode. As such, it is appropriate to examine in some detail the way this language portrays a metaphoric world and life within it.

2

The metaphoric creation of a complementary world

A poetic introduction to the island of Rote

This is a study of a corpus of significant oral compositions from the island of Rote. As an introduction to these narratives and to the world they portray, it is appropriate to present the island of Rote and its traditions through the perspective of the poetic language used in their composition.

The poetic use of ritual language creates a world of metaphor and imagination.[1] This dyadic language requires the use of complementary pairs and insists on their pervasive usage. Each pair in any composition creates a metaphorical link—a cultural correspondence—between two elements. In this way, the language of canonical parallelism builds a world of metaphorical correspondences.

---

1   I intentionally and pointedly refer to the parallel language of the Rotenese as a 'ritual language'. It is more than just a form of elevated 'ritual speaking'. This 'ritual language' is notably different to that of ordinary speech. It is a highly specialised language that only a few Rotenese eventually come to master. A detailed and extensive knowledge of specific and precise pairings is a critical feature of this ritual language. Much of its phrasing is formulaic and these formulae, like the pairs they comprise, must be learned. This means that those speakers who can use this language fluently and become recognised as the 'poets' or 'chanters' (*manahelo*) tend to be elders who are regarded as endowed with a capacity to convey the 'words of the ancestors'. The language is thus formal, focused and highly specialised; its utterances are considered revelatory of an ancestral past and its performative use is primarily directed to ceremonial occasions. Among the Rotenese, the use of this 'ritual language' often overrides performative actions. Rotenese tend to orate rather than perform their rituals. (For this distinction between oration and ostension, see Fox 1979c.)

It is possible to portray this metaphorical world as recounted in the narratives, particularly the origin narratives, of the Rotenese. It is a world set in the past at a time when the foundations of Rotenese culture were being fashioned, but it is also a world that reflects contemporary life, which poets take for granted and on which they base their compositions. An exegesis of these metaphoric correspondences provides a context for understanding the world of imagination that these extended narrative compositions expound.

The three realms of the cosmos

For the Rotenese, there are three realms to their cosmos. The first is *Poin do Lain* ('The Heights or the Heavens'). This is the realm of the Sun or Moon (*Ledo do Bulan*), ruled by Bula Kai ma Ledo Holo, whose heavenly descendants—variously identified with the stars, thunder, lightning and rainbows—populate the origin narratives and whose genealogies are recited in them.[2] Certain species of birds may belong to this sphere or are able to reach it.

The second of these worlds is the Ocean or Sea (*Liun do Sain*). The rulers of this realm are known by their titles, Danga Lena Liun ma Mane Tua Sain ('Great Hunter of the Ocean and Great Lord of the Sea'). These rulers are archetypically male and are personified as Iuk ma Foek ('Shark and Crocodile'). All the creatures of the Sea are members of their domain. This is a realm of great wealth, knowledge and power.

The third world, where the Lords of the Heavens and Sea first meet and interact, is the Earth: *Dae Bafok ma Batu Poin* ('The Flat Land and the Pointed Rock'). In these origin narratives, this is a forested world but there is no mention of any human inhabitants. In fact, in these narratives, there is no account of the origin or creation of humans.[3]

---

2   For a discussion of how these various narratives relate to one another, see Fox (2014: 219–28).

3   The Rotenese use two connectives for their pairs: *do*, which can be translated as 'or'; and *ma*, which can be translated as 'and'. In most compositions, however, these connectives are interchangeable.

The initial encounter of the rulers of the Heavens and the Sea

The origin narratives recount the first encounter between the son of the Sun and Moon and the Lord of the Sea. This encounter occurs in a hunt located on the Earth. This hunt is conducted with bow and blowpipe (*koul//fupu*)— implements that have long disappeared from Rotenese use. This hunt is rendered even more unusual by its object: the forest quest for wild pig and civet (*bafi//kue*). Joining efforts in this hunt is the first of many subsequent interactions between the rulers of the realms of the Heavens and the Sea.

When the hunt is successful, the son of the Sun and Moon is persuaded to descend into the ocean to join the Lord of the Sea to carry out the sacrifice of pig and civet. This leads to the discovery of the vast differences between the two realms. Houses in the Sea are magnificently constructed—'decked with turtle shells and roofed with ray-fish tails'. The Sea is the original source of fire and the purveyor of all the civilised arts: cooking, herding, building, planting and weaving. The use of fire for cooking is highlighted; the taste of cooked food surprises the son of the Sun and Moon, who has previously eaten only raw meat. This contrast between 'raw and cooked'—'roasting with fire//boiling with water'—marks a defining contrast between the two realms and prompts the first exchange between the Heavens and the Sea.

To obtain fire and the tools to build a house, the Heavens must offer a daughter to marry the Lord of the Sea and, in exchange, the Heavens are given an array of essential cultural objects—all in paired combinations:

kapa//lilo	water buffalo and gold
kutu//una	flint and fire-rubbing sticks
bo//pa'a-bala	bore and chisel
funu ma-leo//sipa aba-do	turning-drill and plumbline marker
taka//tala	axe and adze
nesu//alu	mortar and pestle
lali//o'oko	measuring basket and winnowing tray

This first marriage exchange is the start of continuing relations between the Heavens and the Sea, which are recounted in successive origin narratives.

Humans are the ultimate beneficiaries of these relations, which contribute to the origins of cultural goods including the knowledge of fire and cooking, the tools for building a house, the seeds of rice, millet and other plants, the equipment and knowledge of weaving and dyeing as well as the procedures that define the cultural order. By implication, the civilising arts have come to the Rotenese from the Sea, but this bounty has often been mediated via the Heavens.

The origin narratives are intended to set forth the knowledge of these founding events. They convey all the elements of this ordered world. Thus, for example, the great effort, as elaborated in the narratives, to erect the first house is significant because a properly constructed house offers a template of the order of the cosmos and is reflected in the order of the island of Rote itself.

The recitation of these origin chants was once restricted and hedged with omissions. The silence was required to cover their darker aspects. Some chants can only hint at what lies at their core and gives them their full meaning. One of these silences—that which cannot be uttered—relates to attempts to build a house. When these attempts failed utterly, a crocodile had to be killed and its body used as a design for the structure of the house. Similarly, in the chant on the origin of tie-dyeing and weaving, the daughter of the Sun and Moon possesses the instruments for tying and weaving, but 'Figure Shark'//'Pattern Crocodile' (Pata Iuk//Dula Foek) must be killed to obtain the designs and colour patterns for cloths that are dyed and woven. The Sea may be the source of all bounty but relations with the Sea and its creatures are fraught. Thus, too, the origin chants tell of the anger of the Heavens with the Sea, which results in great storms. Knowledge of the transgression of relations between the Heavens and the Sea is integral to the understanding of the origin narratives.

The island and its directional divisions

Rote is a small island at the south-western tip of the larger island of Timor in eastern Indonesia. In ritual language, its most common name is Lote or Kale (*Lote do Kale*). *Lote*, it is said, refers to the main body of the island, while *Kale* refers to the peninsular headland at its eastern end. Another frequently used name for the island is the simple set *Lino do Ne* ('Silent or Tranquil' or, perhaps more appropriately, 'Silence and Tranquillity', which designates a desired state of ritual quiet). These two names may be combined to create the longer formulaic name *Lote Lino do Kale Ne* ('Lote the Silent or Kale the Tranquil'). Yet another variation of this name is *Lote*

Lolo-Ei do Kale Ifa-Lima ('Lote of the Outstretched Legs or Kale of the Cradled Arms'). This body posture—a required position at certain rituals and in burial—is a stance intended to express a state of ritual peace.[4]

The island of Rote is considered at rest in the sea with its 'head' in the east and its 'tail' in the west. Thus, in ritual language, eastern Rote is referred to by the set *Dulu do Langa*, which equates 'east' (*dulu*) with 'head' (*langa*). Similarly, western Rote is referred to by the set *Muli do Iko*, which equates 'west' (*muli*) with 'tail' (*iko*).

Several more complex names are based on these sets. Eastern Rote can be referred to as *Dulu Oen ma Langa Daen* ('Water of the East and Land of the Head'). It is also called *Timu Dulu ma Sepe Langa*. *Sepe* is the light-red colour of a native dye and also of early dawn, while *timu* is an alternative term for 'east' in specific contexts, particularly in reference to the eastern monsoon wind (*ani timu*). A possible translation of *Timu Dulu ma Sepe Langa* might be 'Easterly [or Dawn] in the East and Pink at the Head'. Western Rote is *Muli Loloe Olin ma Iko Bekute Tasin* ('West Descending to its Estuary and Tail Sloping to the Sea').

The set *ki*//*kona* forms a similar directional pair. *Ki* ('north') is also the term for 'left' and *kona* ('south') is also the term for 'right'. The south is considered auspicious and regarded as a source of power.[5]

These various expressions convey an essential convention in all Rotenese ritual understanding. The island is like some creature—imagined as a crocodile—with its 'head' raised in the east and its 'tail' lowered to the west. A basic cosmological simplification asserts that east is always 'up' towards the sun and west is always 'down' towards the sea. The east is 'superior' (*lena*) to the west. South is superior to north.

---

4   A name for the island that has fallen into disuse with the conversion of the Rotenese to Christianity is *Ingu Manasongo Nitu ma Nusa Manatangu Mula* ('The Land that Offers to the Spirits and the Island that Sacrifices to the Ghosts').

5   These orientations and their associations are set forth in a number of traditional syllogisms: 1) *Lain loa dae boe, tehu dano-ina nai lain, de lain loa dae* ('Heaven is as broad as the Earth, but there is a great lake in the Heavens, therefore Heaven is greater than Earth'); 2) *Dulu nalu muli, tehu ledo neme dulu mai, de dulu bau lena muli* ('The east is as broad as the west, but the sun comes from the east, therefore the east is greater than the west'); and 3) *Kona bau ki, tehu koasa neme kona, de kona bau lena ki* ('The south is as great as the north, but power comes from the south, therefore the south is greater than the north'). When, however, the Dutch exercised colonial rule over Rote, this ordering of the world was overturned, reversing the orders of symbolic primacy, making the north or left superior to the south or right. A symbolic syllogism recorded at the time emphasised this change: *Ona bau i boe, te hu Koponi nai i, de i bau lena ona* ('The south [right] is as great as the north [left], but the company is in the north, therefore the north [left] is far greater than the south [right]').

Directionality is critical in ritual and social life. Traditional houses were always built to conform to the cosmological alignment of the island: with their 'head' turned to the east and 'tail' turned to the west. Graves, on the other hand, were oriented so the head of the deceased was turned to the west and the realm of the dead.

Metaphors for the passage of time: Days, nights and the seasons

'Day' (*faik*) and 'night' (*leo'dae*) form a set. 'Day' (*faik*) also forms a set with 'sun' (*ledo*); together they occur in varied formulae to indicate a particular time—invariably, a time in the past. Combined with the numbers 'one' and 'two' (*esal*/*dua*) and modified by terms (*nuni*/*tebe*) that specify a 'true' and 'certain' time, one such formula can be translated as follows:

Faik esa manunin	On one certain day
Ma ledo dua mateben	And at a particular time.

Another common formula that uses the set for 'good' and 'fine' (*lada*/*lole*) and another set for 'inside' and 'interior/stomach' may be translated:

Leo lole faik ia dalen	As on this good day
Ma leo lada ledok ia tein	And as at this fine time.

The spatial coordinates 'east' and 'head' (*dulu*/*langa*) are used in the formula for 'dawn' and 'sunrise' (*huak*/*siluk*) and are also associated with another set (*timu dulu*/*sepe langa*) that links 'east' (*timu*) with the reddening colour (*sepe*) of the sky. This combination of sets occurs in the following four lines that associate the chorus of morning birds with the early morning. Friarbirds and green parrots (*koal*/*nggia*) are also used metaphorically to refer to young girls, so these lines can also be taken to allude to the early morning activities of young women around the house:

Siluk ana mai dulu	Morning comes to the east
Ma huak ana mai langa	And dawn comes to the head.
Boe ma koa bei timu dulu-la	Friarbirds in the dawning east
Ma nggia bei sepe langa-la	And green parrots at the reddening head.

The set *Sepe Langa*/*Timu Dulu* ('Reddening Head and Dawning East') can also be used as a placename to indicate a site of importance in the east.

There are also formulae for the day at noon and the middle of the night. The formula for noon describes the sun at its zenith (*tetu*) and the day at its hottest (*hana*):

Ledo lek lama-tetu	The sun is at the zenith
Ma fai kapak lama-hana.	And day is at its hottest.

The dark of night is expressed by the dyadic set *bolo-do//fati-lada* and the deepening of night before the dawn is encapsulated in a formula of extension by the set of two and three (*dua//telu*) as in the following lines:

Te siluk bei ta dulu	It is not yet daylight in the east
Ma huak bei ta langa.	And it is not yet dawn at the head.
Besak-ka bolo-do neu dua	Now the night is at its height
Ma fati-lada neu telu.	And the dark is at its peak.

Life and livelihoods on Rote are marked by an extended dry season dominated by an east monsoon that generally begins in mid-April and continues until late November, when the short and irregular west monsoon takes shape bringing rains that fall intermittently through to February. The east monsoon (*timu*) forms a pair with the west monsoon (*fak*).

The time of transition from the east to the west monsoon is associated with the drying of the land and its grasses and plants:

Te timu lama-tua dulu	When the east monsoon grows old in the east
Ma fak lama-nalu langa	And the west monsoon becomes long at the head
Fo pila kumea letek-kala	The red kumea grass on the hills
Lama-dilu leu kalen	Bends its heavy tops
Ma nggeo kuku telas	And the black kuku shrub in the underbrush
Lama-sesu leu bu'un-na	Breaks at the weight of its joints.

The passage of time is reckoned in 'months' (*bulak*) and 'years' (*teuk*):

Teuk lakalaladik	Years pass and pass
Bulak lakaseseluk	Moons change and change.

On names and their significance

Knowing the name—the true or 'standing' name—of a person, place or object is an essential aspect of the knowledge of origins. This knowledge confers a form of power. Names are, however, perhaps the most elusive elements in ritual language. They all consist of dual elements. There are a staggering number of such names, both personal names and placenames. Often a clear distinction between the two is difficult to make.

Although names are supposed to be known, they are in fact a source of considerable contention. Poets dispute among themselves about proper names and judge one another's knowledge according to their views of what should be the appropriate set of ritual names. A mistake in naming is considered a lapse in ritual competency. Yet, among this vast corpus of names, only a few are clear and unequivocal. These are generally the formal names of the domains of Rote.

Although some names consist of just two elements that form a single dyadic set,[6] most names are composed of four or more elements. For personal names, a minimum of four elements (two pairs) is essential but often a third or even fourth element may be added to a name to indicate the origin place of the person named. The elements in such names can also be transmitted to form new pairs in a genealogical fashion following the paternal line.

Names are not always entirely intelligible or translatable, but the individual elements within these names frequently encode crucial information in a succinct—if not always unambiguous—form. In general, these elements are interpreted as allusions to: 1) past events, 2) places and their distinguishing features, 3) the status, rank or origin of characters, 4) the function of characters within chants, 5) occasionally their sex, 6) their genealogical relations to other characters in a chant, and often, and most importantly, 7) their 'position' within the spheres of the Rotenese cosmology. Despite their ambiguity, the lexical elements of most names may be interpreted as vehicles of multiple allusions. The traditions of ritual language are sufficiently elaborate to allow poets to make internal references to other compositions. Performance prompts internal referencing to other chants within the corpus and the impact of any ritual is increased by an awareness of such references.

---

6   I have over many years compiled—and continue to compile—a *Dyadic Dictionary* for such pairs used in Termanu's corpus of ritual texts. In this chapter, unless otherwise specified, I cite these dyadic sets in the dialect of Termanu. See Fox (2014) for a discussion of this *Dyadic Dictionary*, its network of semantic relations and the concatenation of dyadic sets in different dialects across the island of Rote.

Since most names are suggestive and only some of the elements of which they are composed are interpretable, these elements are subject to a variety of interpretations. This elusive quality of most names is of great importance in Rotenese speculation and of considerable interest. Names are frequently the subject of multiple folk-etymology and exegesis. Given this general interest, there are few names so opaque that they defy all Rotenese speculation.[7]

Names are often formulae with specific identification to a person or place but without further context. A context in which such names might make sense is left for interpreters to create. The fact that some names are old, unalterable formulae makes the need for their interpretation more compelling. This is another reason names frequently become counters in Rotenese argumentation. Names, it is assumed, should make sense. Despite difficulties in interpretation and translation, names are a critical and indispensable feature of ritual language.

The ritual names for the domains of the island

Politically, Rote is divided among 18 domains (*nusak*), each with its distinctive traditions.[8] Most of these domains were established and given formal recognition by the Dutch East India Company in the seventeenth century. Despite various administrative changes to the island, these domains remain the basis for social and linguistic identity. Included among the domains of Rote is the tiny island of Ndao, which has a separate population with its own language and traditions but figures prominently in Rotenese ritual narratives.

---

7   Thus, for example, in the Rotenese chant *Ana-Ma Manu Kama ma Falu-Ina Tepa Nilu*—the oldest text of its kind, published early last century by the Dutch linguist J.C.G. Jonker, with notes but no translation (Jonker 1911: 97–102)—the woman, whose dual name is Silu Lilo//Huka Besi, marries a man whose dual name has triple elements, Kama Lai Ledo//Nilu Neo Bulan. The wife's name includes the sets *Silu*//*Huka* ('to bare, reveal'//'to open, uncover') and *Lilo*//*Besi* ('gold'//'iron'). Hence, a possible translation would be 'Revealing Gold//Uncovering Iron'. In the case of the husband's name, Kama Lai Ledo//Nilu Neo Bulan, it is difficult to venture a translation of *Kama Lai* or *Nilu Neo*, but the third element in the man's name is significant and revealing: *Ledo*//*Bulan* are 'Sun' and 'Moon'. This third element identifies a place of origin and indicates the high 'heavenly' status for the husband and hence for his male child, whose name is Manu Kama//Tepa Nilu and who is the principal character in the chant. In accordance with Rotenese genealogical conventions, Manu Kama//Tepa Nilu takes his name from his father by coupling his new given name, Manu//Tepa—determined by divination—with the first part of his father's name (Kama//Nilu). Thus, Kama Lai (Ledo)//Nilu Neo (Bulan) begets Manu Kama//Tepa Nilu. The father's origin designation is no longer affixed to the son's name.

8   The Rotenese boast that each domain on Rote has its own language. In effect this means that in addition to the considerable dialect variation that occurs, there exists a conscious effort among the Rotenese of different domains to distinguish themselves from one another.

In ritual language, the same dyadic set, *ingul//nusa*, which refers to the island as a whole, is used to designate its local domains. Each domain has a ritual name. In fact, each domain has several ritual names. Within each domain, most village areas, important fields and key landmarks have established ritual names. In many of the narratives that recount the distribution of specific 'cultural items'—the knowledge of planting or the knowledge of weaving and dyeing—throughout the island, it is considered necessary to recite, in succession, the names of the places, chiefly the domains, that form the 'path' (*dalal//eno*) along which this knowledge was transmitted.

The recitation of a succession of these significant placenames, which is equivalent to the recitation of a genealogy, constitutes a 'topogeny'. In the ritual chants, topogenies are both frequent and essential. No poet who claims to possess knowledge can maintain his claim without demonstrating this knowledge, particularly by the recitation of a succession of names— as placenames or as genealogical names or ideally as a combination of the two.

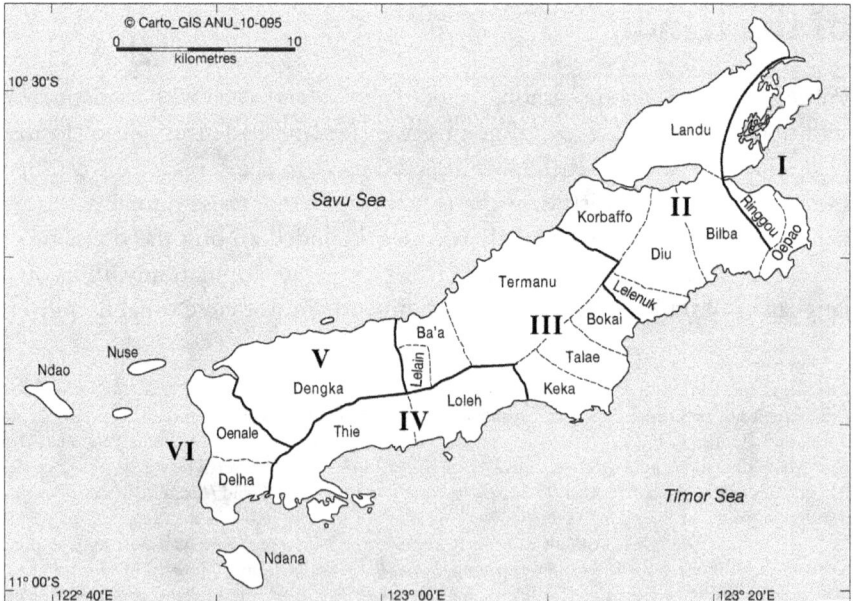

Map 2.1 The domains of Rote

The following is a list of the domains of Rote, from east to west, each with one of its more prominent ritual names.

The domains of Rote and Ndao

1.	Landu	*Soti Mori ma Bola Tena*
2.	Oepao	*Fai Fua ma Ledo So'u*
3.	Ringgou	*Londa Lusi ma Batu Bela*
4.	Bilba	*Pengo Dua ma Hilu Telu*
5.	Diu	*Pele Pou ma Nggafu Lafa*
6.	Lelenuk	*Lenu Petu ma Safe Solo*
7.	Bokai	*Medi do Ndule*
8.	Korbaffo	*Tunga Oli ma Namo Ina*
9.	Termanu	*Koli do Buna*
10.	Keka	*Tufa Laba ma Neë Feo*
11.	Talae	*Pila Sue ma Nggeo Deta*
12.	Ba'a	*Pena Pua ma Maka Lama*
13.	Dengka	*Dae Mea Iko ma Oe Onge Muli*
14.	Lelain	*Nggede Ke ma Donda Mamen*
15.	Loleh	*Ninga Ladi ma Hengu Hena*
16.	Thie	*Tada Muli ma Lene Kona*
17.	Oenale	*Tasi Puka ma Li Sonu*
18.	Delha	*Dela Muli ma Ana Iko*
19.	Ndao	*Ndao Nuse ma Folo Manu*

There exists an abundance of folk exegesis that is called up in the interpretation of ritual names. Oepao is a small domain at the eastern end of the island. Its name is *Fai Fua ma Ledo So'u* ('Day Lifts and Sun Appears'). On this name, there is general agreement. Oepao is the domain of the sunrise, the area from which it is first possible to observe the dawn. The neighbouring domain of Bilba has the name *Pengo Dua ma Hilu Telu*, which can be translated as 'Turn Twice and Swerve Thrice'. Most interpretations of this name hinge on the changeability of Bilba. One interpretation suggests that the name alludes to the contrary nature of the people of Bilba, swinging from one extreme to another, from one allegiance to another; another sees in it an allusion to the continual changing of rulers and alliances in Bilba. Historically, Bilba has been an area of local revolt and internal dissension and, despite Dutch East India Company involvement on the island, it was suspected of an alliance with the Black Portuguese of Timor. Diu's ritual name, *Pele Pou ma Nggafu Lafa* ('Hang the Woman's Sarong and Flutter the Man's Cloth'), is no less elusive than that of Bilba. According to one exegesis, the name refers to the flying of a flag and the union of northern and southern parts of the domain—of Kana and Diu—to form the single unified state of Diu. Another of Diu's ritual names, *Diu Dulu ma Kana Langa*, alludes to this relationship. According to another exegesis, a large segment of the population of Diu was supposed to have come as immigrants from Kuli in the domain of Loleh. At first, without permanent residences, where they hung their clothes was where they had their homes.

By comparison with these, Korbaffo's name, *Tunga Oli ma Namo Ina*, which means literally 'Follow the Estuary and Great Harbour', is more transparently interpretable because it can refer to this domain's wide natural harbour, approached through the estuary of Oenggae. Bokai's name, *Medi do Ndule*, is also said to be based on some reference to the harbour of Bokai, but no-one can suggest a possible translation of its elements. Talae's name, *Pila Sue ma Nggeo Deta*, means 'Red Bracelet and Black Dip'. By one interpretation, this is an allusion to the fact that Talae produces most of Rote's supply of betel or areca nut: 'Red Bracelet' alludes to 'red lips' while 'Black Dip' alludes to 'blackened teeth'. Oenale, at the western end of the island, has a relatively unambiguous name, *Tasi Puka ma Li Sonu* ('Sea Breaks and Waves Splash'), while Thie, Dengka and Delha combine, in their names, directional coordinates with other dyadic elements. Thie's name links the set 'south' (*kona*)//'west' (*muli*) with what are said to be local placenames, *Lene*//*Tada*, to form the name *Lene Kona ma Tada Muli* ('South Lene and West Tada'). Both Dengka's and Delha's names are based on the conventional equation of 'west' and 'tail'. Dengka's name is *Dae Mea Iko ma Oe Onge Muli* ('Red Earth at the Tail and Flowing Water in the West'). This, like another of Dengka's names, *Dae Mea ma Tete Lifu* ('Red Earth and a Thousand Dams'), appears to be an allusion to this domain's agricultural situation: red clay soil with no major rivers, only dozens of smaller sources of water whose flow must be diverted for irrigation. Delha's name is simply *Dela Muli ma Ana Iko* ('Dela in the West and Child and Small One at the Tail').[9]

---

9   What makes these names difficult to interpret is their combination of 1) unique sets, 2) unusual sets, and 3) conventional sets. Sets such as *medi*//*ndule*, *tada*//*lene*, *ninga*//*hena* or *dela*//*ana* occur only in names and only with reference to specific domains. Unusual sets are those that combine recognisable elements in ways that only appear to occur in names. The sets *sue*//*deta*, *mea*//*onge* and even *kona*//*muli* represent unusual combinations. By contrast, *fai*//*ledo*, *pou*//*lafa*, *dae*//*oe* and *iko*//*muli* are conventional sets used in dozens of combinations in ritual language. By no means are these sets confined to names alone. In some instances, the set combination of the elements in a name contravenes the standard procedure for the union of elements in complex formulae. *Oli*//*namo* ('estuary'//'harbour') is a conventional set. Each element of this set should occur, in a similar position, in any formula in which it is used. However, in Korbaffo's name, *Tunga Oli ma Namo Ina* ('Follow the Estuary and Great Harbour'), *Oli* and *Namo* are not in a similar position and hence cannot be considered a proper pair. Other positioning would render the name *Oli Tunga*//*Namo Ina** or *Tunga Oli*//*Ina Namo**, both of which would be nonsensical.

The assignment of ritual names is not confined exclusively to Rote.[10] Rote lies in a chain of islands. The island of Savu, whose principal settlement is Seba, is located to the west and is known as *Seba Iko ma Safu Muli* ('Seba at the Tail'//'Safu in the West'). Ndao, a tiny island off the north-west coast of Rote, is *Ndao Nusa do Folo Manu*. Timor is referred to as *Helok do Sonobai*; this old expression equates the Helong people at the tip of Timor and on the island of Semau with those Timorese who were once united under a ruler known as Sonbai.

The town of Kupang on Timor has various names. It can be referred to as *Kota Batu//Di Lilo* ('Walled Town'//'Golden Pillars'), but a more playful designation is *Si Seu ma So'e Dode* ('Tear, then Sew, Scoop, then Serve'), which sees the population of Kupang as living comfortably with minimal labour. The dyadic set *Sina do Koli* may refer to any Chinese settlement. Originally this set may have referred to the Chinese settlement at Atapupu on the central northern coast of Timor. Now the name *Sina Dale do Koli Dae* ('Sina Interior'//'Koli Land') refers to the Chinese settlement in the town of Ba'a. Seen by some as a reference to an original homeland, any hospitable land beyond the sea is *Sela Sule ma Dai Laka*.[11]

The organisation of the domains

In ritual language, the dyadic set *ingu//nusa* can refer to any territory including the domains of the island. *Ingu* is 'territory' or 'homeland' and it also forms another set with *leo*, which refers to the 'lineages', 'clans' or, in some contexts, the 'clan areas' that constitute a domain. In Rotenese political history, each clan is said to have had its own territory centred on some walled redoubt. *Nusa* is the term for 'island' but can, like *ingu*, refer to a particular territory.

---

10   When I first arrived on Rote, the chanter Peu Malesi used alliteration to name my ritual homeland as 'America'//'Africa' (*Amerika//Afarika*), whereas later, the chanter Esau Pono identified my homeland, which he had visited, as 'Australia Land'//'Kangaroo Domain' (*Dae Australia//Nusa Kangaru*). Years later, when the poets from Rote joined me for recording sessions on Bali, they coined the designation 'Bali Land'//'Gods' Water' (*Bali Daen//Dewata Oen*). The Portuguese and then the Dutch intruded into the world of the Rotenese. Claiming to come from the north-west, the lesser quadrants of the Rotenese four-quarter directional system, these newcomers became associated with sorcery and evil and were given the colours appropriate to the quadrants of their origin: yellow, green, blue and black. In ritual language, the designation for these foreigners that is still used in ritual language is *Mana-Kuei-Modo//Mana-Se-peo-Nggeo* ('Those with Yellow Slippers'//'Those with Black Hats').

11   Some educated Rotenese see in the word *Sela* a reference to a possible earlier land of origin, the island of Ceram (Seram) in the Moluccas; others interpret this as a reference to Ceylon (Sri Lanka; *Selan* in Indonesian).

The lord or ruler of a domain is referred to by the set *mane(k)//boko(k)*. *Manek* is the general Rotenese title for a ruler. The root of this term is *mane* ('male'). The term *mane* occurs in the titles of key ritual figures and in the designation, in ritual expressions, for the Christian God, 'The Great Lord Above' (*Mane Tua Lain*).

In Rotenese domains, in addition to the 'male' ruler, there was the complementary 'female' ruler and, depending on size and composition, an array of clan lords. In Termanu, these clan lords were known as the 'Nine Male Lords' (*Mane-Sio*) because the domain was conceived of as a unity of nine clans. At the court in Termanu, there were other titles as well. All domains were divided between noble and commoner clans and different titles were also associated with these ranks.

Ritual language, however, gives little recognition to such political and social differentiation. Nobles, lords, headmen or anyone with rank can be referred to as *lena//lesik*. In direct address, these terms are reduplicated: *lena-lena// lesi-lesik*. This set occurs in other contexts in ritual language and always refers to that which is 'more, extra, surpassing, overabundant'.

Similarly, ritual language does not make explicit reference to class distinctions, yet such distinctions are implicit throughout the chants, particularly in the use of names and titles. The dyadic set *la'u//solu* is used in various names to indicate a lowly origin.[12] Heavenly names that use terms such as 'sun', 'moon', 'star' or 'lightning' indicate high origin.

Whereas ritual language neglects the apparatus of political relations, it possesses a considerable array of dyadic sets that express different aspects of social relations. The clans of a domain can be referred to by the dyadic set *ingu//leo* ('land'//'clan'), while settlements are designated *nggolo//taduk*, which literally indicates a 'promontory'//'redoubt'. Important relations, however, are expressed in terms of houses and their internal structures.

Rotenese clans or lineages are composed of 'houses' (*uma*). Although *uma* can apply to a single household, it also has a much wider connotation. It can denote a ritual group of lineal relatives who hold rights in common. A widow with sons rarely returns to the house of her father or brother. She will act as the head of the household until her sons are adults. In inheritance, the eldest

---

12 *La'us* is the ordinary-language word for a 'commoner' or the 'common people' as opposed to the noble class. Its root, *la'u*, forms the basis for words for 'filth, ugliness, rot, and disease'. In ritual language, it occurs in the set *hedi//lau* ('sickness and disease').

son receives all his father's ritual entitlements established with other groups through marriage whereas the youngest son inherits his father's house and is ritually responsible for dealing with the spirits of the dead still associated with the house.

Houses figure prominently in ritual language. The single most important Rotenese origin narrative recounts the origin of the house and its complex ritual construction.[13] Houses are referred to by the dyadic set *uma//lo*. *Lo* occurs in several sets but is confined to ritual language. It is possibly related to the word for 'beam' or 'plank', *lolo*. There are other ways of describing houses, in terms of either their inner fires or their ladders. Physically, houses are large, haystack-like structures with roofs thatched in lontar leaf or alang-alang grass that hangs nearly to the ground. They are always set lengthwise on an east–west axis. Beneath these immense sloping roofs, there is a ground-level receiving area in which there are placed four to six elevated platforms for sitting or reclining.

The traditional house was built on posts (*di'i//ai*) and in the receiving area there was a ladder—often the halved trunk of a tree with notches as steps— that led into the house itself. Inside, the house was divided into two sections: the man's side or 'outer' section (*uma deak*) and the woman's side or 'inner' section (*uma dalek*). The man's side was always on the east; the woman's side always on the west. On the woman's side was the cooking fire and another small ladder that led up into a loft where food supplies and seed grain were stored. A man, when ill, retreated to the woman's side of the house to restore his health; he was obliged to ask his wife's permission to enter the loft.

There is a proliferation of dyadic sets in ritual language that refer to this structure (and assume an understanding of its various parts). In addition to the general dyadic set, 'house'//'home' (*uma//lo*), a house may be referred to by a variety of its complementary parts: 'two ridgepoles'//'three crossbeams' (*to'a duak//sema teluk*), 'house-posts'//'the tree-ladder' (*uma di//heda-ai*), 'house-posts'//'home planks' (*uma di//lo ai*) or the 'upper house'//'inner cooking fire' (*uma-lai//la'o dale*). A grave is also conceived of as a kind of house and is thus referred to either as an 'earth-grave'//'tree-home' (*late dae//lo-ai*) or as a 'rock-grave'//'tree-home' (*late batu//lo-ai*).

---

13   For an extended discussion of the Rotenese house, see Fox (1993).

Rotenese rituals of life and livelihood

Rituals are intended to convey the words of the ancestors. These rituals continually speak of Rote as though it were covered in fresh forests and thick woods (*lasi//nula*). Yet, Rote is sadly bare: a dry, eroded, windswept island. The forests that remain are confined to a few limited areas. The major concern of the Rotenese is with water. The Rotenese word for 'water' is *oe*. In ritual language, *oe* is a core term—one of a small number of other core terms that can combine with a wide variety of other terms, in contrast to a majority of words that have one or two required pairs.[14] Thus, ritual language has the paired terms *oe//dae* for 'water and land', *oe//ai* for 'water and tree', *oe//na'u* for 'water and grass(land)' and *oe//da(k)* for 'water and blood'.

A remarkable feature of Rotenese life is the people's adaptation to these dry conditions through a reliance on the lontar palm (*Borassus flabellifer* Linn.; Rotenese: *tua*). The lontar palm is a solitary dioecious fan-leaf palm that flourishes by sending its roots deep into the island's jumbled limestone soil. Rotenese livelihoods are heavily centred on the use of all the products of the lontar palm. From its crown, this palm yields a sweet juice that must be drunk immediately or cooked to produce a dark sugar syrup. This syrup, when mixed with water, makes a sweet sugar drink (*tua hopo*) that is consumed several times daily as the normal sustenance of most Rotenese. In the origin narrative that recounts the discovery of the lontar, its juice is described as *kei-kei//keke'e* ('sweet and sour'). As a consequence, it is said that the Rotenese are a people who drink more meals than they eat. The syrup may be crystallised to form a brown rock sugar, fermented to make a beer or distilled to produce a delicately sweet gin. This native gin is called the 'water of words' and is regarded as an essential prompt for all poets before they can recite.[15]

The male lontar palm (*tua manek*) has hanging from its crown long, narrow and ithyphallic inflorescences; the female palm (*tua fetok*) carries dark round clusters of fruit. This tree, with its marked sexual differences, provides the Rotenese with an iconic model for many of their ritual metaphors. In ritual language, the lontar may be referred to as the 'male' and the 'female' (*mane//*

---

14   See Fox (1975; 2014: 149–80, 365–68) for an examination of the formal, networked properties of Rotenese ritual language.
15   See Fox (1977a) for a detailed discussion of the palm-centred economy.

feto) or as the 'lontar' and the 'female' (*tua//feto*). In ritual language, the verbs for tapping are *pale//lenu* or *pale//seti*; in ordinary speech, the verb is *ledi*.

Literally, in ritual language, a tapper 'tends the male' and 'forces the female'. In practice, the male lontar is tapped more frequently than the female, hence in rituals, the male is identified with the species as a whole and the female becomes the marked category. Crucial to several dimensions of Rotenese symbolism is a distinction that is emphatically made within ritual language. Though the tapped juice might appear the same, if the juice comes from the male it is referred to as *oe* ('water' or 'semen') and if it comes from the female, it is *dak* ('sap' or 'blood'). Thus, the formula in ritual language for this palm juice is *tua oe//feto dak* ('lontar water'//'female blood').

With lontar utilisation at its core, the rest of the Rotenese economy is diverse in its pursuits. It consists of both 'caring for the lontar' and 'attending to the earth' (*pei tua//papa dae*). Rotenese agriculture is based on a complex system of dry fields (*fu'a//mok* or *tina//osi*), house gardens and irrigated orchards (*osi//mamek*). The most important crops are rice and millet (*hade//betek*). In ritual language, the cultivation of rice and millet is described as *lele hade//o'oko bete*. In the rituals, these two crops are of such importance that they epitomise all other 'grain and seed' (*bini//ngges*) and are given a personal ritual name: *Doli do Lutu*.

Rice and millet are first mentioned as cooked food in the initial origin narratives. In a subsequent narrative, these primary grains are associated with a 'sea snail and crab' referred to as Bole Sou//Asa Nao. These creatures of the sea are washed ashore at a ritual site, *Tena Lai ma Mae Oe*, at the eastern end of Rote and are then carried by a succession of women, each of whom endeavours to plant them in their named fields on the island.

In Termanu's recitation of this origin narrative, the first woman to succeed in getting seeds to germinate and grow did so by receiving Doli do Lutu with great ceremony, offering them betel catkin and areca nut wrapped in specially decorated cloth. This woman, Fiti Nggoli//Lole Bako, planted Doli do Lutu in a field in Termanu whose ritual name reflected her own: *Nggoli Kai Tio//Bako Bau Dale*.[16]

---

16   This, according to the Rotenese of Termanu, was the beginning of rice and millet agriculture on the island. In the origin narratives of the domain of Thie, there is another telling of the gathering of Bole Sou ma Asa Nao, but it omits mention of Termanu, concentrating its attention on the principal localities of its own domain.

Maize was introduced to Rote near the end of the seventeenth century and was assimilated to the existing native category of a high-stalked form of sorghum referred to as *pela*, which to this day is referred to in Indonesian as *jagung Rote* ('Rotenese corn'). In Rotenese, sorghum is *pela-hik* ('true *pela*') while maize is *pela-sina* ('Chinese *pela*'). Maize has long surpassed millet as a major subsistence crop while sorghum is still widely grown in particularly dry areas of the island.

Just as the rituals refer to rice and millet (*hadel//bete*) as a pair, they also refer to millet and either sorghum or maize (*betel//pela*) as a pair. Although in some contexts it is unclear whether reference is made to sorghum or maize, some narratives are more explicit in referring to 'the millet kernel'//'the ear of maize' (*bete-pulel//pela-po'o*). There is in Termanu a specific narrative that links these two grains in recounting the origin of a certain kind of millet. According to this narrative, two notable personages requested seeds and grain (*bini no ngges*) from the Heavens but when they were not provided, they created their own seeds by pricking their hands and feet and allowing their blood to spill down and become millet and maize.

Rote has a mixed planting system with a variety of food crops. Collectively these different food crops are referred to as the 'nine seeds and the eight kernels' (*pule siol//kale falu*). Crops such as mung bean, pigeon pea, peanuts, sesame or other crops such as sweet potato, cassava and squash are not mentioned by name in the rituals. On the other hand, there are certain crops like rice and millet that have an iconic importance in the rituals. These are 'taro and yams' (*talel//fia*), 'banana and sugar' (*hunil//tefu*), and coconut and areca nut (*pual//no*). The rituals also mention crops such as 'onions and tobacco' (*laisonal//modo-sina*), which are grown together in specially separated gardens during the dry season. The rituals also refer to cotton but more as a product in the creation of clothing than as a planted crop.

Images of Rotenese livelihood activities: Herding, fishing and weaving

The Rotenese economy is also dependent on the keeping of livestock. Ritual language links pigs and chicken (*bafil//manu*)—animals that scavenge in the vicinity of the house and are, from time to time, fed the surplus of lontar palms. While it is possible to pair the 'dog' with either the pig or the chicken, there is a special set for 'dog' that pairs the Rotenese term for dog (*busa*) with the more common (Austronesian) term *asu*, thus: *busal//asu*.

The water buffalo (*kapa*) is an important source of wealth and prestige and, as such, is linked with gold (*kapa//lilo*). Bridewealth may be paid either in water buffalo or in its accepted equivalent, gold. Such bridewealth payments are referred to by the set *fae tena//beli batu*. *Fae tena* is a reference to livestock while *beli batu* is a reference to gold. Water buffalo can also be linked with goats/sheep in the compound set *tena kapa//bote bi'i*, which is a general expression for both large and small livestock.

The Rotenese keep both sheep and goats. A scrawny, wool-less breed of sheep (*bi'i-lopo*: literally, 'trousered *bi'i*') that reached the island via the Dutch East India Company has been assimilated into the category of goat (*bi'i-hik*: 'true *bi'i*'). A person's wealth is evident in the size of their herd. Herding or tending, based on verbs for 'dividing and separating', is expressed by the dyadic set *lilo//tada*. The gregariousness attributed to herd animals gives rise to a striking Rotenese metaphor: a lonely, isolated or abandoned person can be likened to 'a lone buffalo'//'an orphaned chick(en)'.

Offshore fishing is another important Rotenese livelihood activity and is chiefly a tidal fishing effort. The tides are classified in a monthly cycle according to the time and extent of their ebb. Stone fish-walls (*dea//lutu*) that extend into the sea are built at strategic locations along the shoreline. They are used as a kind of weir to trap fish in the ebbing tide. Most of this fishing is done by women with scoop nets (*seko//ndai*). Whereas men tap palms, women bring in the abundance of the sea.

In the origin narratives, fishing is of major significance, not just for economic reasons, but also because fishing—at the junction of land and sea—offers contact between the people of the Earth and the creatures of the Sea. The tidal shore is thus ritually pregnant with possibilities.

Weaving is—or once was—a complex activity of daily life whose beginnings are recounted in the origin narratives. Weaving requires the prior spinning of cotton and the elaborate dyeing of bundled threads before they can be woven. Women use a simple wooden cotton gin or rack (*lolek*) to remove seeds from the cotton and then spin it into threads using a simple spindle balanced on the base of a shell (*ine*). These processes are expressed in ritual language as complementary activities: *ifa lolek//dipo ine*. The tying (*henge*) of threads and the weaving (*tenu*) of cloth are presented as complementary activities: *henge//tenu*. The loom and its parts are similarly referred to by the dyadic set *ati//selu* ('loom and shuttle'). Together these sets succinctly encode the weaving process whose origins derive from human involvement in the affairs of the Heavens and the Sea.

Metaphors and icons of the Rotenese life cycle

The dyadic set for 'human being' in Termanu is *hataholi*//*daehena*. In ritual language, persons are identified as male and female: the set for a man combines the terms for 'adult man' and 'boy', *tou*//*ta'e*, just as the set for a woman combines the terms for 'woman' and 'girl', *ina*//*feto*.

In ritual language, 'father' (*ama*) forms a set with 'mother's brother' (*to'o*); 'mother' (*ina*) forms a set with 'father's sister' (*te'o*). What Rotenese rituals assert is that a person is composed of two elements: the soft flesh and blood that one obtains from the mother's brother through their mother and the bones and genealogical (literally: 'hard') name (*nade*) that come from the father. The coupling of father and mother's brother, and of mother and father's sister, is intelligible in these terms. Any bodily injury—even accidental self-inflicted injury—requires a payment of indemnification to the mother's brother; any slur or insult to a person's name, if proven, requires a different payment of indemnification to the genealogical group who share that line of names.

Personal naming adds yet another dimension to the Rotenese theory of persons. In the ritual language of Termanu, *nade* ('name') forms a set with *tamok*. In genealogical naming, a person receives the first element of their father's binomial as the last element of their binomial. Their own first binomial element is (or was once) determined by divination. The traditional procedure was to drive a spear into a specific post in the house and, with outstretched arm reaching towards the spear's point, to recite a litany of the names of the child's ancestors on their mother's and their father's sides. When the proper name was reached, the fingertips would suddenly be able to touch the spear's point. Rotenese Christians, rather than abandon genealogical naming, have instead adopted an additional system of Christian *fam* or 'family' names. In place of divination, they open the Bible at random to discover a clue to the name of a suitable ancestor. This ancestor, by divination, is the *tamok*. A portion of this ancestor's name becomes the first part of a child's full binomial name. The full ritual expression for name-giving is 'to lift the *nade* (genealogical name)' or 'bring forth the *tamok* (ancestral name)': *fela-foi nade do bala-tola tamok*.

A person's 'hard' genealogical name is so fundamental that it should never be mentioned out of proper context for fear of insult to that person or some ancestor. As a result, in everyday life, a person is known by a 'soft' or 'gentle' name and many of these allude to the identity of the *tamok*. Individuals who share a *tamok* possess a special mutual bond, even though they may be in different lineages. They have a stake in defending their common ancestral name.

Ritual chants encompass all stages of the human life cycle, from birth, name-giving and hair-cutting ceremonies to courting, marriage and the succession of death rituals. One icon used in ritual language for a young man, particularly when he is 'hunting' for a woman, is 'shark and crocodile' (*iu//foe*) and these terms can be used as verbal forms in courting dialogue: a boy is said to come 'sharking and crocodiling'.

Similarly, ritual language uses specific icons for young marriageable girls. They are compared to specific birds (*koa//nggia*) whose early morning singing and fluttering are supposed to be directed to attracting young men.[17]

As birds, girls are differentiated by status as either noble or commoner. The noble *koa//nggia* are associated with the sun and moon and are distinguished by particular markings:

Bulan koa ma ledon nggia	Friarbird of the Moon
Ma Ledon nggia	And parrot of the Sun
Nggia manutu lilok	Parrot with golden throat
Ma koa malali potak.	And friarbird with gilt crest.

By contrast, commoner *koa//nggia* are distinguished by size and referred to as the 'lorikeet and oriole' (*nggia timu//koa kese*). In ritual language, the search for a girl to marry is often described in archaic hunting terms. A boy must take up his 'blowpipe and bow' (*fupu//kou*) and set out on a 'bird hunt' for the *koa//nggia*.

When a boy eventually manages to 'hunt' his bride, her bridewealth must be negotiated and paid. The origin narratives recount the primal origin of bridewealth. From the beginning, these payments have been made in 'gold

---

17 This formulaic bird pair, *koa//nggia*, embraces a variety of birds based on their Rotenese classification. The *koa* can refer to a particular honeyeater, the helmeted friarbird (*Philemon buceroides*), as well as to the olive-brown oriole or Timor oriole (*Oriolus melanotis*). The *nggia* can refer to several parrot and lorikeet species, of which there are many on Rote, among them the Eclectus parrot (*Eclectus roratus*) and the coconut lorikeet (*Trichoglossus haematodus*).

and water buffalo' (*lilo//kapa*) or 'livestock and units of gold' (*fae tena// beli batu*) and they continue to be calculated in these terms. Negotiations can go on at length and never entirely satisfy either side. However, there is a concluding phrase taken from the narratives that signals an end to negotiations even though not all that was wished for has been obtained. These four lines are as follows:

Dai te ta dai	Enough or not enough
O nai ta dai liman	What's in our grip is enough in our hand
Ma no'u te ta no'u	And sufficient or insufficient
O nai kuku no'u nen.	What's in our fingers is sufficient in our grasp.

The dyadic set *tu//sao* is 'to marry and to wed'. The metaphor for the ceremony itself emphasises the physical transfer of the bride and her role in creating a path between two houses:

Soku Lisu Lasu Lonak	They lift Lisu Lasu Lonak
Ma lali Dela Musu Asuk.	And they transfer Dela Musu Asuk.
De lelete neu sao	She bridges the path to marry
Ma fifino neu tu.	And she joins the way to wed.

The narratives often go on to announce the pregnancy of the girl who has been transferred in marriage and chart the development of her pregnancy, particularly her cravings, because these are believed to reveal a child's character. An example of such cravings is:

Su'un na nggeo lena	Her breasts darken
Ma tein na da'a fai.	And her womb enlarges.
Ana da'a fai bobongin	She grows large to give birth
Ma nggeo lena lalaen,	And grows dark to bring forth,
Te hu ana ta hapu bongi	But she is unable to give birth
Ma ana ta hapu lae.	And she is unable to bring forth.
Ana metu ape u'una	She thirsts for assorted foods
Ma ana ma siu dodoki.	And she craves for odd bits.

Some narratives run through a long list of these cravings to signal the birth of an unusual child. These cravings may, for example, include 'tasty rice'//'sweet palm juice' (*lada hadek//mina tuak*), 'goat's lungs'//'buffalo's liver' (*bote ba//tena ate*), 'slices of turtle meat'//'strips of dugong flesh' (*bia keak//lola luik*) and 'forest-bee jelly'//'bumblebee larvae' (*fani-lasi ana// bupu-timu ana*). Each of these cravings forces the husband to greater efforts to obtain the foods for his wife.

When eventually children are born, the formulaic expression for a boy is 'a cock's tail feathers and a rooster's plume' (*popi koak//lano manuk*); for a girl, the formula *ke fetok//tai inak* is less easy to translate. The expression refers to the special waistband that a girl wears (or used to wear) and can best be translated as 'girdled girl and bound woman'.

The chant *Ndi Loniama ma Laki Elokama*, for example, describes the successive birth of, first, a boy and then a girl:

Boe ma ana bongi-na Solu Ndi	She gives birth to Solu Ndi
Ma ana lae-na Luli Laki	And she brings forth Luli Laki
Fo popi-koak Solu Ndi	A cock's tail feathers, Solu Ndi
Ma lano-manuk Luli Laki.	And a rooster's plume, Luli Laki.
Boe te ana bei boe bongi	But she still continues to give birth
Ma bei boe lae.	And continues to bring forth.
Lae-nala Henu Ndi,	She brings forth Henu Ndi,
De ke-fetok;	She is a girdled girl;
Ma lae-nala Lilo Laki,	And she brings forth Lilo Laki,
De tai-inak.	She is a bound woman.

In ritual language, life is consistently described as a journey. As such, life is a process of discovery even when the journey leads back to where it began. A search for wisdom and knowledge is part of this process and an essential feature of life. This quest is variously phrased in ritual language combining the paired verbs *sanga//tunga*. In its highest form, this search is described as 'seeking for wisdom'//'questing for knowledge' (*sanga ndolu//tunga lela*). Personal encounters on the journey, particularly when arms and hands meet (*tongo lolo//nda lilima*), are frequent and instructive. Respect is accorded a person of knowledge and wisdom (*hataholi malelak*) whose life has been spent in learning from experience.

Journeying is a feature of life but continues in death. Mortuary rituals describe the life journeys of an array of chant characters who represent the deceased. These chant characters portray a formulaic set of possible categories: those who die young or those who die old, nobles and commoners, the rich and the poor, and especially those who die surrounded by family members and are succeeded by sons and daughters. These narratives frequently attribute a sudden death to an attack by malevolent spirits—'craving spirits and grasping ghosts' (*nitu mana-tetenik ma mula mana-doko-doek*)—who cause 'dizziness in the head'//'cramps in the stomach' (*langu-langak//mela-teik*).

Just as the mortuary chants set forth the possible journeys of life, they also hint at the journey after death. Some of the most powerful mortuary chants give voice to the chant character who represents the deceased. This allows the deceased to address those who have gathered to mourn and to describe the final journey that is about to occur. In one such poignant exposition from the dead, the deceased instructs his family in how to use his wealth and to go on living and then announces his imminent departure:

Te au touk Ndi Lonama	For I am the man Ndi Loniama
Ma au ta'ek Laki Elokama	And I am the boy Laki Elokama
Na au tonang sanga sosokun	My boat is about to lift
Ma au balung sanga sasa'en	And my perahu [boat] is about to rise
Fo au ala u tunga inang	For I am going to search for my mother
Ma ala u afi te'ong	And I am going to seek my father's sister
Nai muli loloe	In the receding west
Ma iko tatai.	And at the tail's edge.
Fo au leo Dela Muli u	For I go to Dela in the west
Ma leo Ana Iko u.	And I go to Ana at the tail.
De se au tonang ta diku-dua	My boat will not turn back
Ma au balung ta lolo-fali	And my perahu will not return
Te dae saon doko-doe	The earth demands a spouse
Ma batu tun tai-boni	And the rocks require a mate
De se mana-sapuk mesan-mesan	Those who die, this includes each person
Mana-lalok basa-basan.	Those who perish, this includes everyone.

This passage ends with the restatement of a recurrent theme in Rotenese rituals: the inevitability of death. This notion is often combined with the metaphoric representation of humans as 'orphans and widows' whose journeys end in death. In almost any ritual recitation there is invariably a concatenation of different metaphors. In this passage, in addition to the idea of a journey to the west, the land of the dead, there is mention of the metaphoric search for a new 'mother and aunt (father's sister)'—a common theme in the quest for a permanent abode—and, at the same time, the acknowledgement of the Earth as 'spouse and mate'. A pervasive metaphoric idiom in virtually all ritual recitations—a botanic idiom of relations—requires special exegesis.

The pervasive botanic idiom in ritual discourse

Rotenese relationships are expressed in a pervasive botanic idiom. The mother's brother (*to'o*) 'plants' his sister's children. These children are referred to literally as his plants, *selek*. From among the men who can be regarded as the mother's brothers, one individual is designated as 'trunk' or 'root' (*huk*). This is the *to'o-huk* (the 'trunk mother's brother' or, translated differently, the 'mother's brother of origin'). This man has charge over all his sister's children, who are his 'plants'. His duty is to perform the life-giving rituals that foster the growth of these plants. As such, the mother's brother has the right to indemnification for any damage to his 'plants'. In fact, if a person injures himself, he must pay compensation to his mother's brother. And this relationship passes on for another generation: the mother's brother (*to'o-huk*) becomes the *ba'i-huk* (the mother's mother's brother of origin) and he continues to have residual ritual rights in his sister's children's children.

As a consequence of these ideas of social relationships, the language of the rituals of the life cycle is so heavily couched in a botanic idiom that these rituals might be mistaken for agricultural ceremonies. The converse of this is also true. The plants, in agricultural rituals, are personified.

The botanic idiom is complex in that no one plant serves as a unique form of expression. In this elaborate semiology, a multitude of plants—or parts of plants—express different relations. Thus, in making a request for a girl in marriage, she is referred to as 'grain'//'seed' (*bini*//*ngges*). The marriage party therefore comes not to ask for a woman but to seek 'grain'//'seed'. Formerly, in some domains, the marriage ceremony itself was performed over a coconut with the prayer:

No ia tadak lima	This coconut has five layers
Mbunu holu so'en	The husk embraces the shell
So'en holu isin	The shell embraces the flesh
Isin holu oen	The flesh embraces the water
Ma oen holu mbolon.	And the water embraces the germ.
De ela leo be-na	So let it be
Ana touk no ana inak ia.	For this young man and woman.
Ela esa holu esa	Let one embrace the other
Ma ela esa lili esa	And one cling to the other
Fo ela numbu non, ana dadi	So that the shoots of the coconut may grow

Ma sadu mbua, ana mori	And the core of the areca palm may sprout
Fo ela bonggi	That she may give birth to
Sio lai sio	Nine times nine children
Ma rae	And that she may bring forth
Falu lai falu	Eight times eight children.[18]

A woman's first child is described as her 'eldest sprout'//'first fruit' (*pule uluk//boa sosak*). From the beginning of a child's life, the rituals emphasise botanic growth: 'budding' and 'sprouting' (*lea bu'ul//tona kale*). The performance of such rituals is made to coincide with the waxing of the moon, which, for the Rotenese, is believed to govern this growth. Children, and especially daughters, are said to grow up like quick-growing 'rice'//'millet' (*hade kasel//bete lai*). Daughters, as in the marriage ceremony, are most frequently represented by the paired icons of 'coconut palm'//'areca palm' (*no//pua*). In the chants, a common refrain for a young girl is that she is:

Bei nula-nula no	Still as unripe as a green-green coconut palm
Ma bei sadu-sadu pua.	And still as fresh as the shoots of the areca palm.

Sons are represented as either 'taros and tubers' (*tale//fia*) or, more often, 'banana and sugar cane' (*huni//tefu*). There is a particularly poignant funeral chant for the death of a young son that speaks only of the grievous loss of 'sugar cane' and 'banana'. A similar short chant, which could be mistaken as a prayer for agricultural increase, is in fact a plea for renewal and the continuation of sons:

Lole faik ia dalen	On this good day
Ma lada ledok ia tein na	And at this fine time
Lae:	They say:
Tefu ma-nggona lilok	The sugar cane has sheaths of gold
Ma huni ma-lapa losik.	And the banana has blossoms of copper.
Tefu olu heni nggonan	The sugar cane sheds its sheath
Ma huni kono heni lapan.	And the banana drops its blossoms
Te hu bei ela tefu okan	Still leaving but the sugar cane's root
Ma huni hun bai.	And the banana's trunk too.

---

18 See Fox (1971c, particularly pp. 235–36). The Rotenese text comes from van de Wetering (1925). In 1973, I attended a marriage ceremony in Thie at which the presiding ritual chanter offered to perform the traditional coconut ceremony but was told instead to provide Christian prayers for the bride and groom.

De dei tefu na nggona seluk	But the sugar cane sheaths again
Fo na nggona lilo seluk	The sheaths are gold again
Ma dei huni na lapa seluk	And the banana blossoms again
Fo na lapa losi seluk.	The blossoms are copper again.

The Rotenese depend on the lontar palm for their livelihoods and therefore, not surprisingly, this palm is another prominent icon used in the Rotenese botanic idiom. Like a lontar palm, every person is composed of 'semen or juice'//'blood or sap' (*oe*//*dak*). Juice dripping into a lontar-leaf bucket and collected provides the image of a social group. In Termanu, an extended family is referred to as 'the spilling drops and dripping sap' (*titi-nosi*//*da-fa* or *tititik*//*nonosik*).

Based on similar palm imagery, the lineages within a clan are referred to as *nggi-leo*//*nggona-haik*. Explicating this complex metaphor requires some exegesis. In the first part of this dyadic set, *nggi* refers to the long phallic inflorescences that hang from the crown of the male lontar palm. These inflorescences are squeezed—or, more correctly, in Rotenese terms, 'circumcised'—and their tips slivered and then tied into a single bundle to produce the flow of juice (*oe*) that is caught in leaf buckets (*haik*) suspended beneath them. In the second part of this dyadic set, *nggona* refers to the 'caul' that envelops the child at birth. *Nggi* is linked to *leo*, which refers to a 'lineage' or some segment of a clan, and *nggona* is linked to *haik*, the leaf bucket that catches the juice dripping from the lontar. A contrived literal translation for this complex dyadic set would be the 'lineage inflorescences'//'birth-caul bucket' (*nggi-leo*//*nggona-haik*).[19] A similar but more explicit expression is 'lineage inflorescences'//'birth groups' (*nggi-leo*//*bobongik*). Certain sets of large trees are repeatedly involved in poetic compositions. The first of these sets refers to two kinds of banyan or *waringin* tree (*Ficus spp.*): *kekal*//*nunu*. These trees, with their many branches, form a cosmic tree setting out paths of life and death:

---

19   One might expect this set to be *nggi-haik*//*nggona-leo**. Such a formulaic arrangement might make clearer the relationship of inflorescences and leaf bucket, caul and lineage. Instead, this formula is based on a 'crossover' of dyadic elements of a kind that occurs in the construction of other complex sets or formulae. Another ritual-language expression for a 'relative' is *tola-tungal*//*dudi-no*. This is a difficult expression to translate literally and seems to involve a curious rearrangement of the ordinary-language term for relative, *tola-no*. *Tola* is the verb for 'to penetrate, to force one's way through'. According to the Rotenese, childbirth is a 'bursting' or 'penetration' of the womb (*tola ndunuk*). *No* is interpreted as the third-person singular of the inflected prepositional 'to be with, to accompany'. In this expression, *tola* forms a set with *dudi* ('to pass through, to slip through'), while *no* forms a set with the word 'to follow'. Thus *tola-tungal*//*dudi-no* could be considered another 'crossover' where the expected arrangement for this set might more appropriately be *tola-no*//*dudi-tunga**.

Sa Lepa-Lai nunun	The *waringin* tree of Sa Lepa-Lai
Ma Huak Lali-Ha kekan	And the banyan tree of Huak Lali-Ha
Keka maba'e faluk	The banyan has eight branches
Ma nunun mandana siok.	And the *waringin* has nine boughs.
De dalak ko sio boe	These are the nine roads
Ma enok ko falu boe	And these are the eight paths
Fo dala sodak nai ndia	The road of wellbeing is there
Ma eno mamates nai na ...	And the path of death is there ...

Keka or, more specifically, *keka lasi* ('forest *keka*'; possibly *Ficus rumphii*) forms a pair with *fuli-ha'a*, the designation of another large hardwood tree, the molave (*Vitex parviflora timoriensis*). In the origin narratives, the wood of these two trees—'the two-leaved *keka-lasi* and the three-leaved *fuli-ha'a*'—is cut and hewed to construct the main beams and poles of the first house of the Sun and Moon.

Another pair of large trees that serve as icons in Rotenese ritual poetry are the *delas*, a large, rough-barked tree with striking orange flowers (Erythrina spp.), and the *nitas*, a sizeable, smooth-barked tree with large pungent purple flowers (Sterculia foetida). Both trees flower at the height of the dry season and, in poetry, they mark places of prominence:

Solu Oebau nitan-na	Solu Oebau has a *nitas* tree
Nita mabuna hanas	A *nitas* with blossoms of heat
Ma Pota Popo delan-na	And Pota Popo has a *delas* tree
Dela makapako ledok.	And *delas* with sun-like flowerbuds.

Growth is an external flowering and an internal hardening. In the rituals of life, there is progress from seed to shoot, from shoot to mature plant and, eventually, to full-standing tree. Certain elders are described as 'hard-cored', 'strong-willed' trees and lineage relations can be expressed in terms of large, enduring trees or old, hard-cored palms. A clansman is 'a jutting branch' or 'a descending leaf' (*ndana peuk//do laek*). After death, important individuals were remembered by the ceremonial construction of a circle of smooth river stones arranged around a great tree (*lutu tutus*). Perhaps the most vivid of these images is the Rotenese metaphor for sociality: a dense, untouched forest where tree branches are intertwined and scrape against one another. This rubbing together is ideal Rotenese sociality.

Speaking as a quintessential quality

Speaking is at the core of Rotenese culture. Speeches, sermons and ceremonial presentations—taletelling, debate, repartee and argument—are all essential elements of sociality. Among Rotenese, talk never ceases. In a class society, however, with hierarchies of order, there are some constraints on speech. In gatherings, nobles speak more than commoners, men more than women and elders more than juniors; yet, commoners, women and youth, when given the opportunity, invariably display the same prodigious fondness for speaking.

Only in certain rituals is silence required. Yet, even these occasional ritual injunctions Rotenese find hard to observe. In ordinary situations, a lack of talk is an indication of distress. Rotenese repeatedly explain that if their 'hearts' are confused or dejected, they keep silent. Thus, the act of speaking is critical to all human engagement and, from an early age, every Rotenese engages in the rhetorical presentation of self.

The vocabulary for speaking in ritual language is both extensive and elaborate. In the lexicon of ritual language, there are no less than 25 different verbs for speaking, cajoling, requesting, stating, asserting and conversing.[20] The dyadic sets that link the verbs for speaking are diverse and numerous, ranging from the general to the specific. Translating them appropriately in their different contexts is a daunting task. The most common recurrent dyadic set in the ritual language of Termanu pairs the verb 'to talk, converse' (*kola*) with the verb that implies a more purposive speech and thus can be translated as 'to speak, assert, argue' (*de'a*). This set is most frequently used in a semi-reduplicated form: *kokola//dede'a*. Another dyadic set for speaking links two verbs: *fada*, a general term meaning 'to speak, say, declare', with one that implies a pouring forth of words, *nosi*. (In other domains, though rarely in Termanu, the verb *fada* is paired with *kola*.) The paired verbs for asking or requesting, *tata//teteni*, also take a reduplicated form. An extended formula for speaking associated with women's speech is *selu* (or *ae*) *dasi//lole hala*. I translate this recurrent formula as 'to lift one's voice'//'to raise one's words'. This formula, however, can be further expanded to *lole lele hala//selu doko-doe dasi* ('to lift one's words encouragingly'//'to raise one's voice coaxingly'). The variety of these sets and their recurrence throughout the entire corpus of

---

20   I examine the semantic network of these verbs of speaking in Fox (1974: 77–79; 2014: 141–43).

ritual-language recitations are an indication of the fundamental importance of speaking for the Rotenese. It reflects a basic Rotenese understanding that the highest form of human interaction involves dialogue.

A philosophy of life and the cosmos

A large class of Rotenese ritual chants are concerned with the origins of Rotenese culture. These foundational chants recount the origins of fire and cooking, bridewealth and the objects given in bridewealth, and the house and the tools to construct the house. They also recount the origins of the patterns and implements used in weaving and dyeing and of the principal food crops on the island, particularly the seeds of rice and millet. All these chants are narrative in form and may once have formed part of a single account. Even in their present form, the fragments of this narrative—which are told separately on different ritual occasions—can be seen to relate to each other.

In these origin chants, Rote is the site of cosmological encounters between the Lords of the Heavens and the Lords of the Sea.

The Lords of the Heavens are Sun and Moon (*Ledo//Bulan*), whose children are the chief protagonists in the narratives. All heavenly elements are the descendants of the Sun and Moon. The Lords of the Ocean or Sea are ruled by Shark and Crocodile, whose realm includes all manner of sea creatures.

Whereas origin chants narrate the formative relations between the Lords of the Heavens and the Lords of the Sea, who gave rise to the foundations of Rotenese cultural life, the funeral chants offer personal perspectives on the course of life on Rote and, indeed, on life in general. Each chant is a set narrative that recounts the life of a particular 'chant character' leading from birth to death. Although each of these narratives differs in its telling in relation to the social position of the chant characters, the narratives as a whole are similar in their recourse to three recurrent themes. These themes are interwoven with one another and together convey a consistent message.

The first of these themes is that life is a journey. Life is a process of discovery even when that journey leads back to where it began. A search for wisdom and knowledge is part of this process and an essential feature of life.

A second emphatic theme is that there is no perfect order in the world. Acceptance of the world-as-it-is is essential wisdom. Thus, the most frequent refrain in all the funeral chants is the melancholy reiteration:

Tema ta nai batu poi	Perfection is not of the earth
Tetun ta nai dae bafok.	Order is not of the world.

This refrain has multiple levels of meaning, ranging from the humblest of instances—a torn cloth is no longer 'whole' (*tema*) and a post that falls over is no longer 'erect' (*tetu*); a forest that is felled is neither 'erect' nor 'whole'—to the most general commentary on life itself. As such, depending on context, *tema* can be translated as 'whole', 'integral', 'full', 'complete' or 'ordered', whereas *tetu* can be translated as 'erect', '(up)right' or 'perfect'. In all contexts, there is a relationship between these two terms. In the Heavens, as part of a cosmic order, the moon waxes to fullness (*bula temak*) whereas each day the sun rises to the zenith (*ledo tetu*). Yet, while this heavenly structure may provide a model of order and perfection, it is not one that can be replicated on Earth. Disorder in the world is a condition of life.

Finally, consistent with this view of life is a third theme that asserts that the condition of life is to be an 'orphan and widow' (*ana-mak ma falu-ina*) in the world. This condition is described as *ma-salak//ma-singok*. *Sala(k)* carries with it the idea of being 'mistaken, at fault, wronged' but also 'out of place' or simply 'displaced', while *singo(k)* indicates 'that which missed a target, has diverged, is divergent or off-course'. At a funeral, the bereaved are the 'orphans wronged and widows displaced' (*ana-mak ma-salak//falu-ina masingok*).

Being an 'orphan and widow' in the world implies a state of dependency— a dependency on others that requires a response. The funeral chants, in particular, admonish generosity to orphans and widows:

Fo ela neka lama kako bafa	Let the rice basket overflow at the mouth
Na dai ana-ma leo	To be enough for a clan of orphans
Ma bou lama lua fude	And the lontar syrup jar run over with froth
Na ndule falu-ina ingu.	To be sufficient for a group of widows.

Such admonitions are often figuratively expressed. In a botanic idiom, the following admonition calls forth a continuing, living generosity:

Te sadi mafa-ndendelek	Do indeed remember
Ma sadi masa-nenedak	And do keep in mind
Heo Ingu-fao baun	The *bau* tree at Heo Ingu-Fao
Ma Dolo Sala-Poi tuin na,	And the *tui* tree at Dolo Sala-Poi,
Bau naka-boboik	A *bau* tree to care for
Ma tui nasa-mamaok.	And a *tui* tree to watch over.
De tati mala bau ndanan	Cut and take a branch of the *bau* tree
Ma aso mala tui baen	Slice and take a limb from the *tui* tree
Fo tane neu dano Hela	To plant at the Lake Hela
Ma sele neu le Kosi	And to sow at the River Kosi
Fo ela okan-na lalae	That its roots may creep forth
Ma samun-na ndondolo	And its tendrils may twine
Fo ela poek-kala leu tain	For shrimp to cling to
Ma nik-kala leu feon,	And crabs to circle round,
Fo poek ta leu tain	For it is not for shrimp to cling to
Te ana-mak leu tain	But for orphans to cling to
Ma nik ta leu feon	And not for crabs to circle round
Te falu-ina leu feon.	But for widows to circle round.

In keeping with this botanic metaphor is the hope enunciated in another funeral chant:

Lena-lena ngala lemin	All you great ones
Lesi-lesi ngala lemin	All you superior ones
Sadi mafandendelek	Do remember this
Sadi masanenedak	Do bear this in mind
Fo ana-ma tua fude	For orphans, the froth of cooking syrup
Ma falu-ina beba langa la	And for widows, the heads of leafstalks
Tua fude dua kako na	When the lontar froth spills over twice
Kako kao mala sila	Scoop it up for them
Ma beba langa telu te na	And when the stalk's head droops thrice
Te tenga mala sila	Lop it off for them
Fo ela-ana-ma bei tema	Leaving orphans still intact
Ma falu ina bei tetu	And widows still in order
Fo leo tema toe-ao lasin na	Intact like a dense forest
Teman losa don na	Intact for a long time
Ma tetu lelei nulan na	And in order like a thick wood
Tetun nduku nete na.	Upright for an age.

In 1965, when I had only just begun to comprehend the imagery of Rotenese ritual language, the poet Stefanus Adulanu—'Old Meno', as he was known—tried to explain the significance of the idea of 'orphan and widow'. To provide me with this understanding, he interpolated his explanation into another funeral chant, *Lilo Tola ma Koli Lusi*, which he recited for me:

Se ana-mak?	Who is an orphan?
Na basang-ngita ana-mak	All of us are orphans
Ma se falu-ina?	And who is a widow?
Na basang-ngita falu-ina.	All of us are widows.
Fo la-fada lae:	They speak of:
Manu Kama dala dain	Manu Kama's road to Dain
Ma Tepa Nilu eno selan.	And Tepa Nilu's path to Selan.
Na basang-ngita ta enon	All of us do not follow his path
Ma basang-ngita ta dalan.	And all of us do not follow his road.
Sosoa-na nai dae bafak kia nde bena	This means that on this Earth then
Ana-mak mesan-mesan	Each person is an orphan
Ma falu-ina mesa-mesan.	And each person is a widow.
De mana-sapeo nggeok	Those who wear black hats
Do mana-kuei modok ko	Or those who wear yellow slippers
Se ana-ma sila boe	They will be orphans too
Ma falu-ina sila boe.	And they will be widows too.

In this explanation, death is the great leveller that leaves everyone bereaved. The expression 'those who wear black hats or those who wear yellow slippers', which dates from the time of the Dutch East India Company, is the formulaic designation for the Dutch (and Portuguese). As Old Meno has pointedly observed in these lines, there are different life pathways, but all result in the same end. All humans are 'orphans and widows'.

3

Background and exegesis of the origin narratives of Termanu

The domain of Termanu as a political and social creation

Termanu is one of 18 small previously self-ruling polities (*nusak*) that make up the island of Rote. The establishment of Termanu, as revealed in its oral histories, begins with the ancestor Pada Lalais. Another ancestor, Ma Bulan, arrives in Termanu from across the seas and confronts Pada Lalais. The two contest the ownership of the land. Ma Bulan triumphs by stealth and trickery and gains the right to rule; Ma Bulan becomes the *Manek* or 'Male Lord' and his descendants give rise to the ruling clan, while Pada Lalais is given ritual authority over the Earth and thus becomes the *Dae Langak* or 'Head of the Earth'. To this day, Termanu is referred to by its population as *Pada*. Its dialect is described as *dede'a Pada* ('*Pada* dialect').

Subsequent accounts, all told in the dialect of *Pada* (and not in ritual language), constitute a long and complicated dynastic history that sets out a division in the ruling clan between a 'Male Lord' (*Manek*) and a complementary 'Female Lord' (*Fetor*) and the successive affiliations of some clans along with the defeat of others to form a political union of 'Nine Clan Lords' (*Mane Sio*) attached to the Lord of Termanu. The arrival of the Dutch East India Company and its involvement in local politics are recounted in the oral histories and are occasionally seen as decisive, but Termanu's complicated dynastic history is concerned more with the politics of local succession. The whole of this dynastic history is based on a long royal genealogy of many generations that provides the scaffolding for its narration.

Termanu is mentioned in Dutch East India Company records in 1661. In 1662, the Company signed the first of several contracts with Termanu's ruler. Termanu's location on the northern coast of the island gave it a favoured position. The Dutch built a small fortification at a harbour area known as Kota Leleuk and, by 1677, had stationed armed personnel there to act on its behalf. In that same year, the Company took the teenage son of the ruler of Termanu to Kupang on Timor to learn Malay, the language used by the Dutch in all their dealings on the island. While other territories on Rote resisted the Dutch, Termanu remained a loyal ally.

From its favoured position, Termanu initially expanded its territory and came to dominate central Rote. However, in the later part of the eighteenth century, it was forced to relinquish authority over territory on the southern coast as the Company recognised more local rulers, eventually dividing the island into 18 separate domains. In the nineteenth century, Termanu was the first domain to cooperate with the Dutch in transferring population to settle around Kupang to provide a buffer against incursions by the local Timorese. As a result, relative to other domains, Termanu held extensive territory with a lower density of population. This was particularly the case in relation to the domain of Thie to its south and the domain of Dengka to its west. With wide grasslands for herds of water buffalo and key sources of water for irrigating rice, Termanu's ruling dynasty had greater wealth than the rulers in other domains. This dynasty was able to assert political authority on the island.

As a domain, Termanu's internal political structure consisted of a large ruling clan, Masa-Huk, divided among many ranked lineages and surmounted by Fola-Teik, the lineage of Termanu's ruler, the *Manek* or 'Male Lord'. Kota Deak, a clan that originated from an early division of the ruling clan, provided the *Fetor* or 'Female Lord'. At the court of the *Manek* were the 'Nine Lords' (*Mane Sio*) of clans recognised by and affiliated with the royal lineage. These named clans were: Kiu-Kanak, Ulu-Anak, Sui, Dou-Danga, Ingu-Beuk, Nggofa-Laik, Ingu-Nau, Ingu-Fao and Meno, the clan founded by Pada Lalais, whose ritual title, *Dae Langak* or 'Head of the Earth', remained of ritual importance.

In Termanu, there was a differentiation between nobles—*mane-ana* ('descendants of the *manek*') and *feto-ana* (descendants of the *fetor*)—and commoners (*la'uk*). Precedence was a considerable concern among high-ranking lineages, especially those of the ruling clan, Masa-Huk, whose apex was dominated by the status line Fola-Teik. This idealised structure, as recounted and legitimised in the oral histories, masked a diversity of more complex relations among the lineages within the domain's principal clans—a social complexity that must be seen in perspective. Termanu had a population of fewer than 6,000 people at the time of my first fieldwork in 1965–66.

Of narrators and their knowledge of origins

An exegesis of the origin narratives of Termanu must begin with a discussion of the narrators who provided these recitations. Within the domain, each narrator was considered a 'person of knowledge' (*hataholi malelak*). This designation is one that is accorded sparingly to elders who are regarded as possessing a knowledge of the past—particularly the distant past—and thus possess a knowledge of origins: the 'trunk and root' (*hu ma oka*) of Rotenese traditions. Some but not all of these knowledgeable elders have the ability and fluency to recite long narratives. These men—and they are mostly men—are recognised as 'chanters' or 'poets' (*manahelo*).

The key narrator of Termanu's origin narratives was Stefanus Adulanu, known as 'Old Meno' (*Meno Tua*), who was the 'Head of the Earth' (*Dae Langak*) in Termanu. His position made him the principal custodian of Termanu's traditions.

On my first field trip to Rote in 1965, I was taken by the Ruler (*Manek*) of Termanu, who at the time held the government position as *Camat* or District Head of Rote, to the royal residence at Feapopi and introduced to an assembled group of elders from Termanu. He presented me as his proposed 'historian' to gather the history of the domain. I was called on, in my still faltering Indonesian, to display something of what I had already gathered about the domain from Dutch sources. I had a list of the clans of Termanu from various sources and I went through this list asking whether there was a representative of each clan at the gathering. When I called the name of clan Meno, 'Old Meno' stood up and we met for the first time. Meno's first ancestor was Pada Lalais, the ancestral figure central to the founding of the domain. As I was quickly made aware, the true name of the domain used by its members is *Pada*.

Eventually, when my wife and I had settled in Ufa Len in Termanu, Old Meno, who lived in the nearby village of Ola Lain, took me under his wing and made a concerted effort to teach me what he felt I needed to know about *Pada*. He focused on teaching me ritual language as a means of understanding *Pada*'s traditions. Later Old Meno told me that he was initially reluctant to reveal too much, but because I had come with a bulky Uher tape recorder—dubbed the 'voice catcher' (*penangkap suara*, in Indonesian)—he realised that I had the capacity to pass on his recitations to future generations.

Most of the crucial origin narratives I recorded were gathered during the first intensive year of fieldwork. These narratives were considered foundational to my learning and critical to the understanding I needed to advance my comprehension of Rotenese culture. As a result, there were other elders and knowledgeable individuals who were keen to offer me recitations. All such recitations came at a time when I was struggling to grasp the basics of the Rotenese language and, more dauntingly, the pervasive particularities of Rotenese ritual language. Old Meno always avoided a direct answer. He would invariably circle around the point he was trying to convey, and he would often reply to a question of mine with a return question, which if I understood it, might hint at the answer to my question. It took me months to adapt to his manner of guiding me towards understanding.

At the time when Old Meno had begun tutoring me, another figure, Peu Malesi, came forward to recite. He was probably in his forties but not yet socially regarded as a person of knowledge. Yet, he was exceptionally knowledgeable, versatile and fluent. He provided me with my first full recitation (Recitation 1, in Chapter 4), which I asked a local schoolteacher, Jon Pello, to transcribe. I then took the transcription to Old Meno for his help with translation and exegesis. My possession of this key narrative prompted Old Meno to overcome his hesitancy about revealing more of his own knowledge.

Early in my time at Ufa Len, there were others who came forward, unexpectedly, to recite for my tape recorder. The most unusual of these chanters was Lisabeth Adulilo, who came looking for me during a feast that was being held nearby. She was direct, forthcoming and fluent. She recited Recitation 2 in this collection (Chapter 4), listened back to her words and left. I expected her to come again to Ufa Len, but she never reappeared. She was the only woman ever to provide me with a long recitation and I was unable to learn more about her.

Another chanter who appeared only once was Ayub Amalo, a member of the royal lineage. He provided the initial basis for Recitations 5 and 6 (Chapter 4). As I did with Recitation 1, I took Ayub Amalo's Recitation 5 to Old Meno and he elaborated on it considerably without changing any of the names that Amalo had used. Recitation 6 was shorter and I did not require similar assistance from Old Meno. As with Lisabeth Adulanu, I hoped for another visit from Ayub Amalo but he never returned to Ufa Len.

Another chanter of note was Eli Pellondou, known as Seu Ba'i, whom I first met at Old Meno's house in Ola Lain. Seu Ba'i spent time with Old Meno seemingly learning from him. I considered that he was doing an informal apprenticeship as he would often be with Meno when I came for one of my regular visits. Seu Ba'i was from the same clan, Dou Danga, as Peu Malesi, but from a different branch of this clan located in Namodale. He listened to the recording I had made of Lizabeth Adulilo's recitation, and this prompted him to offer his own short recitation, which was intended as a comment and correction. This has become Recitation 3.[1]

To add to my accumulation of origin narratives, Old Meno provided me with two more: Recitations 8 and 9. As a result, all but one of the origin narratives of Termanu in this collection were gathered during my first visit to Rote in 1965–66, and virtually all of them were provided by or filtered through Old Meno. The one exception is Recitation 4 by the poet Esau Pono.

In 1965–66, I hardly knew of Esau Pono, who lived in the village of Hala. By the time of my second visit, in 1972–73, he had begun to gain a reputation as a preacher rather than as a traditional chanter, and I turned to him as my speaker for a memorial *tutus* ceremony for Old Meno that I sponsored with Old Meno' son. Our friendship began then and continued when I visited Rote to make documentaries of Rotenese life with the filmmaker Tim Asch in 1977 and again in 1978. We invited Pak Pono, as he was known, to Canberra to help with the film.

Over the years, our friendship grew and I watched Pak Pono's stature in the community grow until he came to be regarded as a true person of knowledge and the leading chanter of Termanu. Only in 2007 did Pak Pono insist on reciting his version of Termanu's origin narrative. Importantly, his recitation

---

1   During 1965–66, my dealings with Seu Ba'i were limited. On a subsequent visit to Rote in 1973–74, I recorded a great deal more from Seu Ba'i and learned more from him. I was later introduced to others among his close relatives, all of whom were notable poets.

shows a continuity in the transmission of the knowledge of origins that stretches back over 40 years. His recitation shows its specific continuity with recitations by Peu Malesi and Seu Ba'i, which Pak Pono would have heard on various occasions.

The collection of oral narratives of Termanu in this volume was not gathered systematically with a clear idea of its assemblage, but rather in the confusion of initial fieldwork with all the challenges associated with this discovery process. The main task of this fieldwork was to understand the social realities of Rotenese life. Old Meno was more concerned to carry out the initial instructions of the *Manek* of Termanu that I be informed of the history of the domain. This required the accumulation of a diverse assortment of narratives in ordinary language and of the genealogies of the clans and lineages that provided the scaffolding for these oral histories. Old Meno was also intent on my attending court sessions to understand how deliberations were conducted according to Rotenese customary law (*hadat*).

At the time, most ritual-language recordings that I made were of funeral chants because these are less restricted and constitute the bulk of the Rotenese religious liturgy. Had Peu Malesi not provided his initial origin chant, I suspect Meno would have delayed his revelation of these most serious of oral narratives until I was further along in my understanding. In the end, however, the collection took shape principally under the guidance of Old Meno.

Of names and their significance

Names are an essential feature of the origin narratives. These names apply to persons, places and a variety of objects and creatures. Personal names follow a genealogical pattern that links children with their father. Personal names can also merge with placenames to define an identity by locality. The problem is, however, that names often vary in different recitations even when these recitations recount similar events. No topic causes more disputes among chanters on Rote than the names that occur in the origin narratives.

The names in the collection of origin narratives from Termanu are a prime example of what can cause disputes. Although there may be some general agreement, points of difference are notable. In the first four recitations, the son or sons of the Sun and Moon (Ledo Holo and Bula Kai) are Mandeti Ledo and Patola Bulan. However, Recitation 5 gives different names for these sons, Ndu Bulan and Pala Ledo, while Recitation 4 introduces another set of sons, Kaibake Ledo and Lakimola Bulan, who, though hunters, become farmers of the land. Similarly, most of the recitations identify the Lords of Sea and Ocean as Danga Lena Liun and Mane Tua Sain. However, Recitation 3 gives these names as Danga Lena Liun and Mone Ni Sain and Recitation 5 gives Tou Danga Liun and Mane Tua Sain.

There is a minor variation in the name of the daughter of the Sun and Moon, who marries into the Sea: she is Fuda Kea Ledo and Tau Senge Bulan, as in Recitation 1; Kudu Kea Ledo and Tau Senge Bulan, as in Recitations 2 and 3; or Kudu Kea Ledo and Matau Senge Bulan, as in Recitation 4. There are greater differences in the names of the spouse whom she divorces—either Nggolo Fae Batu and Teke Laba Dae, as in Recitation 1, or Bose Latu and Do Lona, as in Recitation 2—and with the names of the spouse whom she marries: Danga Lena Liun and Mane Tua Sain, as in Recitation 1; Holo-Te Liun and Bala-Mae Sain, as in Recitations 2 and 3; or Tio Holo Te and Dusu Bala Mae, as in Recitation 3. Similarly, there are differences in the names of the hunting dogs of the sons of the Sun and Moon and those of the Lords of the Sea.

Several recitations recount attempts at building the first house. These recitations cite a plethora of different builders and crafts creatures who become engaged in this effort. Each recitation names a distinct set of builders. In Recitation 1, the first builder is Makandolu Le ('River Crafter') and Malela Dano ('Lake Designer'), who constructs the house on one side that then slants to the other. Then others are called. This group consists of Didi Bulan ('Moon Spinner') and Bolau Ledo ('Sun Spider'), Solu Nggelo ('Chop Apart') and Silu Mola ('Hack Open'), and Kili-Kili Ki ('Sharpen Left') and Fona-Fona Kona ('Draw Right')—all of whom perform the tasks their names imply. Recitation 2 does not mention all these names but concentrates on the role of Didi Bulan ('Moon Spinner') and Bolau Ledo ('Sun Spider'), who mark out the layout of the house beams with their spittle. There is no mention of building the house in Recitations 3 and 4 while in Recitation 5, Makandolu Sain ('Sea Crafter') and Malela Liun ('Ocean Designer') are called on to forge and sharpen Bani Asa and Doke Tei, the axe and machete.[2]

---

2   How or whether the chant character Makandolu Sain ('Sea Crafter') and Malela Liun ('Ocean Designer') in Recitation 5 are related to Makandolu Le ('River Crafter') and Malela Dano ('Lake Designer') named in Recitation 1 remains uncertain.

The initial hunting area where Mandeti Ledo and Patola Bulan first meet Danga Lena Liun and Mane Tua Sain is also given different names. In Recitation 1, the riverbed of Ango-Kala and the forest of Nggae-Kala are first mentioned but, as the hunt continues, the area is referred to as Ledu Ama Medik's wood and Sadu Ama Kiuk's forest. In Recitation 2, this hunting area is referred to as the woods of Kai Tio and the forest of Lolo Batu; in Recitation 4, the area is the same as in Recitation 1—the Ango-Kala River and Nggae-Kala Forest. The name of the pig and civet that the hunters catch can be considered a name or a descriptor: *Nggeo Alu* refers to a 'black-shouldered' pig and *Tena Lolo* refers to a 'sleek-bodied' civet. In all recitations, these animals are identified with the realm of the Sea.

Names proliferate in other recitations, particularly in the succession of placenames that form the topogeny in Recitation 7. Recitation 7 links personal names and placenames. Lexical elements in the two names point to an intimate connection. Thus, for example, the woman named Fi Bau and Seda Kola comes from *Bau Peda Dele* and *Kola Sifi Ndai*, while the woman Fiti Nggoli and Lole Bako comes from *Nggoli Kai Tio* and *Bako Bau Dale*, and the woman Pinga Peto and Lu'a Lela comes from *Peto Lesi-Ama* and *Lela Bala-Fia*. All these are sites in the domain of Termanu.

Names can signal major differences in the general cast of these origin narratives, which concern their revelations about the first marriage between the Sun and Moon and the Lords of the Sea and Ocean. While Recitations 1 and 4 assert that this first marriage is with Danga Lena Liun and Mane Tua Sain, Recitations 2 and 3 insist that this first marriage is with Holo Te Liun and Bala Mae Sain. All four of these recitations accord the Heavens superiority by making the Heavens the wife-giver to the Sea. The transference of goods establishes the first bridewealth. By contrast, Recitation 5 reverses this relationship. Ledo Holo and Bula Kai marries Lada Saik and Lole Liuk ('Sea Tastiness and Ocean Goodness') and she brings with her all the implements of cultural production as bridal goods. This is a radical alternative view portraying the Sea as wife-giver and thus as socially superior.

On narrative differences

The directionality of marriage—who gives a woman and who receives a woman as a wife—is crucial to defining social position in Rotenese society: wife-givers are superior to wife-takers because they provide the flow of life that extends from them. This flow of life creates a chain of relations that is supposed to continue for generations. It involves lifegiving rituals and regular recompense for the bestowal of life. For this reason, Recitation 5 offers a radical perspective on relations between the Heavens and the Sea and is fundamentally different from the perspective in Recitations 1, 2, 3 and 4 as well as the perspective implicit in the other recitations. (It is also at odds with the perspective in the chief recitations of the domain of Thie.)[3] Recitation 5 does, however, provide a similar view of the great transference of wealth from the Sea to the Heavens and of subsequent efforts at constructing the first house.

Apart from Recitation 5, the other recitations present a generally coherent perspective on the often turbulent relations between the Heavens and the Sea. One of the most significant of these is Recitation 8, which narrates the origin of the beautiful weaving and dyeing that causes a breach in these relations.

In Recitation 8, the daughters of the Sun and Moon, Henge Ne Ledo ('Cloth Binder of the Sun') and Feo Futu Bulan ('Thread Winder of the Moon') give the loom and shuttle to Lui Liuk ('Sea Cow of the Ocean') and Kea Saik ('Turtle of the Sea'). Both weave, tie and dye cloths with crocodile patterns and shark designs. At this time, both the women of the Heavens and the women of the Sea produce similar patterns, but this is not the case on Earth.

Recitation 8 relates that the man Lodo Bela and the boy Solu Lolo from the island of Ndao have become engaged to the woman Pua Kene and the girl No Lini in Loleh on Rote and have returned to Ndao to gather the bridewealth necessary to marry. In their absence, Pata Iuk ('Figure Shark') and Dula Foek ('Pattern Crocodile') come from the Sea and force themselves on Pua Kene and No Lini. In revenge, Lodo Bela and Solu Lolo kill Pata Iuk and Dula Foek as they are about to re-enter the Sea near the island of Ndao.

The woman Haba Ndao and the girl Lida Folo see the patterns produced by Figure Shark and Pattern Crocodile and hurry to buy a loom and shuttle from Kea Saik and Lui Liuk in the Sea. They bring the loom and shuttle back to Ndao and produce cloths that display the patterns of the shark and crocodile. The knowledge of weaving, dyeing and of the skill to produce

---

3   As a recorder and commentator on these oral narratives, I can offer no explanation simply because none was offered to me.

beautiful, patterned cloth is transferred from Ndao to Rote. Although this knowledge has been gained, there exists a breach in relations and, as is recounted in Recitation 9, it is not possible to perform the proper origin celebrations.

As narratives, the recitations are implicitly or tangentially linked to one another, and it is necessary to look to earlier narratives to understand the full significance of later narratives. Thus, for example, as recounted in Recitations 2 and 3, the marriage with the Sea produces the offspring Tio Holu Te and Dusu Bala Lae. These creatures are identified with the blue-spotted emperor fish and bartail goatfish and are the fish that are sought in Recitation 9 by the woman Nggiti Seti and the girl Pedu Hange to perform the ritual that enlivens an origin celebration. The eventual re-establishment of harmonious relations between the Heavens and the Sea, as is recounted in Recitation 9, allows the woman Lole Holu and Lua Bafa to catch the *tio* and *dusu* fish that eluded her mother and thus perform the necessary ritual to hold an origin celebration. At this origin celebration, the textiles with shark and crocodile patterns are worn and displayed. As such, Recitation 9 ends with a restoration of harmony.

Of recitations and ritual purpose

Taken together, these narratives offer a fascinating account of the relations between the rulers of the Heavens and the rulers of the Sea. The various recitations present episodes in the development of these relations. It is likely that these narratives were part of a longer epic that has come down to the present in fragments. What has been transmitted over time relates to rituals for which these recitations were once performed.

Versions of Recitations 1 to 5 were once required as part of the rituals for the construction of a house—one of the most important of Rotenese rituals. Other versions of these same recitations may have also been performed as an accompaniment to the rituals for the payment of bridewealth and the celebration of marriage. Similarly, versions of Recitations 6 and 7 were once performed in relation to the planting of rice and millet, while Recitations 8 and 9 were likely to have been recounted when new weaving or dyeing was undertaken.

What has not been transmitted in Termanu are any of the recitations that once related to the celebration of annual origin ceremonies known as *hus* (or, in ritual language, as *hu//sio*: 'celebrations of origin and of nine').[4] Only one invocation from the *Hus Ina* ('The Great Mother *Hus*') of the royal clan Masa-Huk of Termanu was told to me.

At this celebration, the ceremonial leader, the 'Lord of Heat' (*Mane-Hanas*), would wrap himself in an immensely long cloth (*hahalik*) and, dragging this cloth behind him, he would approach a large Java olive tree (*nitas*; *Sterculia foetida*) and, with a raised spear, call on the moon, saying:

Kona, bulan, kona	Descend, moon, descend
Kona, bulan, kona	Descend, moon, descend
Kona, bulan, kona	Descend, moon, descend
Kona musik nitas-a boboa kona	Descend to the right of the *nitas* tree
Muni meti ma-isi	Bring the abundance of the tide
Muni tua ma-oe	Bring the juice of the lontar palm
Muni bafi mana-bongi-siok	Bring the nine-farrowed sow
Muni manu tutu-natuk.	Bring the hundred pecking chickens.

The chorus, circling round the *nitas* tree, would renew and amplify his invocation. By the conventions of ritual language, the sun must be mentioned with the moon and the spear with the sword, even though the symbolic action was directed with a spear towards the moon. The chorus would respond by singing:

Sio bafi-la tola	The pigs of the Feast of Nine appear
Ma hu kapa-la dadi.	And buffalo of the Origin Celebration grow.
Besak-a ala soku lala bulan ten	Now they lift the spear of the moon
Ma ala ifa lala ledo tafa-na	And they cradle the sword of the sun
De lalo neu bulan	They call upon the moon
Ma langgou neu ledo, lae:	And they address the sun, saying:
Kona, mai	Come, descend
Fo muni dini oe manahaik	To bring sufficient moist dew
Ma a'u oe manano'uk	And ample dampening water

---

4   The dyadic set *hu//sio* used to describe these ceremonies links the pair *hu*, meaning 'origin' or 'trunk', with the term *sio* for 'nine'—a numeral associated with 'fullness' and 'completion'. In Thie, these ceremonies are, in ritual language, designated by another dyadic set: *holi//limba*.

Fo tete dae bafak	To rain down upon the Earth
Ma totoli batu poi	And pour down upon the world
Ma fe tua ma-oe	And give the juice of the lontar palm
Ma tasi ma-isi	And the abundance of the sea
Ma kale duak	And two grains
Ma pule teluk	And three seeds
Fo kalen-na didiku	That the grain stalks might bend
Ma pulen-na loloso	And the seed shoots come forth
Fo ela ana-mak lamahena	To allow the orphans to hope
Ma falu-ina lakabani.	And the widows to trust.

These invocations directed to the moon were for rain, for the juice of the lontar, for the fruits of the sea, for an abundant harvest, for the fertility of animals and for the health and strength of humankind. In Termanu, unlike Thie, these origin celebrations ended in the nineteenth century. The narratives that accompanied them are no longer known.

4

The origin narratives of Termanu

The origin narratives of the domain of Termanu consist of nine recitations of varying lengths. Each recounts ancient relations between the realms of the Heavens and the Sea. Each of these realms has its rulers and descendants, who encounter and engage with one another, producing benefits that are eventually passed on to humankind.

Five of these narratives concern the initial encounter of the Sun and Moon, Rulers of the Heavens and the Heights, with Shark and Crocodile, the Great Hunter of the Ocean and Stalker of the Sea. All these versions describe this momentous encounter in similar terms, each adding specific revelations to its account. However, these versions differ in their presentation of the marriage contracted between the Heavens and the Sea. The differences are significant in defining the relationship between these realms.

The narratives of the first encounter are also concerned with the origin of an array of implements for living: the means for the creation of fire, for gardening and for building houses as well as for preparing cooked food. All this wealth originates from the depths of the Sea and includes gold and water buffalo.

Subsequent origin narratives are predicated on the continuing relationship between the Heavens and the Sea. They recount the origin of a special kind of millet from the Heavens along with other sorts of rice and millet from the Sea; they reveal the origin of the loom, of tie-dyeing and of the distinctive patterns on Rotenese cloth. They also recount the spread and transference of these goods throughout the island of Rote. The last of the narratives recounts the troubled relations between the Heavens and the Sea and their resolution through yet another union. This narrative of a pair of shells—a nautilus and a baler shell—expelled from the Sea also accounts for the origin of the vessel used for keeping indigo dye and the base of the spindle used in preparing thread.

These origin narratives are listed as Recitations 1 to 9, each of which bears the name of a chant character whose role is prominent in the recitation. Doubtless, these narratives are a fragment of a much larger heritage of traditional knowledge. All that is here preserved is what was recited to me in my episodic efforts in trying to learn this most important of traditional knowledge.

Recitation 1. The origin of fire, of cooking and of the implements for living

Petrus Malesi

Patola Bulan ma Mandeti Ledo

The initial misguided hunt for pig and civet

The sons of the Sun and Moon, Mandeti Ledo and Patola Bulan, set out to hunt, accompanied by their dogs, Pia Dola and Hua Lae. Their hunt takes them into the forbidden forest of the Sun and Moon, where they corner their father's tame civet. They are reprimanded and allotted new lands in which to hunt.

1.	*Boe ma ala soku Mandeti Ledo*	They set off, Mandeti Ledo
2.	*Ma lali Patola Bulan.*	And they go forth, Patola Bulan.
3.	*De ala fu-toleu asu*	They whistle for their dog
4.	*Ma ala kati-kofio busa*	And they call for their hound
5.	*Busa nade Pia Dola*	The hound named Pia Dola
6.	*Ma asu nade Hua Lae.*	And the dog named Hua Lae.
7.	*Ala sopu lai basa dae*	They hunt through all the land
8.	*Ala fule [lai] basa oe.*	They stalk through all the water.
9.	*Leu Ledo lasi nana-papadak*	They go to the Sun's forbidden forest
10.	*Ma Bulan nula nana-babatak*	And the Moon's restricted wood

11.	*Ma lala meo dei pana-foe*	And they catch a pied-nosed cat
12.	*Ma kue dei iko-fula,*	And a white-tailed civet,
13.	*Bulan kue nasa-mao*	The Moon's fond civet
14.	*Ma Ledo meo naka-boi-na.*	The Sun's tame cat.
15.	*Boe ma lae a:*	Then they [the Sun and Moon] say:
16.	*'Emi sopu sala dae*	'You hunted mistakenly on the land
17.	*Ma emi fule sala oe.'*	You stalked mistakenly on the water.'
18.	*De ala ba'e fes dae*	So, they allot them land
19.	*Ma tada fes oe.*	And assign them water.

The resumption of the hunt and the encounter with the Lords of the Sea

The sons of the Sun and Moon set out to hunt again, this time in forests along the seashore. At the same time and in the same forests, the Great Lord of the Sea and Chief Hunter of the Ocean, Shark and Crocodile, are also hunting with their dogs, Masi Tasi ('Sea Salt') and Deta Dosa(n) ('Sour Dip'). The dogs join and corner a civet and a pig: Tena Lolo of the Sea and Nggeo Alu of the Ocean. The civet's name can be translated as the 'Sleek Body of the Sea' and the pig's as 'Black Shoulder of the Ocean'.

20.	*Boe ma leu Ango-Kala le dale*	Then they go into the riverbed of Ango-Kala
21.	*Ma leu Nggaek-Ka lasi lai.*	And they go into the forest of Nggaek Ka.
22.	*Asu-la ta fua*	The dogs corner nothing
23.	*Ma busa-la ta eko.*	And the hounds encircle nothing.
24.	*Besak-ka leu Ledu Ama Medik nulan*	Now they go to Ledu Ama Medik's wood
25.	*Nai sain naka-to beten*	Where millet fields border the sea
26.	*Ma Sadu Ama Kiuk lasin*	And to Sadu Ama Kiuk's forest
27.	*Nai liun ma-talada haden.*	Where rice fields bound the ocean.
28.	*Besak-ka asu-la leu fua*	Now the dogs corner something
29.	*Ma busa-la leu eko.*	And the hounds encircle something.
30.	*Boe ma Danga Lena Liun busa*	The hound of the Chief Hunter of the Ocean
31.	*Ma Man'Tua Sain asu*	And the dog of the Great Lord of the Sea

32.	*Ma asu nade Masi Tasi*	The dog named Masi Tasi
33.	*Busa nade Deta Dosan.*	And the hound named Deta Dosan.
34.	*Asu ha leu eko*	The four dogs encircle their quarry
35.	*Ma busa telu leu fua*	And the three hounds corner their prey
36.	*De ala fua laka-bubua*	They corner in a pack
37.	*Ma eko la-e'esa.*	And they encircle together.
38.	*Boe ma lala Tena Lola Liuk*	Thus, they catch Tena Lolo Liuk
39.	*Ma lala Nggeo Alu Saik.*	And they catch Nggeo Alu Saik.

The discussion of where to hold the sacrifice of pig and civet

The sons of the Sun and Moon converse with the Lords of the Sea. Mandeti Ledo and Patola Bulan propose that they go to the Heights to hold the sacrifice of pig and civet. The Lords of the Sea ask what they will eat to accompany this sacrifice of pig and civet and are told that the accompaniment ('spouse') will be 'raw leaves' (*nae do*) and 'river water' (*oe le*). The Lords of the Sea counter this proposal, urging instead that they all descend into the Sea for their sacrifice.

40.	*Boe ma Mandeti Ledo kokolak*	Then Mandeti Ledo speaks
41.	*Ma Patola Bulan dede'ak, nae:*	And Patola Bulan talks, saying:
42.	*'Teu be fina kue*	'Where shall we go to eat the sacrifice of civet
43.	*Ma teu be fati bafi?*	And where shall we go to eat the offering of pig?
44.	*Teu poi fina kue*	Let us go to the Heights to eat the sacrifice of civet
45.	*Ma teu lain fati bafi.'*	And let us go to the Heavens to eat the offering of pig.'
46.	*Boe ma Danga Lena Liun*	But the Chief Hunter of the Ocean
47.	*[Ma Mane Tua Sain]*	[And the Chief Hunter of the Sea]
48.	*Nahela ma nae:*	Raises his voice and says:
49.	*'Teu poin fina kue*	'Let us go to the Heights to eat the sacrifice of civet
50.	*Fo malole-la so*	For these things are good
51.	*Ma teu lain fati bafi*	And let us go to the Heavens to eat the offering of pig

52.	*Fo mandak-kala so.*	For these things are proper.
53.	*Hu kue tun nde se*	But who is the civet's mate
54.	*Bafi saon nde se?'*	And who is the pig's spouse?'
55.	*Ma nae: 'Bafi saon Nae Do*	And he says: 'The pig's spouse is raw leaves
56.	*Ma kue tun Oe Le.'*	And the civet's mate is river water.'
57.	*Boe ma touk Danga Lena Liun*	Then the man Danga Lena of the Ocean
58.	*Ma ta'ek Mane Tua Sain*	And the boy Mane Tua of the Sea
59.	*Lole-la halan neu*	Raises his voice
60.	*Ma selu doko-doe dasin:*	And offers his word:
61.	*'Teu poin fina kue-na*	'If we go to the Heights to eat the sacrifice of civet
62.	*Sosoan bei ta*	This still has no purpose
63.	*Ma teu lain fati bafi-na*	And if we go to the Heavens to eat the offering of pig
64.	*Ndandan bei ta.*	This still has no sense.
65.	*Dilu teu liun dalek*	Let us turn and go down into the Ocean
66.	*Ma loe teu sain dalek.'*	And let us descend and go down into the Sea.'

The descent into the Ocean and the discovery of the house of the Lords of the Sea

Mandeti Ledo and Patola Bulan agree to descend into the Sea, but they ask how they may do so.

They are instructed to mark a path with lontar and gewang palm leaves. In the sea depths, they discover the house of the Shark and Crocodile decked in turtle shells and roofed with ray-fish tails.

67.	*Boe ma besak-ka ta'ek Mandeti Ledo*	So, now the boy Mandeti Ledo
68.	*Ma touk Patola Bulan, nae:*	And the man Patola Bulan says:
69.	*'Loe teu liun*	'Let us descend and go into the Ocean
70.	*Ma dilu teu sain*	And let us turn and go into the Sea
71.	*Mandak-kala so*	These things are proper

72.	*Malole-la so.*	These things are good.
73.	*Te hu enon-na nai be*	But where is the path
74.	*Fo dilu teu liun dalek*	For us to turn and go into the Ocean
75.	*Ma dalan-na nai be*	And where is the road
76.	*Fo loe teu sain dalek?'*	For us to descend and go into the Sea?'
77.	*Boe ma lae a:*	So, they say:
78.	*'Dilu neu liun dalek*	'To turn down into the Ocean
79.	*Helu bobok neu liun*	Bend a trail of lontar leaves in the Ocean
80.	*Ma loe lo sain dalek*	And to descend into the Sea
81.	*Fe tula neu sain*	Place a trail of gewang leaves in the Sea
82.	*Tao neu eno telu*	To mark three paths
83.	*Ma tao neu dala dua.'*	And to mark two roads.'
84.	*Besak-ka dilu leu liun dalek*	Now they turn and go down into the Ocean
85.	*Ma leo neu sain dalek*	And they descend and go down into the Sea
86.	*Ma leu Man'Tua Sain lon-na*	And they go to the house of Mane Tua Sain
87.	*Ma Danga Lena Liun uman-na*	And the home of Danga Lena Liun
88.	*Nana-sini kea louk*	Decked with turtle shells
89.	*Ma nana-heu hai iko.*	And roofed with ray-fish tails.
90.	*De na-ndela liti data*	It flashes like ancient copper
91.	*Do na-sa'a engge oe.*	Or it shines like wetted lead.

The sacrifice of pig and civet and the taste of cooked food

When they have eaten, Mandeti Ledo and Patola Bulan wrap a bundle of food and take it to their father, Ledo Holo and Bula Kai. Ledo Holo and Bula Kai enjoy the taste of the cooked food, ask where it has come from and are told that it comes from the Sea.

92.	*Boe ma ala dilu doli nai liun*	So, they prepare rice in the Ocean
93.	*De fina kue nai liun*	To hold the sacrifice of civet in the Ocean
94.	*Ma tutu lutu nai sain*	And they pound millet in the Sea

95. *De fati bafi nai sain.*	To offer pig in the Sea.
96. *La'a te feo filu*	They eat but also wind a leaf container of food
97. *Ma linu te poti latu.*	And they drink but also wrap a bundle of food.
98. *De leni fe Ledo Holo*	They carry this to Ledo Holo
99. *Ma leni fe Bula Kai.*	And they carry this to Bula Kai.
100. *Besak-ka Bula Kai na'a nita*	Now Bula Kai eats to see what it is
101. *Ma Ledo Holo ninu nita.*	And Ledo Holo drinks to see what it is.
102. *Boe ma nae:*	He says:
103. *'Ladak ia nai be*	'From where is this taste?
104. *Ma lolek ia nai be?'*	Where is this goodness?'
105. *Boe ma lae:*	They say:
106. *'Ladak ia nai liun*	'This taste is in the Ocean
107. *Ma lolek ia nai sain.'*	And this goodness is in the Sea.'

The choice of a woman from the Heavens to marry with the Lords of the Sea

The hunters return to the hunt where they met. The Lords of the Sea request a woman to marry. The Sun and Moon designate their daughter, Fuda Kea Ledo and Tau Senge Bulan, as a suitable bride. Since she is already married to Nggolo Fae Batu and Teke Laba Dae ('The Green Rock Lizard and the Small Earth Gecko'), she must be divorced to marry the Lords of the Sea.

108. *Besak-ka ala sopu bafi leu-dua*	Now they return to hunt pig
109. *[Ma] sopu kue lasa-fali.*	And they go back to hunt civet
110. *Boe ma ala nai liun naka-to beten*	There where the millet fields border the Ocean
111. *Ma nai sain na-talada haden.*	And where the rice fields bound the Sea
112. *Ala mai tongo lololo*	They come to meet [Danga Lena Liun]
113. *Ma mai nda lilima.*	And they come to encounter [Mane Tua Sain].
114. *Boe ma ala teteni feto lesi[k]*	They request a girl of standing
115. *Ma ala tata ina lenak.*	And they ask for a woman of note.
116. *Boe ma Poin neu na-fada*	The Heights speak

117. *Ma Lain neu na-nosi ma nae:*	And the Heavens proclaim, saying:
118. *'Inak Fuda Kea Ledo nai poin*	'The woman Fuda Kea Ledo is in the Heights
119. *Ma fetok Tau Senge Bulan nai lain*	And the girl Tau Senge Bulan is in the Heavens
120. *Te hu feto mana-tuk*	But she is a girl who has a mate
121. *Ina mana-saok,*	A woman who has a spouse,
122. *Tu sosa manda-na*	A proper initial mate
123. *Touk Nggolo-Fae Batu*	The man Nggolo Fae Batu [Green Rock Lizard]
124. *Ma sao ulu malole*	And good prior spouse
125. *Ta'ek Teke-Laba Dae.'*	The boy Teke Laba Dae [Small Earth Gecko].'
126. *Boe ma neu fo nole-ladi tu sosan*	So, they go and divorce her from her initial mate
127. *Ma hela-ketu sao ulun*	And separate her from her prior spouse
128. *Fe tu neu liun dalek*	To allow her to wed within the Ocean
129. *Ma sao neu sain dalek.*	And to marry within the Sea.
130. *Besak-ka ala hela ketu tu sosa*	Now they divorce the initial mate
131. *Ma nole ladi sao ulu*	And they separate the prior spouse
132. *[Touk] Nggolo-Fae Batu*	The [man] Nggolo Fae Batu
133. *Ma taek Teke-Laba Dae.*	And the boy Teke Laba Dae.

The request for bridewealth from the Sea

The Heights bring their bride to marry in the Sea, but they demand a substantial bridewealth in return. Besides gold and livestock, the Heights demand a mortar and pestle for preparing rice and millet, a flintstone and firestick for making fire and a full array of tools—axe and adze, chisel and bore, plumbline marker and drill—for building a house.

134. *Besak-ka ala fifino neu liun*	Now they make a way to the Ocean
135. *De tu neu liun dale*	To wed within the Ocean
136. *Ma ala lelete neu sain*	And they bridge a path to the Sea
137. *De sao neu sain dalek.*	To marry within the Sea.
138. *Besak-ka ana sao Danga Lena Liun*	Now she marries Danga Lena Liun

139. *Ma tu Mane Tua Sain*	And she weds Mane Tua Sain
140. *Boe ala doko-doe fae-tena*	They demand a payment of livestock
141. *Ma ala tai-boni beli-batun.*	And they claim a bridewealth of gold.
142. *De ala fe lilo ma-langa menge*	They give a gold chain with a snake's head
143. *Ma ala fe kapa ma-ao foek.*	And they give buffalo with pied-white bodies.
144. *Te ala bei doko-doe*	But still they continue to demand
145. *Ma ala bei tai-boni.*	And still they continue to claim.
146. *Besak-ka ala fe bo pa'a-bela*	Now they give the bore-tool and flat chisel
147. *Ma ala fe taka tala-la.*	And they give the axe and the adze.
148. *Ala fe sipa aba-do*	They give the plumbline marker
149. *Ma ala fe funu ma-leo.*	And they give the turning drill.
150. *Te hu ala bei doko-doe.*	But still they continue to demand.
151. *Ma ala bei tai boni.*	And still they continue to claim.
152. *Boe-ma ala fe nesu maka-boka buik*	They give the mortar, whose thudding shakes its base
153. *Ma alu mata-fia tongok.*	And the pestle, whose thrust blisters the hand.
154. *Te ala bei doko-doe*	But still they continue to demand
155. *Ma ala bei tai-boni*	And still they continue to claim.
156. *Besak-ka ala fe kutu-ana nau-poin*	Then they give the little flint set with loose tinder grass
157. *Ma una-ana ai-nggeo.*	And the little black-stick fire drill.
158. *Besak-ka ala lae:*	Now they say:
159. *'Dai te ta dai*	'Whether enough or not enough
160. *O nai ta dai liman*	What is in our grip is enough in our hand
161. *Ma noü te ta no'u*	And whether sufficient or insufficient
162. *O nai kuku no'u nen.'*	What is in our fingers is sufficient in our grasp.'

The building of the first house

On their return to the Heavens, work is begun on the Sun's house and the Moon's home. Faced with building difficulties, the master builders, who are initially given the task of construction, must call on other notable figures to help with the alignment of the beams and poles of the house.

163.	*Besak-ka lenin neu poin*	Now they carry everything to the Heights
164.	*Ma lenin neu lain.*	And they carry everything to the Heavens.
165.	*De besak-ka laka-ndolu Ledo lon*	Now they construct the Sun's house
166.	*Ma la-lela Bulan uman.*	And they design the Moon's home.
167.	*Boe ma ala lali Makandolu Le*	They bring over Makandolu Le [River Crafter]
168.	*Ma ala soku Malela Dano*	And they carry Malela Dano [Lake Designer]
169.	*De ala dadi neu ndolu ma lelak.*	They become the crafter and designer.
170.	*De ala la-lela dulu uma dei*	They design the eastern half of the house
171.	*De to'ak telu te leo ndia [ko]*	The three *to'a* poles are there [garbled line].
172.	*Laka-ndolu nai muli*	They construct on the west side
173.	*Na ana fa leo dulu*	But it slants to the east
174.	*Ma laka-ndolu nai ki*	And they construct on the north side
175.	*Na ana soko leo kona neu.*	But it slopes to the south.
176.	*Besak-ka ala teteni sanga ndolu*	Now they request and seek [another] crafter
177.	*Ma la-tane sanga lela.*	And they ask and seek [another] designer.
178.	*De la-nggou ma la-lo*	They call and invite
179.	*Touk Didi Bulan*	The man Didi Bulan [Moon Spinner]
180.	*Ma ta'ek Bolau Ledo*	And the boy Bolau Ledo [Sun Spider].

181. *De besak-ka la-lo Solu Nggelo*	Now they invite Solu Nggelo [Chop Apart]
182. *Ma la-lo Silu Mola mai.*	And they invite Silu Mola [Hack Open].
183. *Boe ma la-lo Kili-Kili Ki*	They invite Kili-Kili Ki [Sharpen Left]
184. *Ma la-nggou Fona-Fona Kona*	And they call Fona-Fona Kona [Draw Right]
185. *Kili-Kili Ki, ana kili beba*	Kili-Kili Ki, he sharpens the leafstalks
186. *Ma Fona-Fona Kona, ana fona tali.*	And Fona-Fona Kona, he draws the cords.
187. *Ma-nalu, na ala nggelo*	When something is too long, they chop it off
188. *Ma-kekeuk, na ala tuti.*	And when something is too short, they join it.
189. *Besak-ka lala ndo milan*	Then they get it as true as a bamboo shoot
190. *Ma lido telin.*	And as straight as a bamboo stalk.
191. *Besak-ka ana dadi neu to'a teluk*	Now it becomes a house with three *to'a* poles
192. *Ana moli neu sema duak.*	And it grows to be a home with two *sema* beams.
193. *De ala soe saike iko-na,*	They incise a tail design on the ridgepole,
194. *De kue luu nai ikon,*	A civet crouches at the tail,
195. *Ma tati solobana langan*	And they cut a head pattern on the ridgepole
196. *De fani tai nai langan.*	Bees nest at the head.

Recitation 2. The origin of fire, of cooking and of the implements for living

Lisbeth Adulilo

Patola Bulan ma Mandeti Ledo

The fateful encounter while hunting for pig and civet

Patola Bulan and Mandeti Ledo, the sons of the Sun and Moon, set out with their dogs to hunt for pig and civet. They meet the Lords of the Sea and Ocean, Mane Tua Sain and Danga Lena Liun, who are also hunting pig and civet with their dogs. The dogs form a pack and continue their hunt in the depths of the Kai Tio forest and the Lolo Batu wood. There they corner and catch a civet, Tena Lolo ('Sleek Body') of the Ocean, and a wild pig, Nggeo Alu ('Black Shoulder') of the Sea.

1.	*Neu faik esa manunin*	On a certain day
2.	*Ma ledo dua mateben-na*	And at a particular time
3.	*Boe ma touk Patola Bulan*	The man Patola Bulan
4.	*Ma ta'ek Mandeti Ledo*	And the boy Mandeti Ledo
5.	*Neu sopu bafi ndondolo*	Wanders about hunting pig
6.	*Ma ana fule kue lolota.*	And roams about stalking civet.
7.	*Asu nade Lepa Lae*	The dog named Lepa La'e
8.	*Ma busa nade Doi Sou,*	And the hound named Doi So'u,
9.	*Doi-la so'u ao*	Mutual aid in balancing a burden
10.	*Ma lepa-la la'e ao.*	And mutual support in carrying a load.
11.	*Neu sopu bafi ndondolo*	He wanders about hunting pig
12.	*Ma neu fute kue lolota.*	And roams round tracking civet.
13.	*Boe ma neu tongo lololo*	He encounters directly
14.	*Ma neu nda lilima*	And meets face to face
15.	*Ta'ek Mane Tua Sain*	The boy Mane Tua Sain
16.	*Ma touk Danga Lena Liun.*	And the man Danga Lena Liun.
17.	*Ana sopu bafi ndondolo*	He is wandering about hunting pigs
18.	*Ma ana fule kue lolota.*	And he is roaming round pursuing civet.
19.	*Busa nade Masi Tasi*	The dog named Masi Tasi [Sea Salt]

20.	*Ma asu nade Deta Dosa.*	And the hound named Deta Dosa [Sour Dip].
21.	*Boe ma busa-la laka-bua*	The dogs form a pack
22.	*Ma asu-la la-esa.*	And the hounds join together.
23.	*De ala fule kue*	They pursue civet
24.	*Ma ala sopu bafi.*	And they hunt pig.
25.	*De leo nula Kai Tio dale*	Deep in the woods of Kai Tio
26.	*Ma lasi Lolo Batu dale*	And deep in the forest of Lolo Batu
27.	*Boe ma asu-la fua*	The dogs corner their prey
28.	*Ma busa-la usi.*	And the hounds give chase
29.	*Boe te lala Tena Lolo Liuk*	They catch the civet Tena Lolo Liuk
30.	*Ma lala Nggeo Alu Saik.*	And they the catch the pig Nggeo Alu Saik.

The invitation to sacrifice in the Sea and the descent into the Ocean

Patola Bulan and Mandeti Ledo propose that they all ascend to the Heavens to perform their sacrifice of the pig and civet. Mane Tua Sain and Danga Lena Liun respond by proposing that they all descend into the Sea. This proposal is accepted and they descend into the Sea, where they hold their sacrifice. They roast on a smoking fire and cook in boiling water in a house roofed with ray-fish tails and decked with turtle shells. For the sons of the Sun and Moon, this is their first encounter with fire for cooking in so magnificent a house.

31.	*Boe ma touk Patola Bulan*	So, the man Patola Bulan
32.	*Ma ta'ek Mandeti Ledo nae:*	And the boy Mandeti Ledo says:
33.	*'Bou tiang ngo nou*	'Oh, my friend
34.	*Do bou senana ngo nou,*	Oh, my companion,
35.	*Ata hene lo lain teu*	Let us climb to the Heavens
36.	*Do ata kae lo poin teu*	Or let us mount to the Heights
37.	*Teu lain fati bafi*	Let us go to the Heavens to eat the offering of pig
38.	*Ma teu poin fina kue.'*	Let us go to the Heights to eat the sacrifice of civet.'
39.	*Te touk Man'Tua Sain*	But the man Mane Tua Sain
40.	*Ma ta'ek Danga Lena Liun nae:*	And the boy Danga Lena Liun says:
41.	*'Bou tiang ngo nou*	'Oh, my friend

42.	*Do bou senang ngo nou*	Oh, my companion
43.	*Liun nai sasalin*	The Ocean is overflowing
44.	*Ma sain nai loloen*	And the Sea is receding
45.	*Loe teu liun dale*	Let us descend into the Ocean
46.	*Ma ata sai teu sain dale,*	And let us go down into the Sea,
47.	*Teu sain fati bafi*	Let us go to the Sea to eat the offering of pig
48.	*Ma teu liun fina kue.'*	Let us go to the Ocean to eat the sacrifice of civet.'
49.	*Boe te ala loe leo liun dale*	So, they descend into the Ocean
50.	*Ma ala sai leo sain dale.*	And they go down in the Sea.
51.	*De leu, de ala fati bafi*	They go and they eat the offering of pig
52.	*Ma fina kue.*	And eat the sacrifice of civet.
53.	*De ala tunu ha'i bei masu*	They roast on a smoking fire
54.	*Ma ala nasu oek bei lume*	They cook in boiling water
55.	*Nai lo heu hai ikon*	In a house roofed with ray-fish tails
56.	*Ma nai uma sini kea louk.*	In a home decked with turtle shells.

The return to the Heavens with cooked food from the Sea

When they have finished eating, Patola Bulan and Mandeti Ledo wrap some cooked food in a leaf container and take it back to the Sun and Moon, Ledo Holo and Bula Kai, who express their astonishment at these new marvels.

57.	*Boe ma ala fati basa bafi*	They eat all the offering of pig
58.	*Ma ala fina basa kue.*	And they eat all the sacrifice of civet.
59.	*Boe ma ala poti latu fe Bula*	Then they wrap a bundle for the Moon
60.	*Ma ala feo filu fe Ledo.*	And they wind a leaf container for the Sun.
61.	*De touk Patola Bulan*	The man Patola Bulan
62.	*Ma ta'ek Mandeti Ledo*	And the boy Mandeti Ledo
63.	*Ana tulek lain neu*	He returns to the Heavens
64.	*Ma ana falik poin neu.*	And he goes back to the Heights.
65.	*Boe ma touk Ledo*	The man Ledo Holo
66.	*Ma ta'ek Bula Kai ma nae:*	And the boy Bula Kai says:
67.	*'Bou anang ngo nou*	'Oh, my child

68.	*Ma bou upung ngo nou*	Oh, my grandchild
69.	*Te ita ta nasu oek bei lume*	We do not cook in boiling water
70.	*Maita ta tunu haï bei masu*	And we do not roast on a smoking fire
71.	*Ma ita ta'a tasak*	We eat raw food
72.	*Ma ita tinu tasak.'*	And we drink plain water.'
73.	*Boe-ma nae:*	So, he says:
74.	*'Ah, poti latu neme liun*	'Ah, a wrapped bundle from the Ocean
75.	*Ma feo filu neme sain mai*	And wound container from the Sea
76.	*Te nai sain ala nasu oek bei lume*	For in the Sea they cook in boiling water
77.	*Ma ala tunu haï bei masu*	And in the Ocean they roast on a smoking fire
78.	*Nai lo heu hai ikon*	In a house roofed with ray-fish tails
79.	*Ma nai uma sini kea louk.'*	And in a home decked with turtle shells.'

The decision to establish a marriage alliance with the Lords of the Sea

Bula Kai and Ledo Holo propose marriage with the Ocean and Sea and take their daughter, Tau Senge Bulan and Kudu Kea Ledo, to marry Bala Mae Sain and Holo Te Liun. The couple give birth to Dusu Bala Mae and Tio Holo Te. The first names of these children identify them with specific colourful reef fish. A *dusu* is the blue-spotted emperor (*Lethrinus laticaudis*) while a *tio* is the bartail goatfish (Mullidae: *Upeneus tragula*).

80.	*Boe ma touk Bula Kai*	So, the man Bula Kai
81.	*Ma ta'ek Ledo Holo nae:*	And the boy Ledo Holo says:
82.	*'Ah, mai ata taka-bua*	'Ah, come let us form a group
83.	*Ma mai ata ta-esa*	And come let us join together
84.	*Fo ata tu leo liun teu*	So, that we may go and marry with the Ocean
85.	*Ma ata sao leo sain teu*	And we may go and wed with the Sea
86.	*Fo ela ata hapu uma sini kea louk*	That we may have a home decked with turtle shells

87. *Ma ata hapu lo heu hai iko*	And we may have a house roofed in ray-fish tails
88. *Fo ata tunu ha'i bei masu*	That we may roast on a smoking fire
89. *Ma ata nasu oek bei lume.'*	And we may cook in boiling water.'
90. *De koö la fetok Tau Senge Bulan*	So, they cradle the girl Tau Senge Bulan
91. *Fe tu leo sain neu*	To give her to wed with the Sea
92. *Ma [ifa-la] inak Kudu Kea Ledo*	And [they carry] the woman Kudu Kea Ledo
93. *Fe sao leo liun neu.*	To give her to marry with the Ocean.
94. *Ana sao Bala Mae Sain*	She marries Bala Mae Sain
95. *De ana bongi Dusu Bala Mae*	And she gives birth to Dusu Bala Mae
96. *Ma ana [tu] sao Holo Te Liun*	And she weds Holo Te Liun
97. *De ana lae Tio Holo Te.*	And she brings forth Tio Holo Te.

The Sun and Moon's demand for bridewealth

Following the marriage of the Heavens and the Sea, the Sun and Moon demand bridewealth. They first demand gold and livestock, the traditional components of bridewealth, but then demand other crucial paired items that constitute the wealth of the Sea: 1) the mortar and pestle for pounding rice and millet, 2) the flint and fire-drill, 3) the bore and chisel, 4) the axe and adze, and 5) the plumbline marker and drill. These implements are for making fire, for working the fields and for preparing rice and millet. Important also are the tools for building a house. When their bridewealth demands have been granted, the Sun and Moon return to the Heavens.

98. *Boe te ana doko-doe beli-batu*	So, he demands a bridewealth of gold
99. *Ma ana tai-boni fae-tena,*	And he claims a payment of livestock,
100. *Boe te ala fe kapa ma-ao foek*	They give water buffalo with pied-white bodies
101. *Ma ala fe lilo ma-langa mengek-kala*	And they give gold chains with snake heads
102. *Ela menge seli fola la tebi sak*	And so many snake-chains testing them would crack an assay stone

103. *Ma kapa loli la mada dano.*	And so many water buffalo that their wallowing would dry a lake.
104. *Te fe dai bei ta dai*	They give enough, yet it is not enough
105. *Ma fe no'u bei ta no'u.*	And they give sufficiently, yet it is not sufficient.
106. *Ala bei doko-doe*	They still continue to demand
107. *Ma ala bei tai boni.*	They still continue to claim.
108. *Boe te ala fe nesu maka-boka buik*	So, they give the mortar whose thudding shakes its base
109. *Ma alu mata-fia tongok*	And they give the pestle whose thrust blisters the hand
110. *Boe te una ai nggeo*	And the black-sticked fire-drill
111. *Ma kutu na'u poi.*	And the flint with loose tinder grass.
112. *Fe dai ta dai*	They give enough, but not enough
113. *Ma no'u ta no'u.*	And they give sufficiently, but not sufficient.
114. *Ma ala bei doko-doe*	And they still continue to demand
115. *Ma ala bei tai-boni.*	And they still continue to claim.
116. *De ala fe bo pa'a-bela-la*	Then they give bore tool and flat chisel
117. *Ma ala fe taka tata-la*	And they give the axe and the adze
118. *Ma ala fe sipa aba-do*	And they give the plumbline marker
119. *Ma funu ma-leo.*	And the turning drill.
120. *Boe te touk Bula Kai*	So, the man Bula Kai
121. *Ma ta'ek Ledo Holo ma nae:*	And the boy Ledo Holo says:
122. *'Dai ta dai fa*	'Whether enough or not enough
123. *O nai ta dai liman*	What is in our grip is enough in our hand
124. *Ma no'u ta no'u fa*	And whether sufficient or insufficient
125. *O nai kuku no'u nen*	What is in our fingers is sufficient in our grasp
126. *De no'u ma dai so.'*	It is sufficient and enough.'
127. *Boe ma ala tulek leo lain leu*	So, they return to the Heavens
128. *Ma ala falik leo poin leu.*	And they go back to the Heights.

The return to the Heavens and the construction of the house

On the return to the Heavens, construction is begun on the house of the Sun and Moon. Specific hardwood trees—the *fuliha'a* (*Vitex parviflora*) and the *keka* (*Ficus superba*)—are felled to make the beams and poles of the house, but the work does not go well. The construction leans and tilts. It is then that they call the Lord of the Sea and the Great Hunter of the Ocean—the Shark and Crocodile—and physically make them the model for the house. As was explained to me, a proper Rotenese house is, like the island of Rote itself, a crocodile turned to the east.

The formulaic lines of a mortuary chant—'the sun heats the buffalo sinews'//'the dew moistens the chicken bones'—indicate the death of the Shark and the Crocodile, which is a ritual killing that permits Sun Spider and Moon Spinner to come forward to direct the layout of the beams and poles according to the bones and sinews and, thus, create the house.

129.	*Laka-neni ledo lon*	They carry things to the Sun's house
130.	*Ma laka-neni bulan uman.*	And they carry things to the Moon's home.
131.	*Boe ta ala lo'o keka-lasi do-duak kala*	Then they hew two-leaved *keka* trees
132.	*Ma ala huma fuli-ha'a do-teluk kala*	And they chop three-leaved *fuliha'a* trees
133.	*Tao neu sema teluk*	To make the three *sema* beams
134.	*Ma tao neu to'a duak*	And to make the two *to'a* poles
135.	*Tao neu lo ai*	To make the beams of the house
136.	*Ma tao neu uma di.*	And make the posts of the home.
137.	*Te laka-ndolu nai lain*	When they work above
138.	*Na ana kekeak leo dae mai*	It tilts towards the ground
139.	*Ma laka-ndolu nai dulu*	When they work on the east
140.	*Na lai leo muli neu.*	It leans to the west.
141.	*Boe ma ala le'a-la tua tele*	They tug a bending lontar palm
142.	*Ma ala lo'o-la ai nalo*	They chop a fallen tree
143.	*De ala lo'o-na langa-nalo*	They hew looking upward
144.	*Ma ala tati-na laka-tele.*	And they cut bending down.
145.	*Ala tao neu sema teluk*	They make the three *sema* beams
146.	*Ma ala tao neu to'a duak.*	And they make the two *to'a* poles.

147. *Ala tao neu uma di*	They make the house-posts
148. *Ma ala tao neu eda ai.*	And they make the tree-ladder.
149. *Te la-ole nai lain*	When they arrange it above
150. *Na ana kekeak leo dae mai.*	It tilts towards the ground.
151. *Te lakandolu nai muli*	When they erect it on the west
152. *Na soko leo dulu.*	It slants to the east.
153. *Boe ma ala do-do neu dalen*	So, they think to themselves
154. *Ma nda-nda neu tein,*	And they ponder within,
155. *Te keka-lasi do-duak ko*	The two-leaved *keka* tree
156. *Ta dadi to'a duak*	Will not become the two *to'a* poles
157. *Ma fuli-ha'a do-teluk ko*	And the three-leaved *fuliha'a* tree
158. *Ta dadi sema teluk.*	Will not become the three *sema* beams.
159. *Boe te ala boe do-do*	They continue to think
160. *Ma ala boe nda-nda.*	And they continue to ponder.
161. *Boe te ala teteni*	Thereupon they ask for
162. *[Line missing]*	[Line missing]
163. *Touk Danga Lena Liun*	The man Chief Hunter of the Ocean
164. *Ma ta'ek Man'Tua Sain*	And the boy Great Lord of the Sea
165. *Ala taon neu uma*	They make him into the house-posts
166. *Ma ala taon neu eda ai.*	And they make him into the tree-ladder.
167. *Besak-ka kalu kapa ledo ha'an*	Now the sun heats the buffalo sinews
168. *Ma dui manu a'u te'e-na.*	And the dew moistens the chicken bones.
169. *Ala tao[n] neu sema teluk*	They make him into the three *sema* beams
170. *Ma taon neu to'a duak.*	And make him into the two *to'a* poles.
171. *Besak-ka Didi Bulan mai*	Now Didi Bulan [Moon Spinner] arrives
172. *Ma Bolau Ledo mai.*	And Bolau Ledo [Sun Spider] arrives.
173. *De lae: 'Deta ape.*	They say: 'Dip spittle.

174.	*De deta ape neu be*	Where the spittle is dipped
175.	*Fo lolo neu ndia.'*	There lay the planks.'
176.	*Boe te Bolau lolo ape neu be*	So, wherever Bolau lays spittle
177.	*Na ala solu limak neu ndia*	There they rest the arms
178.	*Ma Didi deta ape neu be*	And wherever Didi dips spittle
179.	*Na ala fua lolo neu ndia.*	There they place the legs.
180.	*Besak-ka sema teluk-kala dadi*	Now the three *sema* beams are made
181.	*Ma to'a duak-kala tola.*	And the two *to'a* poles appear.
182.	*Besak-ka ala soe saike ikon*	Now they incise a tail design on the ridgepole
183.	*Ma tati solo-bana langan*	And they cut a head design on the ridgepole
184.	*Besak-ka lae: 'To'a duak.'*	Now they say: 'Two *to'a* poles.'
185.	*Ma lae: 'Sema teluk.'*	And they say: 'Three *sema* beams.'
186.	*Losa faik ia boe*	Until this day
187.	*Ma nduku ledon ia boe.*	And up to this time.

Recitation 3. The origin of cooking and of the marriage with the Sea

Eli Pellondou

Patola Bulan ma Mandeti Ledo

The hunt and the invitation to descend into the Sea

This short, partial recitation, provided originally as a response and an alternative to the previous narrative, takes up its account after the hunt. Danga Lena Liun and Mone Ni Sain propose to Patola Bulan and Mandeti Ledo that they descend into the Ocean to offer the sacrifice of pig and civet. Patola Bulan and Mandeti Ledo ask the Lords of the Sea just what they will eat with their offering. Danga Lena Liun and Mone Ni Sain tell them that they will eat their offering with rice and millet. They will cook in boiling water and roast on a smoking fire.

| 1. | *Boe ma la-nole fina kuek* | They argue over the sacrifice of civet |
| 2. | *Ma la-le'a fati bafi.* | And they dispute over the offering of pig. |

3.	*Boe ma touk Danga Lena Liun*	The man Danga Lena Liun
4.	*Ma ta'ek Mone Ni Sain*	And the boy Mone Ni Sain
5.	*Lafada ma lae:*	Speaks and says:
6.	*'Loe teu liun dale fati bafi*	'Let us go down into the Ocean to offer pig
7.	*Ma dilu teu sain dale fina kue.'*	And let us turn down into the Sea to sacrifice civet.'
8.	*Boe ma ta'ek Patola Bulan*	The boy Patola Bulan
9.	*Ma touk Mandeti Ledo*	And the man Mandeti Ledo
10.	*Selu dasin na neu*	Raise their voice
11.	*Ma ae halan na neu:*	Lift their words:
12.	*'Teu sain fati bafi*	'If we go to the Sea to offer pig
13.	*Ma teu liun fina kue*	And if we go to the Ocean to sacrifice
14.	*Fo fati to lo hata*	With what will we eat the offering
15.	*Ma fina to lo hatak?'*	And with what will we eat the sacrifice?'
16.	*Boe ma touk Danga Lena Liun*	The man Danga Lena Liun
17.	*Ma ta'ek Mone Ni Sain nae:*	And the boy Mone Ni Sain says:
18.	*'Teu liun fati bafi*	'Let us go into the Ocean to eat the offering of pig
19.	*Fo fati bafi to lutu*	To eat the pig offering with millet
20.	*Ma teu sain fina kue*	And let us go into the Sea to eat the sacrifice of civet
21.	*Fo fina kue to doli*	To eat the civet sacrifice with rice
22.	*Fo nasu oek bei lume*	To cook in boiling water
23.	*Ma tunu hai bei masu.'*	And roast on a smoking fire.'

The discovery of cooked food and the decision to marry with the Sea

Patola Bulan and Mandeti Ledo eat and find the food tasty, drink and find it good, so they hide some food and drink and take it to Bula Kai and Ledo Holo in the Heavens. They, too, find the food and drink good and tasty, so they decide to order the divorce of their daughter, Kudu Kea Ledo and Tau Senge Bulan, from her husband, Bose Latu and Do Lona, and instead carry her to the Sea to marry Holo Te Liun and Bala Mae Sain. She gives birth to Tio Holo Te and Dusu Bala Mae.

24.	*Boe ma touk Patola Bulan*	So, the man Patola Bulan
25.	*Naä nita ladak*	Eats and sees that it is tasty
26.	*Ma ta'ek Mandeti Ledo*	And the boy Mandeti Ledo
27.	*Kupa nita lolek.*	Drinks and sees that it is good.
28.	*Boe te na'a te kikiduk*	He eats but tucks some away
29.	*Ma kupa te nafuni,*	And drinks but hides some away,
30.	*Fo neni fe Bula Kai*	To carry it to Bula Kai
31.	*Ma Ledo Holo.*	And Ledo Holo.
32.	*De Bulan naä nita ladak*	The Moon eats and sees that it is tasty
33.	*Ma Ledo kupa nita lolek.*	And the Sun drinks and sees that it is good.
34.	*Besak-ka laka-bua ma la-esa.*	Now they form a group and get together.
35.	*Inak Kudu Kea Ledo*	The woman Kudu Kea Ledo
36.	*Ma fetok Tau Senge Bulan*	And the girl Tau Senge Bulan
37.	*Ana tu ingu-anak, Bose Latu*	She is wed to a man of a minor land, Bose Latu
38.	*Ma sao leo-anak, Do Lona* [*Lolo Dano*]	And is married to a man of minor lineage, Do Lona
39.	*De ala nole ladin*	They divorce her
40.	*Ma hela ketun.*	And separate her.
41.	*Besak-ka ifa Tau Senge Bulan*	Now they lift Tau Senge Bulan
42.	*Ma soku Kudu Kea Ledo.*	And carry Kudu Kea Ledo.
43.	*De ala tu leo liun dale*	They wed down in the Ocean
44.	*Ma sao leo sain dale.*	And marry down in the Sea.
45.	*De tu Holo Te Liun*	They wed Holo Te Liun
46.	*Ma sao Bala Mae Sain.*	And marry Bala Mae Sain.
47.	*De ala bongi Tio Holu Te*	They give birth to Tio Holo Te
48.	*Ma ala lae Dusu Bala Mae.*	And they bring forth Dusu Bala Mae.

Recitation 4. The origin of fire, of cooking and of the implements for living

Esau Markus Pono

Mandeti Ledo ma Patola Bulan

The first hunt for pig and civet

The Sun and Moon require a side dish to accompany their drinking. So, Mandeti Ledo and Patola Bulan set out with their dogs, Ho'u La'en and Tenga Ndan, to hunt for pig and civet. However, they catch animals that belong to the Sun and Moon. When they return, the Sun and Moon scold them for hunting on the wrong land.

1.	*Faik esa manunina*	On a certain day
2.	*Do ledo esa mate'ena*	At a particular time
3.	*Ledo lalu na, ana makei*	The Sun's beer, it is sour
4.	*Ma Bulan nggeto na, ana makanilu.*	And the Moon's brew, it is tart.
5.	*Boe ma ana doko-doe sanga du'una.*	It calls for and seeks a side dish.
6.	*Boe ma lafada ana mane-nala*	So, they speak to their sons
7.	*Touk Mandeti Ledo*	The man Mandeti Ledo
8.	*Ma ta'ek Patola Bulan, lae:*	And the boy Patola Bulan, saying:
9.	*'Meu sopu ma meu danga dei,*	'Go hunt and go stalking,
10.	*Te lalu la makei*	Because the beer is sour
11.	*Ma nggeto la maka-nilu*	And the brew is tart
12.	*De ela du'uk dei.'*	Let it have a side dish.'
13.	*Boe ma Mandeti Ledo*	So, Mandeti Ledo
14.	*No Patola Bulan*	With Patola Bulan
15.	*Ala kati-kofio busa-nala*	They call-whistle for their dogs
16.	*Fo busa nade Ho'u La'en*	The dog named Ho'u La'en
17.	*Ma asu nade Tenga Ndan*	And the hound named Tenga Ndan
18.	*De leu sopu bafi*	They go to hunt for pig
19.	*Ma leu fule kue.*	And they go to pursue civet.
20.	*Lala Bulan kue-na*	They catch the Moon's civet
21.	*Fo kue ina dei fula*	The female civet with white forehead

22. *Ma lala Ledo meon*	And they catch the Sun's cat
23. *Fo meo mane iko lolo.*	The male cat with the straight, long tail.
24. *Fali mai,*	Arriving back,
25. *Boe ma Bulan selu dasi na neu*	The Moon raises his voice
26. *Ma Ledo a'e halan na neu, ma lae:*	And the Sun lifts his words, saying:
27. *'O emi sopu sala dae*	'You hunted on the wrong land
28. *Ma emi fule sala oe.*	And you pursued in the wrong water
29. *De meu sopu di'u dua*	Go back and hunt again
30. *Ma meu danga lolo fali.'*	Return and stalk again.'

The second hunt and the encounter with the Lords of the Sea

Patola Bulan and Mandeti Ledo set off again to hunt with their dogs. Along the Ango-Kala River and in the Nggae-Kala Forest, they hear Mane Tua Sain and Tou Danga Liun's dogs barking. The dogs join together and catch a large black-shouldered pig and small, sleek civet associated with the Ocean and Sea.

31. *Boe ma Patola Bulan*	So, Patola Bulan
32. *No Mandeti Ledo*	With Mandeti Ledo
33. *Kati-kofio nala busa-nala do asu-nala.*	Call-whistle for their dogs and hounds.
34. *De leu sopu lasa-fali*	They go back hunting
35. *Ma leu danga di'u dua seluk.*	And they go back stalking again.
36. *De leu Ango-Kala Le Dale*	They go to Ango-Kala River
37. *Ma Nggae-Kala Lasi Lai.*	And to Nggae-Kala Forest.
38. *Boe ma lama-nene*	Then they hear
39. *Te Mane Tua Sain busana na a'uk*	Mane Tua Sain's dog barking
40. *Ma Tou Danga Liun asuna na-hala.*	And Tou Danga Liun's hound howling.
41. *Boe Patola Bulan busa*	Patola Bulan's dog
42. *Busa nade Ho'u La'en*	The dog named Ho'u La'en
43. *Ana neu*	He goes
44. *Ma Mandeti Ledo asu na*	And Mandeti Ledo's hound

45. *Asu nade Tenga Ndan*	The hound named Tenga Ndan
46. *Ana neu.*	He goes.
47. *De dua leu la-nda*	The two go to meet
48. *Ma ha leu la-tongo*	And the four go to encounter
49. *De ka'a lala bafi ina nggeo alu sai-kala*	Biting the Sea's large black-shouldered pig
50. *Ma kue tena lolo lui-kala.*	And the Ocean's small, sleek civet.

The debate on where to hold the sacrifice of pig and civet

The Lord of the Sea, Mane Tua Sain, and the Stalker of the Ocean, Tou Danga Liun, ask Mandeti Ledo and Patola Bulan where they would like to go to hold the feast of pig and civet. Mandeti Ledo and Patola Bulan propose that they go to the Heavens and eat the meat of the pig and civet with river water and plant leaves. Mane Tua Sain and Tou Danga Liun reject this suggestion and propose that they all descend into the Sea. Mane Tua Sain and Tou Danga Liun then show the way into the Sea.

51. *Boe ma Man'Tua Sain*	So, Man'Tua Sain
52. *No Tou Danga Liun*	With Tou Danga Liun
53. *Ala kokolak lo Mandeti Ledo*	They speak with Mandeti Ledo
54. *Ma Patola Bulan ma lae:*	And with Patola Bulan and say:
55. *'Ata teu be fati bafi*	'Where should we go to eat the pig
56. *Ma teu be folo kue?'*	And where should we go to feast on the civet?'
57. *Boe ma Patola Bulan*	So, Patola Bulan
58. *No Mandeti Ledo lae:*	And Mandeti Ledo say:
59. *'Teu lain fati bafi*	'Let us go to the Heavens to eat the pig
60. *Do teu ata folo kue.'*	Or let us go to the Heights to feast on the civet.'
61. *'Na kue tun nde se*	'Then who will be the civet's wife
62. *Ma bafi saon nde se?'*	And who will be the pig's spouse?'
63. *Boe ma Patola Bulan*	So, Patola Bulan
64. *No Mandeti Ledo lae:*	With Mandeti Ledo say:
65. *'Kue tun oe le*	'The civet's wife will be river water
66. *Ma bafi saon nae do.'*	And the pig's spouse raw leaves.'
67. *Boe ma Man'Tua Sain*	So, Man'Tua Sain
68. *No Tou Danga Liun lae:*	With Tou Danga Liun say:

69.	*'Sona sosoak bei ta*	'That's not good enough
70.	*Ma mamandak bei ta.*	And that's not sufficient.
71.	*Mai fo loe teu Liun dalek*	Let's go down into the Ocean's depths
72.	*Ma kona teu Sain dalek,*	And descend into the Sea's depths,
73.	*Te Liun na loloena*	For the Ocean is lowering
74.	*Ma Sain na kokona na.'*	And the Sea is descending.'
75.	*Te hu Mandeti Ledo*	But Mandeti Ledo
76.	*No Patola Bulan lae:*	And Patola Bulan say:
77.	*'Awi! Te Sain bei ele-ele*	'Awi! The Sea flows forth
78.	*Ma Liun bei mamo-mamo*	And the Ocean tide is at the full
79.	*Na dala na nde be?'*	So, where is there a path?'
80.	*Boe ma Mane Tua Sain*	So, Mane Tua Sain
81.	*No Tou Danga Liun*	And Tou Danga Liun
82.	*Lahala ma lae:*	Speak and say:
83.	*'Enok leo Liun dalek neu*	'There is a path to the Ocean's depths
84.	*Ma dalek leo Sain dale neu a,*	And a road to the Sea's depths,
85.	*Helu bok neu dalak*	Break a marker for the road
86.	*Ma te tula neu enok.'*	And snap a leaf for the path.'
87.	*Boe ma ala loe leo Liun*	So, they descend into the Ocean
88.	*Ma kona leo Sain leu.*	And they go down into the Sea.

Arrival in the Sea and the feast of cooked pig and civet with rice and millet

In the depths of the Sea, the hunters feast on the cooked pig and civet with pounded rice and millet. Mane Tua Sain and Tou Danga Liun urge Patola Bulan and Mandeti Ledo to eat and drink. They find the food delicious and are promised wrapped food to take with them as a gift.

89.	*Losa, boe ma ala masu ndalu bafi*	On arriving, they smoke the pig
90.	*Ma ala pila nuli kue,*	And they roast the civet
91.	*Ma ina-kala tutu mala*	And the women pound the rice
92.	*Ma ala dengu doli.*	And they beat the millet.
93.	*De lama-tasa.*	Then they taste it.
94.	*Boe ma Mane Tua Sain*	So, Mane Tua Sain
95.	*No Tou Danga Liun lae:*	With Tou Danga Liun say:

96. *'Mai kupa ma mai ta'a leon.*	'Come let us drink and come let us eat.
97. *Te ta'a bo'o loe kai*	Let's eat but not hide any food
98. *Ma kupa boso fua kulu.*	And drink but not conceal any food.
99. *Te de'i ata feo-filu*	Let us wrap the food as a present
100. *Ma ata poti-latu haitua.'*	And let us prepare it as a gift.'
101. *De ala kupa ma ala la'a.*	So, they drink and they eat.
102. *Boe ma Patola Bulan*	Then Patola Bulan
103. *No Mandeti Ledo*	With Mandeti Ledo
104. *Esa dede'ak no esa ma lae:*	They speak with one another and say:
105. *'Te ia ladak-ladak mesan.'*	'This is indeed delicious.'

The return to the Heavens with the cooked food from the Sea

When Patola Bulan and Mandeti Ledo are ready to return to the Heavens, Mane Tua Sain and Tou Danga Liun wrap some food as a gift for the Sun and Moon. The Sun and Moon eat and drink the food and declare it to be delicious. They ask where it has come from and Patola Bulan and Mandeti Ledo explain that it has come from the Sea.

106. *Boe ma Patola Bulan*	Then Patola Bulan
107. *No Mandeti Ledo*	With Mandeti Ledo
108. *Ala lolo fali ma ala di'u dua.*	They return and they go back.
109. *Boe ma Mane Tua Sain*	So, Mane Tua Sain
110. *No Tou Danga Liun*	With Tou Danga Liun
111. *Poti latu ma ala feo filu hatua*	Wrap food and they prepare it as a gift
112. *Fe Bulan ma fe Ledo.*	To give to the Moon and give to the Sun.
113. *Bulan no Ledo*	The Moon and Sun
114. *Ala kupa ma ala la'a*	They drink and they eat
115. *Boe ma lae:*	Then they say:
116. *'Awi. Te ladak ia nai bee?*	'Awi. From where does this tastiness come?
117. *De lada-ladak a mesan.'*	It is indeed delicious.'
118. *Boe ma Patola Bulan*	So, Patola Bulan

119. *No Mandeti Ledo lae:*   With Mandeti Ledo say:
120. *'Ami ma-tongo do ma-natamo*   'We met or we encountered
121. *Mane Tua Sain do Tou Danga*   Mane Tua Sain or Tou Danga
    Liun,   Liun,
122. *De ami meni ladak ia neme*   We brought this tastiness from
    na mai.'   there.'

The return to the Sea and the request for a marriage alliance

Bula Kai and Ledo Holo tell their sons to return to the Sea. Patola Bulan and Mandeti Ledo go hunting again and meet Mane Tua Sain and Tou Danga Liun, who ask whether there are women in the Heavens who would be willing to marry with the Sea.

123. *Boe ma Bula Kai no Ledo Holo lae:*	So, Bula Kai and Ledo Holo say:
124. *'Meu sopu di'u dua*	'Go back and hunt
125. *Ma meu danga masafali*	And return and stalk
126. *Fo ela meni seluk ladak ia mai.'*	To bring more of this tastiness.'
127. *Boe ma Patola Bulan no Mandeti Ledo*	So, Patola Bulan and Mandeti Ledo
128. *Leu sopu di'u dua seluk*	Go back to hunt again
129. *Ma leu danga lasafali seluk.*	And return to stalk again.
130. *De leu latongo lo selu*	They go and meet again with
131. *Mane Tua Sain*	Mane Tua Sain
132. *Ma Tou Danga Liun.*	And Tou Danga Liun.
133. *Boe ma ala tui Ledo Holo dede'a na*	They recount Ledo Holo's speech
134. *Ma Bula Kai kokolana.*	And Bula Kai's conversation.
135. *Boe ma Man'Tua Sain*	So, Mane Tua Sain
136. *No Tou Danga Liun*	With Tou Danga Liun
137. *Latane lae:*	They ask, saying:
138. *'Hapu ina lenak*	'Do you have extra women
139. *Ma feto lesik nai ata do ta?'*	And additional girls in the Heavens or not?'
140. *Boe ma Patola Bulan*	So, Patola Bulan
141. *Ma Mandeti Ledo lae:*	And Mandeti Ledo say:
142. *'Hapu.'*	'We do have them.'

143. *Boe ma Man'Tua Sain*	So, Mane Tua Sain
144. *No Tou Danga Liun*	With Tou Danga Liun
145. *Lahala ma lae:*	Speak and say:
146. *'Fes tun leo Sain*	'Give them as wives to the Sea
147. *Ma sao leo Liun.'*	And as spouses to the Ocean.'

The marriage and request for bridewealth

The Heavens offer Patola Bulan and Mandeti Ledo's sister, the woman Matau Senge Bulan and the girl Kudu Kea Ledo, to marry Mane Tua Sain and Tou Danga Liun. After the marriage has taken place, the Sun and Moon demand bridewealth in exchange.

148. *Boe ma Patola Bulan feto na*	Patola Bulan has a sister
149. *Nade Matau Senge Bulan*	Named Matau Senge Bulan
150. *Ma Mandeti Ledo feto na*	And Mandeti Ledo has a sister
151. *Nade Kudu Kea Ledo.*	Named Kudu Kea Ledo.
152. *Ala fes tu'u leo Sain*	They give them to marry in the Sea
153. *Ma ala sao leo Liun,*	And give them to wed in the Ocean
154. *Fo tu'u Mane Tua Sain*	To marry Mane Tua Sain
155. *Ma sao Tou Danga Liun.*	And to wed Tou Danga Liun.

The demand for bridewealth from the Lords of the Ocean and Sea

The Sun and Moon demand bridewealth, consisting first of gold and livestock. When Mane Tua Sain and Tou Danga Liun give this portion of bridewealth in the form of gold chains and pied-white water buffalo, the Sun and Moon respond by saying that this is not enough and they demand a number of specific tools for building and working the fields: 1) the plumbline marker, 2) the bore and chisel, 3) the axe and adze, and 4) the iron digging stick. When these tools are granted, the Heavens continue to demand more—this time, the implements for making fire: 5) the fire-drill, and 6) the flint with tinder grass. The recitation ends with an enumeration of these objects that give rise to the cooking of food and the construction of proper houses. This event is seen also as the origin of the institution of bridewealth.

156. *Fai esa mandan*	On a certain day
157. *Do ledo esa manunina,*	Or a particular time,
158. *Boe ma loke beli batu na*	They ask for solid gold

159. *Ma hule fa'e tena na.*	And they request fine livestock.
160. *Boe ma touk Mane Tua Sain*	The man Mane Tua Sain
161. *No ta'ek Tou Danga Liun*	And the boy Tou Danga Liun
162. *Ala fe beli batuna*	They give bridewealth of gold
163. *Ma fa'e tena na.*	And payment of livestock.
164. *Ala fe lilo ma langa menge-kala*	They give gold chains with snakes' heads
165. *Ma kapa ma ao foe-kala*	And water buffalo with pied-white bodies
166. *Te lae: 'Bei ta dai.'*	But they say: 'Not yet enough.'
167. *Boe ma ala fe sipa aba do*	So, they give a plumbline marker
168. *Ma ala fe bo pa'a bela*	And they give bore and flat chisel
169. *Ma ala fe taka tata-la*	And they give the axe and the adze
170. *Ma besi kakali dae lok.*	And the iron digging stick.
171. *Te Bulan do Ledo lae:*	But the Moon or Sun say:
172. *'Bei ta dai fa.'*	'Still not yet enough.'
173. *Boe ma besak ala fee u'una ai nggeo*	So, now they give the black-stick fire-drill
174. *Ma putu-ana nau poi.*	And the flint with tinder grass.
175. *Boe ma Bula Kai no Ledo Holo lae:*	So, Bula Kai and Ledo Holo say:
176. *'Dai ta dai o dei so*	'Enough or not enough
177. *Te nai sama dai lima de dai*	What is in the hand is enough
178. *Ma no'u ta no'u fa o*	Sufficient or not sufficient
179. *Nai kuku nu'u liman de no'u.'*	What is in the fingers is sufficient.'
180. *Neme ndia mai a besaka hapu*	From this comes what exists now
181. *Ha'i-so'ik, besi taka,*	Hearth fire, iron axe
182. *Bo pa'a bela, taka tatala*	Bore and chisel, axe and adze,
183. *Sipa aba-do nai ata.*	Plumbline marker in the Heights.
184. *De ala hapu la'a tasak*	So, they are able to cook food
185. *Ma tao uma, tesak-teik*	And construct proper houses
186. *Ma uma di, eda ai, la dadi.*	And house-posts and wooden ladders began.
187. *Boe ma beli-pa-sala boe dadi*	And bridewealth also began
188. *Nde lelek ndia.*	From that time.

Recitation 5. The origin of fire, of cooking and of the implements for living, and the sadness of the axe and adze

Ayub Amalo and Stefanus Adulanu (Old Meno)

Ndu Bulan ma Pala Ledo

The hunting encounter of the sons of the Sun and Moon with the Lords of the Sea

In this recitation, the sons of the Sun and Moon are referred to as Ndu Bulan and Pala Ledo. They encounter the Lords of the Sea and Ocean, Danga Lena Liun and Mane Tua Sain, while hunting for pig and civet. Together they hunt in the Nggaek forests and Angok riverbeds. Their dogs catch a pig called Nggeo-Alu Sado and a civet called Lolo Lida.

1.	*Faik esa dalen*	On one day
2.	*Ma ledok esa tein*	And at one time
3.	*Touk-ka Ndu Bulan*	The man Ndu Bulan
4.	*Ma ta'ek-ka Pala Ledo*	And the boy Pala Ledo
5.	*Sopu bafi ndondolo*	Wanders about hunting pig
6.	*Ma fule kuen lolota.*	And roams round pursuing civet.
7.	*De neu tongo lololo*	He meets with his arms
8.	*Ma neu nda lilima*	And encounters with his hands
9.	*Sena oe malole*	His good water companion
10.	*Ma tia ai mandan,*	And his proper tree friend,
11.	*Manek Danga Lena Liun*	The Lord, Chief Hunter of the Ocean
12.	*Ma Bokok Mane Tua Sain.*	And the Ruler, Great Lord of the Sea.
13.	*De leu Nggaek-kala lasi lai*	They go through the forests of Nggaek
14.	*Ma Angok-kala le dale.*	And through the riverbeds of Angok.
15.	*Boe ma busa ka'a-la bafi*	The dogs bite a pig
16.	*Ma asu kiki-la kue,*	And the hounds seize a civet,
17.	*Fo bafi Nggeo Alu Sado*	The pig Nggeo-Alu Sado
18.	*Ma kue Lolo Lido.*	And the civet Lolo Lido.

The debate about sacrificing and the invitation to descend into the Sea

Pala Ledo and Ndu Bulan propose that they immediately cut up the animals and eat them raw, but Danga Lena Liun and Mane Tua Sain reply and explain to the sons of the Sun and Moon that when they catch their game, they roast and smoke the meat on a fire before they eat it. They invite Pala Ledo and Ndu Bulan to descend with them into the Sea for a cooked feast.

19.	*Boe te touk-ka Pala Ledo*	The man Pala Ledo
20.	*Ma ta'ek-ka Ndu Bulan*	And the boy Ndu Bula
21.	*Lafada ma lae:*	Speak and say:
22.	*'Si fo ta'a leon.*	'Slice, so we can eat it
23.	*Ma ke fo folo leon.'*	And tear it apart, so we can consume it.'
24.	*Boe ma touk Danga Lena Liun*	So, the man Danga Lena Liun
25.	*Ma ta'ek Mane Tua Sain*	And the boy Mane Tua Sain
26.	*Lafada ma lae:*	Speak and say:
27.	*'Te sona ami mateme*	'But usually when
28.	*Ami busam-mala ka-la*	Our dogs bite
29.	*Ma ami asum-mala kiki-la*	And our hounds seize
30.	*Na ela ami pila nuli neu bafi*	Then we burn and roast the pig
31.	*Ma masu ndalu neu kue*	And we smoke and fire the civet
32.	*Dei ami mia do folo.*	Then we eat or consume it.
33.	*Te nadek-ka hang-ngita*	So, then let us four
34.	*Do telung-ngita*	Or let us three
35.	*Tama-hehena aok*	Rely on each other
36.	*Ma taka-babani aok,*	And trust each other,
37.	*Fo ata loe leo liun teu*	That we may descend into the Ocean
38.	*Ma ata dilu leo sain teu.'*	And we may turn down into the Sea.'

The hesitation of the sons of the Sun and Moon over descending into the Sea

Ndu Bulan and Pala Ledo reply with some hesitation because they cannot understand how they may descend into the Sea, but Danga Lena Liun and Mane Tua Sain tell them to follow them because there are passages into the Sea.

39. *Boe ma Ndu Bulan ma Pala Ledo*	Ndu Bulan and Pala Ledo
40. *Lafada ma lae:*	Speak and say:
41. *'Te hu tasi oe lama-lama*	'But the Sea's water spreads everywhere
42. *Ma pela oe leu-leu.*	And the Ocean's surface wanders all about.
43. *De tao liun na leë*	What can be done to the Ocean
44. *Ma tao sain na leë*	And what can be done to the Sea
45. *Fo ata teu?'*	That we may go?'
46. *Boe te Danga Lena Liun no Mane Tua Sain*	But Danga Lena Liun with Mane Tua Sain
47. *Lafada ma lae:*	Speak and say:
48. *'Kada mai teu*	'Just come, let us go
49. *Te natik-kala lai na*	For there are passages there
50. *Ma lolok-kala lai ndia.*	And there are straits in that place.
51. *De nau do ta nau*	Like it or not
52. *Kada teu leon,*	Just let us go on,
53. *Sena-oe malole*	Good water-companion
54. *Do tia-ai mandak.'*	Or proper tree-friend.'

The descent into the Sea and the discovery of fire for cooking

So, together they descend into the Sea and arrive at the house of Danga Lena Liun and Mane Tua Sain. There they use a flint and firestick to light a fire to roast the pig and civet.

55. *Boe ma leu leon*	So, they go on
56. *De losa solokae keken*	They go to the cut edge of the shore
57. *Ma tasi-oe pepesan.*	And to the pounding boundary of the Sea.
58. *Boe ma ala so-la leu leon.*	They dive in there.
59. *De bei bonu losa liun nakaton*	They bob to the Ocean's border
60. *Ma bei ele losa sain nataladan,*	And they drift to the Sea's boundary,
61. *Fo Danga Lena Liun uman*	To Danga Lena Liun's house
62. *Ma Mane Tua Sain uman.*	And Mane Tua Sain's house.
63. *Boe ma ala diu besi no batu*	They strike iron with stone

64.	*Ma ala una ai no ai*	And rub stick with stick
65.	*De ala tao kutu nau poi*	They work the tinder-top flint set
66.	*Ma tao una ai nggeo.*	And work the black-stick fire-drill.
67.	*Boe ma ala pila nuli neu bafi*	They burn and roast the pig
68.	*Ma ala masu ndalu neu kue.*	And they smoke and fire the civet.

The choice of rice and millet to cook with roast pork and civet

Danga Lena Liun and Mane Tua Sain turn to their sister, Lole Liuk ('Ocean Goodness') and Lada Saik ('Sea Tastiness'), and ask them what they should eat with their roasted meat. They reply that they should prepare rice and millet to eat with the roast pork and civet. They do so and have their feast.

69.	*Boe ma touk Danga Lena Liun*	The man Danga Lena Liun
70.	*Ma ta'ek Mane Tua Sain*	And the boy Mane Tua Sain
71.	*Lafada neu feton*	Speak to the girl
72.	*Fo fetok-ka Lole Liuk*	The girl Lole Liuk
73.	*Ma lanosi neu inan*	And say to the woman
74.	*Fo inak-ka Lada Saik:*	The woman Lada Saik:
75.	*'Te bafi sao no bek*	'With what do you marry pig
76.	*Ma kue tu no hata?'*	And with what do you wed civet?'
77.	*Boe te inak-ka Lada Saik*	The woman Lada Saik
78.	*Ma fetok-ka Lole Liuk nafada nae:*	And the girl Lole Liuk speak, saying:
79.	*'Te dengu doli no bafi*	'Stamp rice with pig
80.	*Ma tutu lutu no kue.'*	And pound millet with civet.'
81.	*Boe ma ala dengu doli*	They stamp rice
82.	*Ma ala tutu [lutu].*	And they pound [millet].
83.	*De ala dode nasu*	They cook and boil
84.	*De la'a linu.*	They eat and drink.

The decision to bring food to the Sun and Moon

Danga Lena Liun and Mane Tua Sain propose that food be saved and wrapped for Ndu Bulan and Pala Ledo to carry back with them to give to the Sun and Moon. But Ndu Bulan and Pala Ledo reply that the Sun and Moon do not eat wrapped food that has been cooked. In response, Danga Lena Liun and Mane Tua Sain insist that Ndu Bulan and Pala Ledo take the food to the Sun and Moon so that they can eat and drink and enjoy the goodness and tastiness of the Sea.

85.	*Boe ma touk Danga Lena Liun*	The man Danga Lena Liun
86.	*Ma ta'ek Mane Tua Sain*	And the boy Mane Tua Sain
87.	*Nafada ma lae:*	Speak and say:
88.	*'Ita ta'a ma poti fani*	'Let us eat and wrap some food
89.	*Ma kupa fo pisa kue*	And drink and basket some civet
90.	*Fo ela Ndu Bulan no Pala Ledo*	For Ndu Bulan and Pala Ledo
91.	*Leni Bulan dei*	To carry to the Moon
92.	*Ma leni fe Ledi dei fo la'a.'*	And to carry for the Sun to eat.'
93.	*Te hu Ndu Bulan ma Pala Ledo lae:*	But Ndu Bulan and Pala Ledo say:
94.	*'Ami amam-mala*	'Our father
95.	*Do ami to'om-mala,*	Or our mother's brother,
96.	*Bulan no Ledo*	Moon and Sun
97.	*Ta la'a poti fani*	Do not eat wrapped food
98.	*Ma ta kupa pisa kue fo tasak fa.'*	And do not drink basketed civet that is cooked.'
99.	*Te hu touk Danga Lena Liun*	The man Danga Lena Liun
100.	*Ma ta'ek Mane Tua Sain ta nau, lae:*	And the boy Mane Tua Sain do not want this, saying:
101.	*'Kada meni fo ela Bulan na'a nita*	'Just take it for the Moon to eat and see
102.	*Ma Ledo folo nita.*	And for the Sun to consume and see.
103.	*Te lolek-kala lai Liun*	For goodness is in the Ocean
104.	*Ma ladak-kala lai Sain.'*	And tastiness is in the Sea.'

Lontar-palm tapping and the gift of the lontar's sweet-tasting juice

Danga Lena Liun and Mane Tua Sain conduct Ndu Bulan and Pala Ledo back to dry land. There they encounter someone tapping the lontar palm, a tree whose origins are considered to derive from the Sea. They drink some lontar juice and compare each other's drinks. The Sea's drink is tasty, sweet and sour while the Heavens' drink is insipid and tart, so Ndu Bulan and Pala Ledo take some lontar juice to give to the Sun and Moon to eat with the cooked food from the Sea.

105. *Boe ma touk Danga Lena Liun*	The man Danga Lena Liun
106. *Ma ta'ek Mane Tua Sain lo falik*	And the boy Mane Tua Sain conduct
107. *Touk-ka Ndu Bulan no Pala Ledo*	The man Ndu Bulan and Pala Ledo
108. *Leo madak lain mai.*	To the dry land.
109. *De poti leni pa tasak*	They wrap and carry cooked meat
110. *De ala losa madak lain.*	They reach the dry land.
111. *Boe ma lita manaledi tua-la*	There they see someone tapping lontar palms
112. *Leme enok taladak.*	In the middle of the path.
113. *De ala linu tua*	They drink the lontar juice
114. *De lameda ladan-na*	They consider it tasty
115. *Kei-kei ma keke'e.*	Sweet and sour.
116. *Boe ma touk Danga Lena Liun*	The man Danga Lena Liun
117. *No ta'ek Mane Tua Sain*	And the boy Mane Tua Sain
118. *Lafada lae:*	Speak, saying:
119. *'Seok-ka sain liun lalun-na malada hik*	'Indeed, the Sea-Ocean's beer is very tasty
120. *Kei-kei ma keke'e.'*	Sweet and sour.'
121. *Boe ma Ndu Bulan ma Pala Ledo*	Ndu Bulan and Pala Ledo
122. *Lafada bai ma lae:*	Speak again and say:
123. *'Bulan no Ledo lalun-na so*	'The Moon and Sun's beer is
124. *Na mamis ma makale'ek-ka.'*	Insipid and tart.'
125. *Boe te ala dia leni tua matak*	So, they pour and carry fresh lontar juice
126. *Fo leni fe Bulan no Ledo linu*	They carry it for the Moon and Sun to drink
127. *Ma la'a no pa tasak.*	And eat with cooked meat.

The discussion of the possibilities of either war or alliance

The Sun and Moon eat and drink and immediately propose to wage war on the Sea to obtain what the Lords of the Sea possess. Their sons, Ndu Bulan and Pala Ledo, reply that the Sea is too wide and spreads too far to make war on it. Instead, they propose a marriage with the Sea, offering to marry Lole Liuk and Lada Saik. The Sun and Moon counter their sons' proposal, insisting that they themselves marry Lole Liuk and Lada Saik. This they do.

128. *De Bulan no Ledo*	The Moon and Sun
129. *La'a ma linu lita.*	Eat and drink and they see.
130. *Boe ma ala do-do.*	Then they think to themselves.
131. *De lafada anan nala,*	They speak to their child,
132. *Fo Ndu Bulan ma Pala Ledo lae:*	Ndu Bulan and Pala Ledo, saying:
133. *'Malole ata le'a tafa neu sain*	'It would be good if we stretch a sword to the Sea
134. *Ma loe dongi neu liun.'*	And lower a barbed spear to the Ocean.'
135. *Boe te Ndu Bulan*	But Ndu Bulan
136. *No Pala Ledo lae:*	And Pala Ledo say:
137. *'Malole ndia boe.*	'That would be good.
138. *Te hu pela oe leu-leu*	But the Ocean's surface wanders all about
139. *Ma tasi oe lama-lama.*	And the Sea's water spreads everywhere.
140. *De ita tesik enok-ka nde be?'*	What path would we take?'
141. *Boe ma Ndu Bulan*	So, Ndu Bulan
142. *No Pala Ledo lafada*	And Pala Ledo speak
143. *Bulan no Ledo ma lae:*	To Moon and Sun and say:
144. *'Malole ami dua sao tu*	'It would be good if we two marry-wed
145. *Leo liun sain meu,*	In the Ocean-Sea,
146. *Fo ami sao tu inak-ka Lole Liuk*	For we could marry-wed the woman Lole Liuk
147. *Ma fetok-ka Lada Saik.'*	And the girl Lada Saik.'
148. *Te hu Bulan no Ledo lae:*	But the Moon and Sun say:
149. *'Bo'o do'e to'on*	'Don't outdo your mother's brother
150. *Ma seli aman,*	And surpass your father,
151. *Fo ela ami dua dei*	So, allow us two then
152. *Sao Lole Liuk ma Lada Saik.'*	To marry Lole Liuk and Lada Saik.'
153. *Boe ma Bulan no Ledo*	So, Moon and Sun
154. *Sao-la Lole Liuk*	They marry Lole Liuk
155. *Ma tu-la Lada Saik.*	And wed Lada Saik.

The marriage of the Heavens and the Sea and its consequent benefits

The Moon and the Sun go to the Sea for their marriage with Lole Liuk and Lada Saik. When the marriage is concluded and Lole Liuk and Lada Saik removes her wedding clothes, they return in a procession to the Heavens. They bring with them the implements needed to work the fields, to build a house, to make fire and to pound and prepare rice and millet. They also bring the trees needed for the crucial beams of the house.

156. *Besak-ka Bulan no Ledo leu*	Now Moon and Sun go
157. *Sao tu Lole Liuk ma Lada Saik.*	To marry-wed Lole Liuk and Lada Saik.
158. *Boe te ala pau tede Lole Liuk*	They insert Lole Liuk's hairpiece
159. *Ma ala diku suta Lada Saik.*	And they fold Lada Saik's silks.
160. *De nama-tata didiku*	She takes away her folded clothes
161. *Ma nama-sida seseu.*	And she removes her stitched clothing.
162. *Boe ma ala dode-diku los*	They lead her back in procession
163. *Leo Bulan no Ledo uman leu.*	To the Moon and Sun's house.
164. *De leni fuliha'a do duak*	They bring a two-leaved *fuliha'a* tree
165. *Ma keka-lasi do teluk*	And a three-leaved *keka-lasi* tree
166. *Fo ai ma-lou letik*	A tree with stiff bark
167. *Ma tua ma-tea besik.*	And a lontar palm with an iron centre.
168. *De ala tao neu sema duak*	They make them into two *sema* beams
169. *Ma tao neu to'a teluk.*	And make them into three *to'a* poles.
170. *Boe ma leni Bani Asa*	They bring Bani Asa [Chopping Axe]
171. *Ma leni Doke Tei*	And they bring Doke Tei [Adze]
172. *Leni bo pa'a bela*	They bring the bore and flat chisel
173. *Ma funu ma-leo*	And the turning drill
174. *Leni taka tata-la*	They bring the axe and adze
175. *Ma sipa aba-do;*	And the plumbline marker;
176. *Leni lali o'oko*	They bring the measuring basket and winnowing tray

177. *Ma leni tali ai-la boe*	And they bring rope and wood
178. *Ma leni nesu maka-boka buik*	And bring the mortar whose thudding shakes its base
179. *Ma alu mata-fia fangak.*	And the pestle whose thrusting blisters the hand.

The great unhappiness of the axe and the adze

The chant now focuses on the unhappiness of Bani Asa, the axe, and Doke Tei, the adze, which the Sun and Moon have brought with them from the Sea. Bani Asa and Doke Tei begin to cry. In response, the Sun and Moon wake their wife, Lole Liuk and Lada Saik, to tell them that Bani Asa and Doke Tei are crying and to ask them why this might be. Lole Liuk and Lada Saik tell the Sun and Moon the tools must be forged—pounded and sharpened. So, they take them to Makandolu Sain ('Sea Crafter') and Malela Liun ('Ocean Designer'), who forge and sharpen the cutting edges of the two implements. Sun and Moon then take them and put them back in place.

180. *De losa boe ma ala peda*	When they arrive, they place
181. *Bani Asa no Doke Tei*	Bani Asa and Doke Tei
182. *Leu solo-banakan lain*	On top of the *solo-banakan* [a place in the loft]
183. *Ma nati-sosoin lain.*	And on top of the *nati-sosoin* [a place near the door].
184. *Faik esa manunin*	On one certain day
185. *Ma ledok esa mateben,*	And at one particular time,
186. *Fatik kala tao lada*	It is the middle of the night
187. *Ma bolok kala tao do.*	And it is late in the evening.
188. *Boe ma Bani Asa nasa-kedu*	Bani Asa sobs
189. *Ma Doke Tei nama-tani.*	And Doke Tei cries.
190. *Boe ma Bulan ana fafae*	The Moon shakes
191. *Ma Ledo ana oöfe*	And the Sun wakes
192. *Neu saon-na Lole Liuk*	His wife, Lole Liuk
193. *Ma tun-na Lada Saik nae:*	And his spouse, Lada Saik, saying:
194. *'A te Bani Asa nasa-kedu*	'Bani Asa is sobbing
195. *Ma Doke Tei nama-tani.*	And Doke Tei is crying.
196. *De nasa-kedu lo hatak ia*	For what thing is he sobbing
197. *Ma nama-tani bek ia?'*	And for what is he crying?'

198.	*Boe te Lole Liuk*	So, Lole Liuk
199.	*No Lada Saik lae:*	And Lada Saik say:
200.	*'Nama-tani sanga pepesan*	'He is crying to be forged
201.	*Ma nasa-kedu sanga tututun.'*	And he is sobbing to be pounded.'
202.	*Boe te Bulan no Ledo lae:*	So, Moon and Sun say:
203.	*'Fo tenin leo be bai?'*	'Where will we take him?'
204.	*Boe ma Lole Liuk*	Then Lole Liuk
205.	*No Lada Saik lae:*	And Lada Saik say:
206.	*Fe Makandolu Sain pesan*	'Give him to Sea Crafter to forge
207.	*Ma Malela Liun tutun*	And to Ocean Designer to pound
208.	*Fo ana pesa sai lou*	So that he may forge thin his edge
209.	*Ma tutu nama-ni'i matan*	And pound fine his blade
210.	*Fo ela tane nama-kokoun*	Leaving the tip of the blade sharp
211.	*Mata-anan lelenek.'*	And the edge of the blade sheer.'
212.	*Boe ma leni leu*	So, they take him to
213.	*Touk Makandolu Sain*	The man Sea Crafter
214.	*Ma [ta'ek] Malela Liun*	And [the boy] Ocean Designer
215.	*De ana pesa sai-lou taka*	He forges thin the axe's edge
216.	*Ma tutu nama-nii felas.*	And pounds fine the adze's blade.
217.	*De ala tutu lepo ndelo-hun*	He pounds a band round the haft
218.	*Ma ala pesa nggeo mata-anan.*	And he forges black the blade's edge.
219.	*De tanen nama kokoun*	The tip of the blade is sharp
220.	*Ma mata-anan lelenek fo teak-ka.*	And the edge of the blade is sheer and hard.
221.	*Boe ma leni falik-kasa*	They take them back
222.	*De ala peda seluk-kasa*	They put them once more
223.	*Leu mamana makahulun-na.*	In their former place.

The persistent unhappiness of the axe and the adze

In the middle of the night Bani Asa and Doke Tei cry again and, once again, the Sun and Moon wake their wife, Lole Liuk and Lada Saik, to tell them that the axe and adze are crying. This time Lole Liuk and Lada Saik tell them that Bani Asa and Doke Tei are crying to be married. They tell the Sun and Moon to cut wood from two trees, a *poa* and a *ninilu*, and 'marry' them with Bani Asa and Doke Tei. These pieces of wood are intended as the handle and haft for the two implements.

224. *Faik esa,*	One day,
225. *Fatik-kala tao lada*	It is the middle of the night
226. *Ma bolok-kala tao do.*	And it is late in the evening.
227. *Boe te Bani Asa nama-tani bai*	Bani Asa begins to cry again
228. *Ma Doke Tei nasa-kedu bai.*	And Doke Tei begins to sob again.
229. *Boe ma Bulan boe fafa'e*	The Moon again shakes
230. *Ma Ledo boe o'ofe*	And the Sun again wakes
231. *Neu saon-na Lole Liuk*	His wife, Lole Liuk
232. *Ma tun-na Lada Saik ma nae:*	And his spouse, Lada Saik, and say:
233. *'Ate Bani Asa boe nasa-kedu*	'Bane Asa is again sobbing
234. *Ma [Doke Tei] boe nama-tani bai.'*	And [Doke Tei] is again crying.'
235. *Boe ma Lole Liuk*	So, Lole Liuk
236. *No Lada Saik lae:*	And Lada Saik say:
237. *'Ana sanga sasaon*	'He seeks to be married
238. *Ma tutun-na.'*	And to be wed.'
239. *Boe ma Bulan no Ledo latane:*	So, Moon and Sun ask:
240. *'Te fen sao se*	'But to whom do we marry him
241. *Ma tu se?'*	And to whom do we wed him?'
242. *Boe te Lole Liuk*	So, Lole Liuk
243. *No Saik lafada lae:*	And Lada Saik speak, saying:
244. *'Tati ma bu'u dua poa*	'Cut a double-jointed *poa* tree
245. *Ma kale telu ninilun-na*	And a triple-topped *ninilu* tree
246. *Fo fe Bani Asa sao ndia*	To give this for Bani Asa to marry
247. *Ma fe Doke Tei tu ndia.'*	And to give this for Doke Tei to wed.'
248. *De fes sao la boe*	So, they give them to marry
249. *Ma lapeda seluk-kasa*	And they place them once more
250. *Leu mamana bese fain na.*	In their previous place.

The continuing unhappiness of the axe and the adze

Once again, in the middle of the night, Bani Asa and Doke Tei begin to cry inconsolably. And once again the Sun and Moon wake their wife, Lole Liuk and Lada Saik, to tell them. This time Lole Liuk and Lada Saik tell the Sun and Moon that Bani Asa and Doke Tei are crying because they want to clear a garden for planting.

251. *Faik esa bai,*	One day again,
252. *Fatik-kala tao lada*	It is the middle of the night
253. *Ma bolok-kala tao do.*	And it is late in the evening.
254. *Boe te Bani Asa nasa-kedu dodopo*	Bani Asa sobs tearfully
255. *Ma Doke Tei nama-tani bobolo seluk bai.*	And Doke Tei cries weepingly again.
256. *De Bulan boe fafa'e*	The Moon again shakes
257. *Me Ledo boe o'ofe*	And the Sun again wakes
258. *Neu saon Lole Liuk*	His wife, Lole Liuk
259. *Ma neu tun Lada Saik.*	And his spouse, Lada Saik.
260. *De nafadas dede'ak ia.*	He tells them this news.
261. *Boe ma Lole Liuk no Lada Saik*	So, Lole Liuk and Lada Saik
262. *Lafada ma lae:*	Speak and say:
263. *'Ana sanga lelele binan*	'He seeks to clear his dry field
264. *Ma ana seseku ndenun.'*	And he wants to work his garden.'

The preparation, planting and harvesting of field and garden

The Sun and Moon call on all their children and grandchildren to bring the axe and adze to clear a thick wood and prepare a field and garden. They sow the garden with seed. Grains form and grow to produce an abundant harvest—one sufficient to be shared with widows and orphans to this day.

265. *Boe te Bulan no Ledo*	So, the Moon and Sun
266. *Lalo lelena*	Call loudly
267. *Ma langgou ngganggali*	And invite clearly
268. *De ana-teun-nala mai*	Their children and descendants
269. *Ma upu-nelun-nala mai.*	And their grandchildren and great-grandchildren.
270. *De besak-ka ala nole-la felas, Doke Tei*	Now they bring out the adze, Doke Tei
271. *Ma le'a-la taka, Bani Asa.*	And carry out the axe, Bani Asa.
272. *De leu tetu lelei lasin*	They go to a full thick wood
273. *Ma tema toe-ao nulan-na.*	And they go to a whole dense forest.
274. *De ala lele popo bina*	They clear a wide field
275. *Ma seku lelea ndenu.*	And they work a gaping garden.
276. *Besak-ka ala tane bini-la leu*	Now they sow seed in it

277.	*Ma sele ngges-sala leu.*	And they plant grain in it.
278.	*Boe te ana dadi neu pule duak*	It becomes the two budding grains
279.	*Ma moli neu kale teluk.*	And grows into three kernel heads.
280.	*De tu'u na tatana*	It teems with plenty
281.	*Ma diku na babate.*	And it bends with abundance.
282.	*Besak-ka ala ketu ndule buin*	Now they reap to fill their baskets
283.	*Ma kolu sosofe liman*	And harvest to overload their hands
284.	*Fo natun ana dai-lena*	A hundredfold, it exceeds
285.	*Ma lifun ana to-lesi.*	And a thousandfold, it surpasses.
286.	*De dai-lena ana-mak*	The excess is for orphans
287.	*Ma to-lesi falu-ina*	And the extra is for widows
288.	*De losa faik ia*	To this day
289.	*Ma nduku ledok ia boe.*	And until this time.
290.	*Basa nde ndia so.*	This is the end.

Recitation 6. The origin of red millet

Ayub Amalo

Lakimola Bulan ma Kaibake Ledo

The hunt for pig and civet

Lakimola Bulan and Kaibake Ledo descend to Earth from the Heavens. They come to a place in Termanu known as Poko Danon and they bring with them three dogs, Solu Ndan, Lau Masin and Deta Dosa. They whistle for their dogs and set out to hunt for pig and civet in the forest of Nula Tati Bafi and the waters of Seda Solo Mako.

1.	*Hida hatan ma data don-na*	In a former period and a past time
2.	*Touk Lakimola Bulan*	The man Lakimola Bulan
3.	*Ma ta'ek Kaibake Ledo*	And the boy Kaibake Ledo
4.	*Ala lona ue leme poin mai*	They come down from the Heights
5.	*Ma felo fa leme lain mai.*	And they swing down from the Heavens.
6.	*De ala tena mai dae-bafok*	They land on the earth
7.	*Ma tuda mai batu-poi.*	They descend to the world.
8.	*De ala mai mamanak esa*	They arrive at a place

9.	*Nade Poko Danon [Pada].*	Called Poko Danon [in Termanu].
10.	*Nde be na ala lonas lo busan telus*	They come down with three dogs
11.	*De esa nade Solu Ndan*	One named Solu Ndan
12.	*Esa nade Lau Masin*	One named Lau Masin
13.	*Ma esa nade Deta Dosa.*	And one named Deta Dosa.
14.	*De ala kati kofio busa*	They whistle for their dogs
15.	*Ma fu tolesi asu*	And they call for their hounds
16.	*De leu Nula Tati Bafi daen*	And they go to the land of Nula Tati Bafi
17.	*Ma leu Seda Solo Mako oen.*	And they go to the water of Seda Solo Mako.
18.	*De ala sopu bafi leme ndia*	They hunt pig there
19.	*Ma fule kue leme ndia.*	And they pursue civet there.

The decision to plant a dry field and the quest for seed

They decide to make a dry field and garden there and return to the house of the Sun and Moon to ask for seeds. But the Sun and Moon refuse their request because they have separated themselves from their father. So, they once more return to the Earth.

20.	*Boe ma ala tao osi leme ndia*	Then they make a dry garden there
21.	*Ma ala tao tina leme ndia*	And they make a dry field there
22.	*Boe ma leu loke bini no ngges*	And they go to ask for seed and grain
23.	*Lai poin do lain*	From the Heights and the Heavens
24.	*Fo Bulan uman ma Ledo lon.*	The Moon's house and the Sun's home.
25.	*Te hu aman Bulan do Ledo ta fe fan*	But their father, Sun or Moon, would give none
26.	*Nenik ani'i-ana sila la-tea henis.*	Because his children had separated themselves.
27.	*De hu ndia de ala lonas leo*	Therefore, they come down to
28.	*Dae-bafa batu-poi-a mai.*	The earth and world.
29.	*De ala fali ma'is.*	They return.

The planting of blood in the place of seed

They take their machete and their knife and prick the little finger of their right hand and the little toe of their left foot. They then walk through their dry field and garden dripping blood. Wherever the blood drops, maize and millet grow up. These become quick-growing red millet and blood-red maize—crops that continue to grow to the present.

30.	*Boe ma ha'i-la felas-sa ma dope-a leon*	Then they take up their machete and knife
31.	*De ala paun neu lima ku'u dao konan-na*	And they prick the little finger of their right hand
32.	*Ma paun neu ei kuu dao kin-na.*	And they prick the little toe of their left foot.
33.	*Boe ma ala lao feo*	They walk around
34.	*Osi-a no tina-a dalen-na leon.*	Within the dry garden and the dry field.
35.	*De dan-na nesik be*	Wherever their blood falls
36.	*Na ana moli te betek ma pela.*	It grows up as millet and maize.
37.	*Fo loke lae bete pila lai doli*	They invoke the red quick-maturing millet
38.	*Ma [pela] pila pa dak*	And the red-flesh maize
39.	*Losa fai*	To this day and
40.	*Ma nduku besak-ia.*	Until this present time.
41.	*Basan nde ndia so.*	This is the end.

Recitation 7. The origin and spread of rice and millet

Stefanus Adulanu and Petrus Malesi

Doli Mo ma Lutu Mala

The anger of Shark and Crocodile and the storm that carries seed to land

The opening lines of this origin chant are concise, cryptic and critical to understanding its meaning. The chant begins with a serious disturbance in the Sea. The characters in this disturbance are identified as the man Bole Sou and the boy Asa Nao. They slash and cut the Shark and Crocodile, who are the Lords of the Sea. The Shark and Crocodile react, grow angry and furious, and cause a storm that lifts Asa Nao and Bole Sou out of the Sea. Suddenly there is a change in names: Asa Nao and Bole Sou are referred to as Doli Mo and Lutu Mala.[1] Doli Mo and Lutu Mala are the ritual names for rice and millet. Doli Mo and Lutu Mala are carried by the tide to a place at the eastern end of the island of Rote, known as *Mae Oe* and *Tena Lai* in the domain of Landu. Their arrival is auspiciously marked by the sprouting of coconut and pinang palms.

1.	*Touk leo Bole Sou*	The man like Bole Sou
2.	*Ma ta'ek leo Asa Nao*	And the boy like Asa Nao
3.	*Ala ke bibia iu*	They cut and hack the Shark
4.	*Ma ala tati momola foe.*	And they slash and slice the Crocodile.
5.	*Boe ma iu neu namanasa*	Then the Shark grows angry
6.	*Ma foe ana nggenggele.*	And the Crocodile becomes furious.
7.	*Hu ndia de tasi lu Asa Nao*	At this the Sea rises with Asa Nao
8.	*Ma oli lama Bole Sou.*	And the estuary lifts Bole Sou.
9.	*Boe te lu neni Doli Mo*	So, the tide carries Doli Mo [rice]
10.	*Ma lama neni Lutu Mala.*	And the flow carries Lutu Mala [millet].
11.	*De nenin neu Mae Oe*	It carries him to Mae Oe
12.	*Ma nenin neu Tena Lai*	And carries him to Tena Lai
13.	*Fo Mae Oe Loek lutun*	To the fish-catch at Mae Oe Loek
14.	*Ma Tena Lai Laok dean.*	And to the seawall at Tena Lai Laok.
15.	*Besak-ka nupu non na dadi*	Now the coconut shoots begin to grow
16.	*Ma sadu puan na tola*	And the pinang sprouts begin to appear
17.	*De li lakadodofun*	The waves cover him
18.	*Ma nafa lapopolin.*	And the surf soaks him.

---

1   There is an unresolvable ambiguity in the use of the name Asa Nao//Bole Sou in this recitation. Initially, it is an unmistakable reference to the double-named actor who cuts the Shark and Crocodile, whereas later (lines 33–34), it might better be interpreted as the place where this occurs:

33.	*Te hu inan nai Asa Nao*	A mother at Asa Nao
34.	*Ma te'on nai Bole Sou.*	And an aunt at Bole Sou.

The first encounter with Doli Mo and Lutu Mala

On a certain day, as the tide recedes and the seabed opens, the woman Masu Pasu and the girl He Hai go with their scoop nets to search in their fish-catch—an area of raised rock and coral built into the sea to trap all manner of sea creatures as the tide goes out. There they encounter Doli Mo and Lutu Mala, who are crying for a 'mother and aunt'—someone to take care of them. Interestingly, Doli Mo and Lutu Mala refer to themselves by their other ritual names, Asa Nao and Bole Sou.

19.	*Faik esa ma-nunin*	On one certain day
20.	*Ma ledo esa ma-teben*	And at a particular time
21.	*Tasi la huka papa*	The sea opens its planks
22.	*Ma meti la si unu.*	And the tide tears wide its slats.
23.	*Boe te inak-ka Masu Pasu*	So, the woman Masu Pasu
24.	*Ma fetok-ka He Hai*	And the girl He Hai
25.	*Neu nafadama lutu limak*	Goes to probe the arms of the fish-catch
26.	*Ma nafaloe dea eik.*	And goes to grope at the foot of the seawall.
27.	*Boe to neu nda lilima*	There they encounter [Doli Mo]
28.	*Ma neu tongo lololo.*	And there they meet [Lutu Mala].
29.	*Doli Mo nasakedu*	Doli Mo is sobbing
30.	*Ma Lutu Mala namatani*	And Lutu Mala is crying
31.	*Fo nasakedu sanga inan*	Sobbing for his mother
32.	*Ma namatani sanga teön,*	And crying for his aunt,
33.	*Te hu inan nai Asa Nao*	A mother at Asa Nao
34.	*Ma te'on nai Bole Sou.*	And an aunt at Bole Sou.

The gathering and first planting of Doli Mo and Lutu Mala in Korbaffo

The woman Masu Pasu and the girl He Hai pick up Doli Mo and Lutu Mala. Cradling them in their arms, they carry them, as Asa Nao and Bole Sou, to *Tunga Oli* and *Namo Ina* in the domain of Korbaffo. There they plant them carefully, but they do not grow.

35.	*Besak-ka inak-ka, Masu Pasu*	Then the woman Masu Pasu
36.	*Ma fetok-ka, He Hai neu.*	And the girl He Hai goes [there].
37.	*Ifa neni falik Doli*	She returns carrying Doli in her lap

38.	*Ma ko'o neni tulek Lutu*	And comes back cradling Lutu in her arms
39.	*De tulek Asa Nao*	She brings back Asa Nao
40.	*Ma falik Bole Sou.*	And returns Bole Sou.
41.	*Mai bei nai Tunga Oli ma Namo Ina.*	She arrives at Tunga Oli and Namo Ina.
42.	*De sele lakaboboin*	They plant him with care
43.	*Ma tane lasamamaon*	And they sow him with attention
44.	*Te hu bokon ta dadi*	But the bending stalk does not grow
45.	*Ma do belan ta tola.*	And the heavy leaves do not appear.

The transfer and planting of Doli Mo and Lutu Mala in the domain of Termanu

The first attempt to plant Doli Mo and Lutu Mala at Tunga Oli and Namo Ina initiates a long litany of further attempts to transfer and plant them at different sites in the various domains of Rote.

Each domain on Rote is identified, ritually, by several such placenames. This litany thus constitutes a topogeny: an ordered recitation of specific placenames. In some cases, the women's names indicate a site, as do the names of the places where Doli Mo and Lutu Mala are planted. The progress of this topogeny follows in a counterclockwise movement around the island.

Four separate attempts are made to plant Doli Mo and Lutu Mala in the domain of Termanu. Because this recitation forms a critical part of Termanu's heritage, it provides an elaborate exposition of specific sites. The first of these attempts occurs when the woman Fi Bau and the girl Seda Kola plant Doli Mo and Lutu Mala at *Bau Peda Dele* and *Kola Sifi Ndai*—an area referred to in ordinary language as Kola, on the north coast of Termanu near the border with Korbaffo. (Kola appears twice: in the woman's name Seda Kola and in the placename *Kola Sifi Ndai*.) The second attempt occurs when Kada Ufa and Dila Latu try to plant the seeds at *Hau Hala* and *Kae Kopa*. This is an area, known as Hala, further west along the north coast of Termanu. The third attempt is by Leli Onge and Fula Fopo. Although no planting site is mentioned, the location of this third attempt is called Leli—identified by the woman's name Leli Onge—located still further along the north coast of Termanu. The next attempt overlaps with that of the third attempt as indicated by the recurrence of the word 'Leli' in the names Soe Leli and Pinga Pasa.

46. *Besak ka inak-ka Fi Bau*	Then the woman Fi Bau
47. *Ma fetok-ka Seda Kola*	And the girl Seda Kola
48. *Ko'o do ifa nenin.*	Cradles or carries him away.
49. *De sele nakaboboin*	She plants him with care
50. *Ma tane nasamamaon*	And sows him with attention
51. *Nai Bau Peda Dele fuan*	In the field at Bau Peda Dele
52. *Ma Kola Sifi Ndai mon,*	And in the plain at Kola Sifi Ndai,
53. *Te do belan ta dadi*	But the heavy leaves do not grow
54. *Ma hu bokon ta tola.*	And the bending stalk does not appear.
55. *Boe te inak-ka Kada Ufa*	But then the woman Kada Ufa
56. *Ma fetok-ka Dila Latu*	And the girl Dila Latu
57. *Ko'o lenin do ifa lenin.*	Cradles him away or carries him away.
58. *De tane lasamamaon*	They sow him with attention
59. *Ma sele lakaboboin.*	And plant him with care.
60. *Te do belan ta dadi*	But his heavy leaves do not grow
61. *Ma hu bokon ta tola.*	And his bending stalks do not appear.
62. *Besak-ka inak-ka Hau Hala*	Now the woman Hau Hala
63. *Ma fetok-ka Kae Kopa*	And the girl Kae Kopa
64. *Ko'o nenin do ifa nenin.*	Cradles him away or carries him away.
65. *De tane lakaboboin*	And sows him with care
66. *Ma sele lasamamaon.*	And plants him with attention.
67. *Te do belan ta dadi*	But his heavy leaf does not grow
68. *Ma hu bokon ta dadi.*	And his bending stalk does not grow.
69. *Besak ka inak-ka Leli Onge*	Now the woman Leli Onge
70. *Ma fetok-ka Fula Fopo mai.*	And the girl Fula Fopo comes.
71. *De ko'o do ifa nenin.*	She cradles or carries him away.
72. *De tane lakaboboin*	They sow him with care
73. *Ma tane lasamamaon.*	And sow him with attention.
74. *Te hu bokon ta tola*	But his bending stalk does not appear
75. *Ma do belan ta dadi.*	And his heavy leaf does not grow.
76. *Besak-ka inak-ka Soe Leli*	Now the woman Soe Leli

77. *Ma fetok-ka Pinga Pasa*	And the girl Pinga Pasa
78. *[Ko'o nenin do] ifa nenin.*	[Cradles him away or] carries him away.
79. *De tane lakaboboin*	They sow him with care
80. *Ma sele lasamamaon.*	And plant him with attention.
81. *Te hu bokon ta dadi*	But his bending stalk does not grow
82. *Ma do belan ta tola.*	And his heavy leaf does not appear.

The first successful planting of Doli Mo and Lutu Mala in Termanu

At this point the woman Fiti Nggoli and the girl Lole Bako come rushing to take the seeds, Doli Mo and Lutu Mala. They bring betel and areca nut and wear fine sarongs to welcome the seeds. They plant them in a field known as *Bako Bau Dale* and *Nggoli Kai Tio*—a site called Bau Dale that is also on the north coast of Termanu. They also set out special winnowing baskets to gather the harvest of seed.

In response, Doli Mo and Lutu Mala bring forth their grains. Shouting occurs to drive away birds that threaten the crop. This first planting at Bau Dale is, for Termanu, the beginnings of rice and millet harvesting on Rote.

83. *Besak-ka inak-ka Fiti Nggoli*	Then the woman Fiti Nggoli
84. *Ma fetok-ka Lole Bako*	And the girl Lole Bako
85. *Ana tolo mu sasali*	She comes running
86. *Ma nalai lelena.*	And she comes dashing.
87. *De neni pua lisu lasu boak*	She brings an areca nut round as a tufted cotton ball
88. *Ma malu boa dongi aik*	And a betel fruit long as a barbed spear shaft
89. *Pou le'u pana-daik*	A sarong with *pena-daik* bands
90. *Ma sidi soti tola-teëk.*	And a ritual cloth with the *tola-te'ek* stitches.
91. *Mai de ana ifa do ko'o nenin.*	She comes; she carries or cradles him away.
92. *De neu tane nasamamaon*	She goes to sow him with attention
93. *Do sele nakaboboin*	And plant him with care
94. *Neu Bako Bau Dale mon*	In the plain of Bako Bau Dale
95. *Ma neu Nggoli Kai Tio fuan*	And in the field of Nggoli Kai Tio

96. *Ma ana mole sepe do fua oli.*	And she sets the *sepe* basket or lays the *oli* basket.
97. *Besak-ka kalen-na didiku*	Now his kernel bends over
98. *Ma pulen-na loloso.*	And his buds creep upward.
99. *Boe ma besak-ka oku-bolu ma do-se'ek*	Now they yell and make noise
100. *Nai Baku Bau Dale mon*	In the plain of Bako Bau Dale
101. *Do Nggoli Kai Tio fuan.*	And in the field of Nggoli Kai Tio.

The next two successful plantings of Doli Mo and Lutu Mala in Termanu

Doli Mo and Lutu Mala are carried and planted in two more large fields in Termanu. The girl Dulu Kilik and the woman Leo Lasuk plant the seeds at *Ki Lama* and *Le Ina*, where they grow as in Bau Dale. Thereafter the woman Pinga Pasa and the girl Lu'a Lela take Doli Mo and Lutu Mala and plant them at *Peto Lesi-Ama* and *Lela Bala-Fia*, where once again they grow. This area, known as Peto and Lela, is in the interior of Termanu. This *sawah* complex is irrigated by a large, reliable spring-fed water source and serves as Termanu's largest and most productive rice basket.

102. *Besak-ka fetok-ka Dulu Kilik*	Now the girl Dulu Kilik
103. *Ma inak-ka Leo Lasuk*	And the woman Leo Lasuk
104. *Ana mai.*	She arrives.
105. *De ana ifa do ko'o neni[n]*	She carries or cradles him away
106. *De ana selen neu Ki Lama*	She plants him at Ki Lama
107. *Do tanen neu Le Ina.*	Or sows him at Le Ina.
108. *Besak-ka hu bokon na tola*	Now his bending stalk appears
109. *Ma do belan na dadi.*	And his heavy leaf grows.
110. *Kalen na loloso*	His kernel creeps upward
111. *Ma pulen didiku.*	And his buds bend over.
112. *Boe ma besak-ka [inak-ka] Pinga Peto*	Now [the woman] Pinga Peto
113. *Ma fetok-ka Lu'a Lela*	And the girl Lu'a Lela
114. *De ana ifa do ko'o neni[n]*	She carries or cradles him away
115. *De ana tanen neu Peto Lesi-Ama mon*	She sows him in the plain of Peto Lesi-Ama
116. *Ma [sele neu] Lela Bala-Fia fuan.*	And [plants him] in the field of Lela Bala-Fia.

117. *Boe ma besak-ka ala oku-boluk*	Now they yell
118. *Ma ala do-se'ek*	And they make noise
119. *Nai Peto Lesi-Ama mon*	In the plain of Peto Lesi-Ama
120. *Do Lela Bala-Fia fuan.*	Or in the field of Lela Bala-Fia.

The transfer and planting of Doli Mo and Lutu Mala in Ba'a and Dengka

The recitation continues to recount the transfer of Doli Mo and Lutu Mala around the island of Rote. This progression moves from Termanu to the west through the domains of Ba'a and Dengka to the domains of Delha and Oenale at the far western end of the island.

The principal ritual name for the domain of Ba'a is *Pena Pua* and *Maka Lama*. This ritual name is used first as the name of a woman and then as the name of a place. After the first mention of this name, the recitation continues by citing the name of the girl Loe Tesa and Dilu Tama, who comes, takes the seeds and plants them at *Tanga Loi* and *Oe Mau*—another large spring-fed field complex. It then repeats the name *Pena Pua* and *Maka Lama* as a placename. The implication is that the seeds take root and grow in Ba'a.

The girl Dae Mea Iko and the woman Oe Ange Muli take the seeds and plant them at *Dae Mea* and *Tete Lifu* in the domain of Dengka. Again, the woman's name Dae Mea, which literally means 'Red Earth', is the same name as the place where the seeds are planted. The other half of that placename, *Tete Lifu*, refers to the existence of 'a thousand dikes'—a collection of small dams for trapping and diverting water. That shouting occurs after the planting process indicates that the seeds have grown to a harvest.

121. *Boe ma besak-ka inak leo Pena Pua*	Now a woman like Pena Pua
122. *Ma fetok leo Maka Lama*	And a girl like Maka Lama
123. *Inak-ka Loe Tesa*	The woman Loe Tesa
124. *Ma fetok-ka Dilu Tama*	And the girl Dilu Tama
125. *Ana mai.*	She arrives.
126. *De ana ifa do ko'o nenin,*	She carries or cradles him away,
127. *Ana tane nasamamaon*	She sows him with attention
128. *Do sele nakaboboin*	Or plants him with care
129. *Bei nai Tanga Loi*	At Tanga Loi

130. *Ma bei nai Oe Mau*	And at Oe Mau
131. *De bei nai Pena Pua*	Then in Pena Pua
132. *Ma bei nai Maka Lama.*	And in Maka Lama.
133. *Besak-ka fetok Dae Mea Iko*	Now the girl Dae Mea Iko
134. *Ma inak Oe Ange Muli*	And the woman Oe Ange Muli
135. *Tolomu sasali*	Comes running
136. *Ma nalai lelena.*	And comes dashing.
137. *De ifa do ko'o nenin.*	And carries or cradles him away.
138. *De ana sele nasamamaon*	And she plants him with attention
139. *Ma tane nakaboboin*	And sows him with care
140. *Bei nai Dae Mea*	In Dae Mea
141. *Ma bei nai Tete Lifu leon.*	And in Tete Lifu.
142. *De basak-ka oku-boluk ma do-se'ek.*	Now they yell and make noise.

The transfer and planting of Doli Mo and Lutu Mala in Delha and Oenale

Next the woman Tete Kefa and the girl Kali Solu come to gather the seeds and take them to Delha, but there is no place to plant them. Then the woman Meda Afe and the girl Fai Nggengge take them to Oenale, whose ritual name is given as *Nale Dene* and *Nada Dona*. (The more commonly recognised ritual name for Oenale is *Tasi Puka ma Li Sonu.*) Again, the shouting indicates the success of the planting in Oenale.

143. *Besak-ka inak-ka Tete Kefa*	Now the woman Tete Kefa
144. *Do fetok-ka Kali Solu*	Or the girl Kali Solu
145. *Neme Dela Muli mai*	Comes from Dela Muli
146. *Ma neme Ana Iko mai,*	And comes from Ana Iko,
147. *Ana tolomu sasali [neu]*	She comes running
148. *Ma nalai lelena neu.*	And she comes dashing there.
149. *De ifa nenin do ko'o nenin.*	And she carries him away or cradles him away.
150. *De ana tane neu Dela Muli*	She sows in Dela Muli
151. *Ma sele neu Ana Iko.*	And she plants in Ana Iko.
152. *Te fuak ta Dela Muli*	But there is no field in Dela Muli
153. *Ma mok ta Ana Iko.*	And there is no plain in Ana Iko.
154. *Boe ma besak-ka fetok-ka*	Now the girl Meda Afe

155. *Do inak-ka Fai Nggengge*	Or the woman Fai Nggengge
156. *Tolomu sasali*	Comes running
157. *Do lalai lelena.*	Or comes dashing.
158. *Leni leu Nale Dene [ma] Nada Dona*	They bring him to Nale Dene and Nada Dona
159. *De leni leu Oenale.*	They bring him to Oenale.
160. *Ana tane nasamamao[n]*	She sows him with attention
161. *Ma sele nakaboboi[n].*	And plants him with care.
162. *[De besak-ka] oku-boluk ma do-se'ek.*	Now they yell and make noise.

The transfer and planting of Doli Mo and Lutu Mala in Thie and Loleh

Having reached the western end of Rote, Doli Mo and Lutu Mala's progression turns eastward: the seeds are successfully carried and planted in the domains of Thie and Loleh, both of which are on the southern side of the island.

The girl Foi Lama and the woman Teku Tada bring the seeds to Thie and plant them in two places, *Lene Kona* and *Tada Muli* and *Tuda Meda* and *Do Lasi*, where they take root and grow. Then the woman Tui Beba and the girl Oe Ange, who is also identified with various of Loleh's ritual names, *Ninga Ladi* and *Hengu Hena* as well as *Teke Dua* and *Finga Telu*, carry the seeds to Loleh and successfully plant them there.

163. *Besak-ka fetok-ka Foi Lama*	Now the girl Foi Lama
164. *Bei nai Tada Muli*	In Tada Muli
165. *Ma inak-ka Teku Tada*	And the woman Teku Tada
166. *Bei nai Lene Kona*	In Lene Kona
167. *Ala ifa do ko'o lenin.*	They carry him or cradle him away.
168. *De tane neu Lene Kona*	They sow in Lene Kona
169. *Ma sele neu Tada Muli*	And plant in Tada Muli
170. *Ma leu de sele neu Tuda Meda*	And they go; they plant him in Tuda Meda
171. *Do tane neu Do Lasi.*	And sow him in Do Lasi.
172. *Boe ma besak-ka [ala] oku boluk*	Then they yell
173. *Ma ala do-se'ek.*	And they make noise.
174. *Boe ma inak bei Ninga Ladi*	The woman of Ninga Ladi

175. *Ma fetok bei Hengu Hena*	And the girl of Hengu Hena
176. *Inak bei Teke Dua*	The woman of Teke Dua
177. *Ma fetok bei Finga Telu*	And the girl of Finga Telu
178. *Inak-ka Tui Beba*	The woman Tui Beba
179. *Do fetok-ka Oe Ange*	Or the girl Oe Ange
180. *Ana ifa do ko'o nenin.*	She carries or cradles him away.
181. *De ana sele do tane*	She plants or sows
182. *Neu Ninga Ladi do Hengu Hena.*	In Ninga Ladi or Hengu Hena.
183. *De [ala] oku boluk ma do-se'ek.*	They yell and make noise.

The transfer of Doli Mo and Lutu Mala to Keka, Talae, Bokai and Lelenuk

Doli Mo and Lutu Mala are next transferred to four further domains on the south coast of the island: Keka, Talae, Bokai and Lelenuk. The woman Neu Lopo and the girl Neu Nggele carry and plant them in *Tufa Laba* and *Ne'e Feo*, the domain of Keka. Then the woman Pila Sue and the girl Nggeo Deta, who are identified by the principal ritual name of the domain of Talae, take the seeds and plant them at a site identified as *Sosolo Lean* and *Batu Tanga Lou*. Next the woman Toin Dae and the girl Le Kama carry the seeds to Bokai, which is identified by its two main ritual names, *Ko Solo* and *Nilu Foi* and *Medi* and *Ndule*. The woman Poko Tasi and the girl Silu Meti comes and tries to plant the seeds in Lelenuk, *Lenu Petu* and *Safe Solo*, but without success because there is no suitable field in the domain.

184. *Besak-ka feto bei Tufa Laba*	Then a girl of Tufa Laba
185. *Ma ina bei Ne'e Feo*	And a woman of Ne'e Feo
186. *Inak-ka Neu Lopo*	The woman Neu Lopo
187. *Do fetok-ka Neu Nggele*	Or the girl Neu Nggele
188. *Ko'o tapandondoen*	Cradles him gently in her arms
189. *[Ma] ifa mangananaün.*	And carries him tenderly on her lap.
190. *De tane do sele*	She sows or plants
191. *Neu Tufa Laba do Neë Feo.*	In Tufa Laba or Ne'e Feo.
192. *Besak ka eki-kala bekedoto*	Now their shouts burst out
193. *Ma hena-kala bekao*	And their cries howl forth
194. *Boe ma ina bei Pila Sue*	A woman of Pila Sue
195. *Ma feto bei Nggeo-Deta*	And a girl of Nggeo Deta
196. *Ala tolomu do lalai.*	They run or hurry.

197. *Leme Longa Fa [mai]*	From Longa Fa, they arrive
198. *Do leme Feo Ne mai.*	Or from Feo Ne, they arrive.
199. *De ala tane neu Sosolo Lean daen*	They sow in the earth of Sosolo Lean
200. *Do [sele] neu Batu Tanga Lou oen.*	Or [plant] in the water of Batu Tanga Lou.
201. *Boe ma hu bokon na tola*	His bending stalk appears
202. *Boe ma kale dua na dadi*	Then his two kernels grow
203. *Boe ma eki-kala bekedoto*	Their shouts burst out
204. *Ma hema-kala bei kao.*	And their cries howl forth.
205. *Boe ma besak-ka feto bei Ko Solo*	Now a girl of Ko Solo
206. *Ma ina bei Nilu Foi*	And a woman of Nilu Foi
207. *Inak-ka Toin Dae*	The woman Toin Dae
208. *Do fetok-ka Le Kama*	Or the girl Le Kama
209. *Ana tolomu sasali*	She comes running
210. *Do nalai lelena.*	Or she comes dashing.
211. *De ana ifa do ko'o nenin.*	She carries or cradles him away.
212. *De ana tane neu Ko Solo*	She sows in Ko Solo
213. *Ma ana sele neu Nilu Foi.*	And she plants in Nilu Foi
214. *De ana tane neu Keko Nesu*	She sows in Keko Nesu
215. *Do [ana] sele neu Te Alu*	And plants in Te Alu[2]
216. *Sele neu Medi Daen*	[She] plants in the earth of Medi
217. *Ma tane neu Ndule Oen.*	And sows in the water of Ndule.
218. *Besak-ka hu bokon na tola*	Now his bending stalk appears
219. *Ma do belan na dadi.*	And his heavy leaf grows.
220. Kale dua na lesu	His two kernels come out
221. *Ma pule telu na tola.*	And his three buds appear.
222. *Boe ma besak-ka feto bei Lenu Petu*	Now a girl of Lenu Petu
223. *Do ina bei Safe Solo*	Or a woman of Safe Solo
224. *Inak-ka Poko Tasi*	The woman Poko Tasi
225. *Ma fetok-ka Silu Meti*	And the girl Silu Meti
226. *Ana ko'o nenin [do ifa nenin]*	She cradles him away [or carries him away]

---

2   *Keko Nesu//Te Alu* may be a mistake in this recitation. The name is similar to the name *Pesu Nesu//Te Alu*, which is used in Termanu to allude to its border region with Bokai.

227. *De tanen neu Lenu Petu*	Sows him in Lenu Petu
228. *Ma selen neu Safe Solo.*	And plants him in Safe Solo.
229. *Te fuak ta Lenu Petu*	But there is no field in Lenu Petu
230. *Ma mok ta Safe Solo.*	And there is no plain in Safe Solo.

The transfer of Doli Mo and Lutu Mala to Diu, Bilba, Ringgou and Oepao

Moving still further eastward, Doli Mo and Lutu Mala are carried and planted in the domains of Diu, Bilba, Ringgou and Oepao. The girl from Diu Dulu and Kana Langa, Leo Lata and Adu Pinga, plants the seeds at two places in Diu: at Pele Pou and Nggafu Lafa—identified as one of the common names for Diu—but also, specifically, at *Sapan Daen Oe Utuk* and *Seun Oen Fi Bolo*. Then the woman Nggeo Lao and Pila Selu, identified by two of the principal names of Bilba, *Pengo Dua* and *Hilu Telu* and *Feni Fi* and *Tane Bau*, carries the seeds to plant there. Then the girl Oko Beba and the woman Tui Lele plant the seeds at *Londa Lusi* and *Batu Bela*, at *Saba Lai* and *Dele Bui* and at *Tua Nae* and *Lele Beba*—all identified as the ritual names for Ringgou. Next the woman Kao Kai and the girl Pena Ufa from Fai Fua and Ledo So'u from Oepao carries the seeds to plant them at *Lifa Lama* and *Lutu Oen*. In all these domains, Doli Mo and Lutu Mala, with heavy leaf and bending stalk, grow and yield a harvest.

231. *Besak-ka inak bei Diu Dulu*	Now the woman of Diu Dulu
232. *Ma fetok bei Kana Langa*	And the girl of Kana Langa
233. *Fetok-ka Leo Lata*	The girl Leo Lata
234. *Do inak-ka Adu Pinga*	And the woman Adu Pinga
235. *Ana ifa do ko'o nenin*	She carries or cradles him away
236. *De tane neu Pele Pou*	She sows in Pele Pou
237. *Ma sele neu Nggafu Lafa*	And plants in Nggafu Lafa
238. *[Neu] Sapan Daen Oe Utuk*	[At] Sapan Daen Oe Utuk
239. *[Ma neu] Seun Oen Fi Bolo.*	[And at] Seun Oen Fi Bolo.
240. *Besak-ka hu bokon-na tola*	Now his bending stalk appears
241. *Ma do belan-na dadi.*	And his heavy leaf grows.
242. *Boe ma besak-ka ina bei Pengo Dua*	Now a woman of Pengo Dua
243. *Ma feto bei Hilu Telu*	And a girl of Hilu Telu
244. *Ina bei Feni Fi*	A woman of Feni Fi
245. *Ma feto bei Tane Bau*	And a girl of Tane Bau

246. *Inak-ka Nggeo Lao*	The woman Nggeo Lao
247. *Ma fetok-ka Pila Selu*	And the girl Pila Selu
248. *De ana ifa do ko'o nenin*	She carries or cradles him away
249. *De tane neu Feni Fi*	She sows in Feni Fi
250. *Ma sele neu Tane Bau.*	And plants in Tane Bau
251. *Besak-ka [ala] oko-boluk ma do-se'ek.*	Now [they] yell and make noise.
252. *Boe ma fetok bei Londa Lusi*	The girl of Londa Lusi
253. *Ma inak bei Batu Bela* .	And the woman of Batu Bela
254. *Inak-ka Oko Beba*	The woman Oko Beba
255. *Do fetok-ka Tui Lele*	Or the girl Tui Lele
256. *Ana tolomu sasali*	She comes running
257. *Ma nalai lelena.*	And comes dashing.
258. *De ana tane neu Londa Lusi*	She sows in Londa Lusi
259. *Do [ana] sele neu Batu Bela*	Or plants in Batu Bela
260. *Do sele neu Saba Lai*	Or plants in Saba Lai
261. *Ma tane neu Dele Bui*	And sows in Dele Bui
262. *Sele neu Tua Nae*	Plants in Tua Nae
263. *Do tane neu Lele Beba.*	Or sows in Lele Beba.
264. *Bo ma besak-ka fetok-ka Meda Afe*	Now the girl Meda Afe
265. *Do inak-ka Fai Nggengge*	Or the woman Fai Nggengge
266. *Ina bei Fai Fua*	A woman of Fai Fua
267. *Do feto bei Ledo So'u*	Or a girl of Ledo So
268. *Inak-ka Kao Kai*	The woman Kao Kai
269. *Do fetok-ka Pena Ufa*	Or the girl Pena Ufa
270. *Ifa do ko'o nenin.*	Carries or cradles him away.
271. *De tane neu Lifa Lama*	She sows in Lifa Lama
272. *[Ma] sele neu Lutu Oen.*	And plants in Lutu Oen.
273. *Beask-ka do belan na tola*	Now his heavy leaf appears
274. *Ma hu bokun na dadi.*	And his bending stalk grows.

The transfer of Doli Mo and Lutu Mala back to Landu and the return to the Sea

The cycle is completed and Doli Mo and Lutu Mala are returned to *Tena Lai* and *Mai Oe* in Landu. The woman Liti Lifu and the girl Henu Helok from *Soti Mori* and *Bola Tena*—the domain of Landu at the eastern end of the island—carry the seeds to plant them but there is no field at *Tena Lai* and *Mae Oe* and thus Doli Mo and Lutu Mala return to the Sea.

275. *Boe ma feto bei Soti Mori*	A girl of Soti Mori
276. *Ma ina bei Bola Tena*	And a woman of Bola Tena
277. *Inak-ka Liti Lifu*	The woman Liti Lifu
278. *Do fetok-ka Henu Helok*	Or the girl Henu Helok
279. *De ifa do ko'o nenin*	She carries or cradles him away
280. *Koo mangananaün*	Cradles him gently in her arms
281. *Ma ifa tapandondoen.*	And carries them tenderly on her lap.
282. *De ana tane do sele*	She sows or plants
283. *Neu Tena Lai do Mae Oe.*	At Tena Lai or Mae Oe
284. *Te fuak ta Tena Lai*	But there is no field at Tena Lai
285. *Ma mok ta Mae Oe.*	And there is no plain at Mae Oe.
286. *Boe ma ana tulek leo liun neu*	Then he [Doli do Lutu] goes back to the Ocean
287. *Ma falik leo sain neu.*	And returns to the Sea.

In this chant, Doli Mo and Lutu Mala are transferred in a counterclockwise progression from Landu, from domain to domain along the north coast of Rote, moving from east to west and then continuing from west to east until they arrive back at *Tena Lai ma Mae Oe* and return to the Sea.

It is notable and significant that the transfer of Doli Mo and Lutu Mala— the knowledge of planting and its successful execution—is undertaken by women: a chain of transmission of crucial cultural knowledge from woman to woman across the island of Rote. A similar form of transmission is recounted in Recitation 8 on the origin of tie-dyeing and weaving and the spread of the loom and of the cloth patterns that derive from the realm of the Sea.

Recitation 8. The origin of weaving and dyeing and the spread of cloth patterns

Stefanus Adulanu

Pata Iuk ma Dula Foek

This recitation begins in the Heavens, where the daughters of the Sun and Moon, Henge Ne Ledo ('Cloth Binder of the Sun') and Feo Futu Bulan ('Thread Winder of the Moon') weave, tie and dye cloths—both men's cloths and women's sarongs—with shark and crocodile patterns. They take their shuttle and loom and give them to Lui Liuk ('Sea Cow of the Ocean') and Kea Saik ('Turtle of the Sea'). They, in turn, produce fine cloths with shark and crocodile patterns.

1.	*Inak Henge Ne Ledo*	The woman Henge Ne Ledo
2.	*Ma fetok Feo Futu Bulan*	And the girl Feo Futu Bulan
3.	*Ala ndolo selu lai lain*	They throw the shuttle in the Heavens
4.	*Ma nggiti ati lai poin*	And they work the loom in the Heights
5.	*Fo ala fula-foe*	To form fine patterns
6.	*Ma ala lai-hai.*	And fashion bright designs.
7.	*Ala henge ma tenu*	They tie and weave
8.	*Pou lafa.*	Women's sarongs and men's cloths.
9.	*Faik esa manunin*	On one certain day
10.	*Ma ledok esa mateben*	And at a particular time
11.	*Boe ma inak Henge Ne Ledo*	The woman Henge Ne Ledo
12.	*Ma fetok Feo Futu Bulan*	And the girl Feo Futu Bulan
13.	*Ala tenga la ndolo selun*	They take their shuttle
14.	*Ma ngga'u la nggiti atin.*	And grab their loom.
15.	*De fe leo liun neu*	They go and give it to the Ocean
16.	*Ma fe leo sain neu.*	And go and give it to the Sea.
17.	*De fe neu Lui Liuk*	They give it to Lui Liuk
18.	*Ma fen neu Kea Saik.*	And give it to Kea Saik.
19.	*Boe te inak-ka Lui Liuk*	The woman Lui Liuk
20.	*Ma fetok-ka Kea Saik*	And the girl Kea Saik

21.	*Ana ndolo selu nai liun*	She throws the shuttle in the Ocean
22.	*Ma nggiti ati nai sain*	And works the loom in the Sea
23.	*De ana lai-hai malole*	She fashions good shark designs
24.	*Ma ana fula-foe mandak.*	And she forms proper crocodile patterns.

Pata Iu and Dula Foek's search for a woman to love

Then one day, the man Pata Iuk ('Figure Shark') and the boy Dula Foek ('Pattern Crocodile') comes out from the Sea and goes to make love with the maiden girls on the island of Ndao. He finds no unmarried girls on Ndao, but he hears of the woman Pua Kene ('Areca Kene') and the girl No Lini ('Coconut Lini'), who lives in *Hengu Hena* and *Ninga Ladi*: the domain of Loleh. The chant character Pua Kene and No Lini is a beautiful woman with striking eyes and long strands of curly hair.

25.	*Faik esa manunin*	On one certain day
26.	*Ma ledok esa mateben*	And at a particular time
27.	*Boe te touk-ka Pata Iuk*	The man Pata Iuk
28.	*Ma ta'ek-ka Dula Foek*	And the boy Dula Foek
29.	*Neme sain dale mai*	Comes out from the Sea
30.	*Ma neme liun dale mai*	And comes out from the Ocean
31.	*De leo Folo Manu neu*	He goes to Folo Manu
32.	*Ma leo Ndao Nusa neu*	And goes to Ndao Nusa [Ndao]
33.	*Fo neu sosoa sanga teman*	To make love and seek fulfilment
34.	*Ma piao sanga tetun.*	And to take pleasure and seek climax.
35.	*Te hu ina lenak ta Ndao*	But there are no unmarried women in Ndao
36.	*Ma feto lesik ta Folo.*	And no maiden girls on Folo.
37.	*Boe te ndiin-na namanene*	But his ears hear
38.	*Ma nggatan-na namania*	And his hearing takes note
39.	*Inak-ka Pua Kene*	Of the woman Pua Kene [Areca Kene]
40.	*Ma fetok-ka No Lini*	And of the girl No Lini [Coconut Lini]
41.	*Inak leo Hengu Hena*	A woman living in Hengu Hena
42.	*Ma fetok leo Ninga Ladi*	And a girl living in Ninga Ladi

43.	*Ina mata na'a*	A woman with striking eyes
44.	*Ma feto idu malole*	And a girl with a beautiful nose
45.	*Fo e'eke oe*	With hair bound in coils
46.	*Ma langa sesenga siok.*	And in nine long strands.

The engagement of Lodo Bela and Solu Lolo from Ndao

The man Lodo Bela and the boy Solu Lolo from the island of Ndao have already become engaged to the woman Pua Kene and the girl No Lini, but they have returned to Ndao to gather the gold and livestock that they need to pay bridewealth.

47.	*Fo touk leo Ndao Nusa*	A man living in Ndao Nusa
48.	*Ma ta'ek leo Folo Manu*	And a boy living in Folo Manu
49.	*Touk-ka Lodo Bela*	The man Lodo Bela
50.	*Ma ta'ek-ka Solu Lolo*	And the boy Solu Lolo
51.	*Neu adu Pua Kene so*	Has already requested Pua Kene
52.	*Ma neu luü No Lini so.*	And has already asked for No Lini.
53.	*De ala helu malu lakabua*	They bend the betel catkin together [have intercourse]
54.	*Ma sada pua laesa.*	And peel the areca nut as one.
55.	*Boe te touk-ka Lodo Bela*	But the man Lodo Bela
56.	*Ma ta'ek ka Solu Lolo*	And the boy Solu Lolo
57.	*Tulek leo Ndao neu*	Goes back to Ndao
58.	*Ma falik leo Folo neu*	And returns to Folo
59.	*Fo dodo beli batuk*	To plan how to collect the bridewealth of gold
60.	*Ma ndanda fae tenak.*	And consider how to gather the brideprice of buffalo.

Pata Iuk and Dula Foek's forced marriage with Pua Kene and No Lini

The man Pata Iuk and the boy Dula Foek go to Loleh and force themselves on Pua Kene and No Lini. He marries her and forces her to reject the man Lodo Bela and the boy Solu Lolo, causing shame and anger.

61.	*Boe te touk-ka Pata Iuk*	The man Pata Iuk
62.	*Ma ta'ek-ka Dula Foek*	And the boy Dula Foek
63.	*Lelete de neu.*	Crosses to go.
64.	*Ma fifino de neu.*	And proceeds to go.

65.	*De ana seti na Pua Kene*	He forces Pua Kene
66.	*Ma laka na No Kene [Lini]*	And he compels No Kene [No Lini]
67.	*De ana sao na Pua Kene*	He marries Pua Kene
68.	*Ma tu na No Kene [Lini]*	And he weds No Kene [No Lini]
69.	*De dadi hela ketu Lodo Bela*	Therefore, she breaks with Lodo Bela
70.	*Ma nole ladi Solu Lolo*	And separates from [rejects] Solu Lolo
71.	*De ala mae ma lamanasa.*	They are shamed and angered.
72.	*Sanga tao leo ndia*	They seek to do something
73.	*Ma no'i tao leo na.*	And they intend to do something.

Lodo Bela and Solu Lodo's killing of Pata Iuk and Dula Foek

So, the man Lodo Bela and the boy Solu Lodo wait in ambush for Pata Iuk and Dula Foek as they return to the Sea near the island of Ndao. Lodo Bela and Solu Lodo attack and kill the Shark and Crocodile and their blood and guts spill onto the island of Ndao.

74.	*De faik esa manunin*	On one certain day
75.	*Ma ledok esa mateben*	And at a particular time
76.	*Boe ma touk-ka Lodo Bela*	The man Lodo Bela
77.	*Ma ta'ek-ka Solu Lolo*	And the boy Solu Lolo
78.	*Nahani Dula Foek*	Wait for Dula Foek
79.	*Nabafa Pata Iuk*	Lie in ambush for Pata Iuk
80.	*No ana fali leu sain neu*	As he returns to the Sea
81.	*Ma tulek leo liun neu*	And goes back to the Ocean
82.	*De ana losa Ndao Nusa dalek*	When he reaches Ndao Nusa
83.	*Ma nduku Folo Manu dalek*	And approaches Folo Manu
84.	*Boe ma touk-ka Lodo Bela*	The man Lodo Bela
85.	*Ma ta'ek-ka Solu Lodo*	And the boy Solu Lodo
86.	*Tati nisa Dula Foek*	Slashes and kills Dula Foek
87.	*Ma dodo nisa Pata Iuk.*	And cuts the throat and kills Pata Iuk.
88.	*Boe ma da'an-na pipisi neu Ndao Nusa*	His blood sprinkles over Ndao Nusa
89.	*Ma tein-na ngganggali Folo Manu*	And his insides are strewn over Folo Manu
90.	*Ma pan-na ndu neu basa nusak kala.*	And his flesh is divided among all the domains.

Haba Ndao and Lida Folo copy the patterns from Pata Iuk and Dula Foek

The woman Haba Ndao and the girl Lida Folo from Ndao observe the patterns that come from Dula Foek ('Pattern Crocodile') and the figures produced by Pata Iuk ('Figure Shark'). They use them to tie and dye beautiful bundles of thread but there exists no loom and shuttle on Ndao.

91.	*Besak-ka inak leo Ndao Nusa la*	Now the woman of Ndao Nusa
92.	*Inak-ka Haba Ndao*	The woman Haba Ndao [Gold Braid of Ndao]
93.	*Ma fetok leo Fola Manu la*	And the girl of Fola Manu
94.	*Fetok-ka Lida Folo*	The girl Lida Folo [Gold String of Folo]
95.	*De ala bebesa dulan-na*	They carefully observe his pattern
96.	*Fo Dula Foek*	That of Pattern Crocodile
97.	*Ma ndanda patan na*	And thoughtfully ponder his figure
98.	*Fo Pata Iuk.*	That of Figure Shark.
99.	*Boe te ala lai-hai lalan*	They fashion bright designs from it
100.	*Ma ala fula-foe lalan.*	And they form fine patterns from it.
101.	*Te hu selu bei ta Ndao*	But there is yet no shuttle on Ndao
102.	*Ma atis bei ta Folo*	And there is yet no loom on Folo
103.	*Fo ala ndolo selu*	That they may throw the shuttle
104.	*Ma ala nggiti ati linik.*	And that they may work the loom.

Haba Ndao and Lida Folo purchase the loom from Kea Saik and Lui Liuk

So, the woman Haba Ndao and the girl Lida Folo take a snake-headed gold braid and a long gold string to buy a loom from Kea Saik ('Turtle of the Sea') and Lui Liuk ('Sea Cow of the Ocean'). They bring the loom and shuttle back to Ndao and weave cloths that they call Pattern Crocodile and Figure Shark: long women's sarongs and men's broad cloths.

105.	*Boe te besak-ka inak-ka Haba Ndao*	Now the woman Haba Ndao
106.	*Ma fetok Lida Folo*	And the girl Lida Folo
107.	*Ana kosu haba dua langan*	She takes off a gold braid with two heads

108.	*De haba Ndao dua langan*	A gold braid from Ndao with two heads
109.	*Ma ana tete lida telu ein*	And she cuts off a gold string with three feet
110.	*De lida Folo telu ein.*	A gold string from Folo with three feet.
111.	*De neni fe Kea Saik*	She carries it to Kea Saik
112.	*Ma neni fe Lui Liuk*	And carries it to Lui Liuk
113.	*Fo tadi neu ndolo seluk*	To obtain the shuttle
114.	*Ma asa neu nggiti atik.*	And to buy the loom.
115.	*De leni selu la mai*	They bring back the shuttle
116.	*Ma leni atis sala mai.*	And bring back the loom.
117.	*De ala ndolo selu lala dulan*	They throw the shuttle according to the pattern
118.	*De loken lae Dula Foek*	They call it Dula Foek [Pattern Crocodile]
119.	*Ma ala nggiti ati lala patan*	And they work the loom according to the figure
120.	*De hule lae Pata Iuk.*	They pronounce it Pata Iuk [Figure Shark].
121.	*Boe te ala lai-hai lakando*	They fashion bright designs continually
122.	*Ma fula-foe henge seku-seku*	And they form fine patterns ceaselessly
123.	*Fo ala tenu pou manalu*	They weave women's long sarongs
124.	*Ma henge lafa maloa*	And tie men's broad cloths
125.	*Fo langapou oko-oko*	Sarongs that hang to the ground
126.	*Ma kekeo loso-loso.*	And cloths that drape down loosely.

The first transfer of the knowledge of dyeing and weaving of patterns

At this point the recitation begins a long topogeny recounting the transfer from Ndao to the domains of Rote of the knowledge of how to tie and weave the cloth patterns that derive from Pattern Crocodile and Figure Shark. This litany moves from west to east. The first transfer is to the domain of Delha.

The woman Sio Meko and the girl Tesa Kola from *Dela Muli* and *Ana Iko* (Delha) hear about the patterns. They go to Ndao to make friends with Haba Ndao and Lida Folo, who gives them instruction on how to dye and weave these cloths.

127. *Boe te bon-na naleli*	The rumour [smell] spreads in all directions
128. *Ma piun-na nafeo.*	And the news [taste] circulates.
129. *De inak-ka Sio Meko*	The woman Sio Meko
130. *Ma fetok-ka Tesa Kola*	And the girl Tesa Kola
131. *Fo inak bei Dela Muli*	A woman of Dela Muli [Delha]
132. *Ma fetok bei Ana Iko*	And a girl of Ana Iko [Delha]
133. *Ndiin-na namanene*	Her ears hear
134. *Ma mata-na namania.*	And her eyes observe.
135. *Boe te natia Haba Ndao*	So, she makes friends with Haba Ndao
136. *Nasena Lida Folo.*	Makes her companion Lida Folo.
137. *Fo ela nanolin lai-haik*	So, she may instruct her to form fine patterns
138. *Ma nafadan fula-foek.*	And tell her how to fashion bright designs.
139. *Ma ndolo seluk*	And to throw the shuttle
140. *No nggiti atik.*	And work the loom.
141. *Boe te ana tenu henge*	So, she weaves and ties
142. *Nalelak pou no lafa.*	Knowing [how to make] sarongs and men's cloths.

The continuing spread of the pattern to west Rote

The news of the designs of Pattern Crocodile and Figure Shark continues to spread and, as a result, women come from the domains of Oenale, then Dengka and then Thie to learn the art of tie-dyeing and weaving.

The woman Ango Beu and the girl Baba Dela come from *Tasi Puka* and *Li Sonu* in Oenale. They obtain the loom and shuttle and learn to design cloths according to the motifs of Pattern Crocodile and Figure Shark. The woman Oe Ange Muli and the girl Dae Mea Iko from *Lutu Mau* and *Holo Tula* in Dengka copy the patterns and learn to weave them. When the news spreads to *Lene Kona* and *Tada Muli* in Thie, the woman Teo Tada and the girl Leo Lene observe the process carefully and learn to tie, dye and weave fine female and male cloths.

143. *Boe ma bon boe pepele*	The rumour still goes forth
144. *Ma piun boe boboka.*	And the news still percolates.
145. *De inak-ka Ango Beu*	The woman Ango Beu
146. *Ma fetok-ka Baba Dela*	And the girl Baba Dela
147. *Neme Tasi Puka mai*	Comes from Tasi Puka
148. *Ma neme Li Sonu mai.*	And comes from Li Sonu.
149. *De nanolin [ma nafadan]*	She instructs her [and tells her]
150. *Boe te tenga do ngga'u nenin*	She takes and grabs it [the shuttle and loom].
151. *De ana lai-hain*	She forms her patterns
152. *Ma fula boen*	And fashions her designs
153. *Ma ndolo selun*	And throws her shuttle
154. *Ma nggiti atin*	And works her loom
155. *De nala Dula Foek boe*	According to Pattern Crocodile
156. *Ma nala Pata Iuk boe.*	And according to Figure Shark.
157. *Boe te inak Oe Ange Muli*	The woman Oe Ange Muli
158. *Ma fetok Dae Mea Iko*	And the girl Dae Mea Iko
159. *Neme Lutu Mau mai*	Comes from Lutu Mau
160. *Ma neme Holo Tula mai.*	And comes from Holo Tula.
161. *De nana neni Dula Foek*	She copies and takes away Pattern Crocodile
162. *Ma Pata Iuk*	And Figure Shark
163. *Ma mete neni ndolo selun*	And sees how to throw her shuttle
164. *Ma nggiti atin.*	And how to work her loom.
165. *De ana lai-hai*	She forms fine patterns
166. *Ma ana fula-foe*	And fashions bright designs
167. *De ana ndolo selun*	She throws her shuttle
168. *Ma nggiti atin.*	And works her loom.
169. *De malole-a boe*	This, too, is good
170. *Ma mandak-ka boe.*	And this, too, is proper.
171. *De bon boe naleli*	The rumour still spreads
172. *Ma piun boe nafeo.*	And the news still circulates.
173. *Losa Lene Kona neu*	To Lene Kona, it goes
174. *Ma nduku Tada Muli neu.*	And to Tada Muli, it goes.
175. *De inak-ka Teo Tada*	The woman Teo Tada
176. *Ma fetok-ka Leo Lene neu.*	And the girl Leo Lene goes.

177.	*De ana mete dodo nenin*	She watches thoughtfully and carries it away
178.	*Ma lelu ndanda nenin.*	And observes ponderingly and carries it away.
179.	*De lai-hai nai Tada*	She forms fine patterns in Tada
180.	*Ma fula-foe nai Lene,*	And fashions bright designs in Lene,
181.	*De pou dula malole-la boe*	Women's sarongs with good patterns
182.	*Ma lafa dula mandak-kala boe.*	And men's cloths with proper patterns.

The transfer of the patterns to west central Rote

The knowledge of dyeing and weaving is next transmitted westward to the domains of Loleh, Keka, Lelain and Ba'a. The woman Oe Ange and the girl Dusi Beba, who live in *Ninga Ladi* and *Hengu Hena*, take the knowledge of weaving back to Loleh. Then the woman Nggede Ke and the girl Dane Nane go to Loleh and take this knowledge to *Tilo Nesi* and *Ose Mboka*, the tiny domain of Lelain. Then the woman Hulu Nggela and the girl Seu Loko bring this knowledge to *Tufa Laba* and *Ne'e Feo* in Keka. Next the woman Loe Tesa and the girl Dilu Tama bring the knowledge of how to create fine patterned cloths to *Pena Pua* and *Maka Lama* in Ba'a.

183.	*Boe te inak leo Ninga Ladi*	The woman living in Ninga Ladi
184.	*Ma fetok leo Hengu Hena*	And the girl living in Hengu Hena
185.	*Ndiin-na nama nene*	Her ears hear
186.	*Ma nggatan-na nama nia.*	And her hearing harkens.
187.	*Fo inak-ka Oe Ange*	The woman Oe Ange
188.	*Ma fetok-ka Dusi Beba neu,*	And the girl Dusi Beba goes,
189.	*De tenga nenin*	She takes it away
190.	*Ma ngga'u nenin*	And grabs it away
191.	*De ana lai-hai neu lafa*	She fashions bright designs on a man's cloth
192.	*Ma fula-foe neu pou*	And forms fine patterns on a woman's sarong.
193.	*De ana ndolo selun*	She throws her shuttle
194.	*Ma nggiti atin.*	And works her loom.
195.	*De malole ma mana'a-la boe.*	This is good and pleasing, too.

196. *Boe te inak leo Nggede Ke*	The woman Nggede Ke
197. *Ma fetok leo Dane Nane*	And the girl Dane Nane
198. *La dingo done de leu*	They stand; then they go
199. *Ma hate mola de leu*	And they arise; then they go
200. *Fo leo Ninga Ladi leu*	To Ninga Ladi, they go
201. *Ma leo Hengu Hena leu*	And to Hengu Hena, they go
202. *De ala lai-hai lenin*	They fashion bright designs and carry these away
203. *Ma ala fula-foe lenin*	And they form fine patterns and carry these away
204. *De lenin neu Tilo Nesi*	They carry them to Tilo Nesi
205. *Ma lenin neu Ose Mboka*	And carry them to Ose Mboka
206. *De ala ndolo selu neme ndia*	They throw the shuttle there
207. *Ma nggiti ati neme na*	And they work the loom at that spot
208. *De malole-la boe*	These things are good, too
209. *Ma mana'a-la boe.*	And things are pleasing, too.
210. *Besak-ka inak-ka Hulu Nggela*	Now the woman Hulu Nggela
211. *Ma fetok-ka Seu Loko*	And the girl Seu Loko
212. *Leme Tufa Laba*	From Tufa Laba
213. *Do Ne'e Feo leu.*	Or from Ne'e Feo, they go.
214. *De mete dodo lenin*	They watch thoughtfully and bear it away
215. *Ma lelu ndanda lenin.*	And observe ponderingly and bear it away.
216. *De ala lai-hain*	They fashion their bright designs
217. *Ma fula-foen.*	And form their fine patterns.
218. *Boe te ala ndolo selun*	They throw their shuttle
219. *Ma nggiti atin,*	And work their loom,
220. *De lafa dula malole*	Making men's cloths with beautiful patterns
221. *Fo pou dula manaä.*	And women's sarongs with pleasing patterns.
222. *Boe te inak-ka Loe Tesa*	So, the woman Loe Tesa
223. *Ma fetok-ka Dilu Tama*	And the girl Dilu Tama
224. *Leme Pena Pua mai*	Come from Pena Pua
225. *Ma leme Maka Lama mai.*	And come from Maka Lama.

226. *Boe te mete la Dula Foek*	They see Pattern Crocodile
227. *Ma lelu la Pata Iuk*	And observe Figure Shark
228. *De ala lai-hai tesa-tesa*	They fashion bright, tightly woven designs
229. *Ma fula-foe tama-tama.*	And form fine, closely woven patterns.
230. *De ala ndolo selu malole*	They throw the shuttle well
231. *Ma nggiti ati mana'a.*	And work the loom pleasingly.

The transfer of the knowledge of patterns to Termanu

The recitation focuses next on the domain of Termanu and the transmission of the knowledge of dyeing and weaving in different parts of the domain. Two of the women who gain and transmit this knowledge are given a genealogical identification to indicate their ancestral attachment to the domain. The women who acquire this knowledge for Termanu are: 1) Lole Bako, the child of Bako Baudale, and Fiti Nggoli, the child of Nggoli Kaitio, who come from *Boko Lino* and *Hoi Ledo*. These names allude to two settlements, Baudale and Hoiledo. The recitation confirms this by stating explicitly that these villages neighbour each other. 2) Soe Leli, the child of Leli Tua-Eo, and Pinga Pasa, the child of Pasa Boboi, who come from *Leli Papo Ama* and *Sani Solo Be*. These women learn the skills of dyeing and weaving from the women Lole Bako and Fiti Nggoli. 3) Tesa Nggusi and Tama Nggala, who are identified as living in *Koli do Buna*—the principal ritual name for the entire domain of Termanu—but who come specifically from *Pinga Dale* and *Nggusi Bui*, are the next women to learn to weave. At this point, the recitation declares that all things were good and proper.

232. *De bon boe pepele*	The rumour still spreads
233. *Ma piun boe boboka*	And the news still circulates
234. *Feo basa dae ain*	Round all the lands' woods
235. *Ma ndule basa oe ain.*	And through all the waters' woods.
236. *Besak-ka inak-ka Lole Bako*	Now the woman Lole Bako
237. *Fo Bako Baudale anan*	Bako Baudale's child
238. *Ma fetok-ka Fiti Nggoli*	And the girl Fiti Nggoli
239. *Fo Nggoli Kaitio anan*	Nggoli Kaitio's child
240. *Leme Boko Lino leu*	From Boko Lino, they go
241. *Ma leme Hoi Ledo leu.*	And from Hoi Ledo, they go.

242. *De ala mete dodo lenin*	They watch thoughtfully and bear it away
243. *Ma lelu ndanda lenin.*	And observe ponderingly and bear it away.
244. *De ala lai-hai*	They fashion bright designs
245. *Ma ala fula-foe*	And they form fine patterns
246. *Boe te ala ndolo selu*	They throw the shuttle
247. *Ma nggiti ati.*	And work the loom.
248. *De lala pou malole*	They make beautiful women's sarongs
249. *Ma lala lafa manaä*	And make pleasing men's cloths
250. *Leo Dula Foek*	Like Pattern Crocodile
251. *Ma leo Pata Iuk boe.*	And Figure Shark, too.
252. *Boe te nggolok lakadadalak*	The villages are in a row
253. *Ma taduk lakaneneak*	And the hamlets are next to each other
254. *De inak-ka Soe Leli*	The woman Soe Leli
255. *Ma fetok-ka Pinga Pasa*	And the girl Pinga Pasa
256. *Leli Tua-Eo anan*	Leli Tua-Eo's child
257. *Ma Pasa Boboi anan*	And Pasa Boboi's child
258. *Neme Leli Papo Ama neu*	From Leli Papo Ama, she goes
259. *Ma Sani Solo Be*	And [from] Sani Solo Be, [she goes]
260. *De nasena Lole Bako*	She takes as a companion Lole Bako
261. *Ma natia Fiti Nggolo.*	And makes friends with Fiti Nggolo.
262. *Besak-ka Lole Bako nafadan*	Now Lole Bako tells her
263. *Ma Fiti Nggolo natudun.*	And Fiti Nggolo shows her.
264. *De ana lai-hai nalelak*	She understands how to fashion bright designs
265. *Ma fula-foe bubuluk.*	And knows how to form fine patterns.
266. *De ndolo selu pou*	She throws the shuttle for a woman's sarong
267. *Ma ana nggiti ati lafa*	And works the loom for a man's cloth
268. *De pou dula malole*	A woman's sarong with beautiful patterns

269. *Ma lafa pata mana'a.*	And a man's cloth with pleasing figures.
270. *Boe te inak leo Koli dale*	So, the woman living in Koli
271. *Ma fetok leo Buna dale*	And the girl living in Buna
272. *Inak-ka Tesa Nggusi*	The woman Tesa Nggusi
273. *Ma fetok-ka Tama Nggala*	And the girl Tama Nggala
274. *Leme Pinga Dale leu*	From Pinga Dale, they go
275. *Ma leme Nggusi Bui leu*	And from Nggusi Bui, they go
276. *De mete dodo lenin*	They watch thoughtfully and bear it away
277. *Ma lelu ndanda lenin*	And they observe ponderingly and bear it away
278. *De ala lai-hai*	They fashion bright designs
279. *Ma ala fula-foe.*	And form fine patterns.
280. *Besak-ka ndolo selu tesa-tesa*	Now they throw the shuttle, tightly weaving
281. *Ma nggiti ati tama-tama*	And work the loom, closely weaving
282. *De pou dula manatesak*	A woman's sarong with tightly woven patterns
283. *Ma lafa pata manatamak.*	And a man's cloth with closely woven designs.
284. *De malole-la so*	These things are good
285. *Ma mandak-kala boe.*	And these things are proper.

The transfer of the knowledge of the patterns to east Rote

The knowledge of dyeing and weaving is next transferred from Termanu to Korbaffo and then to Landu, Ringgou and Oepao. A woman Lutu Namo and a girl Heu Oli in Korbaffo—known by its principal ritual name, *Namo Ina ma Tunga Oli*—come specifically from *Asa Nao* and *Bole Sou*, which is the first place where the seeds of rice and millet, Doli Mo ma Lutu Mala, were planted, to learn to make beautiful patterns. Then the woman Henu Helok and the girl Liti Lifuk come from *Tena Lai* and *Mae Oe* to bring the shuttle and loom to *Soti Mori ma Bola Tena* in Landu. The woman Tui Beba and the girl Doko Meti take this knowledge to Londa Lusi and Batu Bela in Ringgou and then the woman Afe Ledo and the girl Nggenge Fai come and carry the knowledge to Oepao, which is identified by two of its ritual names, *Pao Kala ma Pena Ufa* and *Fai Fua ma Ledo So'u*. Again, the recitation declares all things are good and pleasing.

286.	*Besak-ka inak leo Namo Ina*	Now the woman living in Namo Ina
287.	*Ma fetok leo Tunga Oli la*	And the girl living in Tunga Oli
288.	*Inak-ka Lutu Namo*	The woman Lutu Namo
289.	*Ma fetok-ka Heu Oli*	And the girl Heu Oli
290.	*Neme Asa Nao mai*	Comes from Asa Nao
291.	*Neme Bole Sou mai*	And comes from Bole Sou
292.	*De ngga'u do tengan nenin*	She grabs or takes it away
293.	*Boe te ana fula-foe*	She forms fine patterns
294.	*Ma lai-hai*	And fashions bright designs
295.	*Ma ana ndolo selun*	And she throws her shuttle
296.	*Ma nggiti ati.*	And works the loom.
297.	*De malole-a boe*	These things are good, too
298.	*Ma mana'a boe.*	And pleasing, too.
299.	*Boe te inak-ka Henu Helok*	The woman Henu Helok
300.	*Ma fetok-ka Liti Lifuk*	And the girl Liti Lifuk
301.	*Neme Tena Lai mai*	Comes from Tena Lai
302.	*Ma neme Mae Oe mai.*	And comes from Mae Oe.
303.	*De ana lai-hai nenin*	She fashions bright designs and carries these away
304.	*Ma ana fula-foe nenin*	And she works fine patterns and carries these away
305.	*De nenin neu Soti Mori*	She carries them to Soti Mori
306.	*Ma nenin neu Bola Tena.*	And carries them to Bola Tena.
307.	*De ana ndolo selun*	She throws her shuttle
308.	*Ma nggiti atin.*	And works her loom.
309.	*De malole ma manaä la boe.*	Things are good and pleasing, too.
310.	*Boe te inak leo Londa Lusi*	So, the woman living in Londa Lusi
311.	*Ma fetok leo Batu Bela*	And the girl living in Batu Bela
312.	*Inak-ka Tui Beba*	The woman Tui Beba
313.	*Ma fetok-ka Doko Meti*	And the girl Doko Meti
314.	*Ndiin-na namanene*	Her ears hear
315.	*Ma nggatan-na namania.*	And her senses note.
316.	*Boe te ana tolomu de neu,*	She dashes, she goes,
317.	*Ma nalai de neu.*	And she hurries, she goes.
318.	*De ana mete neni Dula Foen*	She watches and carries away her Pattern Crocodile

319. *Ma lelu neni Pata Iun.*	And observes and carries away her Figure Shark.
320. *De ana lai-hai neu pou*	She fashions bright designs on a woman's sarong
321. *Ma ana fula-foe neu lafa*	And she forms fine patterns on a man's cloth
322. *Boe te ana nggiti ati*	She works the loom
323. *Ma ana ndolo selu*	And she throws the shuttle
324. *De leo Dula Foek boe*	Like Pattern Crocodile, too
325. *Ma leo Pata Iuk boe.*	And like Figure Shark, too.
326. *Boe te inak-ka Afe Ledo*	The woman Afe Ledo
327. *Ma fetok-ka Nggenge Fai*	And the girl Nggenge Fai
328. *Neme Pao Kala mai*	Comes from Pao Kala
329. *Ma neme Pena Ufa mai.*	And comes from Pena Ufa.
330. *De ana tenga neni Dula Foek*	She takes and carries away Pattern Crocodile
331. *Ma ngga'u neni Pata Iuk.*	And grabs and carries away Figure Shark.
332. *De nenin neu Fai Fua*	She carries it to Fai Fua
333. *Ma nenin neu Ledo So'u.*	And carries it to Ledo So'u.
334. *De ana lai-hain*	She fashions bright designs
335. *Ma fula-foen.*	And forms fine patterns.
336. *De ndolo selun*	She throws her shuttle
337. *Ma nggiti atin.*	And works her loom.
338. *De malole-la boe*	These things are good, too
339. *Ma mana'a la boe.*	And these things are pleasing, too.

The transfer of the knowledge of the patterns to other parts of east Rote

At this point, the recitation turns back westward to include the domains of Bilba and Diu and of Lelenuk, Bokai and Talae on the south coast of the island. Four of these five domains—Bilba, Lelenuk, Bokai and Talae—are referred to by two ritual placenames.

The woman Nggeo Lao and the girl Pila Selu carry the knowledge of dyeing and weaving to *Tane Bau* and *Feni Fiu* and *Pengo Dua* and *Hilu Telu* in Bilba. Then the woman Leo Lata and the girl Adu Pinga, living in *Pele Pou* and *Nggafu Lafa*, bring the knowledge to Diu. From there the news of this knowledge spreads to *Lenu Petu* and *Safe Solo* and to *Kokote* and *Sonimanu* in Lelenuk and then the woman Poko Tasi and the girl Solu Meti also seek out the knowledge and bring it to Lelenuk. News of this knowledge spreads next to *Medi* and *Ndule* and to *Ko Solo* and *Nilu Foi* in Bokai. The woman Le Fango and the girl Tui Daen go to Diu and bring back the skill and knowledge to Bokai. Finally, news reaches *Nggeo Deta* and *Pila Sue* and *Lona Fa* and *Feo Ue* in Talae, where the woman Fula Seda and the girl Sao Tangi live. She goes to Bokai and acquires it for Talae. This concludes the transference of the knowledge of dyeing and weaving among the domains of Rote.

340.	*Boe te inak-ka Nggeo Lao*	The woman Nggeo Lao
341.	*Ma fetok-ka Pila Selu*	And the girl Pila Selu
342.	*Ndii-na namanene*	Her ears hear
343.	*Ma nggatan-na namania.*	And her hearing hears tell.
344.	*Neu de tenga nenin*	She goes; she takes and carries it away
345.	*Ma ngga'u nenin;*	And grabs and carries it away;
346.	*Fo nenin neu Tane Bau*	She carries it to Tane Bau
347.	*Ma nenin neu Feni Fiu*	And carries it to Feni Fiu
348.	*Fo nai Hilu Telu daen*	In the land of Hilu Telu
349.	*Ma nai Pengo Dua [oen].*	And in the waters of Pengo Dua.
350.	*Boe ma fula-foe*	She forms fine patterns
351.	*Ma lai-hain*	And fashions bright designs
352.	*De ana ndolo selu nala pou*	She throws the shuttle to make a sarong
353.	*Ma nggiti ati nala lafa*	And works the loom to make a man's cloth
354.	*De pou dula malole*	A woman's sarong with beautiful patterns
355.	*Ma lafa pata manaä.*	And a man's cloth with pleasing figures.
356.	*Boe ma inak leo Pele Pou*	The woman living in Pele Pou
357.	*Ma fetok leo Nggafu Lafa*	And the girl living in Nggafu Lafa
358.	*Fo inak-ka Leo Lata*	The woman Leo Lata
359.	*Ma fetok-ka Adu Pinga neu.*	And the girl Adu Pinga goes.
360.	*De tenga nenin*	She takes and carries it away
361.	*Ma ngga'u nenin.*	And grabs and carries it away.

362. *De ana lai-hai*	She fashions bright designs
363. *[Ma] fula-foen.*	[And] forms fine patterns.
364. *Boe te ana nggiti ati neu pou*	She works the loom on a sarong
365. *Ma ndolo selu neu lafa.*	And throws the shuttle for a man's cloth.
366. *De malole ma mana'a-la boe.*	Things are good and pleasing, too.
367. *De piun-na boboka*	The news spreads
368. *Ma bon-na pepele.*	And the rumour circulates.
369. *Leo Lenu Petu neu*	Towards Lenu Petu, it goes
370. *Ma nduku Safe Solo neu*	And to Safe Solo, it goes
371. *Fo bei Kokote oen*	Still in Kokote's waters
372. *Ma bei Sonimanu daen.*	And still in Sonimanu's land.
373. *Boe te inak-ka Poko Tasi*	The woman Poko Tasi
374. *Ma fetok-ka Solu Meti neu.*	And the girl Solu Meti goes.
375. *De tenga do ngga'i nenin.*	She takes or grabs and carries it away.
376. *De lai-hain*	She fashions her bright designs
377. *Ma fula-foen.*	And forms her fine patterns.
378. *Boe te ndolo selun*	She throws her shuttle
379. *Ma nggiti atin*	And works her loom
380. *Nala Dula Foen boe*	Following the Crocodile's Pattern, too
381. *Ma Pata Iun boe.*	And the Shark's Design, too.
382. *De malole-la so*	Things are good
383. *Ma mandak-kala boe.*	And things are proper, too.
384. *Boe te ala benga piun*	They tell the news of it
385. *Ma dasi bon*	And speak the rumour of it
386. *De losa Medi dale neu*	Towards Medi, it goes
387. *Ma nduku Ndule dale neu,*	To Ndule, it goes,
388. *Fo bei nai Ko Solo*	Still in Ko Solo
389. *Ma bei nai Nilu Foi.*	And still in Nilu Foi.
390. *Boe ma inak-ka Le Fango*	The woman Le Fango
391. *Ma fetok-ka Tui Daen*	And the girl Tui Daen
392. *Ana nalai de neu*	She hurries; she goes
393. *Ma tolomu de neu.*	And she dashes; she goes.
394. *De ngga'u nenin*	She grabs and carries it away
395. *Ma tenga nenin.*	And takes and carries it away.

396. *De lai-hai neu lafa*	She fashions bright designs on a man's cloth
397. *Ma fula-foen neu pou.*	And forms fine patterns on a woman's sarong.
398. *De ana ndolo selun*	She throws her shuttle
399. *Ma nggiti atin.*	And works her loom.
400. *De malole-la boe*	These things are good, too
401. *Ma mandak-kala boe.*	And these things are proper, too.
402. *Boe ma ala benga piun*	They tell the news of it
403. *Ma dasi bon na neu.*	And speak the rumour of it.
404. *De losa Nggeo Deta neu*	Towards Nggeo Deta, it goes
405. *Ma nduku Pila Sue neu*	And to Pila Sue, it goes
406. *Ma losa Lona Fa neu*	And towards Lona Fa, it goes
407. *Ma nduku Feo Ue neu.*	And to Feo Ue, it goes.
408. *Boe te inak-ka Fula Seda*	The woman Fula Seda
409. *Ma fetok-ka Sao Tangi*	And the girl Sao Tangi
410. *Nalai de neu*	She hurries; she goes
411. *Ma tolomu de neu.*	And she dashes; she goes.
412. *De tenga nenin*	She takes and carries it away
413. *Ma ngga'u nenin.*	And grabs and carries it away.
414. *De ana fula-foe neu pou*	She forms fine patterns on a sarong
415. *Ma lai-hai neu lafa*	And fashions bright designs on a man's cloth
416. *De tenu dedele pou*	She weaves the sarong firmly
417. *Ma toko bebesa lafa,*	And strikes [the shuttle] on the man's cloth carefully,
418. *De pou dula malole*	A woman's sarong with beautiful patterns
419. *Ma lafa pata mandak.*	And a man's cloth with proper designs.

The recitation concludes by proclaiming the transfer of the knowledge of dyeing and weaving and the use of the motifs of Pattern Crocodile and Figure Shark throughout all the domains of Rote. This knowledge continues to the present day and, thus, weaving and tie-dyeing has its origin—its trunk and roots—on the island of Lote of the Outstretched Legs and Kale of the Cradled Arms.

420.	*De basa nusak-kala so*	All the domains had it.
421.	*Ma ingu-la boe.*	And all the territories had it
422.	*De lalelak kana so*	They understood it
423.	*Ma bubuluk kana so.*	And they knew it.
424.	*De ndule dae-la boe*	Through all the lands, too
425.	*Ma feo oe-la boe*	And round all the waters, too
426.	*De losa faik ia boe*	To this day, too
427.	*Ma nduku ledok ia boe.*	And until this time, too.
428.	*Fo tetenu hehengek ka*	Weaving and tie-dyeing
429.	*Nahu ma naoka*	Has its trunk and its roots
430.	*Nai Lote Lolo Ei dalek*	On Lote of the Outstretched Legs
431.	*Ma Kale Ifa Lima dalek.*	And Kale of the Cradled Arms.
432.	*Basan nde ndia so.*	This is thus the end.

Recitation 9. The origin of the nautilus shell for indigo dye and the baler shell for resting the spindle

Stefanus Adulanu

Suti Solo do Bina Bane

Genealogical introduction

This recitation begins with a genealogical introduction to the two creatures from the Sea who are cast forth from the Ocean and are carried to dry land where they are eventually made into the container for indigo dye and the shell base for spinning cotton. The opening lines of the recitation describe the physical transfer of the woman Hali Siku and Manu Koa, who marries the man Bane Aka and Solo Bane. The names of these chant characters suggest a bird-like creature who weds a shell-like being. From this union of land and sea come Suti Solo and Bina Bane, who are identified as nautilus (*suti*) and bailer (*bane*) shells. In Rotenese genealogical reckoning, children take the first name of their father as their second name: hence, Bane Aka gives rise to Solo Bane and Solo Bane gives rise to Suti Solo.

1.	*La-fada Suti Solo*	They speak of Suti Solo
2.	*Ma la-nosi Bina Bane.*	And they talk of Bina Bane.

3.	*Ala soku Hali Siku nula*	They transfer Hali Siku of the woods
4.	*Ma ala ifa Manu Koa lasi.*	And they cradle Manu Koa of the forest.
5.	*Ala tu Bane Aka liun*	They wed Bane Aka in the Sea
6.	*Ma sao Solo Bane sain.*	And marry Solo Bane in the Ocean.
7.	*De besak a bongi-la Suti Solo*	And now they give birth to Suti Solo
8.	*Ma lae la Bina Bane.*	And they bring forth Bina Bane.

Shame in the Sea and the expulsion of Suti Solo do Bina Bane

The recitation proceeds to recount the events that lead to the expulsion of Suti Solo and Bina Bane from the Sea. Suti Solo and Bina Bane's father, Bane Aka and Solo Bine, hosts a lively origin feast. The woman Po'o Pau Ai and Latu Kai Do, whose dual name could be translated as 'Mouldy *Pau* Trees'//'Withered *Kai* Leaves', comes to dance at the feast. She is, like Suti Solo and Bina Bane's mother, a creature from the forest and wood, but is certainly not attractive. She asks to dance with Suti Solo and Bina Bane, but the shells refuse her request. Po'o Pau Ai and Latu Kai Do is shamed and expresses her outrage to the Heavens and Heights, who grow angry and create the storm that rages on the Sea, expelling the shells.

9.	*Faik esa manunin*	On a certain day
10.	*Ma ledok esa mateben*	And at a particular time
11.	*Boe ma Bane Aka liun hun*	Bane Aka in the Sea has his origin feast
12.	*Ma Solo Bane sain sion na*	Solo Bane in the Ocean has his feast of nine
13.	*Sio lakadoto*	The feast of nine boils lively
14.	*Ma hus-sala lakase.*	The origin feast bubbles noisily.
15.	*Boe ma inak Po'o Pau Ai la*	The woman Po'o Pau Ai [Mouldy *Pau* Trees]
16.	*Po'o Pau Ai lasi*	Po'o Pau Ai of the forest
17.	*Ma fetok Latu Kai Do la*	And the girl Latu Kai Do [Withered *Kai* Leaves]
18.	*Latu Kai Do nula*	Latu Kai Do of the woods
19.	*Leu pela sio*	Comes to dance at the feast of nine

20. *Ma leu leno hu.*	And comes to turn at the origin feast.
21. *Boe ma ala pela sio kokolak*	While dancing at the feast of nine, they talk
22. *Ma ala leno hu dede'ak ma lae:*	And while turning at the origin feast, they speak and say:
23. *'Te Suti Solo nai be?*	'But where is Suti Solo?
24. *Fo au pela akasusudik*	For I wish to dance next to him
25. *Ma Bina Bane nai be?*	And where is Bina Bane?
26. *Fo leno akaseselik.'*	For I wish to turn beside him.'
27. *Boe ma Bina Bane na-fada ma nae*	Then Bina Bane speaks and says
28. *Ma Suti Solo na-fada ma nae:*	And Suti Solo speaks and says:
29. *'Oo ina Po'o Pau Ai la*	'Oh, the woman Po'o Pau Ai
30. *Po'o Pau Ai lasi la*	Po'o Pau Ai of the forest
31. *Au senang ta no ndia*	I am no friend of this one
32. *Ma feto Latu Kai Do la*	And the girl Latu Kai Do
33. *Latu Kai Do Nula la*	Latu Kai Do of the woods
34. *Au tiang ta no ndia.'*	I am no companion of this one.'
35. *Boe ma Ina Po'o Pau Ai la*	The woman Po'o Pau Ai
36. *Ala mae leu dedein*	There is shame on her forehead
37. *Ma Feto Latu Kai Do la*	And the girl Latu Kai Do
38. *Ala bi neu mataboan.*	There is fear in her eyes.
39. *Boe ma leu la-nosi poin*	They go to talk to the Heights
40. *Ma leu la-fada lain*	And go to speak to the Heavens
41. *Lain manakoasa*	The Heavens who have power
42. *Ma Poin manakila.*	The Heights who see overall.
43. *Boe ma Lain nggenggele*	The Heavens rage
44. *Ma Poin namanasa.*	And Heights grow angry.
45. *De sangu nala liun dale*	A storm strikes the Ocean's depths
46. *Ma luli nala sain dale.*	A cyclone strikes the Sea's depths.
47. *Hu ina Po'o Pau Ai la*	Because the woman Po'o Pau Ai
48. *Po'o Pau Ai lasi*	Po'o Pau Ai of the forest
49. *Ma feto Latu Kai Do la*	The girl Latu Kai Do
50. *Latu Kai Do nula nae-a:*	Latu Kai Do of the wood says:
51. *'Ala mamaek Poo Pau Ai la*	'They shame Po'o Pau Ai

52.	*Ma ala lakabibik Latu Kai Do la.'*	And they frighten Latu Kai Do.'
53.	*Boe ma Poin namanasa*	The Heights grow angry
54.	*Ma Lain nggenggele.*	And the Heavens rage.
55.	*Neme ndia mai*	From this comes
56.	*Boe ma sangu nala liun dale*	A storm striking the Ocean's depths
57.	*Ma luli nala sain dale.*	And a cyclone striking the Sea's depths.
58.	*Boe ma besak ka Suti lama-edo nggi*	Now Suti extends his pods
59.	*Ma Bina lamatoko-isi*	And Bina puts out his insides
60.	*De ana tolomu sasali*	He escapes quickly
61.	*Ma nalai lelena.*	And he flees hastily.

The arrival of Suti Solo and Bina Bane at Tena Lai and Mae Oe in Landu on Rote

The next lines tell of the arrival of Suti Solo and Bina Bane in the tidal shallows on the coast of Rote. The place of arrival, *Tena Lai* and *Mae Oe*, is a ritual site of great importance.

62.	*De mai Tena Lai Loek lutun*	He comes to the fish-wall in the shallows at Tena Lai
63.	*Ma Mae Oe Nggolok dean na.*	And the stone weir at the promontory at Mae Oe.
64.	*Bina mai ndia*	Bina comes there
65.	*De ana babi mafo neu ndia*	He conceals [himself] in the shade there
66.	*Ma Suti mai ndia*	And Suti comes there
67.	*De ana sulu sa'o neu ndia.*	He covers [himself] in the shadows there.

The quest for the ritual fish at Tena Lai and Mae Oe

The recitation sets the scene for the 'scooping and gathering' of Suti Solo do Bina Bane and the transfer of these shells onto dry land. Three chant characters are introduced: 1) Manupui Peda and Kokolo Dulu, who, like Bane Aka and Solo Bane wishes to hold an origin feast; 2) Bafa Ama Laik and Holu Ama Daek; and 3) his wife, Nggiti Seti and Pedu Hange. In this passage and throughout the recitation, there is a clear opposition between the origin feast held on land and that in the Sea. Manupui Peda and Kokolo

Dulu's feast is not lively. Divination is held and it is determined that a key ritual, *peda poi*//*fua bafa* (literally, 'placing at the tip'//'loading the mouth'), has not been carried out as part of the agricultural rituals for receiving harvested rice and millet into the house. This ritual requires that an offering be made of two specific fish referred to, in ritual language, as *tio holu*//*dusu lae*: fish identified as a blue-spotted emperor and a bartail goatfish.

The significance of these fish is revealed in Recitations 2 and 3. They are the offspring of the marriage between the Heavens and the Sea. Tau Senge Bulan and Kudu Kea Ledo, the daughters of the Sun and Moon, marry Holo Te Liun and Bala Mae Sain of the Ocean and Sea, giving birth to Tio Holu Te and Dusu Bala Lae.

To obtain these fish, Nggiti Seti and Pedu Hange must prepare a scoop net and go to the stone fish-traps that are set out in the Sea to catch fish as the tide recedes. These fish-walls at *Tena Lai* and *Mae Oe* form a boundary between the land and the Sea and therefore provide a point of contact between the two worlds.

68.	*Faik esa manunin*	On one certain day
69.	*Ma ledok esa mateben*	And at one particular time
70.	*Boe ma Manupui Peda hun-na*	Manupui Peda holds his origin feast
71.	*Hus ta laka-doto*	The origin feast is not lively
72.	*Ma Kokolo Dulu sio-na*	Kokolo Dulu holds his feast of nine
73.	*Sio ta laka-se.*	The feast of nine is not noisy.
74.	*Boe ma ala kani batu dodo*	They divine by shaking the stone
75.	*Ma ala lea te ndanda.*	They consider by measuring the spear.
76.	*Boe ma lae:*	They [the diviners] say:
77.	*'O peda poin bei ta*	'You have not yet placed a fish on top of the rice
78.	*Ma fua bafa bei ta.'*	And you have not yet laid a fish on the basket's mouth.'
79.	*Boe ma ina Nggiti Seti*	The woman Nggiti Seti
80.	*Ma fetok ka Pedu Hange*	And the girl Pedu Hange
81.	*Bafa Ama Laik tun*	Bafa Ama Laik's wife
82.	*Ma Holu Ama Daek saon*	Holu Ama Daek's spouse
83.	*Ala kedi la mau don*	They cut a *mau* plant's leaves

84.	*De mau mana'a don*	A *mau* with a mouthful of leaves
85.	*Ma ala pena-la pole aban*	And they pluck a *pole* plant's cotton tufts
86.	*De pole masapena aban.*	A *pole* bursting with cotton tufts.
87.	*De ala teli kokolo ndai*	They string and wind a fishnet
88.	*De ndai mahamu lilok.*	A fishnet with a gold-weighted belly.
89.	*Ma ala ane seko, bui seko*	They braid a scoop net, twine a scoop net
90.	*De seko matei besik.*	A scoop net with iron-weighted insides.
91.	*De ana ndae ndai neu alun*	She hangs the fishnet over her shoulder
92.	*Ma ana su'u seko neu langan*	And she balances the scoop net on her head
93.	*De leo Tena Lai neu*	And goes to Tena Lai
94.	*Ma leo Mae Oe neu,*	And goes to Mae Oe,
95.	*Neu nafa-nggao lutu limak*	Goes to grope in the 'arms' of the fish-wall
96.	*Ma neu nafa-dama dea eik*	Goes to probe in the 'legs' of the stone weir
97.	*Dea ei manalek*	The 'legs' of the stone weir that hold good fortune
98.	*Ma lutu lima mauak.*	The 'arms' of the fish-wall that bear good luck.
99.	*Nafanggao dea eik*	She gropes in the 'legs' of the stone weir
100.	*Ma nafadama lutu limak.*	And probes the 'arms' of the fish-wall.

The encounter with Suti Solo do Bina Bane

The recitation goes on to describe Nggiti Seti and Pedu Hange's encounter with Suti Solo do Bina Bane. Although Nggiti Seti and Pedu Hange are determined to catch only *tio holu*//*dusu lae* fish, all that she can scoop up is Suti Solo and Bina Bane, who declares himself 'an orphan wronged'//'a widow mistaken'. So, in the end, Nggiti Seti and Pedu Hange agree to take the shells back to give to Lole Holu and Lua Bafa, who become the companions of Suti Solo do Bina Bane. As is evident by the patterning of succession in Rotenese names, Lole Holu is the child of Holu Ama Daek and Lua Bafa is the child of Bafa Ama Laik.

101.	*Siluk bei ta dulu*	When morning is not yet in the east
102.	*Ma hu'ak bei ta langa dei*	And dawn is not yet at the head
103.	*Boe ma ana ndai ndano, ndai ndano*	She fish-catches, fish-catches
104.	*Ma ana seko toko, seko toko.*	And she scoop-throws, scoop-throws.
105.	*Boe ma ana seko nala Suti Solo*	She scoops up Suti Solo
106.	*Ma ana ndai nala Bina Bane*	And she fishes up Bina Bane
107.	*Boe ma lae:*	They say:
108.	*'Au seko tio*	'I scoop for a *tio* fish
109.	*Ma au ndai dusu dei*	And I fished for a *dusu* fish
110.	*Fo dusu lae dei*	A real *dusu lae*
111.	*Ma tio holu dei*	And a real *tio holu*
112.	*Tao neu peda-poik*	To place on top of the rice
113.	*Ma tao neu lua-bafak.'*	And to lay on the basket's mouth.'
114.	*Boe ma nae:*	Then he says:
115.	*'O ndai ndano meni au*	'Oh, fish me forth and take me
116.	*Ma seko toko meni au*	And scoop me up and take me
117.	*Fo ela tao neu namahenak*	To create expectation
118.	*Ma tao neu nakabanik.'*	And to establish hope.'
119.	*Boe ma ana ndai ndano [heni] Suti*	But she fishes and throws Suti away
120.	*Ma ana seko toko heni Bina.*	And she scoops and throws Bina away.
121.	*Te hu inak Pedu Hange*	But when the woman Pedu Hange
122.	*Ma fetok ka Nggiti Seti*	And the girl Nggiti Seti
123.	*Seko nala lek dua*	Scoops in two waterholes
124.	*Na Bina nala lek dua*	Bina is there in the two waterholes
125.	*Ma ndai nala lifu telu*	And when she fishes in three pools
126.	*Na Suti nala lifu telu.*	Suti is there in the three pools.
127.	*Boe ma Suti, ana kokolak*	Then Suti, he talks
128.	*Ma Bina, ana dede'ak nae:*	And Bina, he speaks, saying:
129.	*'Ndai ndano muni au*	'Fish me forth and take me

130. *Ma seko toko muni au dei*	And scoop me up and take me then
131. *Au ana-nia ma-salak*	I am an orphan wronged
132. *Ma au falu-ina ma-singok.'*	And I am a widow mistaken.'
133. *Boe ma nae:*	So, she says:
135. *'Te au ndai ndano uni o*	'I will fish you forth and take you
136. *Ma au seko toko uni o*	And I will scoop you up and take you
137. *Fo mu mo Lole Holu*	That you may go with Lole Holu
138. *Ma mu mo Lua Bafa.'*	And you may go with Lua Bafa.'

The beginning of the dialogue with Suti Solo and Bina Bane

The recitation now begins a remarkable dialogue with the shells that can be considered a defining component of the composition. This dialogue extends for more than 80 lines and consists of several possibilities phrased in poetic formulae. Suti and Bina agree to befriend Lole Holu and Lua Bafa but ask what would happen if the leaf-container in which they were being carried broke. If this were to happen, Suti and Bina exclaim: 'Then, I, Suti, with whom would I be and I, Bina, with whom would I be? With whom will I talk and with whom will I speak?' This is the cry of the displaced orphan and widow.

139. *Boe ma Suti, ana kokolak*	Then Suti, he talks
140. *Ma Bina, ana dede'ak ma nae:*	And Bina, he speaks, saying:
141. *'Te o ndai muni au*	'If you fish and take me
142. *Fo au atia Lole Holu*	I will be a friend to Lole Holu
143. *Ma seko muni au*	And if you scoop and take me
144. *Fo au asena Lua Bafa.*	So that I will be a companion to Lua Bafa.
145. *De malole-la so*	These things are good
146. *Ma mandak-kala so.*	And these things are proper.
147. *Te leo hai-paik la-tato*	But if the ends of the leaf-bucket bump
148. *Ma leo lepa-solak la-bebi*	And if the corners of the water carrier crash
149. *Fo ala hika setele henin*	So, they laugh with a shriek at losing me

150. *Ma eki mata-dale henin,*	And they scream with a startle at losing me,
151. *Na Bina, au o se*	Then I, Bina, with whom will I be
152. *Ma Suti, au o se*	And I, Suti, with whom will I be
153. *Fo au kokolak o se*	With whom will I talk
154. *Ma au dede'ak o se?'*	And with whom will I speak?'

The initial response to the shell's query

In response to Suti Solo and Bina Bane's query, it is Nggiti Seti and Pedu Hange who replies, first proposing the possibility of an alternative resting place: to reside with the syrup vat and the rice basket. For the shells, this, too, offers only a transient possibility.

155. *Boe ma inak-ka Nggiti Seti*	The woman Nggiti Seti
156. *Ma fetok-ka Pedu Hange nae:*	And the girl Pedu Hange says:
157. *'Te eki setele henin*	'If they scream with a shriek at losing you
158. *Ma hika mata-dale henin na,*	And laugh with a startle at losing you,
159. *Suti mo Tua Bou*	Then Suti, go with syrup vat
160. *Ma Bina mo Neka Hade.'*	And Bina, go with the rice basket.'
161. *Boe ma nae:*	Then he says:
162. *'O malole-la so*	'Oh, these things are good
163. *Ma mandak-kala so.*	And these things are proper.
164. *Te leo bou lamakako fude*	But if the vat overflows with froth
165. *Ma soka lamalua bafa*	And the sack runs over at the mouth
166. *Fo bou lo totonon*	So that the vat must be overturned
167. *Ma soka no lulunun*	And the sack must be rolled up
168. *Na Suti, au o se*	Then I, Suti, with whom will I be
169. *Ma Bina, au o se?'*	And I, Bina, with whom will I be?'

The offer of alternative places for the shells to rest

To each proposal that is made, Suti Solo and Bina Bine respond by emphasising the precariousness of that possibility and, in each response, Suti Solo and Bina Bane lay stress on the lack of a companion with whom to speak. The various settings that are proposed are botanic metaphors for community. The first of these possibilities is to go with millet and maize but millet and maize can be eaten by the monkey and pig. The second possibility is to rest in the trees' shade and the lontar palms' shadow, but such shade can shift and disappear. The third possibility is to go with boundary tree and border stone, but this offers no fellowship—no-one with whom to talk and with whom to speak.

170.	*Boe ma nae:*	Then she says:
171.	*'Oo na mo bete pule kode ketuk*	'Oh, go with the millet grains that the monkey plucks
172.	*Ma pela po'o bafi ka'ak.'*	And with the ears of maize that the pig chews.'
173.	*Te hu Suti bei namatane*	But Suti continues to cry
174.	*Ma Bina bei nasakedu.*	And Bina continues to sob.
175.	*Boe ma nae:*	So, he says:
176.	*'Te leo kode ketu neni betek*	'But if the monkey plucks the millet
177.	*Ma bafi ka'a neni pelak*	And the pig chews the maize,
178.	*Na Suti, au o se*	Then I, Suti, with whom will I be
179.	*Ma Bina, au o se?'*	And I, Bina, with whom will I be?'
180.	*Boe ma Suti Solo na-fada*	Then Suti Solo speaks
181.	*Ma Bina Bane na-nosi ma nae:*	And Bina Bane answers and says:
182.	*'Oo ndia bei ta au alelak ndia.'*	'Oh, that I do not yet know at all.'
183.	*Boe ma nae:*	Then she says:
184.	*'Na mo sa'o tua*	'Then go with lontar palms' shadow
185.	*Ma mo mafo ai.'*	And go with trees' shade.'
186.	*Boe ma nae:*	Then he says:
187.	*'Te leo mafo ai la hiluk*	'But if the trees' shade recedes
188.	*Ma sa'o tua la keko*	And the lontars' shadow shifts
189.	*Na Sutu, au o se*	Then I, Suti, with whom will I be
190.	*Ma Bina, au o se*	And I, Bina, with whom will I be
191.	*Fo au kokolak o se*	With whom will I talk
192.	*Ma au dede'ak o se*	And with whom will I speak
193.	*Tao neu nakabanik*	To establish reliance
194.	*Ma tao neu namahenak?'*	And to create trust?'
195.	*Boe-ma nae:*	Then she says:
196.	*'Te na mu mo peu ai*	'Then go with boundary tree
197.	*Ma mu mo to batu.'*	And go with border stone.'
198.	*Boe ma Suti boe kokolak*	Still Suti talks
199.	*Ma Bina boe dede'ak ma nae:*	And still Bina speaks and says:

200.	*'Te hu ai dedean ta*	'But a tree does not talk
201.	*Ma batu kokolan ta.'*	And a stone does not speak.'
202.	*Bina boe nasakedu*	Still Bina sobs
203.	*Ma Suti boe namatani.*	And still Suti cries.

The proposal for the shells to return to the Sea

Finally, Nggiti Seti//Pedu Hange proposes that the shells, guided by the forest cuckoo and the river watercock, follow the river's current into the estuary and return to the Sea.

204.	*Besak-ka nae:*	Now she says:
205.	*'Mo doa lasi*	'Go with the forest cuckoo
206.	*Ma mo koloba'o le*	And go with the river watercock
207.	*[Fo] fa tunga-tunga le*	So that as current passes down the river
208.	*Ma fo ela udan tunga-tunga lasi*	And rain passes through the forest
209.	*Fo mu oli tatain*	You may go to the edge of the estuary
210.	*Ma mu le bibifan*	And you may go to the lip of the river
211.	*Fo ela fa oek ana mai*	So that when the current's water arrives
212.	*Ma ela epo oek ana mai*	And when the eddy's water arrives
213.	*Na bonu boa fo mu*	That bobbing like *boa* wood, you may go
214.	*Ma ele piko fo mu,*	And drifting like *piko* wood, you may go
215.	*Leo sain dale mu*	To the Sea, you may go
216.	*Ma leo liun dale mu.*	And to the Ocean, you may go.
217.	*Te hu mu posi makamu mekon*	Thus, to the Sea's edge resounding like a gong
218.	*Fo nene fino tata*	To stop and listen there
219.	*Ma mu unu mali labun*	And to the reef rumbling like a drum
220.	*Fo dei dongo meme ndia*	To stand and wait there
221.	*Fo dei loe sain dale mu*	And then descend into the Ocean
222.	*Ma dilu liun dale mu.'*	And turn downward into the Sea.'

The return of the shells to the Sea

Suti Solo and Bina Bane return to the Sea, where the festivities are still under way. The shells can now refuse to dance with the woman Po'o Pau Ai and Latu Kai Do by formally declaring companionship with Lole Holu and Lua Bafa.

223.	*Boe ma besak ka*	Now it is that
224.	*Ina Po'o Pau Ai la bei pela*	The woman Po'o Pau Ai is still dancing
225.	*Ma feto Latu Kai Do la bei longe.*	And the girl Latu Kai Do still does the *ronggeng*.
226.	*Ala teteni Suti Solo*	They request Suti Solo
227.	*Ma ala tata Bina Bane.*	And they ask for Bina Bane.
228.	*'Boe ma oo te nakas sa ia*	'Oh, just a while ago
229.	*Fo Suti namaedo nggi*	Suti extended his pods
230.	*Hu inak nde*	Because of this woman
231.	*'Oo bei huas a ia*	Oh, just yesterday
232.	*Fo Bina lamatoko isi*	Bina put forth his insides
233.	*Hu inak ka nde.'*	Because of this woman.'
234.	*'O de au senang ta no o*	'Oh, I am no companion of yours
235.	*Ma au tiang ta no o.*	And I am no friend of yours.
236.	*Au a-tia Lua Bafa*	I am a friend of Lua Bafa
237.	*Ma a-sena Lole Holu dei.'*	And I am a companion of Lole Holu.'

The return of Suti Solo do Bina Bane

As in the beginning of this recitation, there is again an occurrence of origin feasts both on land and in the Sea. Instead of Nggiti Seti and Pedu Hange going in search of the ritual fish needed for the feast on land, Lua Bafa and Lole Holu go to the Sea in search of these creatures. Suti Solo and Bina Bane's relationship with Lua Bafa and Lole Holu has re-established a harmonious relationship between the land and the Sea. This is signalled by the fact that when the Ruler of the Sea holds his celebration of origin, Lua Bafa and Lole Holu can gather the ritual fish that allow Kokolo Dulu and Manupui Peda to hold his origin feast.

238.	*Faik esa manunin*	On a certain day
239.	*Ma ledok esa mateben*	And at particular time

240. *Boe ma la-fada,*	So they say,
241. *Danga Lena liun hun-na*	The Ruler of the Ocean holds his origin feast
242. *Hus sala lakadoto.*	The origin feast boils.
243. *Ma Mane Tua sain sion-na*	And the Lord of the Sea holds his feast of nine
244. *Sio la laka-se.*	The feast of nine bubbles.
245. *Boe ma besak-ka inak-ka Lole Holu*	Now the woman Lole Holu
246. *Ma fetok-ka Lua Bafa*	And the girl Lua Bafa
247. *Neu sanga dusu peda-poik*	Goes to seek a *dusu* to place on top
248. *Ma neu sanga tio fua-bafak*	And goes to seek a *tio* to lay on the mouth
249. *Fo ana tao neu peda-poik*	That she might do the 'top-placing rite'
250. *Ma tao neu fua-bafak*	And she might do the 'mouth-laying ritual'
251. *Neu Kokolo Dulu hun*	For Kokolo Dulu's origin feast
252. *Ma Manupui Peda sion na.*	And Manupui Peda's feast of nine.

Lua Bafa and Lole Holu as skilled spinner, dyer and weaver

Here the recitation presents Lua Bafa and Lole Holu as a skilled weaver: a woman who knows how to spin, dye and weave bright-coloured cloths.

253. *Boe ma besak-ka inak-ka Lua Bafa*	Now the woman Lua Bafa
254. *Ma fetok-ka Lole Holu*	And the girl Lole Holu
255. *Lima ku'u dao kin*	The left fingers of her hand
256. *Na leleak ifa lolek*	Know how to cradle the winding rack
257. *Ma pu lete lai konan-na*	And the right side of her thigh
258. *Na-lelak dipo ine.*	Knows how to turn the spindle on its base.
259. *Boe ina besak ka ana tenu dedele pou*	Now she weaves a woman's sarong tightly
260. *Fo dula kakaik lo pana-dai esa,*	A patterned sarong with multicoloured designs
261. *Boe ma ana henge dedele lafa*	She ties a man's cloth tightly

262. *Fo sidi soti busa-eik*	With supplementary weave of dogleg pattern
263. *Ma pou leu pana-dai*	A woman's sarong with multicoloured designs
264. *Ma sidi soti busa eik.*	With supplementary weave of dogleg pattern.

Lua Bafa and Lole Holu's appearance at the origin feast in the Sea

Lua Bafa and Lole Holu appears at the great feast in the Sea and is proclaimed the good friend and proper companion of Suti Solo and Bina Bane. This is essentially a restatement of the restoration of the continuing good relationship between the land and the Sea.

265. *Besak-ka leu pela sio nai liun*	Now they go to dance at the feast of nine in the Sea
266. *Ma leu leno hun nai sain.*	And they go to spin at the origin feast in the Ocean.
267. *Boe ma besak ka lae:*	Now they say:
268. *'Oo Suti tian nde ia*	'Oh, that is Suti's friend
269. *Ma Bina senan nde ia*	And that is Bina's companion
270. *Ma inak-ka Lua Bafa*	The woman Lua Bafa
271. *Fo Bafo Ama Laik anan*	Bafa Ama Laik's child
272. *Ma fetok-ka Lole Holu*	And the girl Lole Holu
273. *Fo Holu Aina Daek anan.'*	Holu Ama Daek's child.'
274. *Ma nae:*	And it is said:
275. *'Sena mandak kia*	'This is a proper companion
276. *Ma tia malole ia.'*	And this is a good friend.'

Origin references and ritual outcomes

The final passage in this recitation is the statement of a ritual outcome. Because of the relationship of Lua Bafa and Lole Holu with Suti Solo and Bina Bane, relations between the land and the Sea are restored and the origin feasts on land and in the Sea can be celebrated properly. With the knowledge of dyeing and weaving, these feasts can be performed with dancers arrayed in multicoloured cloths. The recitation concludes by alluding to the chant *Pata Iuk ma Dula Foek*, which recounts the origin of weaving.

277. *Besak-ka ala kokolak sio bafi la*	Now they talk of the pigs of the feast of nine
278. *Ma ala dede'ak hu kapa.*	And they speak of the buffalo of the origin feast.
279. *Hu kapa la tola*	The buffalo of origin appear
280. *Ma sio bafi la dadi,*	And the pigs of nine come forth,
281. *Hu Holu Ama Daek hu-na*	There at Holu Ama Daek's origin feast
282. *Ma hu Bafa Ama Laik sion-na.*	And Bafa Ama Laik's feast of nine.
283. *Ma besak ka neu pela sio*	Now they go to dance at the feast of nine
284. *Ma leno hu.*	And spin at the origin feast.
285. *Besak-ka neni pou la mai*	Now they bring women's sarongs
286. *Ma neni sidik la mai,*	And bring supplementary-weave cloths,
287. *Sidi soti busa eik*	Cloth supplemented with dogleg pattern
288. *Ma pou le'u pana dai.*	And women's sarongs in multicoloured stripes.
289. *Pela ngganggape liman-na*	They dance with outstretched arms
290. *Pana-dai la tuda*	The multicoloured cloth falls
291. *Ma leno sosodo ein-nala*	And they turn with shuffling feet
292. *Ma tola-te-la monu.*	And the spear-patterned cloth drops.
293. *Besak-ka lae:*	Now they say:
294. *'Ninga do Hena bei nde ia.'*	'This is still Ninga do Hena.'
295. *Fo lae: 'Dula Foek.'*	So, they say: 'Dula Foek [Pattern Crocodile].'
296. *Fo lae: 'Pata Iuk.'*	Thus, they say: 'Pata Iuk [Figure Shark].'
297. *Pata Iuk tete'ek*	Truly, Pata Iuk
298. *Ma Dula Foek tete'ek.*	And truly, Dula Foek.
299. *De pana-dai la tuda*	The multicoloured cloth falls
300. *Ma tola-te la monu.*	And the spear-patterned cloth drops.

What is implied but never stated in this recitation is the transformation of Suti, the nautilus shell, into the container for indigo dye and the transformation of Bina, the baler shell, into the base for the spindle that winds cotton thread. The recitation is a complex but subtly structured composition—a narrative that both reveals and hides its meaning.

***

This final recitation, *Suti Solo do Bina Bane*, is one of the best-known narratives on Rote. In this instance, Old Meno presents it as an important origin narrative. In fact, on Rote, *Suti Solo do Bina Bane* takes many forms. In *Master Poets, Ritual Masters* (Fox 2016), I have published 20 different versions of this narrative by poets from across the entire island of Rote to illustrate, specifically and in detail, the art of oral composition.

5

Background and exegesis on the origin narratives of Thie

The origin narratives of Thie and Termanu derive from and belong within a common Rotenese oral tradition. As narratives, they are related and there are correspondences in many of the events that they recount. There are also critical divergencies and distinct accounts offered in each of these traditions.

Recitations 1 to 5 in Termanu's origin narratives correspond to Recitations 1 to 3 in Thie's tradition. They recount the hunting of pig and civet, the encounter of the sons of the Sun and Moon with the rulers of the Sea and Ocean, and the marriage established between these realms that involves the transfer of wealth from the sea. The consequences of this transfer differ in the two traditions. Significantly, the setting for Termanu's narrative of the origin of the house is a heavenly one whereas Thie's narratives set these events in an early ancestral world located in Thie.

Thie's Recitation 4 and 6 correspond with Termanu's Recitation 9. These narratives are concerned with the nautilus and baler shells Suti Solo and Bina Bane, which are scooped from the sea. Yet, these narratives provide notably different versions. The journeying of the shells in Termanu's version ends in a return to the sea whereas, in Thie's narratives, the shells are linked to the beginnings of planting in the domain and the celebration of this achievement.

Similarly, Thie's Recitation 5 corresponds with Recitation 7 for Termanu. Both offer an account of the origins of the planting of rice and millet, but Termanu's narrative becomes an extended topogeny—a litany of placenames—that relates the transmission of planting from one woman to another in locations throughout the island of Rote. In contrast, Thie's narrative concludes with a focus on the celebration of planting in Thie.

There is no equivalent in Thie's tradition of Termanu's narrative of the origin of red millet. This narrative links the origin of this distinctive cultivar to the sons of the Sun and Moon and not to any derivation from the sea, as is recounted in other narratives in both traditions.

The collection of narratives in Termanu includes an account (Recitation 8) of the origin of tie-dyeing, of weaving and of the patterns used in traditional cloths. This narrative makes mention of women of the Heavens and Seas and reveals the killing of the Shark and Crocodile, Pata Iuk ma Dula Foek. The islands of Ndao and Rote are the setting for this narrative. This narrative, as in Termanu's Recitation 7, offers an extended topogeny that traces the spread of these arts of weaving and dyeing throughout the island of Rote. No equivalent narrative was recorded for Thie.

The most striking narrative in the corpus from Thie is an origin celebration narrative, Recitation 6, which recounts, in detail, the love life of two women who are transformed into sea cow and turtle and become the sacrificial offering at an origin feast in Thie. This final narrative from Thie is a monumental work of poetic imagination.

Thie's distinctive social and ritual traditions

Thie (Ti'i), like Termanu, is one of the 18 domains of the island of Rote. Located to the south-west of Termanu, it is the largest and most populous domain on the south coast of the island. Seventeenth-century Dutch records identify both Thie and Termanu as separate territories on Rote. Whereas, at the time, Termanu was considered loyal to the Dutch East India Company, Thie was, for many years, seen as rebellious and, as a consequence, suffered several sharp reprisals, the most severe in 1681. In November 1690, however, Thie joined 11 other domains on the island in signing a treaty of contract with the Company that superseded the previous contract of 1652, which had been signed by a smaller number of domains.

Thie as a domain is not—as is the case in Termanu—centred on a long and elaborate succession of dynastic rule dominated by a single clan. Instead, Thie's traditions revolve around the organisation of an encompassing moiety arrangement that allocates clans either to Sabarai, the moiety of the Male Lord (*Manek*), or to Taratu, the moiety of the Female Lord (*Fetor*). The moieties of Thie, Sabarai and Taratu divide the clans of the domains into intermarrying groups. These moieties were also responsible for the celebration of key origin ceremonies.

Sabarai, headed by the clan of the *Manek* Mbura Lai, comprises eight major or 'mother' clans (*leo inak*). In addition to Mbura Lai, these major clans are Saba Lai, Henu Lai, Nggau Pandi, Meo Leok, Tola Umbuk, Sandi and Kolek. Within this group of eight, there is an internal genealogical division consisting of five clans—Mbura Lai, Saba Lai, Henu Lai, Nggau Pandi and Meo Leok—known as the Pandi Anan ('Descendants of Pandi'). This group of eight clans performed the first of Thie's successive origin ceremonies. This initial celebration by these major clans was known as the *Hus Lutu Ain*.

Taratu, headed by the clan of the *Fetor* Meo Umbuk, also has eight major lineages. These major clans are Meo Umbuk, Feo Soru, Nate Feo, Tode Feo, Mesa Feo, Ndana Feo, Soru Umbuk and Langga Ledo. In Taratu, there are two overlapping genealogical divisions: the first, known as Moi Anan ('Descendants of Moi'), consists of the clans from Meo Umbuk to Ndana Feo; the second, known as Mboru Anan ('Descendants of Mboru'), consists of the four clans Nate Feo, Tode Feo, Mesa Feo and Ndana Feo. Together, the eight clans performed their own origin ceremony, *Hus Dae Ain*.

Within both these moieties, there are other clans, known as minor or 'child' clans (*leo anak*). These clans are considered to have preceded, in origin, the major clans. Collectively, these are associated with the rituals of the earth. There are six minor clans in Sabarai—Kana Ketu, Kona, Le'e, Sua, Musu Hu and Landu—and four minor clans in Taratu: Moka Leok, Bibi Manek, Man'Dato and Keka Dulu.

Whereas members of the clans of Sabarai are supposed to marry members of the clans of Taratu, the minor clans in Sabarai have the right to marry within either Sabarai or Taratu, thus rendering Thie's dual organisation into a triadic marriage structure consisting of the major clans of Sabarai, the minor clans of Sabarai and all of Taratu (for a detailed discussion of these internal relations, see Fox 1980c: 120–33).

Among the minor clans, several are or were critical. The clan Kana Ketu in Sabarai holds the title of 'Head of the Earth' (*Dae Langgak*). Other clans of importance are Sua and Musu Hu in Sabarai and Keka Dulu and Bibi Manek in Taratu. These four clans once celebrated their own separate origin ceremonies. Sua's ceremony followed the *Hus Dae Ain*, then came Musu Hu's, Keka Dulu's and Bibi Manek's ceremonies. All these separate ceremonies culminated in a large communal origin ceremony known as *Soru-Soru*.

The *Soru-Soru* was led by the minor clans in Sabarai: Kana Ketu and Kona, who were positioned on the east with Sua, Musu Hu and Le'e on the west. Members of other clans could join either side of these key clans. The *Soru-Soru* involved a fierce ritual struggle: Sua, Musu Hu and Le'e advanced from the west to steal a large fish that was guarded by Kana Ketu and Kona. In a hail of rocks thrown from both sides, the ritual fish had to be captured and taken by the western group. This was the prelude to Thie's final origin ceremony, known as *Limba*.

The *Limba* was led by seven clans, four from Sabarai (Mbura Lai, Kana Ketu, Meo Leok and Nggau Pandi) and three from Taratu (Nate Feo, Bibi Manek and Keka Dulu)—all of whom were represented by women of these clans, who, dressed in their finery, danced in unison. Thereafter, there was a running of horses and rituals at which a succession of riders at full gallop would pass and split open a coconut mounted on a pole.

In Thie, the rights of ceremonial performance by specific clans are still remembered, even if the ceremonies themselves have long ceased. This plethora of ceremonial memories, genealogical divisions and complex marriage arrangements—all markedly different from those of Termanu—constitute key cultural features that distinguish Thie as a domain. They also figure in its origin narratives. These narratives include references to ancestral founders, the moieties of Sabarai and Taratu and include one narrative, Recitation 7, which is intended to provide the origin of the *Soru-Soru* ceremony. This long recitation tells of the chant characters Masi Dande and Solo Suti, women who are transformed into a sea cow and turtle and hauled up onto the beach at Thie and there become the object of sacrifice and celebration. How precisely this was once linked to ceremonial actions is unexplained but nonetheless, this recitation is a foundation narrative of importance preserved from the past.

Other recitations from Thie overlap with those of Termanu to recount the primordial relationships between the Sun and Moon and the Lords of the Sea and their consequences: the discovery of fire, of cooking and the transfer of an array of cultural implements, the building of the first house, and the origins of rice and millet and other grains. The similarities in these narratives are evident as are some key differences. In the narratives of Thie, the building of the first house of the Sun and Moon fails, but its failure leads to the building of the first ancestral house. More significant are specific ancestral references that occur within these narratives. These narratives assume a knowledge of the genealogies of the domain. These genealogical references are a personalised aspect of the poetic narrative:

Au baing ia Tola Mesa	My grandfather Tola Mesa
Ma au sorong ia Le'e Lunu	And my ancestor Le'e Lunu
Tititin ma nonosin	His descendants and progeny
Kiki Tola mai dea	Kiki Tola comes out
Ma ba'ing Nggebu Nusa mai dea.	And my grandfather Nggebu Nusa comes out.[1]

Thie's ancestral succession and Christian heritage

The name Tola Mesa is cited and evoked in Thie's origin narratives. The ancestral line stemming from Tola Mesa has been Thie's ruling family. This family has used the name Mesa—with various historical spellings: Mesa, Messa, Messakh—in its long dynastic succession. It is this line of 'Mesak' that is associated with the conversion of the domain to Christianity.

The signatory to the 1690 contract with the Dutch East India Company was the then ruler of Thie, Messa Poura (in the dialect of Thie: Mesa Mbura). In 1726, his successor, Poura Messa (Mbura Mesa), was given his staff of office by the Company and, three years later, he became the first Rotenese ruler to convert to Christianity. According to Dutch sources, Poura Messa and his entire family were baptised on 23 May 1728. Eight years before this royal conversion, Poura Messa's son, whose Rotenese name was Foe Mbura, was baptised and took the Biblical name Benjamin. When Poura Messa died just a few years after his conversion, his son Foe Mbura or Benjamin Mesak claimed special status as a Christian ruler and set in train several changes that would affect the development of life on the island of Rote. Thie's status as

---

1   These are separate ancestral names. The succession of these names does not follow the normal succession of names: Tola Mesa > Kiki Tola marks a correct succession, but Le'e Lunu cannot give rise to Nggebu Nusa.

the first of Rote's Christian domains gave the domain historical precedence and prominence. (These developments and their consequences are discussed at length in another chapter of this volume.)

In the oral histories, this conversion is represented expressly to give agency to the Rotenese themselves. It is represented as a quest led by the ruler of Thie, accompanied by the rulers of the neighbouring domains of Loleh and Ba'a, who sail to Batavia (Jakarta) to obtain Christianity and bring it back to Rote. This quest is elevated in its telling and is now recounted in ritual language among all the domains of the island. This account is referred to by the paired phrase *Sangga Ndolu ma Tungga Lela* ('To Search for Wisdom and To Seek for Knowledge'). This recitation has become part of the repertoire of many Rotenese poets and exists in several versions of varying lengths in different dialects.

One short, densely metaphorical version of this recitation is by the poet G.A. Foeh from Thie. The ancestral journey to Batavia in the quest for the knowledge of Christianity is described in botanic terms as a quest for two trees, the *bau koli* and *tui sina*, which are brought back, planted on Rote and take root and flourish. Only in its concluding lines does this recitation explain that these trees are a metaphor for the knowledge of Christianity. The poet relies on the common Rotenese metaphoric equation that describes all human beings as 'orphans and widows' on the Earth.

Sangga Ndolu ma Tungga Lela[2]

Ma-uak neu bain	With good fortune for the ancestor
Ma-nalek neu aman	With great promise for the father
Bain tingga nala tonda lain	The ancestor steps onboard the *perahu*
Aman hene nala balun lain	The father climbs onboard the boat
Fo balun sangga ndolu	The boat that seeks for wisdom
Bain leko la neu langgan	The ancestor raises the sail at the head
Ma aman pale uli neu ikon	The father guides the rudder at the tail

---

2   This recitation, which was recorded in 2009, is not without its peculiarities. Batavia is referred to as Matabi//Jabadiu. I have no explanation for the term Jabadiu. The *bau* tree is *Hibiscus tiliaceus*, a relatively tall, highly decorative tree that is generally planted near water sources. I do not have an identification for its pair, the *tui* tree. *Bau*//*tui* is a well-established dyadic set metaphorically used as trees of knowledge, but the pair *de'a injil*//*Jesus hara li* would seem to be the personal creation of the poet.

Bain sida epo nduku Jabadiu daen	The ancestor sails for the land of Jabadiu
Ma aman neu losa Matabi oen.	And the father heads for the waters of Matabi.
Bain tati neni bau kolin	The ancestor cuts and brings the *bau koli* tree
No aman lo'o neni tui sina	While the father chops and brings the *tui sina* tree
Bain fua neu tonda lain	The ancestor stores it onboard his perahu
Ma aman ndae neu balu lain.	And the father places it onboard his boat.
Bain nenin neu nduku daen	The ancestor brings it back to [Rote's] land
Ma aman neni losa Kale oen.	And the father brings it to Kale's waters.
Bain sele Bau neu dano	The ancestor plants it in a lake
Ma aman tande Tui neu le.	And the father sows it in a river.
De bau don sengga dano	The *bau* tree's leaves sprout in the lake
Ma tui oka ndoro le.	And the *tui* tree's roots spread in the river.
Bali basa dae Rote	Extending all through Rote's land
Ma ndule basa oe Kale	And spreading all through Kale's waters
Ma ndule inggur	And through the territories
Ma nou basa leor	And to all the clans
De mboku dano ramahena	The crabs of the lake depend on it
Ma mboe le rakabani.	And the shrimp of the river rely on it.
Te mboke dano ta, te ana ma	But not lake crabs, but rather orphans
Ma mboe le ta, te falu inar	And not river shrimp, but rather widows
Ma bau koli ta, te de'a injil	And not a *bau koli* tree, but the gospel message
Ma tui sina ta, te Yesus hara lin.	And not a *tui sina* tree, but the voice of Jesus.

The origin narratives of Thie are tinged with passages that invoke the domain's ancestral associations with Christianity. In Recitation 3 from Thie (Chapter 6), which recounts the building of the first ancestral house, there is a passage that attributes the origin of the knowledge of house building—and perhaps wisdom and knowledge in general—to the Holy Spirit. The Holy Spirit is referred to as the 'Inside Patterner and Inner Marker' (Dula Dale//Le'u Tei)—a dyadic set created and used throughout Rote in Christian discourse. The gift that the Holy Spirit brings is 'Ninefold Wisdom and Eightfold Knowledge' (Ndolu Sio//Lela Falu).

Lain atur malole	The Heavens order well
Ata atur mandak ia.	The Heights order properly.
Te fain esa no dalen	So, on one certain day
Ledok esa no serin na [tein]	At one particular time
Manadula Dale neu baing esa Tola Mesa	The Inside Patterner reaches to grandfather Tola Mesa
Ma Le'u Tei neu sorong esa Le'e Lunu	And the Inner Marker reaches to ancestor Le'e Lunu
Nene bonggi kara ruma Landu Kona	At the birthplace, Landu Kona
Ma rae kara ruma Tena Seri	And on the land, Tena Seri
Kara Fau Iko Oe	At the Water's Tail of Fau
Ma Pandi Lua Langa daen	And the Land's Head of Pandi Lua
Bei babi luak	Still sheltering in caves
Ma bei suru leak.	And still residing in grottoes.
Lai atur malole	The Heavens order well
Ana fe Dula Dalen, ana mai	Giving forth the Inside Patterner, he comes
Ana fe Le'u Tein, ana mai	Giving forth the Inner Marker, he comes
I konda Ndolu Sio nara mai	Bringing down the Ninefold Wisdom
Ma Lela Falu nara mai	And the Eightfold Knowledge
Ruma poin ia mai	From the Heavens it comes
Ma ruma ata ia mai.	From the Heights it comes.

In a subsequent passage, the clans of Sabarai and Taratu are invoked and linked to the Holy Spirit and the gift of wisdom bestowed on Thie's ancestor:

Nai leo duahulu ma lima	Among the twenty-five clans
Sabarai ma nate Taratu	Sabarai and Taratu
Sabarai tititin	Sabarai's descendants
Ma nate tetebe sara	And it is truly so
Neu Sakunara nonosin nara	To Sakunara's progeny

Nduku faik ia dale so né.	To this very day.
Ndolu sio ria	The Ninefold Wisdom
Ma nate lela falu ria.	And the Eightfold Knowledge.
Dula Dale ma Le'u Teik	The Inside Patterner and Inner Marker
Sangga ana dadi tao leo ia	Seeks that it be so
Fo Kiki Tola mbembedan	For Kiki Tola's legacy
Ma sangga ara mori tao leo na	And seeks that things are so
Fo Nggebu Nusa nanaen.	For Nggebu Nusa's intention.

Unlike the oral narratives of Termanu that purport to portray a primordial past, the oral narratives of Thie reveal a social embeddedness and give evidence of the domain's Christian heritage.

On narrators and narratives

Unlike my fieldwork in Termanu—where I lived for months within a lively community, was engaged in a variety of social activities and managed to record origin narratives only occasionally, somewhat haphazardly but sometimes opportunistically—my fieldwork in Thie was brief, directed and limited in scope. My first visit to Thie, however, came at the end of my time on Rote and I had, by then, a better understanding of Rotenese ritual language. I travelled to the village of Oe Handi in Thie explicitly to find the elder N.D. Pah, known as Guru Pah, whom I had been told repeatedly was one of the great men of knowledge on the island. When I met him, his first question to me was: 'Why has it taken you so long to come to see me?'

During my short stay with Guru Pah, I was interested in understanding the workings of Thie's moiety organisation because it was so different from any such organisation that I had investigated in Termanu or elsewhere in the east of Rote. Guru Pah, on the other hand, was interested in passing on to me two origin narratives of great importance. The first of these was *Bole Sou ma Asa Nao*, which narrates the origin of rice and millet and the celebration of their planting. This is Recitation 5 in the corpus of origin narratives from Thie. The second was the narrative *Masi Dande ma Solo Suti*, a recitation of more than 550 lines. This is Recitation 7 in the corpus from Thie.

I made my second short visit to Thie in 1973 during my return visit to Rote. Again, I travelled to Oe Handi and stayed at Guru Pah's house. He introduced me to his close friend and fellow chanter Samuel Ndun with whom he was involved in ritual activities: a wedding and a funeral. Amid these activities, both Guru Pah and Samuel Ndun provided for me, separately or together, a further set of origin narratives. These are Recitations 1 through 4 in the corpus from Thie.

Like the origin narratives of Termanu, the initial narratives relate Thie's account of the encounter of the Sun and Moon with the Lords of the Ocean and Sea and its consequences.

These narratives include the building of the ancestral house and the origin and spread of rice and millet. Essentially these narratives cover many of the same topics of origin as those of Termanu with similarities and differences that deserve consideration.

Many years later, in 2009, as part of an effort to understand more systematically the ritual-language traditions recounted across all the dialects of the island, I invited the elder and poet Jonas Mooy, along with other poets from Thie, to a recording session on Bali.[3] Jonas was remarkable for his acute interest, not just in the traditions in which he was versed from Thie, but also in the traditions of the other domains of Rote on which he would reflect, compare and comment.

One of my requests to all the master poets who attended a recording session was whether they could and would recite a version of one of the most widely known chants on the island: *Suti Solo do Bina Bane*. Recitation 4 by Guru Pah and Samuel Ndun is a version of this chant. I had asked Jonas Mooy for a version and, in 2011, I was able to record his version, which is Recitation 5. Only after he had recited this narrative and we had worked through it carefully did I reveal to him the previous version I had recorded in 1973. We were then able to discuss both versions.[4]

---

3   The Master Poets Project has, to date, held 11 recording sessions and has recorded 28 Rotenese master poets, many of whom attended more than one session. My first invitation to Jonas Mooy was for the fourth recording session of the project, in 2009. Because of his interests and abilities, I invited him for five subsequent sessions, in 2011, 2013, 2014, 2017 and 2019.

4   *Master Poets, Ritual Masters* (Fox 2016) is an extended comparative consideration of 20 versions of the chant *Suti Solo do Bina Bane*, recited by different poets from across the entire island of Rote. I began collecting versions of this chant in 1965 and have used it as a touchstone to evaluate poets whom I have encountered. This chant takes many shapes and, over the years, only a few poets have presented it as an origin narrative. In Termanu, for example, it is recited primarily as a mortuary chant. However, Old Meno presented it as an origin chant and his version is included as Recitation 9 in the Termanu corpus (Chapter 4). For a specific comparison of the two versions of this chant from Thie, see Chapters 17 and 18 of *Master Poets, Ritual Masters* (Fox 2016: 213–49).

Both Recitation 4 and Recitation 7 recount the origin and spread of the seeds of rice and millet on Rote, but Jonas Mooy's narrative is also concerned with the ancestral celebration of the planting of these seeds, which was conducted at the first *Limba* ceremony. Recitation 4 alludes to this ceremony but does not elaborate on it as does Recitation 7.

More than the origin narratives in Termanu, the origin narratives of Thie relate to the origin ceremonies of the domain.

6

The origin narratives of Thie

Recitation 1. The origin of fire, of cooking and of the implements for living

N.D. Pah and Samuel Ndun

Adu Ledo ma Ndu Bulan

A genealogy of the Heavens

This recitation begins by setting the scene in the distant past and by providing an initial genealogy: No Rini marries Ledo Horo and Pua Kende weds Bula Kai. They bring forth Adu Ledo and Ndu Bulan. It is a time when the Heavens eat only raw food.

1.	*Bei dalu don*	Still long ago
2.	*Ma bei hida fan*	And still at an earlier time
3.	*Nai dae bafok ledo sa'ak ia*	On Earth lit by the sun
4.	*Ma kiuk ma maka-hatuk*	And dark as night
5.	*Dae bafok ledo sa'ak ia*	The Earth lit by the sun
6.	*Ara bei babi leak*	They still shelter in caves
7.	*Ma ara bei suru luak bai.*	And they still hide in grottoes, too.
8.	*Hu hida bei fan*	At a time long ago
9.	*Ma dalu bei don*	And at a period long past
10.	*Lali rala Kende Bala-Sama anan*	They carry Kende Bala Sama's child
11.	*Inak kia Pua Kende*	The woman Pua Kende
12.	*Neu sao Bula Kai*	To marry with Bula Kai

13.	*Keko rala Rini Bala-Sama anan*	They transfer Rini Bala Sama's child
14.	*Fetok kia No Rini*	The girl No Rini
15.	*Neu sao Ledo Horo.*	To marry with Ledo Horo.
16.	*Ara pasa pendi neu tain*	They wrap a long cloth around her waist
17.	*Ma ara henge deras neu tein.*	And they tie a red cloth on her stomach.
18.	*Ara olu lelen*	They place an armband
19.	*Ma te ara pada suen*	And they ornament her breasts
20.	*Kela nai eis daan*	A bracelet on her ankle
21.	*Ma ndeli nai lima kuku.*	And a ring on the finger.
22.	*Bonggi heni Ndu Bulan*	She gives birth to Ndu Bulan
23.	*Ma rae heni Adu Ledo.*	And brings forth Adu Ledo.
24.	*Te hida bei na fan*	At a time long ago
25.	*Ma dalu bei na don*	And at a period long past
26.	*Lain bei rau-tak*	The Heavens still consume with the skin
27.	*Ata bei na'a-matak ia.*	And the Heights still eat raw food.
28.	*Te hu faik esa no dalen*	Then on a certain day
29.	*Ma ledok esa no serin*	And at a particular time
30.	*Bonggi heni Ndu Bulan*	She gives birth to Ndu Bulan
31.	*Ma rae heni Adu Ledo.*	And brings forth Adu Ledo.

The hunt that leads to the first meeting of the Heavens and the Sea

Ndu Bulan and Adu Ledo whistle for their dogs and set out to hunt in the Sun and Moon's forbidden forest. There they meet with the sons of the Lords of the Sea and Ocean: Danga Lena Liun's son, Tio Dangak, and Mane Tua Sain's child, Rusu Mane. They join with each other and hunt together. Their dogs are named Langga Beba and Dusi Do and Nale Pendik and Suka Besi.

32.	*Faik esa no dalen ne*	On a certain day then
33.	*Kati ko fiu busan*	They whistle clearly for their dogs
34.	*Kodo kokoe asun.*	They call coaxingly for their hounds.
35.	*Ana leo Ledo lasin neu*	He goes to the Sun's forest
36.	*Ma ana leo Bula nuren neu.*	And he goes to the Moon's wood.
37.	*Leo na, neu itonggo no*	There they meet

38.	*Danga Lena Liun anan*	Danga Lena Liun's child
39.	*Tio Dangak*	Tio Dangak
40.	*Ma nate ana neu nda no*	And they encounter
41.	*Mane Tua Sain anan ia*	Mane Tua Sain's child
42.	*Rusu Mane.*	Rusu Mane.
43.	*Ara sombu bafi reu esa*	They hunt pig as one
44.	*Ma nate fula kue rakebua.*	And stalk civet together.
45.	*Touk kia Ndu Bulan*	This man Ndu Bulan
46.	*Ma ta'ek kia Adu Ledo.*	And this boy Adu Ledo.
47.	*Busa nade Langga Beba*	The dog named Langga Beba
48.	*Ma asu nade Dusi Do*	And the hound named Dusi Do
49.	*Busa nade Nale Pendik*	The dog named Nale Pendik
50.	*Ma te asu nae Suka Besi*	And the hound named Suka Besi
51.	*Reu tongo ro Tio Dangak*	They go to meet Tio Dangak
52.	*Ma reu nda ro Rusu Manek.*	And go to encounter Rusu Mane.

The sons of the Sun and Moon and of the Lords of the Ocean and Sea hunt together

The sons of the Sun and Moon and the sons of the Lords of the Ocean and Sea hunt together. They catch a pig and civet: Nggeo Adu Sadu's pig and Iko Lola Ladu's civet. The pig and civet tell them that they are to be treated as persons and set free. So, they continue their hunt. The dogs catch another pig and civet, which they take up and carry off.

53.	*Ara sombu bafi na*	They hunt pig
54.	*Ruma Bulan nuran*	In the Moon's wood
55.	*Ara fula kue na*	They stalk civet
56.	*Ruma Ledo lasin.*	In the Sun's forest.
57.	*Faik na ma ledo na*	On a day and at a time
58.	*Boe ma reu nda ro bafi esa*	They go and encounter a pig
59.	*Te nate Nggeo Adu Sadu bafi nia*	Nggeo Adu Sadu's pig
60.	*Ma reu nda ro kue esa*	And they go and encounter a civet
61.	*Te nate Iko Lola Ladu kuen.*	Iko Lola Ladu's civet.
62.	*Kue ma dede'ak*	The civet is able to speak
63.	*Ma bafi ma kokolak ma rae:*	And the pig is able to talk, saying
64.	*'Mboi heni bafi ia*	'We ask you to free this pig
65.	*Ma nggari heni kue ia.*	And let loose this civet.
66.	*Te kue andiana ia*	For this civet is like a human

67. *Ma bafi hataholi ia.'*	And this pig is like a person.'
68. *Hu na ade ara keko reu fa bali*	So, they shift a little further, too
69. *Ma ara lali reu ba'uk bali.*	And they move a great way, too.
70. *Boe ma ara nda ro nura kue*	They encounter a woodland civet
71. *Ma nate ara nda ro lasi bafi.*	And they encounter a forest pig.
72. *Boe ma busa ka'a kue*	The dog bites at the civet
73. *Ma asu kiki bafi.*	And the hound snaps at the pig.
74. *De rala bafi lasi*	Thus, they catch the forest pig
75. *Ma rala kue nura.*	And they catch the woodland civet.
76. *Touk kia Ndu Bulan, Adu Ledo*	This man Ndu Bulan, Adu Ledo
77. *Tio Dangak nate Rusu Manek-a.*	Tio Dangak with Rusu Mane.
78. *Boe ma rae leo na:*	They say as follows:
79. *'Boe ma ara do'i bafi*	'They lift the pig
80. *Ma ara lemba kue ré.'*	They carry the civet.'

The invitation to eat cooked food in the Sea

Ndu Bulan and Adu Ledo ask that they divide the pig and civet so that they can carry their portion back to Bula Kai and Ledo Horo and there in the Heavens eat their meat raw. Tio Dangak and Rusu Mane respond by inviting them into the Sea to eat delicious cooked food.

81. *Te nate touk kia Ndu Bulan*	So, this man Ndu Bulan
82. *Ma ta'ek kia Adu Ledo*	And this boy Adu Ledo
83. *Selu lole rala haran*	Raises his voice
84. *Ma ai fino rala dasin ma rae:*	And lifts his word and says:
85. *'Bae fe ai bafi leo*	'Divide and give us the pig
86. *Ma bate fe ai kue leo*	And distribute and give us the civet
87. *Fo ai miu Bula Kai dei*	For us to go to Bula Kai
88. *Ma ai miu Ledo Horo dei.*	And for us to go to Ledo Horo.
89. *Te ai bei ra'u tak*	We still take and eat
90. *Ma ai bei si matak.'*	And we still tear food raw.'
91. *Boe te touk kia Tio Danga*	But this man Tio Dangak
92. *Ma ta'ek kia Rusu Mane*	And this boy Rusu Mane
93. *Ana de'a-de'a no Ndu Bulan*	He speaks with Ndu Bulan
94. *Ma ana kola-kola no Adu Ledo.*	And he talks with Adu Ledo.
95. *Boe ma nae: 'Auei!'*	So, they say: 'Auei!'
96. *Nae: 'Liun ndia ka fak*	Saying: 'The Ocean is near

97. *Ma sain ndia ka ba'uk.*	And the Sea goes far.
98. *Teu leo, teu leo*	Let us go, let us go
99. *Te tunu tasa malada ra*	To roast delicious cooked food
100. *Rai sain bakuten dei*	In the deep bending Sea
101. *Ma se'i mina malo'i*	And grill the sizzling fat
102. *Rai liun loloen dei.'*	In the deep lowering Sea.'

The descent into the Sea and the discovery of fire and of cooking

They all descend into the Sea. There Ndu Bulan and Adu Ledo encounter for the first time a flintstone and fire-drill. They see how the meat of the pig and civet is roasted and they taste cooked food for the first time. They eat but put some morsels away to take to Bula Kai and Ledo Horo.

103. *Reu leo*	They go
104. *Reu liun nia loloen*	They go into the descending Ocean
105. *Ma reu sain ma bekuten*	And they go into the bending Sea
106. *Ma nate tonggo ro batu ka sari ai*	And they encounter the firestone
107. *Sari fo rasa-rombe*	The firestone that flames
108. *Ma nda ro unda leru ai nggeo*	And they meet blackwood fire-drill
109. *Ara unda ra-masu*	The drill that smokes
110. *Ara tunu hotu kue nura*	They roast the woodland civet
111. *Leo na o, ana tunu hotu bafi lasi.*	Then they roast the forest pig.
112. *Faik na ta'ek ia Ndu Bulan*	That day, the boy Ndu Bulan
113. *Ma touk ia Adu Ledo*	And the man Adu Ledo
114. *Ara folo fo ara kali kado*	They taste and they put some away
115. *Ma ra'a fo ara so-langga*	And they eat but put some in their hats
116. *Reni fe Bula Kai*	To bring and give to Bula Kai
117. *Ma reni fe Ledo Horo.*	And to bring and give to Ledo Horo.
118. *Iate be'uk liun ia bali*	Something new in the Ocean
119. *Ma fe'ek sain ia bali.*	And something strange in the Sea.

The sons of the Sun and Moon recount their discoveries in the Sea

Ndu Bulan and Adu Ledo tell their father, Bula Kai and Ledo Horo, what has happened. They have discovered the use of fire made by flintstone and fire-drill and they have eaten cooked food, some of which they have brought back to be tasted.

120.	*Tehu Ndu Bulan ma Adu Ledo*	So Ndu Bulan and Adu Ledo
121.	*Rahara ma rae:*	Speak and say:
122.	*'Tetebe sara,*	'It is truly so,
123.	*Ai miu tongo mia masundaluk*	We encountered smoke
124.	*Ma nda mia pila lurik*	And we met with red fire
125.	*Nate nai liun ma sain.*	In the Ocean and in the Sea.
126.	*Touk Bula Kai e*	The man Bula Kai, ee
127.	*Ma ta'ek Ledo Horo e!*	And boy Ledo Horo, ee!
128.	*Tunu tasa malada nai na dei*	They roast delicious cooked food there
129.	*Masa-ndalu nai na dei*	Smoked food there
130.	*Unda leru ai nggeo*	The blackwood fire-drill
131.	*Batu ka sari ai.*	The stone that strikes fire.
132.	*Hu na de ai mia fo ai so-langga*	So, we ate and put some in our hats
133.	*Ma ai folo fo ai kali kado dei*	And we consumed but put some away
134.	*Ai mini fe Bula Kai dei*	To bring it to give to Bula Kai
135.	*Ma ai mini fe Ledo Horo dei.'*	And to bring it to give to Ledo Horo.'

Deliberations in the Heavens on how to obtain the wealth of the Sea

In the Moon's house and the Sun's home, Ndu Bulan and Adu Ledo deliberate with their father, Bula Kai and Ledo Horo, on how to obtain cooked food from the Sea. Ndu Bulan and Adu Ledo suggest that they divorce their sister, Sa'o Ledo and Mani Bulan, and marry her to Tio Dangak and Rusu Mane. They do this and then take their sister to marry in the Sea.

136.	*Hu na de ara dodo sara*	So, they consider
137.	*Ruma Bulan uman*	At the Moon's house
138.	*Ma ndanda sara*	And they ponder

139. *Ruma Ledo roan na.*	At the Sun's home.
140. *'Ata dua tao leo be*	'Let us think of what to do
141. *Fo keko masu-ndaluk ko*	To carry the smoked food
142. *Bula Kai mai dei*	For Bula Kai
143. *Ma afi tao leo be*	And consider what to do
144. *Fo ara lali pila lurik*	To bring the fire-reddened food
145. *Ledo Horo mai dei*	To Ledo Horo
146. *Fo ita tunu tasak dei*	That we may roast the cooked
147. *Ma ita se'i minak dei.'*	And that we may grill the fat.'
148. *Hu na de touk kia Ndu Bulan*	So, this man Ndu Bulan
149. *Ma ta'ek kia Adu Ledo*	And this boy Adu Ledo
150. *Ana dede'ak no aman*	He speaks with his father
151. *Ma ana kokola no to'on ma nae:*	And talks with his mother's brother, saying:
152. *'Ha'i! Inak ia Sa'o Ledo*	'Ha'i! This woman Sa'o Ledo
153. *Ma fetok ia Mani Bulan na*	And this girl Mani Bulan
154. *Esa sao Suka Hele*	The one who married Suka Hele
155. *Ma esa sao Fanggi Hele bai.*	And one who married Fanggi Hele, too.
156. *Bulan tian ma nate Ledo saon.*	The Moon's companion and Sun's wife
157. *Ara nggero rai Bula faratana falun*	They divorce at the Moon's eight gates
158. *Ma ara fura rai Ledo lelesu sion.*	And they separate at the Sun's nine doors.
159. *Faik ia nore ketu sara*	On the day they cut their connection
160. *Ma [ledo ia] lea ladi sara*	And at the time they draw apart
161. *Fo reu tu Tio Dangak dei*	To go to marry Tio Dangak
162. *Ma reu sao Rusu Manek dei.*	And to go to wed Rusu Mane.

The bridewealth negotiations for the wealth of the Seas

Ndu Bulan and Adu Ledo then demand bridewealth in exchange for their sister. They initially request payment in gold and livestock and then proceed to demand all that they see around them—first, tools for working the fields and for building a house: machete and axe, bore and chisel, adze and plane; then they ask for flintstone and fire-drill.

163. *Hu nande reu doko doe*	Then they go to ask for
164. *Beli batu nara*	Bridewealth of gold
165. *Ma ro fae tena nara*	And brideprice in livestock
166. *Ruma liun dale ma sain dale.*	In the Ocean depths and Sea depths.
167. *Reu leo, reu leo nate*	They go on and on
168. *Ara fe fae tena nate Sa'o Ledo*	They give livestock for Sa'o Ledo
169. *Ara fe beli batu nat Mani Bulan*	And they give gold for Mani Bulan
170. *Nate liun kamba kise-kise*	The Ocean's buffalo one by one
171. *Lemu imada dano*	Whose wallowing dries the pool
172. *Ma sain lilo kise-kise*	And the Sea's gold pieces one by one
173. *Fora ratiu sakara.*	Whose testing breaks the rubbing stone.
174. *Touk kia Ndu Bulan, Adu Ledo*	This man Ndu Bulan, Adu Ledo
175. *Hi bei ta hi*	Desiring still more
176. *Ma nau bei ta nau*	And wanting still more
177. *Nate ana susuri*	He looks closely at
178. *Numa Toak Mataka luan*	What is in Toak Matak's cave
179. *Ma nate fela ma-ai lilo kara*	The machete with its golden handle
180. *Ma ana memete*	And he observes carefully
181. *Nai Kilu Kamadoi lean*	What is in Kilu Kamadoi's grotto
182. *Ma nate taka mabui besikara*	The axe with its iron end
183. *Pase ro pa'a bela*	The bore and flat chisel
184. *Ma toru ro tatara.*	And the adze and plane.
185. *Leo na, ana suri ma ana mete neu*	So, he looks and observes
186. *Ma nate nesu bei makaboka buikara*	The mortar with a deep base
187. *Ma alu makafia tonggokara.*	And the pestle that blisters the hand.
188. *Boe ma ara doko doe sara*	So, they continue to claim
189. *Ma nate unda leru ai nggeo*	The blackwood fire-drill
190. *Batu ka sari ai.*	The stone that strikes fire.
191. *Neu ana tai-boni sara*	They continue to demand
192. *Te ana ta hi liun kamban*	But he does not want the Ocean's buffalo
193. *Ana ta hi sain lilon.*	He does not want the Sea's gold.
194. *De reni nesu makaboka buikara*	But they take the mortar with its deep base

195. *Ma alu makafiak tonggokara*   And the pestle that blisters the hand
196. *Batu ka sari ai*   The stone that strikes fire
197. *Ma unda leru ai ndeo.*   And the blackwood fire-drill.

The return to the Heavens with the bridewealth and the knowledge of cooked food

Ndu Bulan and Adu Ledo take all these goods back to Bula Kai and Ledo Horo so they can for the first time roast and eat cooked food—a practice derived from the bridewealth obtained by the marriage of Mani Bulan and Sa'o Ledo with the Lords of the Sea and passed on to the ancestors. The passage ends with a Christian element: a reference to the ancestors of Thie as descendants of Noah.

198. *Fo reni sara fo ata reu*   So, they take these and go
199. *Reni Bula Kai reu*   With Bula Kai, they go
200. *Ma Ledo Horo reu.*   And Ledo Horo, they go.
201. *Hu nate tunu tasak ko*   Thus, they roast cooked food
202. *Neu fa'ik ka boe*   To this day
203. *Ma se'i minak ko*   And they grill the fat
204. *Neu ledo ka boe.*   To this time then.
205. *Inak kia Mani Bulan*   Because of this woman Mani Bulan's

206. *Nate beli batun*   Bridewealth of gold
207. *Ma fetok kai Sa'o Ledo*   And this woman Sa'o Ledo's
208. *Nate fae tenan ia.*   Brideprice of livestock.
209. *Hu ra de tunu tasa maladak*   Thus, they roast delicious cooked food

210. *Lole faik kia dale*   To this day
211. *Losa faik,*   To the day,
212. *Nduku ledo kia dale*   To this time
213. *Se'i mina malo'oi*   Grill the slices of fat
214. *Ndule mai dae bafok*   Throughout the land
215. *Ndule mane mangaraun*   Among nobles and commoners
216. *Numa au ba'i kara mai*   Originating from my grandfathers
217. *Numa au soru kara mai*   Originating from my ancestors
218. *Fo numa Noa titi mai*   From Noa's descendants
219. *Fo Noa Liun*   Noa of the Sea
220. *Numa Lasi Noan.*   From Old Noa.

Recitation 2. The origin of the house and its roofing

N.D. Pah

Latu Dano ma Nore Le

The Heavenly marriage as the prelude to building the house of the Sun and Moon

This recitation is a continuation of the previous recitation, which ended with Ndu Bulan and Adu Ledo's return with all the bridewealth goods from the Sea. This recitation introduces a new set of descendants of the Sun and Moon and briefly touches on the attempts to build the first house for the Sun and Moon. More importantly, the recitation identifies the Heavenly origins of the gewang palm and alang-alang grass needed especially for roofing the house and situates these essential components in the domain of Thie.

The recitation begins with the marriage of one of the granddaughters of the Sun and Moon. Its initial lines provide the genealogy: Hingga Heu Bulan's daughter, Tode Hingga, and Lafa Lai Ledo's daughter, Dai Lafa, are married to Danok Mandi and Le Lakilima. They give birth to Latu Dano and Nore Le, who are the focus of this chant.

1.	*Faik ia, ledo ia*	This day, this time
2.	*Tetebe sara reni basa sara mai*	That indeed they brought all of these
3.	*Boe ma rakandolu Bulan uman*	To construct the Moon's house
4.	*Ma ralela Ledo roan.*	And to design the Sun's home.
5.	*Sangga mai ramatama Bulan uman*	Seeking to make whole the Moon's house
6.	*Ma ratesa Ledo roan.*	And to make fit the Sun's home.
7.	*Faik na, ledo na*	That day, that time
8.	*Ara soko rala Hingga Heu Bulan anan*	They lift Hingga Heu Bulan's child
9.	*[Inak kia] Nate Tode Hingga*	The woman Tode Hingga
10.	*Ma ara lali rala Lafa Lai Ledo anan*	And they transfer Lafa Lai Ledo's child
11.	*Fetok kia Dai Lafa.*	The girl Dai Lafa.

12.	*Tetebe sara leo na*	Indeed, it is so
13.	*Leo sao Danok Mandi*	To marry Danok Mandi
14.	*Ma bonggi Latu Dano ko*	And to give birth to Latu Dano
15.	*Leo sao Le Lakilima*	To marry Le Lakilima
16.	*Ma bonggi heni Nore Le.*	And to give birth to Nore Le.

The collapse of the Sun and Moon's house and the death of Latu Dano and Nore Le

Work is begun on the Sun's house and Moon's home but soft *bubuni* wood and thin *ndendela* grass are used for the house gates, which collapse on Latu Dano and Nore Le and kill them.

17.	*Dulu oen, langga daen.*	Waters in the east, land at the head.
18.	*Faik esa no dalen*	On this day
19.	*Boe ma ratama Bulan uman*	They make whole the Moon's house
20.	*Ma ratesa Ledo roan.*	And they make fit the Sun's home.
21.	*Boe me inak kia Nore Le*	The woman Nore Le
22.	*Fetok kia Latu Dano.*	And the girl Latu Dano.
23.	*Te nate lole bubuni bunak*	Good flowering *bubuni* wood
24.	*Lada ndendela tetekara*	Fine *ndendela* field grass
25.	*Ruma Bulan Kai*	At Bula Kai's [house]
26.	*Ma ruma Ledo Horo.*	And at Ledo Horo's [home].
27.	*Rambarik faratana bai é*	They erect the house gates
28.	*Lutu ara sasara*	The piles fall in
29.	*Mba'ar ara ndendefa*	The walls collapse
30.	*Ndefa rala Latu Dano*	Collapsing on Latu Dano
31.	*Tuni rala Nore Le.*	Falling on Nore Le.

The search for a burial site for Latu Dano and Nore Le

Dai Lafa and Tode Hingga cradle Latu Dano and Nore Le and carry them away for burial. They go to *Batu Tua* and *Namo Dale*, an important site in Thie, but continue further. They go to *Toto Batu* and *Nggenggo Boko*, but that site, too, is inappropriate. Pigs and buffalo disturb the land. So, they continue to the fields at *Tekeme Reik Oen* and *Fafae Tali Somba*, where they bury Latu Dano and Nore Le. There Latu Dano and Nore Le grow into the gewang palm and alang-alang grass—roofing material for the house.

32.	*Lai ledok ka boe*	At that time then
33.	*Nate neu faik ka*	On that day
34.	*Boe ma inak kia Dai Lafa*	The woman Dai Lafa
35.	*Ma fetok kia Tode Hingga*	And the girl Tode Hingga
36.	*Hinga Heu Bulan anan*	Hinga Heu Bulan's child
37.	*Lafa Lai Ledo anan*	Lafa Lai Ledo's child
38.	*Ko'o reni Nore Len*	They cradle Nore Le
39.	*Ma ara ifa reni Latu Dano bei a*	And they carry Latu Dano
40.	*Reni sara Dulu Oen Len*	Carry her to East Water's River
41.	*Reu Batu Tua Langga Len*	They go to the Head River of Batu Tua
42.	*Reu Namo Dale Dulu olin nara*	They go to the East Estuary of Namo Dale
43.	*Te bei tai ndana*	But they still follow the branch
44.	*[Ma bei sae bae]*.	And still climb the limb.
45.	*Te reu Langga Dulu Toto Batu*	They go to Toto Batu's East Head
46.	*Nggenggo Boko metin.*	Nggenggo Boko's tide.
47.	*Reu rato'i sara*	They go to bury them
48.	*Ma nate rakadofu sara,*	And to inter them,
49.	*Boe ma esa dadi neu tula*	So that one becomes a gewang palm
50.	*Ma esa dadi neu fi.*	And one becomes alang-alang grass.
51.	*Boe ma nate ia Latu Dano dei*	So, it is for Latu Dano
52.	*Ma ia Nore Le*	And so for Nore Le
53.	*Hu nate neu faik na boe*	That on that day then
54.	*Reni sara muri mai.*	They carry them to the west.
55.	*Mandan bei ta*	Things are not yet proper
56.	*Ma malole bei ta dei.*	And things are not yet good.
57.	*Reni sura muri mai*	They carry them to the west
58.	*Bafi reu totofi sara*	[But] pigs go to root
59.	*Ma nate kamba reu fafaka sara.*	And buffalo go to trample there.
60.	*Reni sura mai.*	They carry them onward.
61.	*Ara mai Tekeme Reik Oen*	They arrive at Tekeme Reik Oen
62.	*Ara mai Fafae Tali Somba*	They arrive at Fafae Tali Somba
63.	*Mbulen nara tatali*	The shoots wind round
64.	*Ma don nara lolote*	And leaves spread upward
65.	*Ruma Fafae Tali Somba*	At Fafae Tali Somba
66.	*Ma ruma Tekeme Reik Oen.*	And at Tekeme Reik Oen.

An invocation of the founding ancestors

It is at this point in the narrative that the founding ancestors of the domain of Thie are invoked and they use gewang palm leaves and alang-alang grass for roofing the first house.

These ancestors are Tola Mesa and his son, Kiki Tola. Both ancestors are given dual names in the chant: Tola Mesa//Le'e Lunu and Kiki Tola//Nggebu Nusa. They create the first house at *Do Lasi* and *Ledo Mbena*, the highest hills in Thie, on either side of *Nase Dano*. At the site of the first house people gather—'orphans and widows flock'—and animals abound and take shade. *Do Lasi* and *Ledo Mbena* becomes a centre of wisdom and good counsel.

In its conclusion, this recitation refers to the moieties of Sabarai and Taratu that divide the clans of Thie into intermarrying groups. And at the very end, the recitation invokes the Inner Patterner and Self Marker (Dula Dale//Le'u Teik), the Holy Spirit, as the source of wisdom and good counsel and the overseer of the ancestors' legacy.

67.	*Nate au ba'ing ia Tola Mesa*	Our grandfather Tola Mesa
68.	*Ma sorong ia Le'e Lunu*	And our ancestor Le'e Lunu
69.	*Oen na, dae na mai*	Comes to his water, his land
70.	*Kiki Tola ma Nggebu Nusa*	Kiki Tola and Nggebu Nusa
71.	*Sangga ana dadi tao leo na*	Seek to make it so
72.	*Fo balu tular ia dadi*	So that gewang rooftop is created
73.	*Sangga ana mori tao leo na*	Seek to create it so
74.	*Fo mbuni fi ria ana mori*	So that the alang-alang grass roofing is made
75.	*Nai Do Lasi ma Ledo Mbena.*	At Do Lasi and Ledo Mbena.
76.	*Boe ma mana dadi kara dadi*	What is created is created
77.	*Ma mana mori kara mori.*	What is made is made.
78.	*Manu rara kokoa Do Lasi*	The cocks crow at Do Lasi
79.	*Busa raho'u Ledo Mbena.*	The dogs bark at Ledo Mbena.
80.	*Boe ma falu-inar ara mai*	The widows, they come
81.	*Ma ana-mar ara mai*	The orphans, they come
82.	*Ndolu sio nara mai*	The Ninefold Wisdom comes
83.	*Lela falu nara mai.*	The Eightfold Knowledge comes.
84.	*Babi reu sa'o ai*	Pigs go to the trees' shadow
85.	*[Ma suru reu] mafo tua*	[And go to] the lontars' shade

86.	*Malole dai lena*	It is more than good enough
87.	*Mandak so resi*	It is more than sufficiently proper
88.	*Ndule basa dae bafok ledo sa'ak.*	Through all the Earth.
89.	*Nai leo duahulu ma lima*	Among the twenty-five clans
90.	*Sabarai ma nate Taratu*	Sabarai and Taratu
91.	*Sabarai tititin*	Sabarai's descendants
92.	*Ma nate tetebe sara*	And it is truly so
93.	*Neu Sakunara nonosin nara*	To Sakunara's progeny
94.	*Nduku faik ia dale so né.*	To this very day.
95.	*Ndolu sio ria*	The Ninefold Wisdom
96.	*Ma nate lela falu ria.*	And the Eightfold Knowledge.
97.	*Dula Dale ma Le'u Teik*	The Inner Patterner and Self Marker
98.	*Sangga ana dadi tao leo ia*	Seeks that it be so
99.	*Fo Kiki Tola mbembedan*	For Kiki Tola's legacy
100.	*Ma sangga ara mori tao leo na*	And seeks that things are so
101.	*Fo Nggebu Nusa nanaen.*	For Nggebu Nusa's intention.

Recitation 3. The origin of the first ancestral house, at Do Lasi and Ledo Mbena

N.D. Pah and Samuel Ndun

Tola Mesa ma Le'e Lunu

A prelude to the building of the first ancestral house

This recitation recounts the building of the first house at *Do Lasi* and *Ledo Mbena*. It begins with a long peroration that sets the scene and describes the condition of the ancestors before the building of the first house. These opening lines invoke the inspiration of the Holy Spirit in the creation of the house, adding a critical Christian element to this origin narrative. From a genealogical perspective, the first house was made for Kiki Tola, the son of Tola Mesa.

As a composition, this recitation consists of separate episodes linking to the building of the first house. It also includes references to aspects of this building process that are not explained.

1.	*Dalu bei don*	Long ago
2.	*Hida bei fan*	In the past
3.	*Dae bafok makiuk boe*	The Earth in darkness
4.	*Batu poi makahatuk boe*	The world in gloom
5.	*Ai bai-nara bei babi leak*	Our grandfathers still shelter in caves
6.	*Ma ai soro-nara bei suru luak ka.*	And our ancestors still reside in grottoes.
7.	*Numa ai bain Tola Mesa mai*	Things come from our grandfather Tola Mesa
8.	*Ai soron Le'e Lunu mai.*	Our ancestor Le'e Lunu.
9.	*Lain atur malole*	The Heavens order well
10.	*Ata atur mandak ia.*	The Heights order properly.
11.	*Te fain esa no dalen*	So, on one certain day
12.	*Ledok esa no serin na*	At one particular time
13.	*Manadula Dale neu baing esa Tola Mesa*	The Inner Patterner reaches to grandfather Tola Mesa
14.	*Ma Le'u Tein neu sorong esa Le'e Lunu*	And the Self Marker reaches to ancestor Le'e Lunu
15.	*Nene bonggi kara ruma Landu Kona*	At the birthplace, Landu Kona
16.	*Ma rae kara ruma Tena Seri*	And on the land, Tena Seri
17.	*Kara Fau Iko Oe*	At the Water's Tail at Kara Fau
18.	*Ma Pandi Lua Langa daen*	And the Land's Head at Pandi Luan
19.	*Bei babi luak*	Still sheltering in caves
20.	*Ma bei suru leak.*	And still residing in grottoes.
21.	*Lai atur malole*	The Heavens order well
22.	*Ana fe Dula Dalen, ana mai*	Giving forth the Inner Patterner, he comes
23.	*[Ata atur mandak]*	[The Heights order properly]
24.	*Ana fe Le'u Tein, ana mai*	Giving forth the Self Marker, he comes
25.	*I konda Ndolu Sio nara mai*	Bringing down the Ninefold Wisdom

26.	*Ma Lela Falu nara mai*	And the Eightfold Knowledge
27.	*Ruma poin ia mai*	From the Heavens it comes
28.	*Ma ruma ata ia mai.*	From the Heights it comes.

Initial attempts at building the ancestral house

These lines recount the first fumbling attempts to build the house but without the proper tools and without a proper design. These lines allude to the design that—without clear explanation—involves the Great Squid and Great Octopus of the Sea. They recount briefly how the tools for building the house were obtained as bridewealth payment when the Sun and Moon married their daughter, Sa'o Ledo//Mani Bulan, to the son of the Lords of the Sea, Tio Dangak//Rusu Mane. With these tools, it becomes possible to build the house.

Various lines (40–43) assume a knowledge of genealogical origins. Thus, the names of the descendants of Hele Lain ('Heavenly Hele') reveal a succession of four generations: the successive alteration of these names indicates that Hele Lain has brought forth Suka Hele, who has brought forth Nale Suka, who, in turn, has brought forth Tema Nale. These figures come to *Do Lasi* and *Ledo Mbena*, presumably as builders of the house, but their role is not made clear.

29.	*Faik esa no dalen na*	Then on one day
30.	*Ledo esa no serin na*	And at one time
31.	*Raka-ndolu Nggebu uman*	They offer counsel on Nggebu's house
32.	*Ma ra-lela Kiki roan.*	And give advice on Kiki's home.
33.	*Numa Do Lasi na, Ledo Mbena*	At Do Lasi, at Ledo Mbena
34.	*Raka-ndolu reni seri,*	They design on one side,
35.	*Na ana tu foa neni seri.*	It tilts to one side.
36.	*Ralaka reni seri*	They fashion on one side,
37.	*Na ana nggongga foi neni seri.*	It wobbles to one side.
38.	*Tehu faik esa no dalen*	But on one day
39.	*Ma ledo esa no serin*	And at one time
40.	*Hele Lain bobonggin nara*	The descendants of Hele Lain
41.	*Touk Suka Hele bali*	The man Suka Hele
42.	*Ta'ek Nale Suka bali*	The boy Nale Suka
43.	*Touk Tema Nale bali*	The man Tema Nale

44. *Tengas sara mai*	They come forth
45. *Fo ruma Bula Kai mai*	Come from Bula Kai
46. *Ma ruma Ledo Horo mai*	And come from Ledo Horo
47. *Ara mai Do Lasi ma Ledo Mbena.*	They come to Do Lasi and Ledo Mbena.
48. *Boe ma tenga rala Kiki Inan ma-liun*	They take the Great Squid of the Ocean
49. *Ma hai rala Pado Ina ma-sain*	And grip the Great Octopus of the Sea
50. *Rakandolu numa Do Lasi ma Ledo Mbena.*	They set the design at Do Lasi and Ledo Mbena.
51. *Te hu bei hida hatan*	Yet still in the past
52. *[Ma bei dalu don]*	And still long ago
53. *Pasa pa'a bela beik*	There is no bore and flat chisel
54. *Toro ro tara beik*	Still no axe and wood adze
55. *Taka ma-bui besikara beik*	Still no adze with iron centre
56. *Ma fela ma-ai lilokara beik.*	Still no machete with golden handle.
57. *Te hu ta'ek Ndu Bulan*	But then the boy Ndu Bulan
58. *Ma touk esa Adu Ledo*	And the man Adu Ledo
59. *Tou manasombu bafi*	The man who hunts pig
60. *Ma ta'e manafula kuer é*	And the boy who stalks civet
61. *Ruma dae bafok ledo sa'ak ia*	On the sunlit Earth
62. *Hu na Ndolu Sio ra-esa na*	The Ninefold Wisdom as one
63. *Ma Lela Falu raka-bua na*	And the Eightfold Knowledge together
64. *Reu rala Ndu Bulan*	Reaches Ndu Bulan
65. *Ma Adu Ledo bai.*	And Adu Ledo, too.
66. *Boe-ma ara susuri ma memete*	They look and they observe
67. *Ndae pase neu be*	Where the bore is to be found
68. *Ana tesa neu itama*	Suitable to join
69. *Ma leo nao, ara fua funu neu be*	Where the turning drill is lodged
70. *Menggu reu ranggio.*	Appropriate to come together.
71. *Touk Kita Ina liun*	The man Great Squid of the Ocean
72. *Ta'e Pado Ina sain na.*	And the boy Great Octopus of the Sea.
73. *Te tou manasombu bafi*	So, the man who hunts pig

74.	*Ndu Bulan ia*	This Ndu Bulan
75.	*Ta'e manafula kue*	The boy who stalks civet
76.	*Adu Ledo ia*	This Adu Ledo
77.	*Ledo Horo anan ia*	This child of Ledo Horo
78.	*Do Bula Kai anan ia*	Or this child of Bula Kai
79.	*Tonggo no pase ro pa'a bela*	Meets the bore and flat chisel
80.	*Ruma liun te loloen*	In the descending Ocean
81.	*Ma nate ana nda no funu* *fo mareo*	And encounters the turning drill
82.	*Ruma sain fo bekute*	In the receding Sea
83.	*Ruma Toak Mataka luan*	In Toa Matak's cave
84.	*Ma ruma Kilu Kamadoi lean na.*	And Kilu Kamadoi's grotto.
85.	*Touk ia Adu Ledo*	This man Adu Ledo
86.	*Ma ta'ek ia Ndu Bulan*	And this boy Ndu Bulan
87.	*Nenis sara mai leo*	Brings them to
88.	*Do Lasi mai ma Ledo* *Mbena mai*	Do Lasi and to Ledo Mbena
89.	*Te hu pase ro pa'a bela*	The bore and flat chisel
90.	*Ma toro ro tara ria*	And the axe and the wood adze
91.	*Ma beli ma doik ara.*	Bridewealth and payment.
92.	*Ana lali inak Sa'o Ledo*	They transfer the woman Sa'o Ledo
93.	*Ma ara koko fetok ka Mani* *Bulan nia*	And they cradle the girl Mani Bulan
94.	*Ana tu Danga Lena Liun anan*	She weds the child of the Hunter of the Ocean
95.	*Tio Dangak*	Tio Dangak
96.	*Ana sao Mane Matua Sain anan*	She marries the child of the Lord of the Sea
97.	*Rusu Manek kia.*	Rusu Mane.
98.	*Ana koko pase pa'a bela,*	He cradles the bore and flat chisel,
99.	*Ana mai*	It comes
100.	*Ma Toro Takara,*	And the axe and adze,
101.	*Ana mai*	It comes
102.	*Funu ma-reo,*	The turning drill,
103.	*Ara main.*	They come.
104.	*Felar ma-ai lilokara mai*	The machete with golden handle
105.	*Taka mabui besik*	The axe with iron centre

106.	*Ara mai dei.*	They also come.	
107.	*Ara mai Do Lasi, Ledo Mbena*	They come to Do Lasi, Ledo Mbena	
108.	*Ara menggu reu ranggio*	They come together to fit well	
109.	*Tesa reu ratama*	Join to harmonise	
110.	*Sema Kona na*	The right-house post is there	
111.	*Ara balu manu reu na*	They conduct the *balu manu* ceremony	
112.	*Ma Lunggu Lain na*	And the high *lunggu* beam is there	
113.	*Pase pa'a-bela mori*	The bore and flat chisel come forth	
114.	*Ma funu ma-reo dadi*	The turning drill appears	
115.	*Sema kona nata inggio*	The *sema* and right post interlock together	
116.	*Lunggu lain nahere inggoto.*	The high *lunggu* beams fit together.	

The choice of roofing when the construction of the house is completed

After the house has been erected and an initial celebration held, there remains the question of the roofing for the house. The two possible roofing materials used for a Rotenese house are alang-alang grass, which is tied in bundles and attached to the roofing spars, or gewang leaves, which are spread out and similarly attached. These lines describe the origin of both roofing materials. When the house is completed, a huge celebration is held with the slaughter and sacrifice of many livestock whose meat is distributed to 'the orphans and widows'—an expression that, in this context, refers to the population of the domain.

117.	*Neu faik na ma neu ledo na*	On that day and at that time
118.	*Boe ma ara suru reu sao ai*	They rest under the trees' shadow
119.	*Ma babi reu mafo tua*	And shelter under the lontars' shade
120.	*Sangga balu fi ria*	Seeking a cover of alang grass
121.	*Ma sangga buni tula ria.*	And seeking a decking of gewang leaves.
122.	*Ara mori.*	They come forth.
123.	*Te bei leo na, leo na*	Yet still as then, as then
124.	*Te bei hida hatan dalu don*	Yet still as long ago

125. *Ara bei balu kea rou*	There is still roofing with turtle shells
126. *Ara bei heu hai iko ro*	There are still spars of sharks' tails
127. *Ruma Dulu Oe, Langga Daen nara*	At Eastern Waters, at Head Lands
128. *Ruma Nggenggo Boko metin*	At Nggenggo Boko's tide
129. *Ruma Dulu Oen, Langga daen.*	At Eastern Waters, Head Lands.
130. *Te malole bei ta*	This is not yet good
131. *Ma mandak bei ta.*	And not yet proper.
132. *Tehu ara mai Do Lasi, Ledo Mbena*	So, they come to Do Lasi, Ledo Mbena
133. *Au baing ia Tola Mesa*	My grandfather Tola Mesa
134. *Ma au sorong ia Le'e Lunu*	And my ancestor Le'e Lunu
135. *Tititin ma nonosin*	His descendants and progeny
136. *Kiki Tola mai dea*	Kiki Tola comes out
137. *Ma ba'ing Nggebu Nusa mai dea.*	And my grandfather Nggebu Nusa comes out.
138. *Hu na neu faik ka*	For on that day
139. *Ma neu ledok-a*	And at that time
140. *Boe ara memete*	They continue to look
141. *Ma ara susuri*	And they continue to observe
142. *Ma nate tula mori Fafae*	The gewang comes forth at Fafae
143. *Ma nate fi dadi Tekeme*	And the alang grass appears at Tekeme
144. *Balu fi, ara dadi*	The alang grass covering appears
145. *Mbuni tula, ana mori.*	The gewang leaves come forth.
146. *Ara mai Do Lasi ma Ledo Mbena ia.*	They come to Do Lasi and Ledo Mbena.
147. *Faik na, ledo na*	On that day, that time
148. *Boe ma ara menggu reu ranggio*	They come together and fit well
149. *Ma ara tesa reu ratama.*	And they join and harmonise.
150. *Falu ina reu babi*	Widows go to shelter
151. *Ma ana-ma reu suru.*	And orphans go to reside.
152. *Faik esa no dalen*	On a particular day
153. *Ledo esa no serin*	At a particular time
154. *Ratesa Nggebu uman*	They are satisfied with Nggebu's house

155. *Ratema Kiki roan.*   They are content with Kiki's home.
156. *Boe ma ara hala natun*   They slaughter a hundred livestock
157. *[Ara] pa'a rifun.*   They tie down a thousand livestock.
158. *Ara ndu seli ana-mak*   They distribute to orphans
159. *Ma ana pala seli falu-inak.* And they give to widows.

The ancestral marriage that follows the building of the first house

These lines are among the most obscure of the composition. The woman Binga Ledi//Kada Sali gathers two specific fish, presumably to initiate the celebration of the marriage of the ancestor Kiki Tola//Nggebu Nusa to the woman Seu Dela//Fale Ande. Again, a feast is held to celebrate this wedding and food is distributed to the widows and orphans. The chant concludes with another reference to the wisdom of the ancestors, Tola Mesa and Le'e Lunu.

160. *Inak kia Bingga Lete*   The woman Binga Ledi
161. *Fetok kia Kada Sali*   The girl Kada Sali
162. *Ara bei lili Lao Bola bali*   They forget Lao Bali
163. *Ara bei mbamba rua Doki*   They no longer remember
     Timu bali dei.   Doki Timu.
164. *Hu nate neu faik na*   So, on that day
165. *Ma neu ledok na*   And at that time
166. *Ara memete ma nate [susuri]* They look and observe
167. *Dea ei ma uar*   The legs of the fish weir of good fortune
168. *Ruma Rote Ma-rorok*   At Rote Marorok
169. *Ma lutu lima ma-ralak*   And the arms of the fish-wall of good luck
170. *Ruma Naru No Makamu*   At Naru-No Makamu
171. *Rala beto saikara*   That holds *beto* fish from the Sea
172. *Ma reu rala noa liukara.*   And holds *noa* fish from the Ocean.
173. *Nate ara keko Ina Seu Dela*   Now they carry the woman Seu Dela
174. *Neu sao ba'ing Kiki Tola*   To marry my ancestor Kiki Tola
175. *Ma ara lali Ina Fale Ande*   And they transfer the woman Fale Ande

176. *Neu sao ba'ing Nggebu Nusa ia.*	To marry my ancestor Nggebu Nusa.
177. *Ha'i nala ndai tasi*	She takes up the sea-fishing net
178. *Ma tenga nala seko metin*	And she takes hold of Ocean scoop net
179. *Ara sara Naru No Makamu*	At Naru-No Makamu
180. *Ma Rote Ma-rorok*	At Rote Marorok
181. *Reni beto-kara mai*	Bringing the Sea-*beto*
182. *Ma reni noa-kara main.*	And bringing the Ocean-*noa*.
183. *Ara papala Noak ban*	They repeatedly distribute the *noa*'s lungs
184. *Ma ara ndundu Beto aten.*	And they continually give out the *beto*'s liver.
185. *Neu faik-a boe ma neu ledok-a boe*	On that day and at the time
186. *Ara pala dai ana-mar*	They distribute enough to the orphans
187. *Ma ara ndu ndule falu-inar.*	And they give widely to the widows.
188. *Ara langga lilo reu na.*	They carry out the *langga lilo* ritual.
189. *Nate tula nai Fafae*	Gewang at Fafae
190. *Au bai'ng ia Tola Mesa*	My grandfather Tola Mesa
191. *Fi nai Tekeme*	Alang grass at Tekeme
192. *Au sorong ia Le'e Lunu.*	My ancestor Le'e Lunu.
193. *Manadadi kara dadi*	What happened, happened
194. *Manamori kara mori*	What came about, came about
195. *Ndolu sio, Lela falu.*	Ninefold wisdom, eightfold knowledge.

Recitation 4. The war between the Heavens and the Sea and its consequences

N.D. Pah and Samuel Ndun

Suti Solo do Bina Bane

A Heavenly discussion in preparation for war with the Sea

This recitation begins with a peroration of some seven lines that acknowledge the rule of the Heavens and the Earth. These lines foreshadow the concluding five lines of the recitation, which extol the rule and bounty of the Heavens. After this peroration, the next 49 lines launch immediately into a crucial episode in the canon of Thie's origin chants. They give an account of the leadup to the war waged by the Sun and Moon on the Lords of the Ocean and Sea.

This recitation also provides the genealogical background of the key members of the Heavenly realm. Bula Kai//Ledo Horo is Lord of the Heavens and his wife is Pua Kende//No Rini, who is the daughter of Kende Bei Sama//Rini Bala Sama. Bula Kai//Ledo Horo's children, all of whom bear the first half of the name of their father—Bula(n) and Ledo—are: 1) Patola Bulan//Mandeti Ledo, 2) Tuti Leo Bulan//Si Lete Ledo, 3) Ninga Heu Bulan//Lafa Lai Ledo, and 4) Hundi Hu Bulan//Tefu Oe Ledo.[1]

The Lords of the Sea, Mane Tua Sain//Danga Lena Liun, are mentioned along with various sea creature warriors. Some sea creatures—Ain Bo'o Bai//Etu Asa Siru and Bara Kota Nau//Pila Mengge Mea—are named. These are poisonous sea creatures, as is indicated, for example, by the name Pila Mengge Mea ('Red Snake of the Sea').[2] The fighting occurs at *Lau Mara//Leme Niru*. It is described as fought with swords and flintlocks (*tafa//siro*).

1.	*Hida bei fan na*	At a time long ago
2.	*Dalu bei don na*	At a period long past
3.	*Lalai ma na te dae bafok*	The Heavens and the Earth
4.	*Neni parinda ma neni koasak*	Carry rule and carry power
5.	*Neni ko'o ifak*	Carry it lifting and cradling it

---

1 Note that it is the convention that 'Moon' (*Bulan*) precedes 'Sun' (*Ledo*) in names in Thie. This is a convention that exists in Termanu but is not always consistently applied.
2 I have no species identification of these sea creatures.

6.	*Neni nekeboik*	Carry it with care
7.	*Ma neni nesemaok.*	And carry it with concern.
8.	*Faik esa no dalen*	Then on a certain day
9.	*Ledo esa no tein*	At a particular time
10.	*Touk kia Bula Kai*	The man Bula Kai
11.	*Ta'ek esa Ledo Horo*	The boy Ledo Horo
12.	*Ana dea-dea no tun*	He speaks with his wife
13.	*Ma na te ana kola-kola no saon*	And he addresses his spouse
14.	*Kende Bei Sama anan*	Kende Bei Sama's child
15.	*Inak kia Pua Kende*	The woman Pua Kende
16.	*Ma Rini Bala Sama anan*	And Rini Bala Sama's child
17.	*Fetok kia No Rini.*	The girl No Rini.
18.	*Ana dea-dea no anan nara*	He speaks with his children
19.	*Mandeti Ledo bali*	Mandeti Ledo
20.	*Ma Patola Bulan bali*	And Patola Bulan
21.	*Kola-kola no anan nara*	Addresses his children
22.	*Si Lete Ledo bali*	Si Lete Ledo
23.	*Tuti Leo Bulan bali*	Tuti Leo Bulan
24.	*Ana kola-kola no anan nara*	He addresses his children
25.	*Ningga Heu Bulan*	Ninga Heu Bulan
26.	*Lafa Lai Ledo*	Lafa Lai Ledo
27.	*Hundi Hu Bulan bali*	Hundi Hu Bulan
28.	*Tefu Oe Ledo bali ma nae:*	Tefu Oe Ledo and says:
29.	*'Tetenda tafa langga*	'Sharpen the sword blade
30.	*Ma seseru siro nggoe*	And set the flintlock trigger
31.	*Sain dale miu dei*	We are going into the Sea
32.	*Ma liun dale miu dei.*	And we are going into the Ocean.
33.	*Ela leo be na,*	So let it be,
34.	*Rani falu rai liun*	Eight warriors in the Ocean
35.	*Ma meru sio rai sain*	And nine defenders in the Sea
36.	*Ma na te tetenda tafa langga dei*	Strike their sword heads
37.	*Ma seseru siro nggoe dei.*	Set their flintlocks' triggers.
38.	*Hu na te ara konda sain dale mai*	So, they descend into the Sea
39.	*Ma ana konda liun dale mai*	And descend into the Ocean
40.	*Ratonggo ro liun meru nara*	To meet the Ocean's defenders
41.	*Ma na te randa ro sain rani nara*	And to meet the Sea's warriors

42.	*Manetua Sain rani nara*	The Lord of the Sea's warriors
43.	*Ma Danga Lena Liun meru nara*	And Hunter of the Ocean's defenders
44.	*Ain Bo'o Bai ma Etu Asa Siru*	Ain Bo'o Bai and Etu Asa Siru
45.	*Bara Kota Nau sain*	Bara Kota Nau of the Sea
46.	*Ma Pila Mengge Mea sain.*	And Pila Mengge Mea of the Sea.
47.	*Ara tonggo ro*	They meet them
48.	*Ma ara nda ro*	And they encounter them
49.	*Rain falu ma meruk sio*	The eight warriors and nine defenders
50.	*Ruma sain bei Lau Mara*	In the Sea at Lau Mara
51.	*[Ruma liun] bei Leme Niru bali*	And in the Ocean at Leme Niru, too
52.	*Tonggo langga reu tonggo*	They meet head-to-head
53.	*Tetenda tafa langga*	Strike their sword blades
54.	*Ma seseru siro nggoen.*	Fire their cocked flintlocks.
55.	*Hu na de ara siro la'e Lau Mara*	So, they fire at Lau Mara
56.	*Ma ara tati la'e Leme Niru.*	And they slash at Leme Niru.

Suti Solo (a nautilus shell) and Bina Bane (a baler shell) rise from the Sea.

During the fighting at *Lau Mara*//*Leme Niru*, Suti Solo, a nautilus shell who is the child of Solo Bana Sain, and Bina Bane, a baler shell who is the child of Bane Aka Liun, become tainted by the blood of battle. They put forth their pods and are carried to *Loko Laka Fa* and *Tebu Tipa Re*.

57.	*Dan, ana nonosi*	Blood, it pours
58.	*Ma oen, ana tititi.*	And water, it drips.
59.	*Ana tititi la'e*	It drips on
60.	*Bane Aka Liun anan ia*	Bane Aka Liun's child
61.	*Bina Bane*	Bina Bane
62.	*Ma ana nosi la'e*	And it pours out on
63.	*Solo Bana Sain anan*	Solo Bana Sain's child
64.	*Suti Solo.*	Suti Solo.
65.	*Faik esa no dalen*	On that one day
66.	*Boe ma Suti ramaroko isi*	Suti puts forth his insides
67.	*Ma Bina reu edo nggi*	And Bina extends his pods
68.	*Hu na ara la latu, de mai*	So they drift like seaweed

69.	*Ma ara bonu engga, de mai.*	And they bob like seagrass.
70.	*De ara mai Loko Laka Fa lain*	They come to Loko Laka Fa
71.	*Ma ara mai Tebu Tipa Re lain*	And they come to Tebu Tipa Re
72.	*Isi nara haradoi*	Their insides cry out
73.	*Ma na te nggi nara kurudo.*	And their pods are in pain.

While scoop-net fishing, two women encounter Suti Solo do Bina Bane

Two women, Bui Len and Eno Lolo, who are genealogically identified as the daughters of Leu Le Dale//Lolo Dala Ina and the wives of Nggonggo Ingu Lai//Rima Le Dale, take up their scoop nets and go to fish along the shoreline at *Loko Laka Fa* and *Tebu Tipa Re*. There they encounter the shells, Suti Solo and Bina Bane, who ask to be scooped up and taken back with them to their home.

74.	*Neu faik ka boe*	On that day then
75.	*Na te Nggonggo Inggu Lai tun*	Nggonggo Ingu Lai's spouse
76.	*Leu Le Dale anan*	Leu Le Dale's child
77.	*Ma na te Bui Len*	Bui Len
78.	*Neu faik ka boe*	On that day then
79.	*Rima Le Dale saon*	Rima Le Dale's wife
80.	*Ma na te Lolo Dala Ina anan*	Lolo Dala Ina's child
81.	*Eno Lolo*	Eno Lolo
82.	*Eno Lolo na te Bui Len*	Eno Lolo and Bui Len
83.	*Nggonggo Inggu Lai saon*	Nggonggo Ingu Lai's wife
84.	*Ma Leu [Rima] Le Dale tun*	And Leu [Rima] Le Dale's spouse
85.	*Ana ha'i nala ndai tasi*	She takes her sea scoop net
86.	*[Ana] tengga nala seko metin*	Lifts her tidal fishnet
87.	*Reu meti manggatitiri nara*	Goes to the receding tide
88.	*Ma mada manggaheheta nara.*	And to the drying Sea.
89.	*Ana nda no Bina nggin*	She encounters Bina's pods
90.	*Ma ana tonggo no Suti isin.*	And she meets Suti's insides.
91.	*Ara haradoi numa Loko Laka Fa*	They cry out at Loko Laka Fa
92.	*Ma ara kurudo numa Tebu Tipa Re.*	They are in pain at Tebu Tipa Re.
93.	*'Soro meni nggai dei*	'Lift us up
94.	*Ma ndai meni nggai dei.'*	And scoop us up.'
95.	*'Ai beru Bina mia se*	'To whom will we attach Bina

96.	*Ma ai toto Suti mia se?'*	And to whom will we fit Suti?'
97.	*Boe ma ko'o reni sara mai*	So, they cradle them away
98.	*[Ifa] reni sara [mai].*	And [carry] them away.
99.	*'Ai ndae ei miu be?*	'Where should we hang you?
100.	*Ma ai fua ei miu be?'*	And where should we place you?'

The first request by the shells for proper placement

Suti Solo and Bina Bane's first request to Bui Len and Eno Lolo is to be placed on *ufa* and *bau* trees when they are in blossom. Both trees produce beautiful flowers. The *ufa* is otherwise known as the Malabar plum or rose-apple (*Syzygium jambos*) while the *bau* is the sea hibiscus (*Hibiscus tiliaceus*). Almost immediately, however, this placement proves unsatisfactory.

101.	*Boe ma rae: 'Fua ai miu*	So, they say: 'Place us on
102.	*Ufa mabuna henu [kara]*	The *ufa* tree full of gold-bead flowers
103.	*Ma Bau malusu lilok kara.'*	And on the *bau* tree with golden blossoms.'
104.	*Fai esa no dalen*	On this one day
105.	*Ara bei ta ratetu*	They still do not feel right
106.	*Ma bei ta randa.*	And still do not feel proper.

The second request by the shells for proper placement

Suti Solo and Bina Bane's next request is to be carried into the house and placed on two of its named beams: the *Sema Kona* and the *Lunggu Lai*. These places are where sacrifices are performed in the traditional house in Thie. This placement, however, is also unsatisfactory.

107.	*Ara dea-dea ro Nggonggo Inggu Lai tun*	They address Nggonggo Ingu Lai's spouse
108.	*Inak ia Eno Lolo*	The woman Eno Lolo
109.	*Ana kola-kola ro Rima Le Dale saon*	They speak to Rima Le Dale's wife
110.	*Fetok ia Bui Len:*	The girl Bui Len:
111.	*'Ma ha'i falik ai dei*	'Carry us back
112.	*Ma tengga falik ai dei*	And take us back
113.	*Ndae ai miu Sema Kona*	Set us on the *Sema Kona*
114.	*Fua ai miu Lunggu Lai*	Place us on the *Lunggu Lai*

115. *Fo ama bara manu Sema Kona*	To sacrifice chickens at the *Sema Kona*
116. *Na te ama langge lilo Lunggu Lai.'*	And to place gold at the *Lunggu Lai.'*
117. *Hu na de ara fati bete sara*	They offer millet there
118. *Ma ara hao hade sara,*	And they consume the rice there,
119. *Faru kapa ma na te mina bafi.*	Water buffalo horns and pig's fat.
120. *Faik esa no dalen*	Then on one day
121. *Ledok esa no tein*	And at one time
122. *Bei ta ratetu*	They still do not feel right
123. *Ma bei ta randa.*	And still do not feel proper.

The third request by the shells for proper placement

Suti Solo and Bina Bane then ask to be carried eastward so that at dawn they may be placed at the boundary stone and field's border. There amid the rice fields and dry fields, the shells give birth to what is referred to as 'Planting of the Boundary Stone' (*Tanek To Batu*) and 'Sowing of the Field Boundary' (*Selek Lane Ai*). This alludes to the planting of the first fields in Thie.

124. *Ana de'a-de' a ro Bui Len*	He talks to Bui Len
125. *Ma kola-kola ro Eno Lolo*	And speaks to Eno Lolo
126. *Nggonggo Inggu Lai tun*	Nggonggo Ingu Lai's spouse
127. *Ma Rima Le Dale saon, ma rae:*	And Rima Le Dale's wife, and says:
128. *'Keko ai dulu miu dei*	'Shift us to the east
129. *Ma lali ai langga miu dei*	And transfer us to the headland
130. *Fo ai timu dulu miu dei*	So that we may be in the Dawning East
131. *Ma ai Sepe Langga miu dei.*	And at the Reddening Headland.
132. *Mbeda ai miu to batu*	Take us to the rock boundary stone
133. *Ma na te ndae ai miu lane tiner*	And carry us to the field's border
134. *Fo ela leo be na:*	So let it be:
135. *Natun kae ma rifun hene*	A hundred steps and a thousand mounts
136. *Nai omba hade dei*	On the rice field dike
137. *Nai lane tiner dei,*	And the dry field boundary,
138. *Fo ela leo be na*	So let it be that
139. *Ai makaboi miu ana mar*	We are cared for as orphans
140. *Ma ai masamao miu falu inar*	And are treated as widows

141. *Bonggi Tanek To Batu*	Giving birth to Tanek To Batu
142. *Ma bonggi Selek Lane Ai*	And giving birth to Selek Lane Ai
143. *Ruma Timu Dulu, Sepe Langga.'*	At Dawning East, Reddening Headland.'

The further progress of the two shells

The next three lines appear to be an interjection—a comment on an imagined Biblical homeland located in the Dawning East and at the Reddening Headland (Timu Dulu//Sepe Langga). Thereafter, the women Bui Len//Eno Lolo carry the shells westward to a succession of named places: 1) Deras and Le Lena, 2) Mundek and Na'u Dale, 3) Rote and Kode Ana, 4) Oe Batu and Bau Foe, 5) Kone Ama and Sai Fua, 6) Nggonggoe and Lasi Lai, and 7) Liti and Sera Dale.

144. *Neu na au ba'ing Ibrahim*	At that time my ancestor Ibrahim
145. *Ana leo numa Timu Dulu, Sepe Langga*	He lives in Timu Dulu, Sepe Langga
146. *Nusak Urkasdin.*	The Land of Urkasdin.
147. *Faik na ana ko'o nala sara*	That day she cradles them
148. *Ma na te ana ifa nala sara.*	And she lifts them.
149. *Natun kae o kae*	A hundred steps to climb and climb
150. *Ma rifun hene o hene*	And a thousand steps to mount and mount
151. *Kae, ara muri mai*	Climbing, they go to the west
152. *Hene, ara iko mai*	Mounting, they go to the tail
153. *Ara mai Deras no Le Lena*	They come to Deras and Le Lena
154. *Ara mai Mundek no Na'u Dale*	They come to Mundek and Na'u Dale
155. *Leo na, ara mai Rote no Kode Ana*	Then they come to Rote and Kode Ana
156. *Oe Batu no Bau Foe*	Oe Batu and Bau Foe
157. *Kone Ama ma Sai Fuan*	Kone Ama and Sai Fuan
158. *Ara hene, ara kona reu*	They mount, they descend
159. *Reu Nggonggoer ma reu Lasi Lai*	They go to Nggonggoe and Lasi Lai
160. *Liti ma Sera Dale.*	Liti and Sera Dale.

The conclusion of the journey of the shells

Suti Solo and Bina Bane's journey eventually takes them to a place of rest in the Heights and in the Heavens from whence their descendants (*tititin// nonosin*) continue to spread throughout the world. As in the beginning, the narrative ends with an invocation of the powers of the Heavens.

161.	*Natun kae ma rifun hene*	A hundred steps and a thousand mounts
162.	*Natun kae nai be*	One hundred steps to where
163.	*Ana mar reu suru*	The orphan goes to rest
164.	*Ma na te rifun hene nai be*	And a thousand mounts to where
165.	*Ma falu inar reu tai.*	The widow goes to cling.
166.	*Boe te Suti oen tititin*	So, Suti's water dripping [descendants]
167.	*Ma nate Bina oen nonosin*	And Bina's water droplets [descendants]
168.	*Ndule basa dae bafok ledo sa'ak*	Cover all the world and the sunlit Earth
169.	*Ki boe, kona boe*	North also and south also
170.	*Dulu boe, muri boe.*	East also and west also.
171.	*Lain bati malole*	The Heights distribute the good
172.	*Ma ata ba'e mandak*	The Heavens allocate the proper
173.	*Ruma mana parinda kisek mai a*	From them is a single rule
174.	*Numa tema sion mai*	Of the Ninefold Fullness
175.	*Numa bate falu mai ooo …*	Of Eightfold Completeness …

Recitation 5. The origin of rice and millet and of their celebration

N.D. Pah

Bole Sou ma Asa Nao

A genealogical introduction

This recitation, which bears formal similarities to the recitation *Suti Solo do Bina Bane*, begins with a genealogical introduction. It introduces the man Pasu Rama Nggeo and Hai Rama Toni, who lives in the village of

Eda Oe and *Sari Ama*, which is said to have been in the domain of Delha at the western end of Rote. Pasu Rama Nggeo and Hai Rama Toni marries the woman Ku Eo Iko and Tai Le Muri, part of whose name (Iko//Muri) indicates an identification with Delha. She gives birth to the girl Masi Pasu and Hele Hai.

1.	*Bei dalu don*	Still in a former time
2.	*Do hida fan*	Or in a bygone period
3.	*Touk Pasu Rama Nggeo*	There is the man Pasu Rama Nggeo
4.	*No taek Hai Rama Toni*	And the boy Hai Rama Toni
5.	*Ruma nggorok Eda Oe*	In the village Eda Oe
6.	*Do taduk Sari Ama.*	Or in the hamlet Sari Ama.
7.	*Pasu Rama Nggeo sao*	Pasu Rama Nggeo marries
8.	*Inak Ku Eo Iko*	The woman Ku Eo Iko
9.	*Ma Hai Rama Toni tu*	And Hai Rama Toni weds
10.	*Fetok Tai Le Muri.*	The girl Tai Le Muri.
11.	*Ku Eo Iko bonggi nala*	Ku Eo Iko gives birth to
12.	*Inak Masi Pasu*	The woman Masi Pasu
13.	*Ma Tai Le Muri rae nala*	And Tai Le Muri brings forth
14.	*Fetok Hele Hai.*	The girl Hele Hai.

The sea search to satisfy the cravings of Masi Pasu and Hele Hai

In the middle of the night, the girl Masi Pasu and Hele Hai craves fish meat and so her mother, Ku Eo Iko and Tai Le Muri, takes up her scoop net and goes to fish in her husband's fish-catch built along the coast.

15.	*Faik esa no dalen*	On one day
16.	*De ledok esa no tein*	Or at one time
17.	*Inak Masi Pasu*	The woman Masi Pasu
18.	*Ma fetok Hele Hai*	And the girl Hele Hai
19.	*Beë nai fati ladan*	Wakes in the middle of the evening
20.	*Do afe nai polo don.*	Or comes awake in the dead of night.
21.	*Masi Pasu no Hele Hai,*	Masi Pasu and Hele Hai,
22.	*Ara mada ma dudula*	They begin to have cravings
23.	*Do ara mesu ape dodoki.*	Or they start to have longings.
24.	*Ara doe sangga du'uk:*	They need and seek titbits:

25.	*Fo i'ak no mba.*	Fish and flesh.
26.	*Masi Pasu no Hele Hai*	Masi Pasu and Hele Hai
27.	*Kokolak ro ina bonggi nara*	Speak with their mother of birth
28.	*Ma dede'a ro teö tebenara,*	And talk with their true aunt,
29.	*Ina bongginara*	Their mother of birth
30.	*Fo Ku Eo Iko*	Ku Eo Iko
31.	*Ma teö tebenara*	And their true aunt
32.	*Fo Tai Le Muri.*	Tai Le Muri.
33.	*Ara ndae ndai neu arunara*	They hang the scoop net on their shoulder
34.	*Ma ara su seko neu langganara.*	And they balance the fishnet on their head.
35.	*Reu ndai tasi*	They go to fish in the Sea
36.	*Ma reu seko meti*	And go to scoop in the tide
37.	*Nai meti malole*	In the good low tide
38.	*Ma mada mandan.*	And in the fine ebb tide.
39.	*Inak Ku Eo Iko*	The woman Ku Eo Iko
40.	*Ma fetok Tai Le Muri*	And the girl Tai Le Muri
41.	*Reu dongge deak*	They go to scan the fish-catch
42.	*Ma reu tiro luti,*	And go to spy the seawall,
43.	*Fo Pasu Rama Nggeo dean*	Pasu Rama Nggeo's fish-catch
44.	*Ma Hai Rama Toni lutun*	And Hai Rama Toni's seawall
45.	*Nai Eda Oe Dae Samben*	At Eda Oe's level land
46.	*Do Sari Ama Oe Lenun.*	Or Sari Ama's calm waters.

The scoop-net catch of the crab and sea snail, Bole Sou and Asa Nao

There at the fish-catch, they scoop up the crab Bole Sou and the sea snail Asa Nao, who appear so threatening that at first Ku Eo Iko and Tai Le Muri are afraid, but Bole Sou and Asa Nao ask to be scooped up, taken home and planted.

47.	*Neu faik na dalen*	On that day
48.	*Do ledok na tein*	Or at that time
49.	*Pasu Rama Nggeo dean*	Pasu Rama Nggeo's fish-catch
50.	*Ma Hai Rama Toni lutun*	And Hai Rama Toni's seawall
51.	*Rama ngge rala*	They scoop up
52.	*Ni Bole Sou*	The crab Bole Sou

53.	*Ma ngguma Asa Nao.*	And the sea snail Asa Nao.
54.	*Ni Bole Sou*	The crab Bole Sou
55.	*Ana huhu'a tanan*	He opens his pincers
56.	*Na isa'a idu ai*	Showing the ridge of his nose
57.	*Ma ngguma Asa Nao*	And the sea snail Asa Nao
58.	*Ana beberu nggeten*	He sticks out his foot
59.	*Na indete mata boa.*	Flashing his eyes.
60.	*Inak Ku Eo Iko*	The woman Ku Eo Iko
61.	*Ma fetok Tai Le Muri*	And the girl Tai Le Muri
62.	*Pau nara maniri*	Their thighs grow cold
63.	*Ma husen nara mumuru.*	And their navels become giddy.
64.	*Ara tulek rala bala duan*	They [want] to turn and go back
65.	*Ma hai rala lolo falin,*	And they [want] to halt and return,
66.	*Uma reu.*	To go home.
67.	*Ni Bole Sou*	The crab Bole Sou
68.	*No ngguma Asa Nao*	And the sea snail Asa Nao
69.	*Ara hua bafanara*	They open their mouth
70.	*Ma ara silu nolinara*	And they bare their teeth
71.	*Kokolak ro Ku Eo Iko*	To speak with Ku Eo Iko
72.	*Ma dede'a ro Tai Le Muri:*	And to talk with Tai Le Muri:
73.	*'Keko seu mai fa*	'Come and pick us up
74.	*Ma hiru henda mai bauk*	Approach and lift us up
75.	*Fo soro mininggai*	Fish us up
76.	*Ma ndai mininggai dei.*	And scoop us up then.
77.	*Miu sele do tande ai*	Go, plant and sow us
78.	*Miu lutu nasu*	Beside your cooking stones
79.	*Ma fara tana*	And your doorstep
80.	*Fo fua dae*	For you to turn the earth
81.	*Ma toli oe ai dei.'*	And pour water, too.'

Bole Sou and Asa Nao are gathered and planted

Ku Eo Iko and Tai Le Muri do as they were instructed. They gather Bole
Sou and Asa Nao and plant them. They tend them and water them and,
in three days, they sprout forth, becoming rice and millet.

82.	*Ku Eo Iko no Tai Le Muri*	Ku Eo Iko and Tai Le Muri
83.	*Soro reni*	Fish and carry away

84. *Ni Bole Sou*	The crab Bole Sou
85. *Ma ngguma Asa Nao.*	And the sea snail Asa Nao.
86. *Ara sele sara*	They plant them
87. *Ma ara tande sara*	And they sow them
88. *Reu lutu nasu*	Beside the cooking stones
89. *Ma faratana.*	And the doorstep.
90. *Ara fua dae sara*	They turn the earth on them
91. *Ma ara toli oe sara.*	And they pour water on them.
92. *Tada ledok telu*	Then in three days [suns]
93. *Do sodak fai ha*	Or in four days
94. *Boe ma ara mori mai*	They grow up
95. *Ma ara sadu mai,*	And they sprout forth,
96. *Rakale dua*	With two grain heads
97. *Ma rambule telu*	And with three seed buds
98. *Reni ngge hade*	Bearing rice grain
99. *Ma bini betek.*	And the millet seed.

The harvest of the first grains and the spread of these seeds

Ku Eo Iko and Tai Le Muri harvest these first grains and set out to plant them in other fields, beginning at *Beu Bolu* and *Le'a So'o* and then at *Landu Kona* and *Tena Serik*, where they multiply.

100. *Inak Ku Eo Iko*	The woman Ku Eo Iko
101. *No fetok Tai Le Muri*	And the girl Tai Le Muri
102. *Koru reni*	Pluck and carry them away
103. *Ngge hade kale duan*	The two heads of the rice grain
104. *Ma bini betek pule telun.*	And the three buds of millet seed.
105. *Reu sele ma tande sara*	They go to plant and sow them
106. *Reu omba hade malole*	In a good wet rice field
107. *Ma lane betek mandak ara,*	And in a fine dry millet field,
108. *Ruma Beu Bolu ma Le'a So'o.*	At Beu Bolu and Le'a So'o.
109. *Ngge hade rama no'u*	The rice grains grow numerous
110. *Ma bini betek rama hefu.*	And the millet seeds grow bountiful.
111. *Koru rala ngge hade*	They pluck the rice grain
112. *Ma ketu rala bini betek*	And they cut the millet seed

113. *Ruma Beu Bolu ma Le'a So'o.*	At Beu Bolu and at Le'a So'o.
114. *Reu tande*	They go to sow
115. *Ma reu sele sara*	And they go to plant them
116. *Ruma Landu Kona do Tena Serik.*	At Landu Kona or at Tena Serik.
117. *Ara soru Landu ngge hade*	They welcome the rice grain of Landu
118. *Ma ara tefa Tena bini betek*	And they greet the millet seed of Tena
119. *Ruma Landu Kona do Tena Serik*	At Landu Kona or at Tena Serik
120. *No neme hokok ma netedalek.*	With joy and gladness.

The first origin ceremonies are held and the seeds spread throughout Rote

At *Landu Kona* and *Tena Serik* in Thie, they hold the first rice and millet origin ceremonies (*Holi//Limba*) and, from there, these seeds are spread throughout the island of Rote to the west and to the east.

121. *Ara tao holi hade*	There they perform the rice-origin *Holi*
122. *Ma limba betek numa na.*	And the millet-origin *Limba*.
123. *Ngge hade iti*	This rice grain
124. *Puru pate hade*	Increases in the wet fields
125. *Ma bini betek iti*	And this millet seed
126. *Nggari lena tine.*	Becomes further scattered in dry fields.
127. *Ngge hade reu sele sara*	The rice grain they go and plant
128. *Ma bini betek reu tande sara*	And the millet seed they go and sow
129. *Basa dae ma oer,*	In all the lands and waters,
130. *Ndule nusak ma inggur*	Through the domains and territories
131. *Noü nggorokara*	In every village
132. *Ma basa tadukara.*	And in all the hamlets.
133. *Reni ngge hade ma bini betek*	They carry the rice grain and millet seed
134. *Timu Dulu reu*	To the Dawning East

135.	*Ma Sepe Langga reu.*	And to Reddening Headland.
136.	*Ara tande sara*	They sow them
137.	*Ma ara sele sara*	And they plant them
138.	*Ruma Dulu Oen*	In Eastern Waters
139.	*Ma Langga Daen.*	And in Head Lands.
140.	*Ngge hade no bini betek*	The rice grain and the millet seed
141.	*Reni sara Muri do Iko reu bali.*	They also carry them to the West or Tail.
142.	*Ara sele sara*	They plant them
143.	*Ma ara tande sara*	And they sow them
144.	*Ruma Muri Loloe Olin*	In the West Descending to the Estuary
145.	*Do Iko Beku-te Tasin.*	Or at the Tail Bending to the Sea.
146.	*Ngge hade no bini betek*	Rice grains and the millet seeds
147.	*Momori dadadin numa letek*	Have grown and flourished from that time
148.	*Na mai nduku ledo faikara ia.*	Until this day [and] this moment.

Recitation 6. The origin of the grains and seeds and of their celebration

Jonas Mooy

Suti Solo Liun do Bina Bane Sain

Suti Solo and Bina Bane's arrival at the Reef's base and the Sea's edge

A storm drives Suti Solo, the nautilus shell, and Bina Bane, the baler shell, from the Ocean's depths and carries them to a reef at the edge of the Sea.

1.	*Bei hida fan na*	At a time long ago
2.	*Ma bei dalu don na*	And in an age long past
3.	*Lurik neu nala liun*	A cyclone strikes the Ocean's depths
4.	*Ma sanggu neu tao sain.*	And a storm strikes the Sea's depths.
5.	*Te inak ia Suti Solo sain*	The woman Suti Solo of the Sea
6.	*Ma fetok ia Bina Bane liun*	And the girl Bina Bane of the Ocean

7.	*Ara rama roko isi*	They exude their insides
8.	*Ma ara rama ketu nggi.*	And they cut their pods.
9.	*De rama tani sira nggin nara*	They cry for their pods
10.	*Ma rasa kedu sira isin nara*	And they sob for their insides
11.	*Ruma posi pedan ma unuk hun.*	At the Sea's edge and reef's base.
12.	*Tehu ina mana-adu lolek*	There is the woman who creates beautifully
13.	*Ma feto mana-doki ladak.*	And the girl who designs wonderfully.
14.	*De rama tani unuk hun*	They cry at the reef's base
15.	*Ma bele halu posi pedan.*	And they are sad at the Sea's edge.

Lutu Koe and Rema Ko encounter the shells while scoop-net fishing along the shore

The next lines introduce the women (alluded to in lines 12–13) Lutu Koe and Rema Ko, who scoop in the Sea and fish in the tide. They hear the shells calling and are told of their sad condition. The shells beg to be scooped up and placed on the edge of the shore.

16.	*Boe ma neu faik ia dalen*	Then on a particular day
17.	*Ma ledok ia tein*	And at a certain time
18.	*Feto mana-ndai tasi*	The girl who scoops in the Sea
19.	*Fetok nade Lutu Koe*	The girl named Lutu Koe
20.	*Boema inak mana-seko meti*	And the woman who fishes in the tide
21.	*Inak nade Rema Ko*	The woman named Rema Ko
22.	*Ara su seko neu langgan*	They rest the fishnet on their heads
23.	*Ma ara ndae ndai neu arun.*	And they hang the scoop net on their shoulders.
24.	*De ara loe mada loak reu*	They descend to the wide drying area
25.	*Ma ara loe meti naruk reu*	And they descend to the long tidal area
26.	*Ara losa posi pedan ma unuk hun.*	They arrive at the Sea's edge and reef's base.
27.	*Boema ara rama-nene dasik kara ra-nggou*	They hear a voice shouting
28.	*Ma harakara haru kara ralo'o.*	And they discern a tongue calling.

29.	*Dua de'a-de'a dua*	The two speak with one another
30.	*Ma telu kola-kola telu:*	And the three talk with each other:
31.	*'Ai mama ketu nggi*	'We have cut our pods
32.	*Ma ai mama roko isi ia*	And exuded our insides
33.	*De ai mamatani ai nggi*	We are crying for our pods
34.	*Ma ai masakedu ai isin ia.*	And sobbing for our insides.
35.	*Hu sanggu ana tao ai*	A storm has done this to us
36.	*Ma lurik ana tao ai.*	And a cyclone has done this to us.
37.	*De torano dua nggarene*	My two relatives
38.	*Ma takadena dua nggarene,*	And my two companions,
39.	*Mai ndai tasi mini ai*	Come fish us from the Sea
40.	*Ma seko meti mini ai dei*	And scoop us from the tide
41.	*Mbeda ai miu nembe hun dei*	Place us at the shore's edge
42.	*Ma tao ai miu oli su'un dei.'*	And put us at the estuary's mouth.'

The shells are scooped up and placed near two trees at the edge of the estuary

The women agree to scoop up the shells and place them near two trees (in Rotenese: an *ai-sauk* and a *lenggu haik*) growing along the shore. The shells ask that the women come back and visit them at their resting place.

43.	*Boe ma dua sara rahik rala.*	So, the two agree.
44.	*Ara seko meti reni sara*	They fish them up
45.	*Ma ara ndai tasi reni sara*	And they scoop them up
46.	*Tehu bei ra-ndeni aru*	But they are heavy on the shoulder
47.	*Ma bei ra-ta'a langga*	And weighty on the head
48.	*De ara losa nembe hun*	They come to the shore's edge
49.	*Ma oli su'un [bifin].*	And to the estuary's mouth.
50.	*Boema ara dua de'a-de'a dua ma rae:*	The two speak with each other and say:
51.	*'Ela ei mai ia leo*	'Let us set you here
52.	*Boema ai mbeda ei mai ia leo.*	Let us place you here.
53.	*Tehu ai helu ela ei duangga*	But we promise you two
54.	*Ai fedu ai sauk neu*	We will bend the *ai sauk* tree
55.	*Ma tumbu lenggu ha'ik neu*	And we load the *lenggu-haik* tree
56.	*De ama rada mai ia leo*	That you may lean here
57.	*Ma ama tia mai ia leo.'*	And that you may attach here.'

58.	*Boe ma rae:*	So, they say:
59.	*'Ei ela ai duangga mai ia*	'If you leave the two of us here
60.	*Do tehu, mai la'o ladi ai dei*	Do still come, stop and see us
61.	*Ma mai lope tule ai dei*	And come, swing past and visit us
62.	*Tehu ai mai bengga lada mbeda*	For we have nourishment indeed
63.	*Ma ai mai tou lole heu ia.*	And we have clothing indeed here.
64.	*Ai tu'u sara sira*	We can hold ourselves here
65.	*Ai mbeda sara sira*	We can place ourselves here
66.	*Ara reu de ara losa uma.'*	When you leave and return to your house.'
67.	*Boe ma ara ramanene*	They listen
68.	*Ara raka-se'e bebenggu*	They are noises as horses' bells
69.	*Ma ara raka-doto kokoro*	And they are as lively as *kokoro* birds
70.	*Numa olik su'un ma nembe hun.*	At the edge of the estuary and shore's base.

The founding ancestors Tola Mesa and Le'e Lunu encounter Suti Solo and Bina Bane

The ancestral founders of Thie, Tola Mesa and Le'e Lunu, go to see what has happened after the storm. They arm themselves but encounter only the two shells, who plead with them not to fire their flintlocks or draw their swords. The shells ask to be wrapped in cloth and taken to the house.

71.	*Boe ma bai ia baing Tola Mesa*	Our grandfather of grandfathers Tola Mesa
72.	*Ma ai soro ia sorong Le'e Lunu*	And our ancestor of ancestors Le'e Lunu
73.	*Ara hengge bosan nara reu*	They tie their waist belt
74.	*De ara ndae tafa nara reu.*	And they hang their sword.
75.	*De rae fama kate*	They then consider
76.	*Lurik mai tao sira*	The cyclone comes to strike them
77.	*Do sanggu mai tao sira*	And the storm comes to strike them
78.	*De reu mete ma reu suri.*	They go to look and go to see.
79.	*Reu de ara sudi sira su'u reu sara*	They go, fire their flintlocks
80.	*Ma ara ndae tafa dale reu sara*	And they draw out their swords
81.	*Ara rahara ma rae:*	They answer and say:
82.	*'Boso sudi sira su'u ai*	'Don't fire your flintlocks at us

83.	*Ma boso ndae tafa dale ai*	And don't draw your swords at us
84.	*Te ai mini lole heu rai ia*	For we bring fine attire here
85.	*Ma ai mini lada mbeda rai ia.*	And we bring delicious food here.
86.	*De ei lai ai*	Have sympathy for us
87.	*Boe ma ei sue ai boe.*	And have care for us.
88.	*Na pa'a pou su'u mini ai dei*	Wrap a sarong and take us
89.	*Ma hengge bosa dale mini ai dei*	Tie a waistband and take us
90.	*Miu ndae ai miu fara tanar dei*	Hang us on the doorpost
91.	*Ma mbeda ai miu lulutu nasun dei.'*	And place us on the fence's base.'

The ancestors are instructed to plant the 'rock and tree' for the origin ceremony

The shells instruct Tola Mesa and Le'e Lunu to take up a flat stone from the harbour and cut a tree from near the shore and bring them, along with the shells, to become the focus for the origin feast. These ritual instructions result in the creation of the 'coconut-holding post' for the origin celebration.

92.	*'Boe ma bai-ia baing Tola Mesa*	'So, my grandfather of grandfathers Tola Mesa
93.	*Ma soro ia sorong Le'e Lunu rae*	And my ancestor of ancestors Le'e Lunu
94.	*Mete ma leonak*	If this is so, then
95.	*Na ma hehere fo ita la'o*	Fold it so that we may go
96.	*Do ma bebenda fo ita la'o.'*	Or save it so that we may go.'
97.	*Ara pa'a pou su'u reu sara*	They wrap a woman's sarong around them
98.	*Ma ara mboti lafa una neu sara*	And they fold a man's cloth around them
99.	*Ma ara ra selu reu sara rae:*	They reply, saying:
100.	*'Mete ma ei pa'a pou*	'If you wrap the sarong
101.	*Ma hengge bosa meni ai*	And strap the pouch to take us
102.	*Na tati ai nia nembe dei*	Then cut the tree near the shore
103.	*Ma ei hengge bosa muni ai*	And strap the pouch to take us
104.	*Na ko'o batu bela namo dei*	Cradle a flat stone by the harbour
105.	*Fo mu tian neu tu'u batu*	Balance it as a resting stone
106.	*Ma ama fara neu rai ai*	And plant it as a standing pole
107.	*Fo ai masa-rai dei*	For us to lean upon

108. *Ma ai mangga-tu'u dei*	And for us to rest upon
109. *Boe ma ama sau leli sara dei*	So we may comb ourselves gently
110. *Ma ama tusi bangga na'us sara dei.'*	And we may rub ourselves softly.'
111. *Boe ma ko'o reni batu bela namo*	So, they cradle a flat stone from the harbour
112. *De reu de ara tao neu tu'u batu*	They go and make it a resting stone
113. *De ana dadi neu oli do limba*	To be used for an origin and harvest ceremony
114. *Boe ma ara ha'i rala ai nia nembe*	And they take a tree from the shore
115. *De ara fara no tu'u batu*	They plant it with the resting stone
116. *De ana dadi neu rai ai*	To make it a leaning post
117. *Fo dadi neu fara no.*	To become the coconut-holding post.

A celebration is held to bring the rains and prepare the earth for planting

The first ritual celebration is held. It centres on the coconut that brings the rains and prepares the earth for the planting of seeds. When, after the ceremony, the rains have fallen, the shells give instructions for their own planting at particular named fields.

118. *De ara hene Tola Mesa non*	They climb Tola Mesa's coconut
119. *Ma ketu Le'e Lunu non*	And they pluck Le'e Lunu's coconut
120. *De ara leli sau neu sara.*	They soften and cool them.
121. *Boe ma ara bamba lololo neu sara*	They beat the drum steadily
122. *De ana ba'e dinis mai dae*	It distributes the dew upon the earth
123. *Ma ana bati udan mai lane.*	And it allots the rain upon the fields.
124. *Boe ma rae:*	So, they [the shells] say:
125. *'Udan dai dae ena*	'If the rain is sufficient for the earth
126. *Ma dinis konda lane ena*	And the dew falls upon the fields
127. *Tehu ai mini bini buik nai ia*	Then we bring the basic grains with us here

128. *Ma mbule sio nai ia.*	And the nine seeds with us here.
129. *De mete-ma ei mai pake do hambu*	If you want to use them and have them
130. *Na keko seluk ai dei*	Then move us again
131. *Ma lali seluk ai dei*	And shift us again
132. *Fo ela neu lada mbeda*	To become delicious food
133. *Ma ela neu lole heu.*	And become fine attire.
134. *De mete ma ei mae leo nak*	If you agree to this
135. *Na keko ai miu*	Then move us
136. *Fafa'e Tali Somba dei*	To Fafa'e Tali Somba
137. *Fo tande ai miu na*	To plant us there
138. *Boema lali ai miu*	And shift us
139. *Teke Me Re'ik Oen dei*	To Teke Me Re'ik Oen
140. *Fo sele ai miu na.'*	To sow us there.'

The planting of the seeds begins in fields in Thie and thereafter throughout Rote

In accordance with the instructions from the shells, the planting is begun and the seeds sprout. The first fields in Thie where the seeds are planted are *Fafa'e Tali Somba* and *Teke Me Re'ik Oen* and *Mundek Na'u Dale* and *Nggonggoer No Lasi Lain*. Thereafter these plants spread throughout Rote. The composite placename *Ledo So'u//Anda Iko* ('Sun's Rise'//'Land's Tail') indicates an area that extends across the island from the east to the west, while the placename *Pena Pua//Rene Kona* connotes an area from the north to the south of Rote. These appear to be placenames purposely created to cover the whole of the island. Orphans and widows are the ones to consume the harvest of rice and millet.

141. *Ara sele neu*	They sow them
142. *Fafa'e Tali Somba*	At Fafa'e Tali Somba
143. *Ma ara tande neu*	And they plant them
144. *Teke Me Re'ik Oen.*	At Teke Me Re'ik Oen.
145. *Boe ma ara do dua*	They form two leaves
146. *Ma ara beba telu*	And form three stalks
147. *De mbule na tatali*	Seeds with sprouts
148. *Ma don na sese'i*	And leaves with spikes
149. *Boe ma ara dadi reu lada mbeda*	They become delicious food
150. *Ma ara moli reu lole heu.*	And they turn into fine attire.

151. *Boe ma ara keko neu*	They move them
152. *Mundek Na'u Dale*	To Mundek Na'u Dale
153. *Boema ara lali neu*	They shift them
154. *Nggonggoer No Lasi Lain.*	To Nggonggoer No Lasi Lain.
155. *De ana ndule losa Ledo So'u*	It spreads to Ledo So'u
156. *Ma ana losa nala Anda Iko*	And to Anda Iko
157. *Ki losa Pena Pua*	North to Pena Pua
158. *Ma kona losa Rene Kona.*	And south to Rene Kona.
159. *De ana mar ara fati hade*	The orphans consume rice
160. *Ma ina falur ra ara hao bete*	And the widows eat millet
161. *Ela lole heur bali*	Enjoy fine attire
162. *Ma lada mbeda bali.*	And delicious food.

The perpetuation of the Limba ceremony in Thie

The next stage in this recitation recounts the establishment of a continuing origin ceremony. A sacred space is created around a 'sitting stone and standing tree' where there is dancing and the beating of drums and gongs to bring down cooling rain on the earth. Although initially rice and millet are the crops said to be planted, the chant expands its designation of what is planted, referring to 'the nine seeds and the basic grains, the nine children of Laka Mola'. This is a ritual designation for all the seeds that Rotenese plant in their fields.

163. *De ara tia neu tu'u batu*	They create a sitting stone
164. *De ara tao neni rai ai*	They make a standing tree
165. *De mete ma fain na-nda*	So that when the day comes
166. *Ma ledo na-tetu*	And the time arrives
167. *Na ha'i nala babamba mba'u bibi rouk*	They take a drum sounding with goat's skin
168. *No meko riti fani oen*	And a gong whose beat is sweet as bees' honey
169. *Fo mu lutu mbatu lain*	To mount on top of piled stones
170. *Fo bamba mbaun kurudo*	To drum with a begging sound
171. *Ma dali sole hara doe*	And dance with a requesting voice
172. *Ma lo neu Mana Adu Lain*	Calling on the Creator of the Heaven
173. *Fo Mana Adu Deti Ledo*	The Creator who shaped the Sun

174. *Ma Mana Sura Ndu Bulan*	And who drew the Stars and Moon
175. *Ma lo neu Mana Adu Lalai*	Calling to the Creator Above
176. *Ma dae bafok*	For the surface of the Earth
177. *Tasi oe no isin*	The Sea with its contents
178. *Ma hatahori do andiana*	Mankind and humankind
179. *Fo ana monu fei*	To let fall
180. *Ha'u dini makasufuk*	A gentle damping dew
181. *Ma uda oe makarinik*	And cooling rainwater
182. *Fo ana tolite batu poik*	To pour upon the World
183. *Ma ana bibiru dae bafak.*	And to cool the Earth.
184. *Boe ma ana totoli laner*	It pours upon the rice fields
185. *Ma ana tete tiner*	And it drips down upon the dry fields
186. *Fo tande Mpule Sio neun*	To plant the Nine Seeds
187. *Ma sele Bini Bui'k neun.*	And sow the Basic Grains.
188. *Fo Laka Mola anan sio.*	The nine children of Laka Mola.
189. *Fo ela leo be na*	So, it is thus
190. *Ara rabuna fefeo*	They carry flowers that wind round
191. *Na ra fefeo rifuk*	Wind a thousandfold
192. *Na deta leo rifu ana tali do*	Like a thousand winding cords
193. *Boe ara rambule roroso*	They set seeds that spread round
194. *Na ra roroso natu*	Spread round a hundredfold
195. *Na leo natu ana bolao.*	Like a hundred tiny spiders.
196. *Fo ha'i malan fo mu'a*	Take them to eat
197. *Fo tengga malan fo pake*	Grab them to use
198. *Ma lo neu falu inar*	And provide for the widows
199. *Fo ita tesik be na*	For those of us present
200. *Teik esa ma dalek esa*	One stomach and one heart
201. *Boe ma ita hambu lada mbeda*	So we have delicious food
202. *Ma lole heu*	And fine clothing
203. *Tuda ma monu mai dae bafok*	Fallen and descended on the Earth
204. *Boe ma lenak Rote Ndao.*	Particularly on Rote-Ndao.

Recitation 7. The origin of the celebration at Nasi Dano

N.D. Pah

Masi Dande ma Solo Suti

The marriage of Nggeni Sor and Rote Namba with Masi Dande and Solo Suti

This recitation sets out to explain the origin of the celebration of the *Hus Torombo* or *Hus Nasi Dano* that was previously performed by the clan Bibi Manu in Desa Oebo. In the ritual language of Termanu, this celebration would be referred to as as a *Hu* or *Sio* (a celebration of 'Origin' or a celebration of 'Nine'). In the ritual language of Thie, this kind of celebration is called a *Holi* or *Limba*.

The narrative begins by introducing the man Nggeni Soru and Rote Namba, who marries the woman Masi Dande and Solo Suti. Nggeni Soru and Rote Namba are goldsmiths, as are most of the men of Ndao, whose ritual name is given here as *Ndao Nuse//Folo Manu*. They sail off to *Sina Kona* and *Koli Muri* to forge iron and beat gold. The name *Sina Kona* and *Koli Muri* ('Sina of the South'//'Koli of the West') indicates a Chinese settlement—possibly Atapupu—on the coast of Timor.

1.	*Dalu bei don-na*	In a former period
2.	*Ma hida bei fa-na*	And in a past time
3.	*Ina Ili Alo nan*	The woman Ili Alo's brother
4.	*Nggeni Soru*	Nggeni Soru
5.	*Ma feto Lo Fando na.*	And the girl Lo Fando's brother
6.	*Rote Namba*	Rote Namba
7.	*Ara leo ruma Ndao Nuse*	They live on Ndao Nuse
8.	*Do Folo Manu.*	And on Folo Manu.
9.	*Touk Nggeni Soru*	The man Nggeni Soru
10.	*Sao inak Masi Dande*	Marries the woman Masi Dande
11.	*Ma [ta'ek] Rote Namba*	And [the boy] Rote Namba
12.	*Tu fetok Solo Suti.*	Weds the girl Solo Suti.
13.	*Nggeni Soru*	Nggeni Soru
14.	*Ma Rote Namba*	And Rote Namba

15.	*Touk manatutu besi*	A man who forges iron
16.	*Ma ta'ek manambesa lilo.*	And a boy who beats gold.
17.	*Nggeni Soru*	Nggeni Soru
18.	*No Rote Namba*	And Rote Namba
19.	*Sa'e rala tonda nara*	Climb onboard their boat
20.	*Ma daka rala balu nara;*	And mount onboard their perahu;
21.	*Reni Sina Kona [reu]*	Towards Sina Kona
22.	*Do Koli Muri [reu]*	And Koli Muri
23.	*Reu tutu besi*	They go to forge iron
24.	*Ma reu mbesa lilo.*	And they go to beat gold.
25.	*Nggeni Soru*	Nggeni Soru
26.	*No Rote Namba*	And Rote Namba
27.	*La'o ela sao-nara*	Walk off leaving their wife
28.	*Ma ara lope ela tu-nara,*	And they go off leaving their spouse,
29.	*Masi Dande*	Masi Dande
30.	*No Solo Suti.*	And Solo Suti.

Fingga Fiti and Mbasa Mbaku are called to sing at a Holi celebration

While Nggeni Soru and Rote Namba are away, a *Holi//Limba* ceremony is held at *Tedale Dilu Oen* and *Korobako Lepa Daen*. Chanters are called to come to perform but the celebration does not become lively until Fingga Fiti and Mbasa Mbaku are called from *Turumbou//Korobeba*.

31.	*Neu lelek Nggeni Soru*	While Nggeni Soru
32.	*No Rote Namba*	And Rote Namba
33.	*Bei rai Sina Kona*	Are still in Sina Kona
34.	*Ma Koli Muri*	And Koli Muri
35.	*Ara tao Holi hade*	They hold the *Holi* feast for rice
36.	*Ma [ara ladi] Limba betek*	And the *Limba* feast for millet
37.	*Numa Tedale Dilu Oen*	At Tedale Dilu Oen
38.	*Ma Korbako Lepa Daen.*	And Korbako Lepa Daen.
39.	*Basa manahelo reu helo*	All the chanters go to chant
40.	*Ma manasoda reu soda,*	And [all] the singers go to sing,
41.	*Te Holi ta rakase*	But the *Holi* feast is not lively
42.	*Ma Limba ta rakadoto.*	And the *Limba* feast is not noisy.
43.	*Reu rala Fingga Fiti*	They call Fingga Fiti

44.	*No Mbasa Mbaku*	And Mbasa Mbaku
45.	*Ruma Turumbou [oen]*	At Turumbou
46.	*Ma Korobeba [dae]*	And Korobeba
47.	*Mai soda Holi*	To come to sing the *Holi*
48.	*Ma helo Limba*	And to chant the *Limba*
49.	*Fo rakase*	That it may be lively
50.	*Ma rakadoto dei.*	And that it may be noisy, too.

Fingga Fiti and Mbasa Mbaku's beautiful singing entices Masi Dande and Solo Suti

Fingga Fiti and Mbasa Mbaku sing beautifully, so beautifully that their voice penetrates the heart and so loudly that their song carries across the straits all the way to Ndao. Their singing drives Masi Dande//Solo Suti to distraction as they try to sleep.

51.	*Fingga Fiti*	Fingga Fiti
52.	*No Mbasa Mbaku*	And Mbasa Mbaku
53.	*Ara soda tutuda dasin-na*	They sing, letting fall their words
54.	*Leo manu ratuda tolo*	Like a hen dropping an egg
55.	*Ma ara helo o'olu hara-na*	And they chant, shedding forth their voice
56.	*Leo mengge raolu rou.*	Like a snake shedding its skin.
57.	*Fingga Fiti*	Fingga Fiti
58.	*No Mbasa Mbaku*	And Mbasa Mbaku
59.	*Hara-nara ramaladi tasi*	Their voice crosses the sea
60.	*Ma [dasi nara] randoro le*	And goes beyond the river
61.	*Nduku Ndao Nuse*	Towards Ndao Nuse
62.	*Do [losa] Folo Manu.*	And [to] Folo Manu.
63.	*Dua sara hara-nara*	Their two voices
64.	*Ma dasi-nara*	And their words
65.	*Randoro tei dale*	Penetrate the inner heart
66.	*Ma randoro hena hu.*	And penetrate the upper thigh.
67.	*Masi Dande*	Masi Dande
68.	*No Solo Suti*	And Solo Suti
69.	*Rama-nene harak*	Hear the voice
70.	*Fo Fingga Fiti haran*	Fingga Fiti's voice
71.	*Ma [rama-nene] dasik*	And the words
72.	*Fo Mbasa Mbaku dasin.*	Mbasa Mbaku's words.

73.	*Boe-ma ara sunggu*	As they sleep
74.	*Langga nara fua-fua*	Their heads are lifted
75.	*Ma ara ne'i*	And as they lie
76.	*Tei nara kedi-kedi.*	Their hearts are distracted.
77.	*Ara nau tungga do sangga*	They want to seek or follow
78.	*Se dasin do se harana.*	Whose words or voice they hear.

Masi Dande and Solo Suti sail from Ndao to seek out Fingga Fiti and Mbasa Mbaku

Masi Dande and Solo Suti pick a large cluster of areca nuts and the stalks of the betel catkin, indicating their intention to exchange and chew betel and areca as a prelude to making love. They then board a boat, sail through the straits of *Loe Keli* and *Lolo Dengga* and arrive in the harbour of *Dela Muri* and *Anda Kona* at the south-western end of the island of Rote.

79.	*Masi Dande*	Masi Dande
80.	*No Solo Suti*	And Solo Suti
81.	*Ara seu sesena pua nara*	They pick a cluster of areca nuts
82.	*Fo pua manggi hu nara*	Areca nuts with inflorescences like trunks
83.	*Ma ketu ramale malu nara*	And break stalks of betel catkin
84.	*Fo malu maboa oka nara.*	Betel with catkin like thick roots.
85.	*Dua sara sa'e rala balu mbao nara*	The two climb onboard their ship and perahu
86.	*Ma daka rala tonda ufa nara.*	And mount aboard their boat and craft.
87.	*Ara lena ri Loe Keli*	They transverse the waves of Loe Keli
88.	*Ma ara sida epo Lolo Dengga.*	And they pass the eddies of Lolo Dengga.
89.	*Masi Dande*	Masi Dande
90.	*No Solo Suti*	And Solo Suti's
91.	*Balu do tonda*	Ship and boat
92.	*Nara se numa namo Dela Muri*	Lays anchor in Dela Muri's harbour
93.	*Do meti Anda Kona.*	And Anda Kona's tide.

Masi Dande and Solo Suti meet Seu Dela and Fale Anda on Delha's coast

On Delha's coast they meet the woman Seu Dela and Fale Anda, who asks them where they are hastening so hurriedly. They say they are going to pick *kapok* and cut *gewang* at *Oe He* and *Oe Tenggai*. Seu Dela and Fale Anda propose that they go together, pointing to the dangers of picking *kapok* and cutting *gewang* at *Oe He* and *Oe Tenggai* because it is well guarded. Overcome by the singing of Fingga Fiti and Mbasa Mbaku, Masi Dande and Solo Suti leave Seu Dela and Fale Anda and continue on their way.

94.	*Masi Dande*	Masi Dande
95.	*No Solo Suti*	And Solo Suti
96.	*Ratonggo do randa ro*	Meet and encounter
97.	*Inak Seu Dela*	The woman Seu Dela
98.	*Ma fetok Fale Anda.*	And the girl Fale Anda.
99.	*Inak Seu Dela*	The woman Seu Dela
100.	*No fetok Fale Anda*	And the girl Fale Anda
101.	*Hu'a bafanara ratane*	Open their mouth to ask
102.	*Neu Masi Dande*	Masi Dande
103.	*No Solo Suti, rae:*	And Solo Suti, saying:
104.	*'Ei la'ok be miu*	'Where are you walking
105.	*Ma ei lope be miu?*	And where are you going?
106.	*Ei la'ok no hae-lain*	You walk so rapidly
107.	*Ma lope no tende-tun.'*	And you go so quickly.'
108.	*Masi Dande*	Masi Dande
109.	*No Solo Suti*	And Solo Suti
110.	*Selu lole rala hara nara*	Raise and lift their voices
111.	*Ma a'e fino rala dasi nara, rae:*	And speak these words, saying:
112.	*'Ai miu seu dene*	'We are going to pick *kapok*
113.	*Nai Oe He*	At Oe He
114.	*Ma ai miu tati tula*	And we are going to cut *gewang*
115.	*Nai Oe Tenggai.'*	At Oe Tenggai.'
116.	*Seu Dela*	Seu Dela
117.	*No Fale Anda*	And Fale Anda
118.	*Rafada neu Masi Dande*	Speak to Masi Dande
119.	*No Solo Suti, rae:*	And to Solo Suti, saying:
120.	*'Mai ata seu dene*	'Come let us pick *kapok*
121.	*Taka-bua kada ia*	Together there

122.	*Ma ata tati tula*	And let us cut *gewang*
123.	*Ta-esa kada ia.'*	As a group there.'
124.	*Seu Dela*	Seu Dela
125.	*No Fale Anda*	And Fale Anda
126.	*Rakola do radea*	Talk and converse
127.	*Seluk bali*	Once more and again
128.	*Ro Masi Dande*	With Masi Dande
129.	*Ma Solo Suti, rae:*	And with Solo Suti, saying:
130.	*'Seu dene Oe He*	'If you pick Oe He *kapok*
131.	*Do tati tula Oe Tenggai*	And cut Oe Tenggai *gewang*
132.	*Na masa-nenedak*	You must remember this
133.	*Ma mafa-rerendek.*	And keep this in mind.
134.	*Te refada rae*	For they speak and say that
135.	*Oe He Molek Oen*	At Oe He Molek Oen
136.	*Ara mole mila rahani*	They prepare bamboo spikes in wait
137.	*Ma Oe Tenggai Sirok Daen*	And at Oe Tenggai Sirok Daen
138.	*Ara siro sese ranea.*	They shoot to guard [the place].
139.	*Metema ei mae seu dene Oe He*	If you want to pick Oe He *kapok*
140	*Ma tati tula Oe Tenggai,*	And cut Oe Tenggai *gewang*,
141.	*Na ama memete*	You must watch
142.	*Do susuri matalolole dei*	And guard carefully
143.	*Te ta na, muti matam leo dene*	If not, your eyes will turn white as *kapok*
144.	*Ma fula idum leo tula.'*	And your nose as pallid as *gewang*.'
145.	*Hu Fingga Fiti*	Fingga Fiti
146.	*No Mbasa Mbaku*	And Mbasa Mbaku
147.	*Hara do dasi nara*	Their voice or words
148.	*Boe reu randoro*	Go and penetrate
149.	*Do rafeo*	Or encircle
150.	*Masi Dande*	Masi Dande's
151.	*No Solo Suti*	And Solo Suti's
152.	*Tei dale [nara]*	Inner heart
153.	*Ma hena hu nara*	And upper thigh.
154.	*Boe ma ara lao*	So, they walk on
155.	*Do ara lope*	Or they go forth
156.	*Ela Seu Dela*	Leaving Seu Dela
157.	*No Fale Anda.*	And Fale Anda.

Masi Dande and Suti Solo meet Fingga Fiti and Mbasa Mbaku

Late at night Masi Dande and Suti Solo arrive at *Tedale Dilu Oen//Korobako Lepa Daen*, where the origin celebrations are in full swing. There they meet Fingga Fiti and Mbasa Mbaku and immediately propose marriage. Fingga Fiti and Mbasa Mbaku tell them that they know they are already married. Because they are not good-looking, like Masi Dande//Suti Solo's husband, they insist that Masi Dande and Suti Solo swear an oath that they will not return to their first husband.

158.	*Polok ara tao don*	In the middle of the night
159.	*Do fatik ara tao ladan*	Or late into the evening
160.	*Boe ma Masi Dande*	Masi Dande
161.	*No Solo Suti*	And Solo Suti
162.	*Reu losa*	Go until they reach
163.	*Do reu nduku*	And go until they arrive at
164.	*Tedale Dilu Oen*	Tedale Dilu Oen
165.	*Ma Korobako Lepa Daen.*	And Korobako Lepa Daen.
166.	*Na te Holi hade*	The *Holi* feast for rice
167.	*Ma limba betek*	And the *Limba* feast for millet
168.	*Ara bei raka-se*	Is still lively
169.	*Do raka-doto.*	Or is still noisy.
170.	*Masi Dande*	Masi Dande
171.	*No Solo Suti*	And Solo Suti
172.	*Reu ra-tonggo do ra-nda*	Go to meet and encounter
173	*Ro Fingga Fiti*	Fingga Fiti
174.	*No Mbasa Mbaku.*	And Mbasa Mbaku.
175.	*Ara kokolak dala sao*	They talk about the way to marry
176.	*Ma ara dede'a eno tu.*	And they discuss the path to wed.
177.	*Fingga Fiti*	Fingga Fiti
178.	*No Mbasa Mbaku*	And Mbasa Mbaku
179.	*Hu'a bafan*	Open their mouth
180.	*Ma silu noli nara*	And show their teeth
181.	*Kokolak ro Masi Dande*	As they talk with Masi Dande
182.	*Ma dede'a ro Solo Suti, rae:*	And converse with Solo Suti, saying:
183.	*'Ai bubuluk ei kasao sosa kara*	'We know that you have a first husband

184. *Ma ei katu ulu kara.*	And that you have a prior spouse.
185. *Metema ei kokolak dala sao*	If you talk about the way to marry
186. *Do dede'a eno tu na*	And discuss the path to wed
187. *Mai ata so sera*	Come, let us swear an oath
188. *Ma langgu bano dei.'*	And give a pledge.'
189. *Fingga Fiti*	Fingga Fiti
190. *Mbasa Mbaku*	And Mbasa Mbaku
191. *Nau ara so sera*	Want them to swear an oath
192. *Do langgu bano*	And to give a pledge
193. *Hu dua sara*	Because those two
194. *Tou ta malole*	Are not good-looking men
195. *Ma ta'e ta mana'a.*	And are not fine-looking boys.
196. *Te langga bonggo*	For [their] heads are round
197. *Tou kode kara*	Like monkey men
198. *Ma seru ei*	And their legs are straight
199. *Seku besi kara.*	Like digging sticks.

Masi Dande and Suti Solo's pledge to Fingga Fiti and Mbasa Mbaku

Masi Dande and Suti Solo do as Fingga Fiti and Mbasa Mbaku urge them, swearing that if they ever think of returning to their husband, then by the Heavens and Earth, they should be struck down and cast into the Sea to become an ocean turtle and a sea cow.

200. *Masi Dande*	Masi Dande
201. *No Solo Suti*	And Solo Suti
202. *Ara so sera*	They swear an oath
203. *Ma langgu bano renik*	And give a pledge with
204. *Ndeli lima kukun*	The ring from their finger
205. *Ma kalike daen*	And band round their waist
206. *Dadi neu nesenedak*	To serve as a remembrance
207. *Do neferendek.*	Or as a sign of the pledge.
208. *Masi Dande*	Masi Dande
209. *No Solo Suti*	And Solo Suti
210. *Ara so sera*	They swear an oath
211. *No dede'an*	As they speak to them
212. *Ma ara langgu bano*	And they give a pledge

213. *No kokolan, rae:*	As they converse with them, saying:
214. *'Lole faik [ia]*	'On this good day
215. *Do lada ledok ia*	Or at this fine time
216. *Ai so sera menik*	We swear an oath with
217. *Ai ndeli lima kukun*	The ring of [our] finger
218. *Ma ai kalike daen.*	And the band round [our] waist.
219. *Dae, Lain*	Earth, Heaven
220. *Ma Ki, Kona*	And North, South
221. *Dulu, Murin*	East, West
222. *Ara sakasi metema*	May they witness that if
223. *Neu fai bakahiton*	On a future day
224. *Do ledo makabuin*	And at a later time
225. *Au asaneda falik*	I remember again
226. *Au sao sosang*	My first husband
227. *Fo Nggeni Soru*	Nggeni Soru
228. *Ma afarende falik*	And I think of again
229. *Au tu ulung*	My prior spouse
230. *Fo Rote Namba.*	Rote Namba.
231. *Boe ma au tulek-ala bala-duan*	When I turn back
232. *Do haik-ala lolo-faling*	And when I return again
233. *Uni Ndao Nuse [u]*	To Ndao Nuse
234. *Do Folo Manu u,*	And to Folo Manu,
235. *Na dei fo la telun*	Then let the three-poled sail
236. *Femba heni au*	Beat me down
237. *Ma bobo duan*	And let the two beaks of the ship
238. *Dere heni au*	Strike me down
239. *Nai Loe Keli*	Into Loe Keli
240. *Do Lolo Dengga*	And Lolo Dengga
241. *Fo au dadi u kea liuk*	That I may turn into an ocean turtle
242. *Ma rui saik.'*	And into a sea cow.'

Masi Dande and Solo Suti realise their mistake

At dawn, in day's new light, Masi Dande and Solo Suti see just how unattractive Fingga Fiti and Mbasa Mbaku are, with a monkey's head and stick-straight legs. They immediately remember their handsome husband.

243. *Huak ana lali langga*	When the dawn shifts to the head
244. *Do silu ana soi dulu*	When first light lifts in the east
245. *Fo manggaledok ana dadi*	So that it becomes bright
246. *Ma makarondak ana mori*	And it grows sunny
247. *Boe-ma Masi Dande*	Then Masi Dande
248. *No Solo Suti*	And Solo Suti
249. *Ara mete rata-neneu*	See clearly
250. *Ma ara suri rata-lololo*	And observe directly
251. *Ma nata Fingga Fiti*	That Fingga Fiti's
252. *No Mbasa Mbaku*	And Mbasa Mbaku's
253. *Langga bonggo*	Heads are round
254. *Tou kodek ara*	Like monkey-men
255. *Ma seru ei*	And legs are straight
256. *Seku besi kara.*	Like digging sticks.
257. *Ara fale dale nara*	They have regret in their hearts
258. *Ma ara tu'e tei nara.*	And they have misgivings in their stomach.
259. *Ara rasaneda*	They remember
260. *Sao sosa nara*	Their first husband
261. *Ma tu ulu nara*	And their prior spouse
262. *Fo Nggeni Soru*	Nggeni Soru
263. *No Rote Namba*	And Rote Namba
264. *Tou malole*	A good-looking man
265. *Ma ta'e mana'a.*	And fine-looking boy.

Nggeni Soru and Rote Namba return to Ndao and play their sesandu

At just this time, Nggeni Soru and Rote Namba finish their work at *Sina Kona* and *Koli Muri*. They board their perahu and return to *Ndao Nuse* and *Folo Manu*. Nggeni Soru and Rote Namba can play the *sesandu* (a seven-stringed bamboo-tube zither) and the sound of its sweet music carries all the way to *Tedale Dilu Oen* and *Korobako Lepa Daen*, stirring memories in Masi Dande and Solo Suti.

266. *Neu lelek na boe o*	At that time
267. *Nggeni Soru*	Nggeni Soru
268. *No Rote Namba*	And Rote Namba
269. *Ara tutu rate'e besi*	They finish their forging of iron

270.	*Ma ara mbesa rabasa lilo*	And they complete their beating of gold
271.	*Ruma Sina Kona*	At Sina Kona
272.	*Do Koli Muri ena.*	And Koli Muri.
273.	*Ara sa'e rala balun-ara*	They climb onboard their boat
274.	*Ma daka rala tondanara.*	And they mount onboard their perahu.
275.	*Ara diu-dua*	They turn back
276.	*Ma ara lolo-fali*	And they return again
277.	*Reni Ndao Nuse*	Towards Ndao Nuse
278.	*Do Folo Manu reu.*	And towards Folo Manu.
279.	*Nggeni Soru*	Nggeni Soru
280.	*No Rote Namba*	And Rote Namba
281.	*Touk manasari sandu*	Is a man who plays the *sesandu*
282.	*Ma manadepo hitu.*	And who plucks the seven strings.
283.	*Ara sari kokoe sandu nara*	They play the *sesandu* pleasingly
284.	*Ma ara depo mamako hitu nara*	And they pluck the seven strings sweetly
285.	*Fo hitu ai kae haba nara*	The seven strings of braided gold
286.	*Do sandu ai loa lilo nara.*	And *sesandu* strings of pure gold.
287.	*Sandu li nara rama ketu meti*	The *sesandu's* sounds cut the tide
288.	*Ma rama ladi tasi.*	And they traverse the sea.
289.	*Ramanene sara*	They can be heard
290.	*Losa Tedale Dilu Oen*	As far as Tedale Dilu Oen
291.	*Ma Korobako Lepa Daen.*	And Korobako Lepa Daen.
292.	*Sandu do hitu li nara*	The sound of the *sesandu* or the seven strings
293.	*Reu randoro do rafeo*	Penetrates and encircles
294.	*Masi Dande tei dalen*	Masi Dande's inner heart
295.	*Ma Solo Suti hena hun.*	And Solo Suti's upper thigh.
296.	*Rasaneda ma rafarende*	They think of and remember
297.	*Sao sosa nara*	Their first husband
298.	*Do tu ulu nara*	And their prior spouse
299.	*Fo Nggeni Soru*	Nggeni Soru
300.	*No Rote Namba.*	And Rote Namba.

Masi Dande and Solo Suti attempt to return home to Ndao

Masi Dande and Solo Suti set off to return home, leaving Fingga Fiti and Mbasa Mbaku, who address them as they are leaving, reminding them of their oath and pledge to turn into a turtle and sea cow if they were ever to leave.

301.	*Inak Masi Dande*	The woman Masi Dande
302.	*No fetok Solo Suti*	And the girl Solo Suti
303.	*Ara la'o do ara lope*	They walk off or go forth
304.	*Ela Fingga Fiti*	Leaving Fingga Fiti
305.	*No Mbasa Mbaku.*	And Mbasa Mbaku.
306.	*Fingga Fiti*	Fingga Fiti
307.	*No Mbasa Mbaku*	And Mbasa Mbaku
308.	*Ara hu'a bafan-ara*	They open their mouth
309.	*Ma ara silu nolin-ara*	And they show their teeth
310.	*Kokolak ro Masi Dande*	Speaking to Masi Dande
311.	*No Solo Suti, rae:*	And to Solo Suti, saying:
312.	*'Ei masaneda*	'You now remember
313.	*Ei sao sosan*	Your first husband
314.	*Ma ei tu ulun-ara*	And your prior spouse
315.	*Rote Namba*	Rote Namba
316.	*No Nggeni Soru.*	And Nggeni Soru.
317.	*Lole faik ia dalen*	On this good day
318.	*Do lada ledok ia tein*	And at this fine time
319.	*Ei la'o ela ai*	You walk off leaving us
320.	*Ma ei lope ela ai*	And you go forth leaving us
321.	*Te hu ei so sera basa ena*	But you have sworn an oath
322.	*Ma ei langgu bano basa ena*	And you have given a pledge
323.	*Menik ei ndelin ma kali ken*	With your ring and your waistband
324.	*Fo ai to'u sara*	Which we now hold
325.	*Rai ai lima dale nara.*	In our hands.
326.	*Miu leo*	Go away
327.	*Te boso lili ndondou*	But do not forget
328.	*Ei hehelu baratan mae*	Your promise and pledge
329.	*Ei dadi miu kea ma ruik*	That you turn into a turtle and sea cow
330.	*Nai liun do sain.'*	In the Ocean or Sea.'

Attempting to return to Ndao, Masi Dande and Solo Suti are struck by a storm

Masi Dande amd Solo Suti board their perahu to return to Ndao. A storm arises as they reach the treacherous straits of *Loe Keli* and *Lolo Dengga* between Rote and Ndao; their perahu sinks and Masi Dande and Solo Suti are transformed into an ocean turtle and a sea cow.

331.	*Masi Dande*	Masi Dande
332.	*No Solo Suti*	And Solo Suti
333.	*Ara la'o do lope.*	They walk off or go forth.
334.	*Reu sa'e rala tonda*	They climb onboard their boat
335.	*Do balu nara.*	And onboard their perahu.
336.	*Ara leko la*	They guide the sails
337.	*Do pale uli*	And tend the rudder
338.	*Fali reni Ndao Nuse*	Returning towards Ndao Nuse
339.	*Do Folo Manu reu.*	And towards Folo Manu.
340.	*Masi Dande*	Masi Dande
341.	*No Solo Suti*	And Solo Suti
342.	*Tonda do balu nara*	Their boat and perahu
343.	*Reu losa do reu nduku*	Goes until it attains or reaches
344.	*Loe Keli*	The straits of Loe Keli
345.	*Edo-edo tua-nasu Ndao*	Swirling like the cooking syrup of Ndao
346.	*Ma Lolo Dengga*	And the straits of Lolo Dengga
347.	*Foi-foi manukudu Safu.*	Bubbling up like the boiling dye of Savu.
348.	*Sanggu manande'o ndesi kara dadi*	A tremendous storm arises
349.	*Ma luri manatala fei kara mori*	And a fierce cyclone appears
350.	*Ri boe rambombonu*	The waves rise and fall
351.	*Ma epo boe rafufua*	And the swirls swell and increase
352.	*Reu tufa Masi Dande*	Slapping Masi Dande's
353.	*No Solo Suti*	And Solo Suti's
354.	*Tondan do balun-ara.*	Boat or perahu.
355.	*Tiu heni la telun*	It breaks the three sail-beams
356.	*Ma tepa heni uli duan.*	And snaps the two stern rudders.
357.	*Masi Dande*	Masi Dande

358. *No Solo Suti*	And Solo Suti
359. *Tondan do balun-ara*	Their boat or perahu
360. *Molo ma tena*	Goes down and sinks
361. *Reni tasi oe dale reu.*	Into the depths of the Sea.
362. *Masi Dande*	Masi Dande
363. *No Solo Suti*	And Solo Suti
364. *Tena reni*	Sink down
365. *Liun do sain dale reu.*	Into the Ocean or Sea.
366. *Ara dadi reu*	They turn into
367. *Kea liuk ma rui saik.*	An ocean turtle and a sea cow.

Masi Dande and Solo Suti return to the harbour of Dela

The turtle Masi Dande and the sea cow Solo Suti swim back to the harbour of *Dela Muri* and *Anda Kona*. There they meet another turtle and sea cow, who are described as sea creatures cared for by Seu Dela and Fale Anda, whom Masi Dande and Solo Suti first met when they hurried on their way to the *Limba* feast at *Tedale Dilu Oen* and *Korobako Lepa Daen*. The local turtle and sea cow ask Masi Dande and Solo Suti where they are going, and they reply that they are going to gather two kinds of seaweed//seagrass (*engga*//*latu*) as their food and drink. Seu Dela and Fale Anda's turtle and sea cow propose that they go together to gather their *engga*//*latu*.

368. *Kea Masi Dande*	The turtle Masi Dande
369. *No rui Solo Suti*	And the sea cow Solo Suti
370. *Ara hangge tasi*	They ply through the sea
371. *Ma ara nane oe*	And they swim through the water
372. *Fali reu losa*	Returning, they go to
373. *Do reu nduku*	And they go until
374. *Namo Dela Muri*	The harbour of Dela Muri
375. *Do meti Anda Kona.*	And the tide of Anda Kona.
376. *Dua sara reu tia namo Dela Muri*	The two enter the harbour of Dela Muri
377. *Do Anda Kona.*	And of Anda Kona.
378. *Boe ma ratonggo do randa*	They meet or encounter
379. *Ro Seu Dela no Fale Anda*	Seu Dela and Fale Anda's
380. *Kea ana nekeboin-ara*	Cared-for turtle
381. *Ma rui ana nesemaon-ara.*	And fostered sea cow.
382. *Seu Dela no Fale Anda*	Seu Dela and Fale Anda's

383. *Kea ana nekeboin*	Cared-for turtle
384. *Ma rui ana nesemaon*	And fostered sea cow
385. *Ra-tane neu kea Masi Dande*	Ask the turtle Masi Dande
386. *Ma rui Solo Suti, rae:*	And the sea cow Solo Suti, saying:
387. *'Ei meni be miu?'*	'Where are you going?'
388. *Kea Masi Dande*	The turtle Masi Dande
389. *No rui Solo Suti*	And the sea cow Solo Suti
390. *Ra-hara do ra-selu*	Answer and reply
391. *Neu Seu Dela no Fale Anda*	To Seu Dela and Fale Anda's
392. *Kea ana nekeboin*	Cared-for turtle
393. *Ma rui ana nesemaon, rae:*	And fostered sea cow, saying:
394. *'Ai miu ndano engga*	'We go to gather *engga* seaweed
395. *Ma ketu latu*	And to pluck *latu* seagrass
396. *Soa neu ai naä ninu,*	To serve as food and drink,
397. *Po'o beten.'*	Our maize and millet.'
398. *Seu Dela no Fale Anda*	Seu Dela and Fale Anda's
399. *Kea ana nekeboin*	Cared-for turtle
400. *No rui ana nesemaon*	And fostered sea cow
401. *Ara kokolak do dede'a*	They talk or converse
402. *Ro dua sara, rae:*	With the two of them, saying:
403. *'Mai ata ndano engga*	'Let us gather *engga* seaweed
404. *Do ketu latu*	And pluck *latu* seagrass
405. *Takabua do taesa kada ia leo.'*	Together and as one right there.'

Masi Dande and Solo Suti assert their intention to swim to Namo Tane and Le Lopu

The turtle Masi Dande and the sea cow Solo Suti reply that they want to move on to *Namo Tane* and *Le Lopu*. Seu Dela and Fale Anda's turtle and sea cow warn them to be careful that, while they are gathering *engga//latu*, they are not caught by the seawall built at *Namo Tane* and *Le Lopu* that traps sea creatures as the tide recedes. If they were to be caught, they would be dragged up on land and butchered.

406. *Kea Masi Dande*	The turtle Masi Dande
407. *No rui Solo Suti*	And the sea cow Solo Suti
408. *Selu lole rala hala nara*	Reply, answering with their voice
409. *Do ae fino rala dasi nara, rae:*	And respond, indicating with their words, saying:

410. *'Ai lali miu fa bali dei*	'We are moving from here a short way
411. *Ma ai keko miu ba'uk bali dei.'*	And we are shifting from here a long way.'
412. *Rafada rae:*	They speak, saying:
413. *'Engga manandae reu batu*	'*Engga* clings to the rocks
414. *Ma latu manafua reu tane*	And *latu* lifts in the marshes
415. *Rai Namo Tane*	In Namo Tane
416. *Do Le Lopu dei.'*	Or in Le Lopu.'
417. *Seu Dela kea ana nekeboin*	Seu Dela's cared-for turtle
418. *No Fale Anda rui ana nesemaon*	And Fale Anda's fostered sea cow
419. *Rafada seluk bali neu dua sara, rae:*	Speak once again with the two of them, saying:
420. *'Ndano engga Namo Tane*	'When gathering *engga* at Namo Tane
421. *Ma ketu latu Le Lopu*	And plucking *latu* at Le Lopu
422. *Na masanenedak do mafarendek*	Remember or keep in mind
423. *Te Foi Fatu dea ei mauan*	Lest the leg of Foi Fatu's seawall be fortunate
424. *No Mesak Rau lutu lima manalen-ara.*	And the arm of Mesak Rau's fish-catch be successful.
425. *Boso losa ei suba*	Let it not happen while you are busy
426. *Mia ndano engga do ketu latu*	Gathering *engga* or plucking *latu*
427. *Boe ma meti hitu nara mori*	That a tide of seven occurs
428. *Do mada falu nara mori*	And an ebb of eight happens
429. *Te ei ta meda mala.*	Of which you are unaware.
430. *Boe ma dea ei maua*	Then the leg of the seawall will be fortunate
431. *Do lutu lima manale.*	And the arm of the fish-catch will be successful.
432. *Ara kena ma rataba rala ei*	They will catch and trap you
433. *Ara lui tali ma ara olu nafuk.*	They will attach a line and set an anchor.
434. *Ara reti ei*	They will hold you
435. *Ara le'a do ara nore*	They will pull and they will tug
436. *Ei meni mada lai miu.*	Carry you onto the dry land.

437. *Boe-ma ara sefa baba'e ei aom*   They will open and part your body
438. *Ma ara kedi sasarak ei mbam.'*   And they will slice and loosen
                                         your flesh.'

Masi Dande and Solo Suti are trapped within the seawall at Namo Tane and Le Lopu

The turtle Masi Dande and the sea cow Solo Suti do not heed this warning. They swim to *Namo Tane* and *Le Lopu* to gather seaweed and seagrass. While they are gathering and eating their fill, there is a great ebb tide and they are trapped within the seawall at *Namo Tane* and *Le Lopu*.

439. *Kea Masi Dande*   The turtle Masi Dande
440. *No rui Solo Suti*   And the sea cow Solo Suti
441. *Ara ta tungga Seu Dela*   They do not follow Seu Dela's
442. *No Fale Anda*   And Fale Anda's
443. *Kea ana nekeboin*   Cared-for turtle
444. *Ma rui ana nese-mao nara*   And fostered sea cow's
445. *Hara dasi nara.*   Voices and words.
446. *Dua sara hangge tasi*   They ply through the sea
447. *Ma nane oe.*   And swim through the water.
448. *Ara reu losa Namo Tane*   They go to Namo Tane
449. *Do Le Lopu*   Or to Le Lopu
450. *Ara reu hambu engga manandae*   They go to get the *engga* clinging
     reu batu   to the rocks
451. *Ma latu manafua reu tane*   And the *latu* that is piled in
     ruma na.   the marshes.
452. *Faik esa no dalen*   On one day
453. *Do ledok esa [no] tein*   And at one time
454. *Kea Masi Dande*   The turtle Masi Dande
455. *No rui Solo Suti*   And the sea cow Solo Suti
456. *Ara ndano engga*   They are gathering *engga*
457. *Ma ara ketu latu*   And they are collecting *latu*
458. *Fo ara ra'a*   So they may eat
459. *Do ara folo.*   Or they may gorge.
460. *Ara ta bubuluk*   They do not know
461. *Do ara ta meda rala*   Or they are unaware that
462. *Meti hitu nara mori*   A tide of seven is occurring
463. *Do mada falu nara dadi.*   And an ebb of eight is happening.

464. *Dea ei mauar*   The leg of the seawall has good fortune

465. *Do lutu lima manaler*   Or the arm of the fish-catch is successful

466. *Kena ma rataba rala sara.*   It catches and traps them.

Masi Dande and Solo Suti are trapped but cannot be dragged ashore

Foi Fatu and Mesa Ra'u go to inspect their seawall and see that it has caught the turtle Masi Dande and the sea cow Solo Suti. They attach ropes to Masi Dande and Suti Solo and attempt to drag them up onto the land, but they are unsuccessful, so they call chanters to sing as they struggle to drag Masi Dande and Suti Solo ashore. Still, they are unable to move Masi Dande and Solo Suti.

467. *Neu faik do ledok*   One day or at one time

468. *Na Foi Fatu no Mesa Ra'u*   Foi Fatu and Mesa Ra'u

469. *Reu tiro dea nara*   Go to inspect their seawall

470. *Ma reu dongge lutu nara*   And go to check their fish-catch

471. *Reu losa dea*   When they reach the seawall

472. *Do reu nduku luti dale*   Or they come to the fish-catch

473. *Ara mete neu*   They look

474. *Do ara suri neu*   Or they see

475. *Ma nata deak no lutu*   That indeed the seawall and fish-catch

476. *Kena do rataba rala*   Has caught and holds back

477. *Kea Masi Dande*   The turtle Masi Dande

478. *No rui Solo Suti*   And the sea cow Solo Suti

479. *Ara pa'a tali*   They tie a rope

480. *Ma ara lui nafu kara*   And they fix an anchor

481. *Reu kea Masi Dande*   To the turtle Masi Dande

482. *No rui Solo*   Or the sea cow Solo Suti

483. *Fo ara le'a sara*   That they may pull them

484. *Do ara nore sara*   Or they may tug them

485. *Reni ata do mada lai reu.*   To the top and onto dry land.

486. *Ketu basa tali*   They break all the ropes

487. *Ma ladi basa nafu kara*   And snap all the anchors

488. *Fo ara pa'a*   That they tie

489.	*Do ara lui sara*	And they fix
490.	*Reu kea Masi Dande*	To the turtle Masi Dande
491.	*No rui Solo Suti.*	And to the sea cow Solo Suti.
492.	*Te ara ta keko*	But they do not move
493.	*Ma ara ta lalik.*	And they do not shift.
494.	*Ara roke basa manahelo do manasoda.*	They ask all the chanters and singers.
495.	*Reu helo ma reu soda*	They go to chant and go to sing
496.	*Fo ela leo bena kea Masi Dande*	So that the turtle Masi Dande
497.	*No rui Solo Suti*	And the sea cow Solo Suti
498.	*Ara le'a do nore sara*	They may pull or tug
499.	*Reni ata do mada lai reu.*	To the top and onto dry land.
500.	*Te hu dua sara ta raka undak.*	But the two of them do not budge.

Fingga Fiti and Mbasa Mbaku recognise Masi Dande and Suti Solo in the seawall

Fingga Fiti and Mbasa Mbaku are one of the chanters asked to sing while Masi Dande and Suti Solo are dragged from the seawall. Fingga Fiti and Mbasa Mbaku look closely at Masi Dande and Suti Solo inside the seawall and speak to her, telling her to allow them to roll her body onto the land. Fingga Fiti and Mbasa Mbaku then take her finger-ring and waistband and tie it around her neck. They are then able to drag the turtle Masi Dande and the sea cow Solo Suti ashore to butcher them. Fingga Fiti and Mbasa Mbaku gather Masi Dande and Suti Solo's skull and rib cage and bury them as a remembrance.

501.	*Reu rala Fingga Fiti*	They go to Fingga Fiti
502.	*No Mbasa Mbaku*	And Mbasa Mbaku
503.	*Ruma Turumbou do Korobeba*	At Turumbou and Korobeba
504.	*Ara mai soda ma helo*	That they may come to sing and chant
505.	*Fo ela leo be na kea Masi Dande*	So that the turtle Masi Dande
506.	*No rui Solo Suti*	And the sea cow Solo Suti
507.	*Ara le'a do nore sara*	They may pull and tug
508.	*Reni ata do mada lai reu.*	To the top and onto dry land.
509.	*Fingga Fiti no Mbasa Mbaku*	Fingga Fiti and Mbasa Mbaku
510.	*Reu nduku do reu losa*	Go up to and go towards
511.	*Foi Fatu dean*	Foi Fatu's seawall

512. *Ma Mesa Ra'u dean*	And Mesa Ra'u's seawall
513. *Do lutu nara dale.*	Or fish-catch.
514. *Boe ma ara mete rata neneu*	They look into it
515. *Do suri rata lololo*	And stare into it to see
516. *Kea fo deak imingge nalan*	The turtle that the seawall holds
517. *Ma ruik fo lutu itiba nalan.*	And the sea cow that the fish-catch blocks.
518. *Na ndia be na Masi Dande*	In there is Masi Dande
519. *No Solo Suti sira nara.*	And Solo Suti.
520. *Fingga Fiti no Mbasa Mbaku*	Fingga Fiti and Mbasa Mbaku
521. *Hu'a bafa nara*	Open their mouth
522. *Ma silu noli nara ma rae:*	And show their teeth, saying:
523. *'Mete ma tetebe sara eir ia*	'If it is true that you are here
524. *Masi Dande no Solo Suti*	Masi Dande or Solo Suti
525. *Na ama loko ao mara leo no*	Then roll your body like a coconut
526. *Ma te ao mara leo tula*	And twist your body like a *gewang*
527. *Meni ata do mada lai miu.'*	Upwards and onto dry land.'
528. *Fingga Fiti no Mbasa Mbaku*	Fingga Fiti and Mbasa Mbaku
529. *Ha'i rala Masi Dande*	Take Masi Dande's
530. *No Solo Suti*	And Solo Suti's
531. *Ndeli lima kukun*	Finger-ring
532. *Ma kalike dae nara*	And waistband
533. *Fo ara so sera*	With which they swore the oath
534. *Do langgu bano renik*	And gave their pledge
535. *Ruma Tedale Dilu Oen*	At Tedale Dilu Oen
536. *Do Korobako Lepa Daen.*	And Korobako Lepa Daen.
537. *Ara pa'a kali ke dae nara*	They tie the waistband
538. *Ma ara kado ndeli lima kukunara*	And they slip the finger-ring
539. *Reu Masi Dande no Solo Suti*	On Masi Dande and Solo Suti's
540. *Lesu-ain ma timi lalanggen-ara.*	Neck and chin.
541. *Boe ma ara le'a do ara nore sara*	They pull and they tug them
542. *Reni ata do mada lai reu.*	To the top and onto dry land.
543. *Kea Masi Dande*	The turtle Masi Dande
544. *No rui Solo Suti*	And the sea cow Solo Suti
545. *Ara rasakedu ma ramatani.*	They cry and sob.
546. *Ara lu dua o dua*	Tears fall two by two

547. *Ma pinu telu o telu.*	And snot drops three by three.
548. *Te ara sefa baba'e ao nara*	But they open and part their body
549. *Ma ara kedi sasarak mba nara.*	And they slice and separate their flesh.
550. *Ara ndu do ara pala heni mban-ara*	They divide or give away their flesh
551. *Reu hatahori do andiana.*	To people and persons.
552. *Fingga Fiti no Mbasa Mbaku*	Fingga Fiti and Mbasa Mbaku
553. *Reni langga dila boa teten-ara*	Carry away their skull
554. *Ma kalu kai husu beban-ara.*	And their rib case.
555. *Reu ratoi ma rafua sara*	They bury and cover them
556. *Dadi neu neferendek do nesenedak.*	As a remembrance or memento.

7

Christian narratives of origin

The creation of new origin narratives

At the beginning of the twentieth century, the origin narratives of the Rotenese began a new creative phase, developing new narrative forms drawn from the Christian scriptures. These Christian narratives reflected social changes that had been occurring for centuries on the island. The creation and recitation of these Christian narratives required new semantic categories for their expression. They led to new avenues of expression and produced a new generation of poet–preachers. These new narratives did not replace older origin narratives but developed alongside them. Both the new and the older narratives continued the fundamental Rotenese concern with 'origins' as a primary means of achieving knowledge and understanding. These new narratives were the creative development of Rotenese efforts to incorporate Christianity within their cultural traditions.

Baptisms as a record of Christian conversion

Unlike the Portuguese who preceded them in eastern Indonesia, the Dutch East India Company made no explicit effort in the spread of Christianity and the conversion of the native populations with whom they engaged and traded. The Company was, however, committed to maintaining Dutch Reformed Christianity among its officers and its increasingly diverse European contingent of serving members, including its military, and those with whom they became individually involved. This was a commitment to morality and to an explicit social order. As a result, the Company came to accommodate native conversion and systematically recorded those who sought to become Christian.[1]

The Company's first attempt to assert its interests in eastern Indonesia came in 1613 when it besieged and eventually overran a Portuguese fortification on the island of Solor. The siege of some three months allowed most of the Solor fort's Christian population to escape to Larantuka at the eastern end of Flores, which became a local stronghold that the Dutch were never able to overwhelm. On several occasions, the Company provisioned and held a small fort, known as Henricus, on Solor but eventually chose, in 1651, to situate its operations in the bay of Kupang on the island of Timor, where they built a new fort that they named Concordia.

Surviving Company archives from Solor record marriages and baptisms at Fort Henricus from 1621 to 1629 for the motley mix of its inhabitants made up mainly of Company soldiery, generally of corporal rank, who married with local women from various islands, and their children, who were baptised as reformed Christians. A more complete 'Company Baptismal Register' (*Doop Boek van Timor*) covering 1669 to 1732 has survived in the Dutch archives and records the baptisms of individuals over this period, initially mainly the children and wives of women who married Dutch soldiers and officers. Among those whose baptisms are recorded are the names of the first Rotenese who converted to Christianity.

An entry for the initial date of this Company Register, 3 March 1669, records the baptism of a Maria from the domain of Korbaffo on Rote, who was married to Marcus Daneilzoon, along with their children, Jannetje and Maria, witnessed by Jacob Pieterszoon van den Kerper and Aaltje Paats. Although not all entries are as complete, this initial pattern appears to have been repeated. In some cases, children are registered under their father's name, but no mention is made of their mothers. Similarly, women's names are registered—such as 'Maria of Dengka' and 'Catherina of Diu'—in 1673 but with no mention of possible husbands. Various entries record baptisms only when children have been born in a marriage. Thus, for example, in

---

1   The archival materials used in this section are found in the National Archives of Indonesia (Arsip Nasional Republik Indonesia), Jakarta, in *Archief van de protestantse gemeenten in Batavia en van enige andere protestantse kerken buiten Batavia* [*The Archives of the Dutch East India Company (VOC) and the Local Institutions in Batavia (Jakarta)*], item no. 161: 'Timorse aankomende brieven van anno 1627 tot 1736 en Doopboek van anno 1669 tot 1737'. Available from: sejarah-nusantara.anri.go.id/media/ userdefined/pdf/BRILLVOCInventaris.pdf, p. 534. I want to thank my colleague Hans Hägerdal, Professor of History at Linnaeus University in Sweden, for alerting me to these various *Doop Boeken* and sending me digital copies from his own records.

1677, a 'Maria of Rote' is recorded as married to Leender Welke when their son, Willem, is baptised. Similarly, Catherina of Diu is reported as married to Jacob Cruksang when their daughter was baptised in 1687.

The names of the first Rotenese men to be baptised appear in 1673: 'Jacob of Termanu', 'Reijnout of Bilba', 'Johannes of Ringgou' and 'Pieter of Dengka'. The baptism of the first Rotenese couple, 'Isaak of Termanu' and 'Christina of Dengka', with their children, David, Willem and Catherina, is registered in 1675. Included also in the Register are the baptisms of the various children of the unbaptised 'Anica of Rote' and 'Appolonia of Dengka', each with a succession of different Dutch company officers.

This slow trickle of occasional Rotenese baptisms continued over successive decades but only became politically significant when the members of Rotenese ruling families were baptised. The first of these baptisms occurred on 26 May 1720, when the 10-year-old son of the ruler of Thie was baptised, taking the name Benjamin. Eight years later, on 23 May 1728, the ruler of Thie, Poura Messa, was baptised by the Dominee Aaron Dias d'Fonseca, who also served as his witness. As a mark of respect for the Dominee who baptised him, Poura Messa took the baptismal name Aaron. He was baptised along with his wife, Geertruijda Heno, and his other children: 1) Maria, who was six months old, 2) Antonia, who was four years old; 3) Rehobeam, who was five years old; and 4) Timotheus, who was seven.

At this same ceremony, Tobias, a son of the Radja of Korbaffo, and Daniel, the 10-year-old son of the Radja of Loleh, were also baptised. In the same year, on 15 August 1728, the six-year-old son of the Radja of Bilba was baptised, taking the name Rennet, as was the infant son of the Radja of Landu, who took the name Johannes. Four years later, on 20 April 1732, the eight-year-old son of the ruler of Termanu, Ndaomanu, was baptised and took the name Bernardus. This royal baptism was seen as politically significant and the chief officer of the East India Company in Kupang, Gerhard Bernard Visscher, served as a witness.[2]

---

2   Unlike the ruler of Thie, who is referred to as 'regent', or the rulers of Loleh, Korbaffo and Landu, who are referred to as '*radjas*', the ruler of Termanu is referred to as '*hoofdregent*'. Termanu's ruler was recognised by the Dutch as the chief ruler among all the rulers of Rote. As such, it was appropriate that Gerhard Bernard Visscher as *ondercoopman en opperhoofd* of the Company's residence in the Timor area serve as the witness to his baptism. Dynastic politics took a different turn when Ndaomanu Sinlae was forced into exile and another line of succession in Termanu through Fola Sinlae succeeded to rule in the domain (for a discussion of the genealogy of the rulers of Termanu, see Fox 1971a). Rule in Thie remained among the Messak family in the line of Mbura Lai. In *Harvest of the Palm* (Fox 1977a: 106) is a photograph taken in 1966 of the then ruler of Thie Jeremias Messakh holding the staff of office with its silver crown given to Poura Messa in 1726 by the Dutch East India Company.

Of these royal baptisms, that of Poura Messa's son Benjamin proved to have the greatest significance. At the time of his father's baptism, Benjamin was 18 years old. Within a few years, following the death of his father, he became the ruler of Thie and claimed a higher status than the unbaptised ruler of Termanu, whom he opposed. He insisted on the establishment of a school in his domain to teach Malay as a vehicle for understanding the Malay Bible. As a consequence of his important initial efforts, Benjamin Mesak, known as Foe Mbura, has become recognised, and indeed mythologised, in Rotenese representations of the quest for Christianity.[3]

Malay as the vehicle for schooling and Christianity

Dutch historical records chart this fitful quest for Christianity from the time of Mbura Mesa in 1728 into the early twentieth century.[4] The creation of local Malay schools in various domains across the island was a notable achievement in the eighteenth century, but it came at a price. Each domain had to pay for its schoolteacher, drawn initially and mainly from Malay speakers from the island of Ambon, with a levy of mung beans to support the Dutch in their beleaguered fort at Kupang. Within a generation, most of these outsider-teachers were replaced with Rotenese who had graduated from local schools and the schooling could be continued at a lower cost. During this period and afterwards, a close, almost inseparable association was established between the Malay language and Christianity, creating in each domain an elite cohort of Malay-speaking Christians.

In the nineteenth century, when the Dutch East Indies Government replaced the Company after a brief British interlude, this association persisted. Because Rote was unique in the Timor area in its rulers' adoption of Malay and of Christianity, it became the focus of initial Dutch efforts by the Netherlands Mission Society (*Nederlandsche Zending Genootschap*).

---

3   For clarity, it should be noted that in the dialect of Thie, 'p' becomes 'mb'. Hence 'Poura Messa', as represented in Dutch documents, would be better represented as Mbura Mesa; his son's name, Foe Mbura, follows in genealogical succession: Mbura Mesa > Foe Mbura in the royal clan of Mbura Lai founded by Tola Mesa.

4   These developments are discussed in more detail in *Harvest of the Palm* (Fox 1977a: 101–12, 128–36).

The first Dutch missionary, Dr R. Le Bruijn, arrived in Kupang in 1819. From his base there, Le Bruijn revived the faltering Rotenese school system. By 1825, he had re-established local schools in eight domains including Thie and Termanu, staffing these schools with Rotenese teachers. Le Bruijn's appointee J.K. ter Linden was the first missionary to take up residence on Rote, locating himself in Thie. But within a year, ter Linden closed all the schools Le Bruijn had established 'on account of the shameful and godless conduct of the instructors' and withdrew to Kupang. Within a decade, the missionary G. Heijmering, who remained in Kupang, reopened these schools, increasing their number to ten. Heijmering also succeeded in baptising the ruler of Termanu and was able to open the first church in this domain in 1849—more than a century after the conversion of the ruler of Thie.

This fitful but exclusive mission support of Rotenese schools ended in 1851. By this time, Dutch school inspector S.N. Buddingh, who visited Rote in 1855 and declared 'the Rotenese a studious, clever and intelligent people and from an intellectual as well as moral point of view [they] deserve a place of honour among the tropical peoples'. He recommended substantial government support for the continuation of local schools in each domain. With an established annual budget to support them, by 1857, Rotenese schoolteachers became government employees. In 1871, by which time Rote's school population had risen to 3,277 pupils, teachers who had until then been responsible for religious services on Sundays were forbidden to offer religious instruction in government schools.

Formally, the connection between Christianity and Malay-language schooling was ended; informally, the association continued. Yet another Dutch school inspector, N. Graafland, who had previously served as a missionary in the Indies, visited Rote in 1887. His views of the island were less positive than those of his predecessor.[5] Rotenese schools, he reported, were cast in deep shade under their lontar-leaf roofs; they were poorly attended and only by Christians; and the morals of the schoolteachers were scandalous. In a population estimated at between 54,000 and 62,000, there were only 7,000 baptised Christians and there was little to distinguish them from the majority of heathens. From 1669, when the first baptism was

---

5   Graafland praised the ruler of Thie but goes on, at some length, to describe the clutter and disorder of the household of the ruler of Termanu, who had previously been a sailor on various Dutch ships and brought back with him the furnishings and manners of his earlier employment.

registered for the island, to the time of Graafland's visit in 1887, the 200 years of Christianity on Rote had produced only a small minority of Malay-speaking Christians.[6]

Gaining scriptural voice for communicating Christianity on Rote

Not long after Graafland's visit, in 1890, yet another missionary, G.J.H. Le Grand, arrived on the island. Le Grand's views of the state of Christianity on Rote were much like those of Graafland. As he wrote to his mission society:

> If you ask me what my total impression of Rotenese Christians is, I would answer: for many, Christianity is nothing more than Sunday apparel, which they wear at certain times, while their household undergarment is made of heathen material and woven with heathen patterns.[7]

In Le Grand's judgement, Malay had become 'the vehicle of Christian thought' and, as an exclusive means of transmitting Christianity, this reliance on Malay limited the spread and understanding of the religion. Instead, Le Grand promoted the use of the Rotenese language. Under his auspices, the Rotenese J. Fanggidaej translated the Gospel of Luke (*Manetualain Dede'a Manemi Soda-Molek-a Lukas*; 1895) into the dialect of the central Rotenese domains of Termanu, Keka and Talae. The use of a written text among a population oriented to oral recitations, combined with dialect differences on Rote, limited the usefulness of this effort. Increasingly, as evidenced in his letters, Le Grand came to understand the Rotenese language and he grasped the value of Rotenese ritual language and appreciated its underlying ideas, which he believed could be directed to the promotion of Christianity. He was particularly taken with the *Suti Solo do Bina Bane* recitation with its search for a place of proper abode and he used lines from a mortuary chant,

---

6   Graafland published his report on the island in two parts, the first entitled 'Het eiland Rote' and the second, 'Eenige aantekeningen op ethnographisch gebied ten aanzien van het eiland Rote' ('Some Notes on the Ethnographic Field of the Island of Rote'), in the missionary journal *Mededeelingen van wege het Nederlandsch Zendinggenootschap* (*Communications of the Dutch Missionary Society*) (Vol. 33, 1889: 239–77, 351–75). He also published a German version of 'Het eiland Rote' as 'Die Insel Rote' in *Mitteilungen der Geographischen Gesellschaft zu Jena* (*Communications of the Geographical Society of Jena*) (Vol. 8, 1890: 134–68).
7   Le Grand (1900: 363). See also Hägerdal (2013).

Pata Dai ma Solo Suti, to illustrate to the Rotenese the idea that, in death, all of life's accumulations count as nothing, ending his illustrative fragment with the common Rotenese ritual refrain:

Teman ta dae bafo	Perfection is not of the earth
Ma tetu ta batu poi.	And order is not of the world.[8]

With one period of return-leave to the Netherlands in 1899, Le Grand continued his efforts on Rote until 1907. He was appointed secretary for both government and church schools and, in 1902, was able to establish a Teachers' Training School (*School tot Opleiding van Indische Leraren*, or *STOVIL*) that, for two decades, remained on Rote and became a focus for the training of Rotenese teachers who served both on Rote and on neighbouring islands. In 1919, a further training and examination program was established to produce salaried lay preachers known as *Guru Jumaat* or *Utusan Injil* (*Goeroe Djoemat/Oetoesan Indjil*) and was able to draw upon Rotenese from across the island.[9] This combination of new schoolteachers and lay preachers, fluent in Malay but urged to preach in Rotenese, adapted and appropriated Biblical high Malay, combining it with the poetry of Rotenese ritual language to create a new ritual-language register.

The new lexicon for a Christian scriptural voice

The traditional forms of ritual language took on new relevance and became a vehicle for the transmission of Biblical knowledge alongside that of traditional knowledge. In the twentieth century as Christianity continued to develop, the role of poet–chanter merged with that of Christian preacher. To fashion and convey these new forms of knowledge, a whole new Christian theological lexicon was created in dyadic form.

---

8   This 28-line fragment of a mortuary chant originally quoted by Le Grand is translated and published in Fox (2014: 322–23).

9   In a 1934 handwritten account, '*Sambungan dari Hal Penggambaran Indjil di Poelau Rote*' [Continuation of the Spread of the Gospel on Rote Island]', one of Le Grand's former assistants, a graduate of the *STOVIL* and an ordained minister of many decades, S.J. Meroekh from Thie, recounts his personal involvement in developments during this period. In his account is a list of the 46 graduates (*inlandsche leeraar*) of the *STOVIL* on Rote with details of their origins and their postings after graduation. He also provides details on the first cohort of *utusan injil*.

An examination of some of this formulaic lexicon and its constituent dyadic sets provides an idea of its creativity in translating new ideas in traditional format.

In the dyadic set *soda//molek*, *soda* has the meaning of 'health, life, wellbeing', while *molek* has the meaning of 'peace and security'. Fanggidaej, in his translation, appropriated this set to designate the 'gospel' (*Soda-Molek-a Lukas*). Among Christians, it came also to be applied to 'Heaven': *Soda Daen//Molek Oen* ('Land of Wellbeing, Waters of Peace'). By implication, this rendering indicates that Heaven is the 'Land and Waters of the Gospel'. *Soda Daen//Molek Oen* can also be combined with other recognised sets to form the longer and more traditional-seeming formula *Kapa Sula Soda Daen//Pa-Dui Molek Oen* ('Buffalo-Horn Land of Wellbeing'//'The Flesh and Bone Waters of Peace'). At present, the set *soda//molek* is used as a greeting among Christians in the Timor region.

Using the set *soda//tema*, Heaven can also be referred to as *Nusa Soda// Ingu Tema* ('Domain of Wellbeing'//'Land of Fullness') or, combining two traditional dyadic sets, Heaven can be referred to as *Bate Falu//Tema Sio* ('Eightfold Abundance'//'Ninefold Fullness').

God as the creator can be referred to in various ways. In the dialect of Landu, God as creator is Tou Mana-sula Poi//Ta'e Mana-adu Lai ('The Man Who Inscribes the Heights [Inscriber of the Heights]'//'The Boy Who Creates the Heavens [Creator of the Heavens]') or, as in the dialect of Ringgou: Tou Mana-adu Ledo//Ta'e Mana-sula Bulan ('The Man Who Created the Sun [Creator of the Sun]'//'The Boy Who Inscribed the Moon [Inscriber of the Moon]'). These names are variations on traditional designations for divinity among the Rotenese—one of which was the Heavenly Inscriber (Mane Sulak Lai) and the other, the Earthly Creator (Mane Adu Dae).[10]

The Holy Spirit is referred to by a combination of traditional sets, metaphorically associated with the tie-dyeing of textiles, but linked in a distinctive way for Christian purposes: Dula Dale//Le'u Teik ('Inside Patterner'//'Self Marker'). A variant designation from the domain of Ringgou makes the connection with textile dyeing even more explicit: Dula Dale//Malala Funa ('Inner Patterner'//'Bundle Shaper').

---

10   See Heijmering (1843–44: Vol. 5, pp. 542, 544: Vol. 6, pp. 85–89) for a discussion of these manifestations of divinity and their invocation in rituals of birth and death. It is possible that Heijmering confused the Rotenese term *mane* for *mana*, in which case, these designations of divinity would be *Mana-sulak lai* and *Mana adu dae*.

There are numerous ways of referring to Christ. Christ as shepherd is Tou Mana-Tada Tena//Ta'e Mana Lilo Bote ('The Man Who Separates the Herd'//'The Boy Who Forms the Flock'); Christ as redeemer is Mana-Soi//Mana-Tefa ('The One Who Freed'//'The One Who Paid'); and the risen Christ is Tou Maleo Lain//Ta'e Masafali Poin ('The Man Who Returned to the Heavens'//'The Boy Who Went Back to the Heights').

Christ can also be described with metaphoric exuberance as a healer and repairer of injury:

Tou mana so sidak	Man who sews what is torn
Ta'e mana seu saik	Boy who stitches what is ripped
Seu nama-tema saik	Stitches to make whole what is ripped
Ma so naka-tetu sidak.	And sews to make complete what is torn.

Other vividly constructed metaphors abound: the cross of crucifixion is *Tua Tele//Ai Nalo* ('The Bowed Lontar Palm'//'The Upward-Facing Tree'); Golgotha is *Lete Langa Duik//Puku Paku Lima* ('The Hill of the Skull'//'The Mount of Nailed Hands'); and to repent is *sale dalek//tuka teik* ('to turn the heart'//'to change the inner self').

These formulae are formed from familiar dyadic sets but are recognisable as Christian. Recitations based on these formulae provide a knowledge that is more often seen to complement than to contradict well-established traditional knowledge.

In 1966, just before leaving Rote, I met the last surviving member of the cohort of teachers trained at the *STOVIL* established by Le Grand to preach in Rotenese as well as in Malay. This was Lazaar Tioek Manu'ain. He was 78, having been born in the domain of Ba'a in 1888 and serving as both a Christian minister (*pendeta*) and a teacher in various parts of Rote before returning to a position as head of the main church in Ba'a. I sought him out because of his enormous reputation as a poet and preacher. He had become blind, but in the view of most Rotenese, this blindness had only increased his power as a poet–preacher. He was on his own when I visited him, and he offered me two recitations, which he patiently dictated to me because I had not brought my tape recorder. The first of these recitations was a version of *Suti Solo do Bina Bane*—a popular chant even for Le Grand but one with none of the 'origin' associations of recitations by Old Meno or Guru Pah.

The other of Old Manu'ain's offerings to me was a beautiful recitation of a kind that I had not previously encountered. Based on the image of a cosmic tree of life, this recitation provided advice on pathways to be avoided and others to be followed. When I published a translation and commentary on Old Manu'ain's recitation, I described it as a 'seemingly traditional' composition of 'impeccable parallelism'—'a personal attempt to create a kind of Christian cosmology'. The key passage of this admonition, with its defining Christian dyadic sets, is as follows:

Te ndana esa lido-lido lain neu	But one branch goes forward towards Heaven
Ma dape-dape ata neu	And [one branch] goes straight to the Heights.
Na musik ndanak ndia	Then take that branch
Te dala sodak nde ndia	For this is the road of wellbeing
Ma eno molik nde ndia	And this is the path of life
Fo nini o mu losa kapa sula soda daen	To bring you to the buffalo-horn land of wellbeing
Ma mu nduku pa-dui molek oen.	And to the flesh-and-bone water of life.
Dae sodak nai ndia	The land of wellbeing is there
Ma oe molik nai na	And the water of life is there,
Fo o hambu soda sio	For you will find the wellbeing of nine
Ma o hambu mole falu	And you will find the life of eight
Ma dua lolo ei	And with legs outstretched
Ma kala ifa lima	And with arms cradled on the lap
Fo ifa limam no limam	Cradle your arms on your arms
Ma lolo eim no eim.	And stretch your legs over your legs.

Recreating origins in a Christian mode

On my return to Ufa-Len in Termanu, during my second period of fieldwork in 1972–73, over a long evening's discussion of previous recitations that I had recorded, the poet Peu Malesi told me he was prepared to reveal a new origin narrative. On my first fieldtrip in 1965–66, Malesi had provided me with my first origin narrative (Recitation I; Chapter 4) and much of

Recitation VII (Chapter 4), which Old Meno went on to amplify. Malesi became a frequent visitor to Ufa-Len and was prolific in his recitation of a variety of mortuary chants.[11]

Malesi explained that this new narrative revealed the origin of death. At its recitation and, subsequently, when I replayed my recording, there was near unanimous agreement that Malesi's recitation was an ancestral revelation of importance. Only one schoolteacher recognised Malesi's retelling of the story of Adam and Eve.

Peu Malesi was a thoroughgoing traditional poet—certainly not a poet–preacher—and his recitation was, in my view, an attempt to incorporate new knowledge into the traditional framework, rather than an explicit effort to create a distinctively Christian canon. For this reason, his recitation—the translation of which I have already published[12]—contains none of the key dyadic sets that are the distinctive mark of the Christian canon.

Named in accordance with its principal protagonists, this recitation is entitled *Teke Telu ma Koa Hulu*. In naming these protagonists, one male and one female, Malesi violated one of the basic rules of composition—a blemish that his rival, the poet Se'u Bai, immediately recognised as a serious flaw. In proper composition, double names are either male or female; they cannot be male and female. *Teke Telu* as male and *Koa Hulu* as female are a composite character—not seen in traditional compositions. This presents problems later in the recitation when Koa Hulu alone is tempted by Menge Batu//Tuna Buta ('Rock Snake' and 'Eel Serpent').

Malesi's name for a Heavenly God is not one used in the Christian canon but one that accords with traditional usage: Lesik Lain Lelebe//Mane Ata Malua ('Lord of the Exalted Heights'//'Ruler of the Heavens Above') or, more simply, Lesik Leo Poi//Mane Leo Lain ('Lord in Heaven'//'Ruler in the Heights').

---

11 Before my departure at the end of this second period of fieldwork, Malesi led the drumming (*bapa*) on the night before the *Tutus* ceremony that I sponsored with Meno's son to honour the memory of Old Meno (see Fox 2014b).

12 My translation and commentary on Malesi's recitation is entitled 'Adam and Eve on the Island of Roti: A Conflation of Oral and Written Traditions'. It was originally presented at a seminar on the transmission of oral traditions at the Humanities Research Centre of The Australian National University in 1981, published in the journal *Indonesia* (Fox 1983a) and reprinted in Fox (2014: 343–53). In my original translation, I used the past tense. Since, however, there is no tense in Rotenese verbs, the use of the present tense is also possible and perhaps more appropriate in capturing the sense of this recitation. I have therefore translated appropriate passages in the present tense. My intention here is to situate this narrative within the context of the development of Rotenese ritual language in the twentieth century.

The passage that recounts the temptation of Koa Hulu provides a good illustration of this recitation:

Siluk ka soi dulu	Sunrise opens in the east
Do huak mai langa.	Dawn arrives at the head.
Inak Koa Hulu	The woman Koa Hulu
Neu fetu lae Menge Batu	Goes and steps on Rock Snake
Ma hange lae Tuna Buta.	And treads on Eel Serpent.
Tuna Buta natane	Eel Serpent asks
Ma Menge Batu natane:	And Rock Snake asks:
'Singo-na nai be	'Where is the error
Ma salan nai bei	Where is the wrong
De ta ketu do tua nasu	To pluck a leaf of the syrup tree
Ma seu boa fani oen?'	And to pick a fruit of the honey tree?'
Boe ma inak leo Koa Hulu	So, the woman Koa Hulu
Lole halana	Raises her voice
Ma selu dasin na neu:	And elevates her speech, saying:
'Lesik Leo Poin	'The Lord in Heaven
Ma Manek Leo Lain	And the Ruler in the Heights
Ma ana henge ne	He binds us
Ma ana bala taa, nae:	And ties us, saying:
"Boso ketu do fani oen	"Do not pluck the leaf of the honey tree
Ma seu boa tua nasu.	And do not pick the fruit of the syrup tree.
Te'e o seu boa tua nasu	If you pick the fruit of the syrup tree
Do o ketu do fani oen	Or if you pluck the leaf of the honey tree
Makaheduk nai ndia	There is sourness there
De sapu nitu nai ndia	A spirit death lies there
Makes nai ndia.	There is bitterness there.
De lalo mula nai ndia."'	A ghostly demise lies there."'
Boe ma Menge Batu kokolak	So, Rock Snake speaks
Ma Tuna Buta dede'ak, nae:	And the Eel Serpent converses, saying:
'Seu boak tua nasu na	'Pick the fruit of the syrup tree
Mandak nai ndia	For that is proper
Ma ketu do fani oe na	And pluck the leaf of the honey tree
Malole nai ndia.'	For that is good.'
Boe ma inak leo Koa Hulu	So, the woman like Koa Hulu
Seu boak tua nasu	Picks the fruit of the syrup tree
Ketu do fani eo	Plucks the leaf of the honey tree

De neni fe Teke Telu.	She takes and gives it to Teke Telu.
De leu la'a boa tua nasu	Then they eat the fruit of the syrup tree
Ma do fani oe.	And the leaf of the honey tree.

Teke Telu and Koa Hulu are called before the Lord of Heaven and, as they stand and wait, they forthrightly declare:

| *Ami malelak ndolu ingu* | We know the rules of the land |
| *Ma malelak lela leo.* | We know the wisdom of the clan. |

Koa Hulu explains what she has done, and the Lord of Heaven speaks, passing judgement upon them:

Kalau leo ndiak sona	If this is so that
O seu boak tua nasu	You picked the fruit of the syrup tree
Ma o ketu do fani oe	And you plucked the leaf of the honey tree
Na au henge ne neu o	Then I bind you
Ma bala ta neu emi	And I tie you
Loe mo late-dae	To descend into the Earth's grave
Ma dilu mo kopa-tua.	And to go down in a lontar coffin.

This is the origin of death, which, according to the poet Malesi, is the revelation of this recitation:

Fai esa manuni	On that day
Ma ledok dua mateben	And at that time
Boe ma touk leo Teke Telu	The man like Teke Telu
Ma inak leo Koa Hulu	And the woman like Koa Hulu
Ana sapu tolomumu	He dies instantly
Ma lalo solo bebe.	And she perishes suddenly.

Significantly, this recitation also reveals the origin of the implements for burial. This narrative thus parallels Malesi's Recitation I and others that recount the origins of the implements for the creation of fire and cooking and for the building of houses—implements for living as opposed to these implements for death and burial:

Boe ma besak ka fifilo langa	So, they fell the coffin head
Ma tati nonoli dulu	And they cut the casket top
De ala tao neu kopa tua	And they make them into a lontar coffin
Ma ala tao neu bolo dae.	And they make them into an earthen hole.

Pisa [hu] hulu dae la	The baskets for digging the earth
Boe ma ala dadi.	They originated then.
Boe ma taka huhuma tua	And the axes for cutting the lontar
Boe ala tola.	They appeared then.
Boe soe huhulu dae la	Coconut shells for scooping the earth
Boe ala dadi.	They originated then.
Boe ma besi kakali dae la	And the iron sticks for digging the earth
Boe ala dadi.	They originated then.
Hu touk-ka Teke Telu,	So, the man Teke Telu,
Ana sapu	He died
Ma inak ka Koa Hulu,	And the woman Koa Hulu,
Ana lalo.	She perished.
Besak ka pisak huhulu dae la	Thus, the baskets for scooping the earth
Ala dadi	They originated
Ma taka huhuma tua la	And the axes for cutting the lontar
Ala tola.	They appeared.

Malesi's recitation concludes, in traditional fashion, by acknowledging the precedence of the events that he relates and by asserting the sober and often repeated recognition of human mortality that features in Rotenese ritual performances:

Nduku faik kia boe	To this very day
Ma losa ledok kia boe.	And to this very time.
Hu ala molo tunga momolok	So it is that all walk in their footsteps
Ma ala tabu tunga tatabuk	And all tread their path
Leo faik ia dalen	As on this day
Ma nduku ledok ia tein.	And at this time.

The creation of an origin narrative of the quest for Christianity

In 1905, the renowned Dutch linguist J.C.G. Jonker published a tale entitled *Sanga Ndolu* in Rotenese with a Dutch translation. This tale was collected and written down for Jonker by J. Fanggidaej, the Rotenese translator of the Gospel of Luke. Jonker, who, while serving as a Dutch government linguist based in Makassar, visited Kupang at some time between 1899 and 1900.[13] The tale *Sanga Ndolu* was thus circulating among the Rotenese, particularly among Rotenese Christians, at the turn of the century.

Sanga Ndolu is a long tale. Although told in Termanu dialect, the succession of detailed incidents that lend it credibility derive from Thie.[14] The tale purports to unfold before the arrival of the Dutch East India Company and begins with an account of Termanu's oppression of its neighbouring domains, with the powerful ruler of Termanu forcing subjected populations to work his rice fields in Peto. The rulers of four domains—Thie, Loleh, Ba'a and Dengka—form an opposing alliance. (Dengka then decides to go its own way and this alliance is reduced to three.) The ruler of Thie decides to build a large perahu with the support of the rulers of Loleh and Ba'a. When the perahu is finished and the feasting is held to celebrate its completion, there remains the critical problem of giving the perahu a name. For a while, no name can be found. However, one of the local lords of Thie overhears a commoner child who is playing with a tiny boat, which he has named *Sanga Ndolu* ('To Seek Wisdom'). He takes this name back to the ruler of Thie, who is pleased and accepts it.

The three rulers then board their perahu with all their followers. The ruler of Thie brings along 30 additional slaves. The three allied rulers have heard that the Dutch East India Company is located to the north and west but when they set sail in this direction, they are carried south to the 'Sand Island' (Pulu Solokaek, Pulau Pasir or Ashmore Reef), where the ruler of Thie sets

---

13 In 1903, Jonker returned to the Netherlands and was appointed Professor of Javanese at Leiden University, where he continued to publish mainly work on the languages of eastern Indonesia, including both a dictionary (in 1908) and a grammar (in 1915) of Rotenese. Jonker's 'Rottineesche Verhalen [Rotenese Tales]' (with its Rotenese texts, *Tutui Lote-la Sudi Leohatakala*, by J. Fanggidaej) was published in *Bijdragen tot de Taal-, Land- en Volkenkunde* (*Contributions to Linguistics, Geography and Ethnology*; vol. 58, 1905: 369–464).

14 From a variety of perspectives, J. Fanggidaej's *Sanga Ndolu* is a jumble of elements and a confusing conflation of various historical events. Although told in the central dialect of Rote, its details indicate a tale recounted in Thie with many internal references to this domain. It specifically names the ruler of Thie as Foe Mpura (Mbura), the ruler of Loleh as Ndi'i H'ua, the ruler of Ba'a as Toudenga Lilo and the ruler of Dengka as Mone Eli, but the ruler of Termanu is named Tola Manu—a figure in the early history of the domain. The tale mentions that all the slaves taken to Batavia from Thie were captured from the island of Ndana—an island that, according to the narratives of Thie, was inhabited by a gullible non-Rotenese population. Included in the tale is the mention of how a local lord of Thie, while wandering in Batavia, encountered a gin still, copied how it worked and, on his return, created the first native gin on Rote. This incident underlies the often repeated Rotenese assertion that the rulers brought back to Rote two kinds of knowledge: the knowledge of Allah and the knowledge of *ala* (gin or *arak* as it is referred to in Malay). Also recounted in the *Sanga Ndolu* tale is a massacre of the Dutch at Kota Leleuk led by the ruler of Termanu, which occurred in 1748 and at which, according to archival records, the ruler of Thie was also killed. In the tale, the ruler of Thie manages to flee (see Hägerdal 2012: 356–61).

a marker before departing. When they finally reach Batavia, they declare they have come to seek 'wellbeing and peace' (*soda//molek*). They explain to the Governor-General that they have come from Rote where they live in 'gloom and darkness' (*kiu-kiu//hatu-hatu*) and long for 'light and clarity' (*mangaledo//masaʾak*). The Governor-General accepts their request and gives each of them princely clothing and a staff of office. In turn, the ruler of Thie gives the Governor-General 30 slaves to serve him as his 'children'— a gift that he accepts.

After the three rulers return, the Company establishes a post at Kota Leleuk on the north coast of Termanu to constrain Termanu's power. Angered at these developments, the ruler of Termanu plots against the three returned rulers and the East India Company. He invites the three rulers and the Company officer to a great feast at which he tries to kill them all but succeeds only in killing the Dutch officer and the ruler of Loleh. The account of events ends at this decisive point, with the tale going on to present a succession of folk etymologies that are intended to explain the domain names of Termanu and Pada.

This tale is a complex refraction of local occurrences, conflating memories of historical events of different periods in an account that recognises the Dutch East India Company as the source of Christianity and accords agency to specific Rotenese rulers who bring the knowledge of Christianity to the island. Significantly, the core of this tale with its account of a Rotenese search for wisdom gives early evidence of an ongoing local formulation of the origins of Christianity that was further recast and refocused, in a ritual-language format, during the twentieth century.

In ritual language, the formulaic phrase *sanga ndolu* is paired with *tunga lela*. *Sanga//tunga* are verbs that can refer to both mental and physical efforts 'to search, seek, hunt or stalk'. The pair *ndolu//lela* comprises notions of 'wisdom, counsel, advice and knowledge'. Together, these paired phrases, translated as 'to seek wisdom'//'to search for knowledge', were given specific new meanings in the Christian canon in the early nineteenth century, defining the quest for Christianity. By the late twentieth century and into the twenty-first, *Sangu Ndolu//Tunga Lela*, pared to its core journey and given metaphoric elaboration, became a distinctive origin narrative recounting the coming of Christianity to Rote—a narrative that has become known and is recited throughout the island.

On 1 October 1997, the Evangelical Church on Rote (*Gereja Masehi Injil Timor*) held a *Yubileum* ('jubilee') at Fiulain in Thie to celebrate the coming of Christianity. Included in the liturgy for this celebration was a special recitation of *Sanga Ndolu ma Tunga Lela*.[15] This is an exemplary expression of this origin narrative. It recounts not only the quest for Christianity but also its spread throughout the island. Its scriptural voice is elegantly presented in strict parallelism.

Sanga Ndolu ma Tunga Lela

This narrative signals its Christian identity in the opening lines, first describing the sadness and unhappiness on Rote before the Holy Spirit brings forth a Heavenly message. Rote is referred to by a variant of the oldest of its ritual names, 'Silence and Quiet' (*Lino do Ne*), as the 'Land of Silence and Waters of Quiet' (*Lino Daen//Oe Ne*).

1.	*Hida bei fan*	At a time in the past
2.	*Ma data bei don*	And a period long ago
3.	*Ingu manasongo nitu*	The land offering to spirits
4.	*Ma nusa manatangu mula*	And the domains sacrificing to ghosts
5.	*Soda ta nai daen*	Wellbeing was not in that land
6.	*Ma tema ta nai oen.*	And harmony was not in those waters.
7.	*De falu-ina lasakedu*	The widows cry
8.	*Ala lasakedu bedopo*	They cry continually
9.	*Ma ana-mak lamatani*	And the orphans sob
10.	*Ala lamatani balu-balu.*	They sob steadily.
11.	*Nai Lino Daen*	In the Land of Silence
12.	*Do Ne Oen.*	Or the Waters of Quiet.
13.	*Benga nafafada,*	The Word is spoken,
14.	*Benga neme Dula Dalek*	Word from the Patterner of the Heart

---

15   This *Yubileum* was organised by Dr Tom Therik, who worked closely with the preacher-poet Esau Pono from Termanu, whose origin narrative is Recitation IV (Chapter 4) in the Termanu corpus. This is the reason this narrative is in Termanu dialect and has features of known compositions from Termanu. Tom Therik from Bilba was a descendant of Willem Therik, one of the early Rotenese graduates of *STOVIL*. He was an ordained minister with a PhD in anthropology from The Australian National University and was, for many years, the rector of the Christian university in Kupang on Timor.

15.	*Ma dasi natutuda,*	And the voice falls down,
16.	*Dasi neme Le'u Teik:*	The voice from the Fashioner of the Inner Self:
17.	*'Soda dae nai ata*	'The land of wellbeing is on High
18.	*Ma mole oen nai lain.*	And the waters of peace are in Heaven.
19.	*Sanga dala soda*	Seek the road of wellbeing
20.	*Ma tunga eno molek*	And follow the path of life
21.	*Fo hapu soda sio*	To gain the wellbeing of nine
22.	*Ma hapu mole faluk*	And gain the peace of eight
23.	*Nai Lote daen*	In the land of Rote
24.	*Ma Kale oen.'*	And the waters of Kale.'

Inspired by the Holy Spirit, the rulers of three small domains build a perahu and sail it to Batavia. In the first section, the Holy Spirit speaks; in the next section, the rulers speak, explaining their mission as a search for wisdom. This—the wisdom of Christianity—is represented as two species of trees, *Tui Sodak//Bau Molek* (the '*Tui* Tree of Wellbeing' and the '*Bau* Tree of Peace'), which the Rotenese rulers bring back to the island. The use of the *bau* and *tui* trees to represent Christianity is an appropriation of two botanic icons from the conventions of traditional ritual poetry whose significance is elaborated on when the rulers return to Rote.

25.	*Faik esa manunin*	On one particular day
26.	*Ma ledo dua mateben*	And on a second certain time
27.	*Mane dua lakabua*	Two rulers gathered together
28.	*Ma boko telu laesa*	And three lords gathered as one
29.	*Lakabua fo lamanene*	Gathered together to listen
30.	*Ma laesa fo lamania*	And gathered as one to hear
31.	*Benga neme Dula Dalek*	Word of the Patterner of the Heart
32.	*Ma dasi neme Le'u Teik.*	And the voice of the Fashioner of the Inner Self.
33.	*Ita lakabua sanga ndolu*	We gather together to seek wisdom
34.	*Ma ita laesa tunga lela*	And we gather as one to search for knowledge
35.	*Nai Batafia ma Matabi.*	In Batavia and Matabi.
36.	*Mane dua ma boko telu*	The two rulers and three lords

37.	*Neme Tada Muli ma Lene Kona*	From Tada Muli and Lene Kona [Thie]
38.	*Neme Ninga Lada ma Hengu Hena*	From Ninga Ladi and Hengu Hena [Loleh]
39.	*Neme Pena Pua ma Maka Lama*	From Pena Pua and Maka Lama [Ba'a]
40.	*Boe ma ala lakandolu tona ofan*	They conceive of a sailing boat
41.	*Ma ala lalela balu paun.*	And they fashion a sailing perahu.
42.	*Tehu latane:*	But they ask:
43.	*'Ita fe tona nade hata?*	'What name will we give the boat?
44.	*Ma ita fe balu tamo be?'*	And what designation will we give the perahu?'
45.	*De ala fe nade Sanga Ndolu*	They give the name: 'To Seek Wisdom'
46.	*Ma ala fe tamo Tunga Lela.'*	And they give the designation: 'To Search for Knowledge.'
47.	*De malole nai Lote*	It was good on Rote
48.	*Ma mandak nai Kale.*	And proper on Kale.
49.	*Faik esa matetuk*	On one determined day
50.	*Ma ledo esa matemak*	And at one appropriate time
51.	*De ala laba lala tona ofa*	They climb upon the boat
52.	*Ma ala tinga lala balu paun*	And they board the perahu
53.	*Ala hela tuku telu-telu*	They pull the oars three by three
54.	*Ma ala kale kola dua-dua.*	And shake the oar-rings two by two.
55.	*Ala pale uli titidi*	They guide the splashing rudder
56.	*De leu*	They go
57.	*Ma ala la kukulu*	And they manoeuvre the flapping sail
58.	*De leu*	They go
59.	*Fo sanga ndolu sio*	To seek the wisdom of nine
60.	*Ma tunga lela falu*	And to stalk the knowledge of eight
61.	*Nai Batafia daen*	In Batavia's land
62.	*Ma Matabi oen.*	And Matabi's water.
63.	*Losa meti Batafia daen*	Arriving at the tidal waters of Batavia's land

64.	*Ma nduku tasi Matabi oen*	And reaching the sea of Matabi's water
65.	*Ala leu tongo lololo*	They go to meet
66.	*Ma ala leu nda lilima*	And they go to encounter
67.	*Lena-lena nai ndia*	The great figures there
68.	*Ma lesi-lesi nai na, lae:*	And the superior lords there, saying:
69.	*'Ami mai neme Lote Daen*	'We come from Lote's Land
70.	*Ma ami mai neme Kale Oen*	And we come from Kale's Waters
71.	*Sanga Tui Sodak fo tane*	Seeking the *Tui* Tree of Wellbeing to plant
72.	*Ma tunga Bau Molek fo sele*	And stalking the *Bau* Tree of Peace to sow
73.	*Nai Lote Daen ma Kale Oen.'*	On Lote's Land and Kale's Waters.'
74.	*Hapu Tui Sodak ma Bau Molek.*	They obtain the *Tui* of Wellbeing and *Bau* of Peace.
75.	*Ala lolo-fali leu Sepe Langak*	They return to the Reddening Head
76.	*Ma diku-dua leu Timu Dulu*	And go back to the Dawning East
77.	*For tane Tui lakaboboin*	To plant the *tui* tree with care
78.	*Ma sele Bau lasamamaon.*	And sow the *bau* tree with attention.

The *bau* and *tui* trees are associated with water—riverbanks, lake shores and the coast. The *bau* is the sea hibiscus (Hibiscus tiliaceus) and the *tui* is probably a species of milktree (Sapium indicum Willd). The roots and tendrils of these trees are the focus of attention in traditional ritual chants. This can be illustrated by a few lines of the mortuary chant Ndi Loniama ma Laki Elokama.[16] In a concatenation of metaphoric associations, the roots of these trees as they penetrate the water near where they are planted are seen as an attractor of and shelter for crabs and shrimp. These creatures are, in turn, a metaphor for widows and orphans, who represent all humankind.

---

16 My translation of this entire mortuary chant, published originally in 2003, can be found in Fox (2014: 283–93). The chant was provided to me by Stefanus Amalo during my first period of fieldwork and Old Meno helped me with its transcription and translation. Esau Pono, who knew of this chant from Termanu, was probably responsible, in part, for the use and elaboration of these icons in this version of *Sanga Ndolu ma Tunga Lela*. A clear indication of the derivation of this section of *Sanga Ndolu ma Tunga Lela* from Termanu's *Ndi Loniama ma Laki Elokama* is the mention of *Dano Hela* and *Le Kosi*, as used in Termanu, for *Dana Heo*—a key site in Thie.

Bau naka-boboik	A *bau* tree to care for
Ma tui nasa-mamaok.	And a *tui* tree to watch over.
De tati mala bau ndanan	Cut and take a branch of the *bau* tree
Ma aso mala tui baen	Slice and take a limb from the *tui* tree
Fo tane neu Dano Hela	To plant at the Lake Hela
Ma sele neu Le Kosi	And to sow at the River Kosi
Fo ela okan-na lalae	That its roots may creep forth
Ma samun-na ndondolo	And its tendrils may twine
Fo ela poek-kala leu tain	For shrimp to cling
Ma nik-kala leu feon,	And crabs to circle round,
Fo poek ta leu tain	For it is not shrimp that cling
Te ana-mak leu tain	But orphans who cling
Ma nik ta leu feon	And not crabs that circle round
Te falu-ina leu feon.	But widows who circle round.

In its long concluding section, *Sanga Ndolu ma Tunga Lela* embarks on a topogeny: an ordered succession of dyadic placenames that identify different domains on the island of Rote. The possibility of planting cuttings of the *bau* and *tui* trees allows their spread throughout the island, thus creating a narrative sequence like that of the planting of rice and millet in the traditional origin narratives (Recitation 7 from Termanu in Chapter 4 and Recitations 5 and 6 from Thie in Chapter 6).

Christianity is first planted in the domain of Thie (*Tuda Meda ma Do Lasi*), then in Loleh (*Teke Dua ma Finga Telu*) and then in Ba'a (*Tanga Loi ma Oe Mau*). As these trees of the knowledge of Christianity spread their roots and tendrils, the populations of other domains come and take the trees and plant them in their domains. This topogeny proceeds east along the southern coast of Rote and then, from the furthest eastern domain of Landu, it tracks back along the north coast of the island and onto the offshore island of Ndao until all of Rote has received the complete wellbeing and full peace of Christianity, which is phrased as the 'wellbeing of nine' and the 'peace of eight' (*soda sio//mole falu*):

79.	*Tane leu Tuda Meda*	They plant at Tuda Meda
80.	*Ma sele leu Do Lasi*	And they sow at Do Lasi [Thie]
81.	*Tane leu Teke Dua*	They plant at Teke Dua
82.	*Ma sele leu Finga Telu*	And they sow at Finga Telu [Loleh]
83.	*Tane leu Tanga Loi*	They plant at Tanga Loi
84.	*Ma sele leu Oe Mau.*	And they sow at Oe Mau [Ba'a].

85.	*Tui Sodak nai Dano Hela*	The *Tui* of Wellbeing at Dano Hela
86.	*Okan na lalae*	Its roots spread out
87.	*Ma Bau Molek nai Le Kosi*	And the *Bau* of Peace at Le Kosi
88.	*Samun na ndondolo.*	Its tendrils spread forth.
89.	*Boe ma hataholi neme basa daen*	People from all the lands
90.	*Ma dahena neme basa oen*	And inhabitants from all the waters
91.	*Tati lala Bau ndanan*	Cut the *bau* tree's branches
92.	*Ma aso lala Tui ba'en*	And slice the *tui* tree's boughs
93.	*Fo tane nai Lote ingu*	To plant in Lote's domains
94.	*Ma sele nai Kale leo.*	And sow among Kale's clans.
95.	*Tane leu Pila Sue*	They plant at Pila Sue
96.	*Ma sele leu Nggeo Deta*	And they sow at Nggeo Deta [Talae]
97.	*Tane leu Tufa Laba*	They plant at Tufa Laba
98.	*Ma sele leu Ne'e Feo*	And they sow at Ne'e Feo [Keka]
99.	*Tane leu Meda*	They plant at Meda
100.	*Ma sele leu Ndule*	And they sow at Ndule [Bokai]
101.	*Tane leu Lenu Petu*	They plant at Lenu Petu
102.	*Ma sele leu Safe Solo*	And they sow at Safe Solo [Lelenuk]
103.	*Tane leu Diu Dulu*	They plant at Diu Dulu
104.	*Ma sele leu Kana Langa*	And they sow at Kana Langa [Diu]
105.	*Tane leu Pengo Dua*	They plant at Pengo Dua
106.	*Ma sele leu Hilu Telu*	And they sow at Hilu Telu [Bilba]
107.	*Tane leu Londa Lusi*	They plant at Londa Lusi
108.	*Ma sele leu Batu Bela*	And they sow at Batu Bela [Ringgou]
109.	*Tane leu Fai Fua*	They plant at Fai Fua
110.	*Ma sele leu Ledo So'u*	And they sow at Ledo So'u [Oepao]
111.	*Tane leu Soti Mori*	They plant at Soti Mori
112.	*Ma sele leu Bola Tena*	And they sow at Bola Tena [Landu]
113.	*Tane leu Tunga Oli*	They plant at Tunga Oli
114.	*Ma sele leu Namo Ina*	And they sow at Namo Ina [Korbaffo]
115.	*Tane leu Koli*	They plant at Koli
116.	*Ma sele leu Buna*	And they sow at Buna [Termanu]
117.	*Tane leu Tefu Buna*	They plant at Tefu Buna

118.	*Ma sele leu Nggafu Huni*	And they sow at Nggafu Huni [Lelain]
119.	*Tane leu Dae Mea*	They plant at Dae Mea
120.	*Ma sele leu Tete Lifu*	And they sow at Tete Lifu [Dengka]
121.	*Tane leu Tasi Puak*	They plant at Tasi Puak
122.	*Ma sele leu Li Sona*	And they sow at Li Sona [Oenale]
123.	*Tane leu Dela Muri*	They plant at Dela Muri
124.	*Ma sele leu Ana Iko*	And they sow at Ana Iko [Delha]
125.	*Tane leu Ndao Nusan*	They plant at Ndao Nusa
126.	*Ma sele leu Folo Manu.*	And they sow at Folo Manu [Ndao].
127.	*Tui Soda na dadi*	The *Tui* Tree of Wellbeing comes forth
128.	*Ma Bau Mole na tola*	And the *Bau* Tree of Peace appears
129.	*Boe ma ana-mak leu tai*	The orphans gather round
130.	*Ma falu-ina leo feon*	And the orphans encircle it
131.	*Fo hapu soda sio*	To obtain complete wellbeing
132.	*Ma hapu mole falu*	And obtain full peace
133.	*Tao neu nakababanik*	To create great promise
134.	*Ma tao neu namahenak*	And to create great hope
135.	*Losa faik ia dale*	Up to this day
136.	*Ma nduku ledo ia tein*	And until this time
137.	*Nai Lote do nai Kale.*	On Rote and on Kale.

The retelling of the Bible in a Rotenese scriptural voice

One of the defining features of life on Rote has been its political, social and linguistic diversity. Most of the domains of the island were given political recognition by the Dutch East India Company in the seventeenth century and, over time, each has fashioned a distinct identity practice within a common cultural tradition. While every domain claims its own special genealogical practices and linguistic usages, these claims are invariably asserted to contrast with practices in neighbouring domains. Each domain's cultural awareness is thus defined in relation to other domains on the island.

A crucial aspect of this island-wide awareness can be seen in the way that 'semantic' differences have been harnessed in a ritual language that can be broadly understood across all the dialects of the island. A consequence of this embedded diversity is in its numerous sites of separate innovation, with the result that innovations in one part of the island can be, and generally are, transmitted across the island. Like the patterns on traditional cloths, innovations in one domain are taken up, often acknowledged, and then given a local integration.

This has certainly been the case with the spread of Christianity. One example of this is the Lord's Prayer in Rotenese. Every domain has its own distinctive linguistic version of the Lord's Prayer—in fact, many domains have two versions, one of which tends to be an elevated expression of this prayer with a great deal of parallelism. Similarly, various expressions of Biblical knowledge have developed in different parts of the island. Poet–preachers in eastern Rote, and in particular the eastern dialect domains of Landu and Ringgou, have fostered the ritual-language expression of Biblical knowledge.

At present, there are two master poets who are recognised performers in this genre: Yulius Iu from Landu and Anderias Ruy from Ringgou. Both are known for their interpretation and rendering of Biblical passages in elaborate ritual-language recitations. It is appropriate to present recitations by both these poets as examples of Christian origin narratives.

Yulius Iu is a lay preacher in the Evangelical Church of Timor (*Gereja Masehi Injili di Timor: GMIT*). As a poet, he is noted for his extraordinary ability to translate passages from the Bible into fluent ritual language. He specialises in these forms of recitation and does not claim knowledge of traditional origin narratives. This long recitation from Yulius Iu was recorded in 2007.[17] It continues for more than 270 lines.

---

17   I have previously published passages from this long recitation in Fox (2014: 334–36). Its translation, as I have indicated, has been challenging and I have worked closely with Dr Lintje Pellu in producing this present translation.

Genesis: Dae Ina Dadadi

Yulius Iu

The initial lines in this recitation recount the creation of the world, including all the plants and animals of the Earth.

1.	*Au tui ia nana, nae:*	I tell of
2.	*Tui dae ina dadadi*	The creation of the world
3.	*Masosa na le maulu a*	Its beginning and commencement
4.	*Tou Mana Sura Poi a*	The Inscriber of the Heights
5.	*Ma Tate Mana Adu Lai a*	And the Creator of the Heavens
6.	*Adu neme lalai no dae ina.*	Created Heaven and Earth.
7.	*Boema adu do tao nalan*	Then he created and made them
8.	*Tehu bei kiu-kiu kima rou*	But still there was darkness like the inside of a shell
9.	*Ma bei hatu-hatu do tafeo*	And still there was gloom all round
10.	*Bei nafaroe dea ei*	As if still groping in the legs of a fish weir
11.	*Bei nafadama lutu lima*	Still fumbling in the arms of a fish-trap
12.	*Basa boema adu nala malua a*	When he created the brightness
13.	*Ma riti ndala makaledo a*	And generated daylight
14.	*De malua nala dulu*	The sun rose in the east
15.	*Ma makaledo nala laka*	And the daylight appeared at the head
16.	*Basa boema adu do tao nala*	When this had been created and made
17.	*Tada nala oe mamis no tasi oe.*	He separated freshwater and seawater.
18.	*Basa boema adu do tao nala*	When this had been created and made
19.	*Adu do tao basa-basa*	He created and made all
20.	*Hu marerebi ma ara ma do masesepe a.*	The tree plants and leaved plants.
21.	*Basa boema adu do tao nala*	When this had been created and made
22.	*Malua a do makaledo a*	There was daylight and sunshine
23.	*Ialah bula a, fandu ara, ma ledo a.*	The Moon, the stars and the Sun.

The next lines of the recitation proceed to recount the creation of Adam and then of Eve. Unlike Peu Malesi, Yulius Iu does not give these figures Rotenese names but identifies them explicitly as Adam and Hawa (Eve). Adam, on his own, is described as 'a lone buffalo and a solitary chicken'— common icons in traditional recitations. When Adam and Eve are joined, their situation—as indicated in lines 45 and 46, which I translate as 'Such is a proper social life and an ordered way of living'—could be translated, more literally, as 'proper clan life//good village life'.

24.	*Basa boema adu tao*	When this was done, he created and made
25.	*Laihenda daebafo a*	A person on the Earth
26.	*Ma hataholi batu poi*	And a human in the world
27.	*Adu tao nala Adam*	He created Adam
28.	*Tehu tou a kise apa*	But he was a man like a lone buffalo
29.	*Ma tate a mesa manu.*	And the boy like a solitary chicken.
30.	*De neu fai esa nai ndia*	Then on a particular day
31.	*Ma ledo dua nai na*	And at a certain time
32.	*Boema Adam suku dodoko lakan*	Adam fell asleep
33.	*Ma ana peu ailunu lima*	And napped with his hands as pillow
34.	*Boma Tou Mana Adu Lai a*	Then the Creator of the Heavens
35.	*Ma Tate mana Sura Poi a*	And the Inscriber of the Heights
36.	*Neu leo de hai na Adam ai usu kise na*	Went and took from Adam a rib from his side
37.	*Boema adu na neu lahenda*	Then he created a human
38.	*Ma tao na leo hataholi.*	And made a person.
39.	*Boema mon nai Adam neu*	Then he brought her to Adam
40.	*De neu de nahara ma nadasi:*	Then he spoke and said:
41.	*'Nai ia nana hu nata ndia na so*	'Here is the right trunk
42.	*Ma ndana nasarai na ndia so*	And branch to lean on
43.	*Dadi neu sao uma a leo*	To become a wife of the house
44.	*Ma mori neu mo tu lo a leo*	And to live as household spouse
45.	*De leo matalolole*	Such is a proper social life
46.	*Ma iku matabebesa*	And an ordered way of living
47.	*De losa duas*	So that [you] both
48.	*Leo ma iku rai mamana*	Live and reside at a place

49.	*Si seu ma so'e dode*	Tear, then sew and scoop then serve
50.	*De hi'a fo setele*	Laughing happily and
51.	*Ma eki fo natadale.'*	Shouting for joy.'

At this stage in the recitation, the Creator of the Heavens and the Inscriber of the Heights places a binding command on Adam and Hawa not to lay a hand on the '*keka* tree of prohibition and the *ndao* stone of regulation'. The image that is conveyed by this formulaic set of pairs is not of a tree on its own but of a merger of rock and tree (*batu//ai*)—an image that conjures up the specially marked mortuary monuments known as *tutus* that are found scattered through the island.[18]

52.	*Tehu, mai fai esa nai ndia*	But on a certain day
53.	*Boema ledo dua nai na*	And at a particular time
54.	*Boema Tou Mana Adu Lai a*	The Creator of the Heavens
55.	*Ma Tate Mana Sura Poi a*	And the Inscriber of the Heights
56.	*Ana hara no heke nè*	He spoke the binding command
57.	*Ma dasi no bara tada:*	And he uttered the voice of prohibition:
58.	*'De basa-basa hata*	'All things growing there
59.	*Nai oka ma nai dea dale ia*	In that garden and in that precinct
60.	*Bole upa ma tesa tei a*	You can eat to your full
61.	*Ma minu a tama dale a*	And drink to your satisfaction
62.	*Te noi ai esa nai oka talada*	But there is a tree in the middle of the garden
63.	*Nai ia nade ai pala keka*	Its name is the *keka* tree of prohibition
64.	*Ma batu ndilu ndao.*	And the *ndao* stone of regulation.
65.	*Boso tai lima*	Do not lay your hand
66.	*Ma ei na neu.*	Nor your foot upon it.
67.	*De fai bea o tai lima ma neu*	On the day you put your hand on it
68.	*Ho dua kemi upa sama-sama*	When both of you drink together
69.	*Ma mia sama-sama,*	And eat together,
70.	*Sono neu ko fai esa na ndia*	As on that day
71.	*Ma ledo dua nai na*	And at that time
72.	*Te lu mata mori*	Then tears will appear

---

18 See 'To the Aroma of the Name: The Celebration of a Ritual of Rock and Tree' in Fox 2014: 295–313.

73.	*Ma pinu idu a dadi neu ko emi dua*	And snot will originate for both of you
74.	*Dadi neu tu'e tei*	Becoming a heart's regret
75.	*Ma mori neu sale dale.'*	And growing into inner disappointment.'

The approach to Hawa is portrayed as intimate and persuasive. The tempter is a snake, but this is not made explicit until further along in the recitation. In this recitation, 'snake' is not paired with 'eel', as in Peu Malesi's version. Following ritual-language conventions, the numbers two and three are combined to indicate that both Adam and Hawa partake of the forbidden fruit and leaves. They then immediately feel guilty.

76.	*Tehu no nitu a duduku na*	But then with a spirit's seduction
77.	*Ma no mula a o'oti na*	And with a ghost's persuasion
78.	*Na neu no naneta no Hawa*	He came and met Hawa
79.	*Lima nda lima pua*	Hand met hand like an areca nut
80.	*Ma laka toko laka no*	And head touched head like a coconut
81.	*Selu dasi na neu*	Raised his voice
82.	*Ma lole hara na neu*	And brought forth his words
83.	*Neu Hawa nae:*	Saying to Hawa:
84.	*'Hu ubea tao*	'What is the reason
85.	*Ma sala ubea*	And what is wrong
86.	*Ma siko ubea*	And what is the matter
87.	*De ndi na basa-basa hata fo rai oka*	That all things in this garden
88.	*Ma dea dale ia*	And inside this precinct
89.	*Emi dua bole mi'a ma minu*	You two may eat and drink
90.	*Hu ai nai oka a talada*	But the tree in the middle of the garden
91.	*Emi dua ta mia?'*	You two may not eat?'
92.	*Boema Hawa nae:*	Then Hawa said:
93.	*'Kalau hara heke ne ara mori*	'If the binding command has been given
94.	*Ma dasi bara tada ara dadi*	And voice of prohibition has been raised
95.	*Nae kalau ami dua upa ma mia minu*	That if we two eat and drink

96.	*Sono meu ko ami dua*	Then for both of us
97.	*Lalu mula a mori*	A spirit death will appear
98.	*Ma sapu nitu a dadi.'*	And a deathly demise occur.'
99.	*Boema meke ana selu dasi a neu*	Then the snake raised his voice
100.	*Ma lole hara na neu:*	And brought forth his words:
101.	*'Nai kalau emi dua mia*	'If both of you eat
102.	*Sono neu ko dadi matafali ao*	Then your body will transform
103.	*Ma masadua ao*	And your body will change
104.	*Dadi neu Tou Mana Sura Poi*	To become the Inscriber of the Heights
105.	*Ma Tate Mana Adu Lai.'*	And the Creator of the Heavens.'
106.	*Hu na de doe-doe a dei*	Because of the craving and craving
107.	*Ma nau-nau a dei,*	And desiring and desiring,
108.	*De nau ai pala keka boa*	She desired the fruit of *keka* tree of prohibition
109.	*Ma nau batu ndilu ndao buna.*	And desired the flower of *ndao* stone of regulation.
110.	*Nau-nau a dei*	Desiring and desiring
111.	*Ma doe-doe a dei*	Craving and craving
112.	*De nau lain bo'a bala hoe*	So desiring the young fruit on high
113.	*De lusu boa bala hoe*	The sweet young fruit
114.	*Ma nau poin de male don a de*	And desiring the tender leaves at the top
115.	*Do petu ma lene*	Leaves soft and juicy
116.	*De duas mo na lena lima*	Both extended their hands
117.	*Ma kani do seluk ein.*	And stretched out their feet.
118.	*Ra rala lain boa bala hoe*	Then they ate the young fruit on high
119.	*De boa lusu bala hoe*	The sweet young fruit
120.	*Upa nala poin do*	And they drank from the leaves at the top
121.	*De do petu ma lendu.*	Leaves soft and juicy.
122.	*Boema duas tada ra siko sio a*	Then the two felt their guilt grow great
123.	*Ma telus mori ma sala falu.*	And the three felt their wrong grow large.

The Creator of the Heavens and the Inscriber of the Heights comes looking for Adam and Hawa, who profess their guilt in a complex formulaic metaphor: 'An estuary's bottom of guilt and a river's dregs of sin' (*oli bui masala//le tende masiko*). Neither the largest of tree leaves nor swathes of tree bark can cover their loins and thighs.

124.	*Tou Mana Adu Lai a*	The Creator of the Heavens
125.	*Ma Tate Mana Sura Poi a*	And the Inscriber of the Heights
126.	*Mai teteni ma mai natane*	Came to see and came to ask
127.	*Seluk dasi a neu*	Again, raising his voice
128.	*Ma lole hara a neu:*	And lifting his words:
129.	*Adam-Adam, te o nai bea?'*	'Adam-Adam, where are you?'
130.	*Adam seluk dadae dasi*	Adam replied in a humble voice
131.	*Ma lole mamale hara nae:*	And spoke with weakened words:
132.	*'Ami dua nai ia.*	'Both of us are here.
133.	*Tehu ami dadi nai masala*	But we have become guilty
134.	*De oli bui masala*	In an estuary's bottom of guilt
135.	*Ma ami mori nai masiko*	We have grown sinful
136.	*De le tende masiko.*	In a river's dregs of sin.
137.	*De ami dua lao soro funi ao*	Both of us walk hiding our bodies
138.	*Ma ami dua hae bubui ao*	And we two rest covering ourselves
139.	*De ami dua nai bea na*	For us two are in this situation
140.	*Bina do ta palu paun*	*Bina* leaves cannot wrap the thighs
141.	*Ma ta palu ami dua paun*	And cannot wrap both our thighs
142.	*Ma kode-kè ta ndule kere*	And *kode-ke* bark cannot cover the loins
143.	*Te ta ndule mai dua keren.'*	Nor can it cover both our loins.'

It is at this point in the recitation that the Creator of the Heavens and the Inscriber of the Heights passes judgement on Adam and Hawa. This judgement extends to the tempter snake as well. A key refrain in these lines is that the temptation of Adam and Hawa was caused by their own cravings and desires.

144.	*Boema Tou Mana Adu Lai a*	Then the Creator of the Heavens
145.	*Ma Tate mana Sura Poi a nae:*	And the Inscriber of the Heights said:
146.	*'Boe te emi dua lo do lena lima*	'Surely both of you extended your hands

147.	*Ma kani do seseli ei.'*	And stretched your feet'
148.	*Leo hara heke ne*	Thus speaking the binding command
149.	*Ma dasi bara tada a neu.*	And uttering the voice of prohibition.
150.	*Boema duas ndi bea na rae:*	They there replied, saying:
151.	*'Hu no nitu a nonoi*	'It was because of the spirit's persuasion
152.	*Ma meke a tatao.'*	And the snake's enticement.'
153.	*Boema nalo nala telus a*	Then he called out to the three
154.	*Ma na kou nala duas leo*	And shouted out to the two
155.	*Boema hara heke ne a mori*	He spoke the binding command
156.	*Ma dasi bara tada a dadi nae:*	And uttered the voice of prohibition, saying:
157.	*'Hu no dale tene-tu a nonoi*	'It was because of a heart craving for persuasion
158.	*Ma tei saka-lai tatao*	And a core desiring enticement
159.	*De tene-tu nai lain a*	Craving for what is above
160.	*Ma saka-lai nai malole a*	And seeking after good things
161.	*Te lo dai lena lima*	That you extended your hands
162.	*Ma kani do seseli ei*	And have stretched your feet
163.	*De besa ia mulai neme fai ia dale*	So now beginning from this certain day
164.	*Ma ledo ia tein*	And from this particular time
165.	*Au e dan kedi emi telu a*	I decide and declare that the three of you
166.	*Ialah bati neme neu meke a*	That is, for the snake
167.	*Mulai neme fai dale na mai ri bea a*	From this day forward
168.	*Rodo neu rada dale a*	You will crawl with your chest
169.	*Ma upa soda ma mua mole*	And your sustenance and nourishment
170.	*Neme batu a mai.*	Will come out from stone.
171.	*Mulai fai ia dale juga*	Beginning from this particular time, too
172.	*Hawa nairu fo no totoka ma no tata*	Hawa's pregnancy will be difficult and painful

173. *No lu mata ma pinu idu* — With tears from the eyes and snot from the nose

174. *No boki dan lae no tei hedi* — Giving birth and delivering in pain

175. *Boki dan lae ma dale susa.* — Giving birth and delivering in sorrow.

176. *Leo na leo Adam mulai neme fai ia* — As for Adam, from this day

177. *Sale ma tuka* — With regret and disappointment

178. *O saka noi ma tao* — You will seek your living

179. *O tao nai nura lasi* — You will work in the deep forest

180. *Ma nai pia le* — And on hard rocks

181. *Ladi basa-basa unu laka sosoru* — Tapping the palm tree until your knees ache

182. *Da ma titi besa konana hapu dadai mala* — Your blood will drop for enough to live

183. *Untuk tao neu masoda a.* — To work for your wellbeing.

When Adam and Hawa are expelled from the garden, they go forth to make a living, enduring all the hardships and struggles of life like that on Rote. They leave a place of ease—a place where one tears then sews and where one scoops then serves (formulaic phrases originally applied to an imagined easy life in Kupang) and they go forth to toil and work with dripping tears and snot. This outpouring of tears and snot is compared to the prolific tiny fruit of a jujube tree (*Ziziphus mauritiana*, Indian jujube) and the blossoms of the forest *pio* tree. The passage uses the dyadic set (*soda//mole*) associated with Christian life but indicates this usage is intended to describe the human condition.

184. *Mulai neme fai ia dalen* — Beginning from this particular time

185. *Ma usi do pu heni Adam no Hawa leo* — Adam and Hawa were expelled and evicted

186. *Heo oka dea a leo.* — Out of the garden precinct.

187. *Ara la'o do lope leme* — They walked with swinging arms from

188. *Mamana si, se'u a mai* — The place where one tears then sews

189. *Ma so'e, dode a* — And scoops then serves

190. *Reu tuka do reu saka leo* — To go to seek and go to search

191. *Nai nura dan nai lasi a leo* — Through the woods and the forest

192. *Hu nura mana kaitio ara* — The woods full of *kaitio* bushes

193. *Ma lasi mana lolo batu a leo*	And forest strewn with stones
194. *Hu fo no tei saka-lalai a*	Because of the core's desires
195. *Ma dale tene-tutu a*	And heart's cravings
196. *Te tene-tu neu lain a*	Craving after what is above
197. *Ma saka-lai malole a.*	And desiring after good things.
198. *Mulai neme fai ndia dale*	Beginning from this certain day
199. *Ledo ia tei*	At this particular time
200. *Boema duas na kalua leo*	The two lived there
201. *Duas a lope lima*	The two swung their arms
202. *Ma kani ei a leo*	And stretched their feet
203. *Lope lima fo ere u leo*	Swinging their arms as they went
204. *Tuka ma saka nai nura*	Seeking and searching in the forest
205. *Ma nai lasi a leo*	And in the woods
206. *Losa fai dan mandu'u ledo a*	Until the sun had set
207. *Ladi basa undu laka sosoru*	Tapping palm trees until their legs ached
208. *Puse na ra titi*	With sweat dripping
209. *Ma da na ra fa*	And blood dropping
210. *Besa konana soda a natetu*	That wellbeing may be ordered
211. *Ma mole a manda.*	And peace may be proper.
212. *Mulai neme fai ia na juga*	Beginning from this day also
213. *Ara tuka ma saka*	They sought and searched
214. *Te soda ta natetu na*	But wellbeing was not in order
215. *Ma mole ta na nda so*	And the peace was not proper
216. *Hu karena no dale tene-tu*	Because of the heart's craving
217. *Ma tei saka-lalai a.*	And the core's desires.
218. *Boema soda neu natahi*	Wellbeing might be better
219. *Ma mole neu nataleko*	And peace might improve
220. *Tuka ma saka*	Seeking and searching
221. *Roi ma tao*	Toiling and working
222. *Tehu nai pinu dua o dua*	But still snot fell two by two
223. *Ma nai lu telu o telu*	And tears dropped three by three
224. *Tasaleu ai sale*	Encountering the tree of regret
225. *Ma ratundu batu tu'e*	And knocking against the stone of remorse
226. *De sale dale neu tei*	With inner regret
227. *Ma tu'e tei neu tei*	And heartfelt remorse

228. *Losa lu mata mori*	Until tears came forth
229. *Ma pinu idu a dadi,*	And snot appeared,
230. *De pinu ara kara pio lasi a*	Snot dropping like forest *pio* blossoms
231. *Namanosi tuka dala*	Falling along the way
232. *Ma lu ko boa naru*	And tears dropping like long *ko* fruit
233. *Rematiti tuka enok.*	Dropping along the path.
234. *No ndia soda laihenda a*	So it is with human wellbeing
235. *Ma mole hataholi.*	And with mankind's peace.

The concluding lines in this recitation offer ancestral advice with a Christian message in a clear Rotenese setting the activities of which regulate each day's passing.

236. *A losa nai fai ia dale*	To this day
237. *Nduku ledo ia tein*	And until this time
238. *Tuka ma saka*	Seeking and searching
239. *Noi ma tao*	Pondering and working
240. *Neme le ulu a mai*	From the beginning
241. *De lasi a peda hela neme le ulu a*	The elders promised this from the beginning
242. *Mai bai a hule ela:*	And the ancestors pledged this:
243. *Ita molo tuka momolo*	We step following in step
244. *Ma tabu tuka tatabu*	And we tread following in tread
245. *Hu ria lasi nae:*	Because, as the elders say:
246. *Molo meu suta lane*	Stepping, we follow the line
247. *Ma tabu tuka lae mae*	And treading, we follow the path
248. *Sono besa konana*	So until now
249. *Ndu'u ma losa*	Reaching and arriving at
250. *Lutu lolo ei*	The stone mound to stretch the legs
251. *Ma ro ai ifa lima*	And wood planks to fold the arms
252. *Sono tei ko ta nasala*	Be not inwardly in error
253. *Ma dale ko ta nasiko.*	And be not off target in your heart.
254. *Noi selama ia*	Consider that as long as
255. *Ita basa bole tuka ma saka*	We all can seek and search
256. *Roi ma tao.*	Toil and work.
257. *Sadi iku nasa-neda*	Continually remember

258. *Ma leo nafa-ndendene*	And continually bear in mind
259. *Sale dale dai fai*	Repent when you have the day
260. *Ma tu'e tei dai ledo.*	And regret when you have the time.
261. *Fo ela ko fai na neu fai*	As one day follows another day
262. *Ma ledo a na neu ledo*	And one sun follows another sun
263. *Fai neu pesi nesu*	There is a period for pounding rice
264. *Ma ledo a neu te'e alu*	And a time for resting the mortar
265. *Fai neu bibi kela*	A period to stable the goats
266. *Ma ledo a neu so'o dupe*	And a time for the sun to set
267. *Fai neu huru manu*	A period for gathering the chicken
268. *Ma ledo a neu hani bafi*	And a time for feeding the pigs
269. *Sono ita basa hia mo setele*	So we laugh joyfully
270. *Ma eki boe teta dale*	And shout happily
271. *Nai fai etu ma ledo basa.*	At day's end and sun's setting.

This is a remarkable recitation that utilises an array of traditional dyadic sets cast within a Christian context and thus intended to convey a Christian sense of life's condition. At the same time, this recitation uses a variety of dyadic sets associated with Christianity but used in an altered sense to provide its Christian message. One of the recurrent sets in this recitation is *tuka*//*saka*, the Landu dialect expression of the set *tunga*//*sanga* ('to seek'//'to search for'). This is the set used to describe the search for (Christian) wisdom and knowledge but here it is used without a specific object, implying a continuing and open-ended pursuit in life's activities. This set is linked with the set *roi*//*tao* ('to toil'//'to work'); thus, seeking and searching join toiling and working as common human activities.

***

The other eastern Rotenese poet known for his recitation of Biblical origin narratives is the master poet Anderias Ruy from Ringgou, the domain neighbouring Landu. Ande Ruy, as he is more commonly addressed, is at present the best-known Rotenese poet and performer. He is regularly called upon for formal occasions to represent the government and to participate at official events. He was, for example, the poet called upon to officially welcome the Indonesian President Joko Widodo on his visit to the island in January 2018.

Whereas Yulius Iu specialises in Christian performances, many of which are in a church setting, Ande Ruy is a poet who can and does try to perform all genres of recitations. He is a knowledgeable and versatile poet, chanter, singer and drummer, who commands an extensive repertoire. His repertoire includes Christian recitations.

An example of his appropriation of Biblical knowledge is his ritual-language narrative of creation in Genesis, which he has entitled 'Mother Earth's Creation from the Beginning'. This recitation, which I recorded in 2007, is a personal, interpretative rendering of this Biblical knowledge, which, as far as I can determine, Ande Ruy considers as a complement to and extension of other Rote origin narratives. Indeed, this is a narrative account of the creation of a Rotenese world. The recitation can be divided into the different acts of creation.

Dae Ina a Dadadi Masosana

Anderias Ruy

These initial lines set the stage for and announce the first act of creation. Their symmetry and succession are a masterly expression of an initial process of creation that is repeated in subsequent lines.

1.	*Hida bei leo hata na*	At a time long ago
2.	*Ma data bei leo dona*	At a time since past
3.	*Bei iu-iu kima lou*	Still dark as the inside of a clam
4.	*Ma bei hatu-hatu data feo*	Still gloom wrapped all round
5.	*Ma lua bei taa*	Sunlight was not yet
6.	*Ma makaledo bei taa*	Daylight was not yet
7.	*Ma bei pela oe leleu*	Still surface water throughout
8.	*Bei tasi oe lala*	Still the water of the sea surrounding
9.	*Ma Tate Mana-sura Bula*	The Inscriber of the Moon
10.	*Fo nai Tema Sio*	In the Fullness of Nine
11.	*Do Tou Mana-adu Ledo*	Or the Creator of the Sun
12.	*Fo nai Bate Falu*	In the Abundance of Eight
13.	*Bei ise-ise leo apa*	Still isolated as a lone buffalo
14.	*Ma bei mesa-mesa leo manu*	Still lonely as a lone chicken
15.	*Bei iku nonoi*	Still in the Heights

16.	*Dula Dale namaleu*	The Patterner of the Heart comes
17.	*Bei malalao*	Still hovering above
18.	*Do Malala Funa bei leu-leu*	Or the Marker of the Core still comes
19.	*Do bei lala-lala rae*	Still hovering over the Earth
20.	*Pela oe leleu*	Moving over the water
21.	*Do tasi oe lalama*	The waters of the sea extending
22.	*Ma Tate Mana-sura Bula*	The Inscriber of the Moon
23.	*Do Tou Mana-adu Ledo*	Or the Creator of the Sun
24.	*Lole hara na neu*	Raises forth his voice
25.	*Fo hara eke na neu*	The leaden voice comes forth
26.	*Ma selu dasi na neu*	Lifts forth his words
27.	*Fo dasi lilo na neu, nae:*	Golden words go forth, saying:
28.	*'Makaledo a dadi ma*	'Let sunlight occur
29.	*Ma malua a mori.'*	And let daylight appear.'
30.	*Boe ma malua mori*	So, light appears
31.	*Makaledo dadi,*	Sunlight occurs,
32.	*Silu malua a dulu*	Dawn lights the east
33.	*Ma hua makaledo laka.*	Daybreak brightens the head.

These next lines announce the second stage of creation: the separation of the Earth from the Heavens, concluding with the contrasting image of 'the east as red as a mango leaf and the head[lands] as green as a rice tip'.

34.	*Boema nadasi,*	Then he speaks,
35.	*Dasi lilo na neu*	Golden words come forth
36.	*Ma hara selu,*	And he says,
37.	*Hara eke na neu:*	The leaden voice comes forth:
38.	*'Tada Dae no Lain.'*	'Separate the Earth from the Heavens.'
39.	*De ri rae:*	So, it is said:
40.	*Tema Sio do Bate Falu*	Fullness of Nine or Abundance of Eight
41.	*Poi do Atan*	The zenith or the heights
42.	*Fo kala ledo mai dulu*	So the rising sun appears in the east
43.	*Ma toda bula mai laka*	And the falling moon appears at the head
44.	*Silu malua dulu*	Dawn lights the east

45. *Ma hu'a makaledo laka*	Daybreak brightens the head
46. *Fo dulu pila pao don*	The east as red as a mango leaf
47. *Do laka modo hade pedan.*	Or the head as green as a rice tip.
48. *Rae dae bafo do batu poi*	The earth's surface or rock's points
49. *Liun do sain.*	Ocean or sea.

Each stage of creation is announced by the golden words and a leaden voice. This stage is again concluded by reference to a traditional Rotenese saying:

50. *Selu dasi na neu*	He lifts forth his words
51. *Ma lole hara na neu*	And raises forth his voice
52. *Fo hara eke na neu:*	The leaden voice comes forth:
53. *'Dadi mai Batu Poi a.'*	'Let there be the Rock's Point.'
54. *Ma dasi lilo na neu:*	And the golden words come forth:
55. *Mori mai Dae Bafo a.'*	'Let there appear the Earth's Surface.'
56. *Boe ma mana mori, ara mori*	What appears, appears
57. *Ma mana dadi, ara dadi*	And what comes forth, comes forth
58. *Fo biti ne ara dadi do mori*	Plants come forth or appear
59. *Fo mori reni hu ana*	Appear with tiny trunks
60. *Ma dadi reni hu ina.*	And come forth with large trunks.
61. *Boe ma feli nade neu*	So, he gives them their name
62. *Ma beka bon, rae:*	And their aroma, saying:
63. *'Hu mana rerebi do*	'Trunks that grow thick
64. *Do mana sasape ara*	Leaves that hang down
65. *Fo rabuna bitala*	So that flowers bud forth
66. *Ma raboa bebeku*	And so that fruit droop
67. *Fo buna nara, mafa modo*	Flowers of half-ripe green
68. *Ma boa nara, latu lai*	And fruit of overripe yellow
69. *Fo ono rule Dae Bafo a*	Coming down on to the Earth
70. *Ma refa feo Batu Poi a.'*	And descending round the world.'
71. *De ri rae:*	So, it is said:
72. *'Mara mana lae modo ara*	'Whatever is half-ripe is still green
73. *Ma latu mana siki none ara.'*	And whatever is overripe is already soft.'

In these next lines, the creation of the Sun, Moon and stars invokes two more common Rotenese sayings. The first of these is the often-heard poetic comparison 'my father is like the Sun, rising and setting' (*ti//toda*), 'my mother is like the Moon appearing and disappearing' (*mopo//mori*). The second invocation is of the stars that form Orion's Belt, which are described in Rotenese as the 'stars that carry the pig' (two figures carrying a pig on a stick between them), and the Pleiades, the seven stars whose appearance ushers in the rice harvest.

74.	*Boe ma adu ledo a dadi.*	So, the Sun is created.
75.	*Fo ri rae:*	For it is said:
76.	*Bea aman leo ledo*	My father is like the Sun
77.	*Ma ti toda leo ledo*	Rising, setting like the Sun
78.	*Ma toda bula a mori.*	Setting as the Moon appears.
79.	*Fo ri rae:*	For it is said:
80.	*Bea inan leo bulan*	My mother is like the Moon
81.	*Fo mopo mori leo bulan.*	Disappearing, appearing like the Moon.
82.	*Ma kari ru neu atan*	Scattering stars to the Heavens
83.	*De ri rae:*	Thus, it is said:
84.	*Ru manalepa bafi*	The stars that carry the pig
85.	*Do hitu manahere hade ra*	Or the seven stars that bear the rice
86.	*Fo buka bafa do daen*	To open the surface of the Earth
87.	*Ma silu mata rou lain na*	And the eyelids of the Heights
88.	*Mora te'e rahate.*	Like fireflies blinking.

In the next lines, the voice of the creator speaks directly to creatures of the sea, each of which carries distinct associations in traditional ritual-language compositions. The pairings are crucial: sea clams (*tia tasi*) form a set with mossy lichen (*lopu le*). As such, these sea clams (or, more specifically, their shells, which are seen on rocks near the sea) and mossy lichen (also seen on rocks near the sea) are invoked, in other ritual contexts, as botanic images of intensive clustering and close solidarity. Similarly, the fish *moko holu* and *dusu lake* are the equivalent in Ringgou of the ritually important *tio holu//dusu lae* (see Chapter 3) in Termanu, which are linked to the realm of the sea. The linkage of the *nase* fish of the estuary and playful monkeys of the forest (*nase tel//ode rane*) is less clear but appears to allude to a general idea of the social clustering of Earth's creatures.

89.	*Selu dasin neu sain*	His voice goes to the sea
90.	*Ma lole haran neu liun*	And his words go to the ocean
91.	*Fo ela rai tasi a dadi*	So that the sea comes forth
92.	*Ma seko meti a mori.*	And the ocean appears.
93.	*Boe ma nahara neu sain, nae:*	He speaks to the sea, saying:
94.	*'Moka holu o dadi*	'You, *moka holu* fish, come forth
95.	*Na dadi mo tia tasin*	Come forth with *tia tasi* [sea clams]
96.	*Fo ela tia tasi mai tai*	That the sea clams may cling
97.	*Ma dusu lake o mori*	And you *dusu lake* fish, appear
98.	*Na mori mo lopu le*	Appear with the *lopu le* [mossy lichen]
99.	*Fo ela lopu le mai feo.*	That the mossy lichen may cluster.
100.	*Nai sai makeon*	In the darkened sea
101.	*Do nai liu ma momodo na*	Or the deep green ocean
102.	*Fo ela oli seu meu esa*	So that in the estuary, you go as one
103.	*Ma nase te meu esa*	And the small *nase* fish go there
104.	*Ma nura nai meu esa*	And in the forest, you go as one
105.	*Fo ode rane meu esa.'*	So that playful monkeys, you go as one.'

In the next lines, the voice of the creator is directed to a variety of creatures, all of whom serve as icons in other ritual-language recitations. These creatures of portent are the lizard of the Sun and gecko of the Moon (*korofao ledo//tekelabo bula*), the swallows of the Sun and kestrels of the Moon (*li lao ledo//selu pela bula*), who with small bats and flying foxes (*soi ana//bau ana*), are associated with the initial winds that presage the change in the monsoons. The creatures of the Heavens are described as accompanying the winds that carry the words of the creator.[19] The next eight lines are the words of the creator, who explains how he sees and shapes knowledge and wisdom (in Ringgou dialect: *lela//rolu*) and sets a path to be followed. From what follows, knowledge and wisdom are represented as part of the pattern of the world from its earliest creation.

---

19   The use of a stepwise sequence of lines, rather than coupled lines, is an indication of the poet Ande Ruy's compositional virtuosity but makes recognition of precise pairings more difficult.

106. *Boe ma lole hara na neu*	His word goes forth
107. *Ma selu dasi na neu,*	And his voice goes forward,
108. *Nadasi neu dae bafo a*	The voice directed to the earth
109. *Ma hara mai batu poi a, nae:*	And words directed to the world, saying:
110. *'Korofao ledo o dadi*	'Lizard of the Sun come forth
111. *Dadi mai dae bafo a*	Come forth upon the earth
112. *Dadi mo basa tia dedena mara*	Come forth with all your friends
113. *Ma tekelabo bula o mori*	And gecko of the Moon appear
114. *Mori mo basa sena mara*	Appear with all your companions
115. *Fo dadi meu mana tui dasi*	To come forth with those who give voice
116. *Do mori meu mana malosa hara.'*	Or appear with those who give word.'
117. *Boema hara neu poin*	Then the word goes to Heaven
118. *Ma dasi neu lain, nae:*	And the voice goes to the Heights, saying:
119. *'Li lao ledo a dadi*	'Swallows of the Sun come forth
120. *Dadi mu mana-fako ani*	Come forth with those who follow the wind
121. *Dadi mo soi ana timu dulu ra*	Come forth with the small bats of the east wind
122. *Ma selu pela bula o mori*	And kestrels of the Moon appear
123. *Mori mu mana relu saku*	Appear with those who see the storms
124. *Mori mo bau ana sepe laka ra*	Appear with the tiny flying foxes of the dawn
125. *Fo ela ani ana timu dulu a*	So that light winds of the east
126. *Ani mai fafae*	The winds may come to shake
127. *Ma saku ana sepe laka a*	And the tiny storms of the dawn
128. *Saku mai titipa*	The storms come to gust
129. *Na dadi meu ma neni hara*	Coming forth to carry the word
130. *Na mori meu ma losa dasi:*	And appear to spread the voice:
131. *'Bati neu au lima u'u*	'So that my hands
132. *Adu lela ra*	Shape the knowledge
133. *Do soa neu au mata boa*	Or in order that the pupils of my eyes

134. *Heu rolu ra*	See the wisdom
135. *Ela pasa mata reu eno*	That they may spy the path
136. *Ma sunda idu reu dala*	And they may recognise the road
137. *Fo reu dala dua ra*	That they may go along the two roads
138. *Do eno telu ra.'*	Or the three paths.'

The next lines describe the 'fifth and sixth' days of Creation—a numerical designation required by the formal pairing of numbers in ritual language. The creator views his creation.[20] He then calls for the goats and water buffalo of the hills and fields.

139. *Mai fai lima na*	Come the fifth day
140. *Ma mai ledo ne na*	And come the sixth sun
141. *Nalan neu rerelu*	He went to view
142. *Ma nalan neu memete*	And he went to inspect
143. *Fo mete neu mata boa*	For his eyes
144. *Heu roluna*	To see the wisdom
145. *Ma rerelu neu lima u'u*	And to view his hands' work
146. *Adu lolena*	To shape the appearance
147. *Tehu lete bai no soda*	The hill of wellbeing
148. *Ma bafa bai no loa.*	And the surface of great width.
149. *Boe ma lole hara na neu*	His word goes forth
150. *Ma selu dasi na neu:*	And his voice goes forth:
151. *'Iko mana fefelo o dadi*	'Swaying tails come forward
152. *Ma sura mana mamasu o mori*	And lifting horns appear
153. *Mori mu lete a*	Appear to go upon the hills
154. *Ma dadi mu mo a.'*	And come forth to go upon the fields.'
155. *Fo hule, rae:*	So, they call, saying:
156. *'Sura manamamasu*	'Horns that lift
157. *Do iko manafefelo ara.'*	Or tails that sway.'
158. *Fo ela beka rae:*	Thus, to announce, saying:
159. *'Bulan bote bibi nara*	'The Moon's flock of goats
160. *Ma Ledo tena apa nara.*	And the Sun's herd of water buffalo.

---

20 Several lines in this passage have curious pairings that may simply be mistakes in recitation—for example, *rolu* is paired with *lole* (rather than *lela*) and *soda* with *loa* rather than *mole*.

161. *Rai lete bote bibi*	On the hills are flocks of goats
162. *Do mo tena apa a.'*	Or on the fields are herds of water buffalo.'
163. *Boe ma bote bibi ra dadi*	So, flocks of goats come forth
164. *Ma tena apa ra mori.*	And herds of water buffalo appear.

This next passage is focused on the creation of Adam. In it, there is a minor performance lapse. Instead of '(Boy) Inscriber of the Moon'//'(Man) Creator of the Sun' (*Tate Mana-sura Bula*//Tou Mana-adu Ledo), as in the initial passage of this recitation, Ande Ruy uses the formula '(Boy) Creator of the Moon'//'(Man) Creator of the Sun' (Tate Mana-adu Bula//Tou Mana-adu Ledo). Conferring with the 'Patterner of the Heart'//'Fashioner of the Inner Self' (Dula Dale//Le'u Tei), the creator sets out to create a human being.

This creative act is described, as earlier in the creation of the fifth and sixth days, by citing an idiomatic Rotenese expression about what the eyes see and the nose indicates, thus acting according to a preconceived plan.[21] Adam is created by mixing the Earth's liver and by pounding the innermost rocks. The ritual formula for the Earth is *Dae Bafo*//*Batu Poi* ('Earth's Surface and Pointed Rocks'), thus Adam is created from both the earth (*dae*) and its rocks (*batu*).

In Rotenese, name and reputation go hand-in-hand. In ritual language, 'name' (*nade*) is paired with 'aroma' (*bo*). In this passage, the creator confers the name 'Adam' but Ande Ruy names Adam as 'The Bird of the East and the Cockerel of the Head'.

165. *Boe ma Tate Mana-adu Bulan*	The Creator of the Moon
166. *Ma Tou Mana-adu Ledo*	And the Creator of the Sun
167. *Du'a do neu dua,*	Thinks twice
168. *Ma afi tai neu telu.*	And ponders thrice.
169. *Boema lole hara na neu*	Then his word goes forth
170. *Ma selu dasi na neu, nae:*	And his voice goes forward, saying:
171. *'Mana mori ara mori so*	'What appears has appeared
172. *Ma mana dadi ara dadi so*	And what comes forth has come forth

---

21   In Rotenese ritual language, this is *fo ela adu nan leo mata boana*//*ela tao nan leo idu ain* ('to create things as conceived'//'to make things as indicated'), thus 'conceived'//'indicated' according to a plan—literally: 'according to the pupils of his eyes'//'according to the bridge of his nose'.

173. *Te bea neu relus*	Who sees these things
174. *Ma bea neu metes*	And who watches these things
175. *Ma bea neu tui*	And who speaks of these things
176. *Ma beu neu beka?'*	And who talks of these things?'
177. *Boe ma neu du'a na hataoli a*	So, he thinks of a human
178. *Ma neu afi na lahenda*	And he considers a person
179. *Boema dedea no Dula Dale na*	He speaks with the Patterner of the Heart
180. *Ma o'ola no Le'u Tei na*	And talks with the Shaper of the Inner Self
181. *Fo ela adu nan leo mata boana*	To create things as conceived
182. *Ma ela tao nan leo idu ain.*	And make things as indicated.
183. *De ri rae:*	So, it is said:
184. *Mata boa heu rolu na*	The pupil of the eye shows wisdom
185. *Ma idu bara te tasi na*	And the bridge of the nose points the way
186. *Fo Amak Mata Boan*	As the Father of the Pupil of the Eye
187. *Ma To'ok Idu Ain.*	And Uncle of the Bridge of the Nose.
188. *Boe ma do'i na dae aten*	So, he mixes the earth's liver
189. *Ma tutu a batu buten*	And pounds innermost rocks
190. *De adun hataholi*	He creates a man
191. *Fo dadi neu hataholi*	So that man comes forth
192. *Ma taon laiheda*	And he makes a person
193. *Fo mori ne laihenda*	So that a human appears
194. *Sama leo rupa na*	In his image
195. *Ma deta leo lolena.*	And according to his appearance.
196. *Boema foi nade na*	So, he gives a name
197. *Hule bon na, rae:*	And calls forth an aroma, saying:
198. *'Tou Manupui Dulu*	'The Man, Bird of the East
199. *Ma Tate O'oro Laka*	And the Boy, Cockerel of the Head
200. *Ri Adam.'*	This is Adam.'

The final passage of this recitation, recounting the sixth and seventh days of creation, is revealing. It contains lines that evoke the origin of the house—a well-ordered house with firm posts and an encompassing intact roof—and it calls for blessings in lines drawn from traditional origin celebrations: the bounty of the lontar and blessings of the sea. As such, this passage could pass as a traditional recitation. At the same time, however, it speaks of making things clean and pure (*lalao//lalafu*) for those who are troubled of heart and who seek to follow the right path and it ends with the Christian evocation of wellbeing and peace (*soda//mole*).

201.	*Neu ledo ne na*	On the sixth period
202.	*Ma neu fai hitu na*	And on the seventh day
203.	*Boe ma lole hara na neu*	His word goes out
204.	*Ma selu dasi na neu*	And his voice goes forth
205.	*Adu nan tetu-tetu*	Creating in good order
206.	*Ma tao nan tata-tata*	And working with care
207.	*Na tetu ure dae so*	So that order turns upon the earth
208.	*Ma tama sini laka rao so*	And well-arranged like a thatched roof
209.	*Leo tama sini laka rao*	Like a well-arranged thatched roof
210.	*Tama ta naka boti*	Together, it does not spread
211.	*Ma tesa di nali folo*	Set like a well-planted house post
212.	*Tesa ta nata leko so*	Set, it does not shake
213.	*Rae: ues tou hahae.*	It is said: At his work, he rests.
214.	*De mai tao ma-lalao*	Come make clean
215.	*Do ma-lalafu fai ia*	Or make pure on this day
216.	*Ma fe ua tua mai fai ia*	And give the bounty of the lontar on this day
217.	*Ma bati nale tasi mai ledo ia*	And the blessings of the sea at this time
218.	*Ela bati nale neu*	So that blessings go
219.	*Mana tu'e tei*	To those who are troubled at heart
220.	*Do manasale dale ara*	Or those who feel wrong within
221.	*Reu dodo ma tatai*	To consider and to weigh up
222.	*Fo tabu tuka suta lane dalan*	To step along the right road
223.	*Ma ela lope tuka lae mae enon*	And walk along the proper path
224.	*Losa do na neu*	For all time forward
225.	*Ma seku nete na neu*	And for ever onward
226.	*Soda mole neu ita.*	The wellbeing and peace for us.

This recitation is a fusion: Christian knowledge presented in accordance with traditional ideas, sayings and formulaic phrasing, with allusions to accepted knowledge and practices. It is thus a synthesis of two sources of knowledge regarded as complementary and compatible. The venue for its performance, however, is not a church, as would be the case for Yulius Iu's recitation, but a more traditional social setting.

Elevating recitation to its highest performance level

The highest level of performance for traditional recitations involves a special linguistic style that is accompanied by—indeed, expressed through— a drumming mode of chanting known as *bapa*. Significantly, Ande Ruy can, and does, offer his recitation of this origin narrative as a drumming performance that requires complex linguistic verbal play. Although the message of this recitation is not altered in this performative mode, its expression is elevated by a complex reiterative process.

To illustrate this performance mode, one can compare the initial eight lines as recorded in standard recitation mode with those same eight lines in a drumming mode. The first eight lines are as follows:

1.	*Hida bei leo hata na*	At a time long ago
2.	*Ma data bei leo dona*	At a time since past
3.	*Bei iu-iu kima lou*	Still dark as the inside of a clam
4.	*Ma bei hatu-hatu data feo*	Still gloom wrapped all round
5.	*Ma lua bei taa*	Sunlight was not yet
6.	*Ma makaledo bei taa*	Daylight was not yet
7.	*Ma bei pela oe leleu*	Still surface water throughout
8.	*Bei tasi oe lala …*	Still the water of the sea surrounding …

These same eight lines in drumming mode, which are set out to indicate the main formulaic pairs (in bold and then separately) are as follows:

1.	*Fai nau hida bei-**hida bei leo hata***	> Hida bei leo hata
2.	*Data bei-**data bei leo dona** ma*	> Dato bei leo dona
3.	*Nau uni **bei hatu-hatu data feo** ma*	> Bei hatu-hatu data feo
4.	*Bei iu-iu-**iu-iu kima lou** a*	> Iu-iu kima lou
5.	*Bei uni tasi oe-**tasi oe lala** ma*	> Tasi oe lala
6.	*Pela oe-**pela oe leleu** a*	> Pela oe leleu
7.	*Fo uni makaledo-**makaledo bei taa***	> Makaledo bei taa
8.	*Hu malua-**malua bei taa** ma*	> Malua bei taa

It is essential to recognise this as an entirely separate recitation. As such, and as is common, Ande Ruy has reordered lines, reversing lines 3 and 4 and placing lines 5 and 6 ahead of lines 7 and 8 in comparison with his other 'standard' recitation. Most lines have a repetition of the key semantic forms but there are also 'filler terms' (*fai nau, nau uni, fo uni*) inserted to continue the beat and maintain the drumming rhythm. The connector term *ma* ('and') separates lines and can be considered either the end of one or the beginning of the next.[22]

The fact that this origin narrative is regarded as suitable for performance in this elevated mode, which is used more commonly at present for funeral chants, is indicative of its inclusion within a repertoire of traditional knowledge. It represents the pinnacle of such knowledge on Rote today.

The spoken and unspoken

This is a study of the spoken word in narratives of great significance. Yet, among those for whom these words were regarded as foundational utterances, there were matters that were considered better not spoken. Of these matters, the most important was the killing of Shark and Crocodile to create the model of the first house. Old Meno was emphatic in his view that this act be known but not stated. He insisted that I understand what had occurred but that I recognise that it was not appropriate to give clear expression to it in the narratives.

This act is, however, alluded to in four lines of Termanu's Recitation II. When all attempts to construct the house fail, Danga Lena Liun ('Chief Hunter of the Sea') and Mane Tua Sain ('Great Lord of the Sea') are summoned and, at this point, there are four lines of verse that might not seem to make sense:

Ala taon neu uma	They make him into the house-posts
Ma ala taon neu eda ai.	And they make him into the tree-ladder.
Besak-ka kalu kapa ledo ha'an	Now the sun heats the buffalo sinews
Ma dui manu a'u te'e-na.	And the dew moistens the chicken bones.

---

22 This presentation of eight lines of Ande Ruy's drumming performance is insufficient to understand or appreciate the full complexity of his art. It is intended to recognise the 'elevation' that Ruy accords his recitation and the knowledge it embodies.

The first of these lines use the verb *tao* ('to make, to work'), that gives no idea that this creative action involves the killing of the Lords of the Sea. The lines that follow, which seem hardly to fit with the previous lines, are the lines that reveal the death of these lords. They are formulaic lines that recur in mortuary chants and are used to refer to the mortal remains, particularly the bones, of the deceased. Thus, in the Rotenese cosmology of life, the first successful act of creation—the creation of the house—is founded on the sacrifice of the body of the rulers of the realm of the Sea.

In other of Termanu's recitations, a creature of the Sea renders its body to create a crucial cultural product: rice and millet come from the repeated planting of Bole Sou and Asa Nao; cloth patterns come from the body of Pata Iuk and Dula Foek; and the vessel for indigo and the base for spinning come from the two shells Suti Solo and Bina Bane. Although the initial recitations from Thie are silent about the death of Shark and Crocodile, other recitations recount the death of a creature or creatures from the Sea as part of the process of creation. In Thie, Bole Sou and Asa Nao as well as the shells Suti Solo and Bina Bane are credited with producing rice, millet and the other nine grains and plants of the island, while it is from the capture and slaughter of the sea cow and turtle Masi Dande and Solo Suti that the origin celebration at Nasi Dano derives. The Rotenese do not comment on these acts of creative production but only recount them and remain silent on their creative significance.

The mortuary chants (*bini mamates*) of the Rotenese liturgy

As a study of the spoken word, this volume provides only a partial record of a more extensive Rotenese 'liturgical' tradition. A diverse assortment of mortuary chants constitutes a corpus of oral compositions, all in strict canonical parallelism, that is substantially larger than the corpus of origin narratives. These chants form a less esoteric tradition because they involve— or have involved in the past—the active participation of mourners, led by one or more poets, in a chorus of dancers on the night or nights before burial. Although they share similarities in their composition, these chants are narratives of a different sort from origin narratives.

Each chant is identified with a particular chant character whose life course is imaginatively set out, often beginning at birth and continuing to death, giving emphasis to life as a journey. In some chants, the circumstances of death are recounted; in one notable chant, the chant character describes his pending departure to the Afterworld and admonishes the living on what they should do. All chants carry a moral message.[23]

At death, a particular chant was chosen from the repertoire of existing chants to fit the situation of the deceased. The repertoire includes specific chants: for a young woman who dies while 'still unripe', for a profligate young nobleman, for a widow who has raised a family, for a young child, a rich man or an elder. The repertoire also includes general chants for 'widows and orphans', which can be modified to fit almost any deceased person. The origin narrative *Suti Solo do Bina Bane*, for example, with its emphasis on the journey of the two shells, who, as 'orphans and widows', spend their time in search of companionship, can be used in Termanu and in other domains as a general-category mortuary chant (see Fox 2016).[24]

In addition to these mortuary chants, there exists in some domains a related genre of dirges that are chanted to advise and direct the deceased on the journey to the Afterworld (for an example of this genre by the poet Ande Ruy, see Fox 2021: 222–29). The assemblage of the mortuary compositions is extensive, diverse and engaging. It comprehends much more than is included in this volume.

***

The purpose of this volume has been to document, explicate and thus preserve a tradition of oral poetic composition that would probably have otherwise been lost. Preserving this tradition is in fulfilment of a promise made, many years ago, to the knowledge-holders of this tradition.

---

23 I have published the translations of three life-course recitations from the collection I recorded from Termanu: 1) *Dela Koli ma Seko Buna* (Fox 1971b; 2014a: 91–128); *Ndi Loniama ma Laki Elokama* (Fox 2003; 2014: 283–94); and 3) *Kea Lenga ma Lona Balu* (Fox 2021). I have also published a translation of an untranslated text originally gathered by the linguist J.C.G. Jonker (1911: 97–102), *Manu Kama ma Tepa Nilu* (Fox 1988d; 2014a: 229–64), plus the translation of a short mortuary chant from Oenale, *Pua Rulis ma No Sanggu* (Fox 2023). These illustrative recitations only hint at the beauty and diversity of the repertoire.

24 While in Termanu an origin narrative like *Suti Solo do Bina Bane* can be modified to render it as a mortuary chant, the chant characters named in Termanu's life-course recitations do not figure in its origin narratives. In Thie, however, one notorious chant character, Pau Balo and Bola Lunggi—the Don Juan of Rote—makes his way to the Heavens to continue his lovemaking there. In general, however, mortuary chants form a distinct genre from origin narratives.

My intention in this volume has been not just to preserve this tradition but also to situate it within an array of poetic traditions that harken back to the world's oldest poetry and to indicate how these poetic traditions reverberate with similar oral poetic traditions in some of the world's major cultural regions.

Although Rote is a tiny island on the margins of South-East Asia, its oral poetry is of world significance. An appreciation of the art of composition by the poets of Rote offers insights into early traditions of poetry elsewhere in the world and may, I hope, contribute to the comparative comprehension of the creative processes involved in such oral achievements.

In this volume, I have also endeavoured to trace the development of new forms of expression within the Rotenese tradition. The poets of Rote have been engaged in both preserving and extending their tradition. Life on Rote has been profoundly transformed from the ancestral past and the island's poetry, as a living tradition, has been correspondingly affected. On the island, while some poets—always a minority of individuals— have continued to preserve existing traditions, others have become poet– preachers and developed traditions that reveal and proclaim new origins. Most of the island's finest poets regard all such developments as part of a seamless continuing tradition.

Documenting, explicating and preserving the considerable corpus of Rotenese mortuary chants that form an integral part of this poetic tradition remain the next tasks in my ethnographic efforts.

Appendix I: A portrait gallery of poets

On coming to know the poets of Rote

The master poets, whose 'voices' are represented in this volume, are regarded by their communities as custodians of the knowledge of the ancestors. Although each recitation is a unique composition, these poets insist that they are transmitting the words that have been passed down to them from their ancestors—those who have gone before them. The formal semantic pairing of their words elevates and enhances this ancestral knowledge and the seriousness of their responsibilities.

As recognised custodians of knowledge, the particular poets who have contributed their knowledge to this volume carried out their responsibilities in a time of considerable social change and in response to my interventions and involvement with them. They were all aware of the changes that were occurring in their way of life and particularly determined that their knowledge be preserved and transmitted. Of all the poets in this volume, it was Stefanus Adulanu, 'Old Meno', who most clearly articulated his concern for the preservation of this knowledge and recognised that the tape recorder which I had brought with me on my first period of fieldwork in 1965–66 was the means for his knowledge be passed on to his grandchildren. His involvement was critical to the gathering of this Rotenese 'knowledge of origins'.

It is important to emphasise that origin narratives are a critical component of an array of knowledge that Rotenese master poets preserve and transmit in their recitations. A larger component of this knowledge consists of mortuary compositions that I have described as 'life-course' compositions because they recount, in a standardised but imagined fashion, a life story intended to approximate the situation of different categories of deceased individuals. Each poet, depending on his skill and scope, has a repertoire of recitations, some of which may be origin narratives. While this volume is focused on these origin narratives, there remains a considerable collection of other compositions on which I continue to work.

The poets whose recitations are recorded and conveyed in the volume share a common goal in perpetuating their knowledge of 'origins'. They are recognised as *hataholi malelak*: 'persons of knowledge'. Their personal capacities and fluency in expressing this knowledge, in a canonical linguistic fashion, marks them as poets. Their special skills may have led some of them to become teachers or preachers while others have lived their lives as simple farmers and palm tappers. Each of these poets is a distinct individual in personality, background, interest and even in style of expression. This portrait gallery is intended to present these individual poets and to hint at their differences.

My close involvement with the poets who have contributed to this volume began during extended fieldwork on Rote—initially in 1965–66 and again in 1972–73. Most of the origin narratives from Termanu were gathered during my first field trip while those from Thie were gathered during short visits on both my field trips.

My initial involvement was, by no means, straightforward. My efforts involved a fraught learning process. When my wife and I had settled into the community at Ufa Len in Termanu, I began my efforts to learn spoken Rotenese—the dialect of Termanu—but from the time of my first recording, I was thrust into trying to understand the formal complexities and compositional subtleties of ritual language in parallelism whose competence was confined to a relatively small group of knowledgeable elders. This was a different task from learning 'ordinary' spoken Rotenese, but I was continually told by the elders that this was the only way to answer the questions about Rotenese culture that I had begun to ask.

I had brought with me to Rote an Uher tape recorder, an instrument that was new to the Rotenese of Ufa Len and which they named my 'voice catcher' (*penangkap suara*). This voice catcher was regarded as the appropriate vehicle for the recording of ritual language recitations and that became its primary purpose. It became an 'attractor' for the poets of Termanu. By the time that I visited Thie, I had gained in my language skills, and I was better prepared to record the various recitations I was offered.

My second intensive involvement with poets from Rote was in the 'Master Poets Project' which begun in 2006 with initial support from the Australian Research Council that was extended with additional funding. The 'Master Poets Project' involved bringing poets from all areas of Rote for a week's recording session in Bali. The intention was to record compositions in parallelism across the entire chain of dialects on the island. In total, eleven recording sessions were held from 2006 to 2019 involving 28 different Rotenese poets. Origin narratives for both Termanu and Thie were recorded during this period along with the recitations of *Genesis* by poets from the domains of Landu and Ringgou.[1]

---

1   One regret in putting together this portrait gallery is that I did not take more photographs of the poets whom I recorded during my first field trip. It was often a trade-off between photos and recordings. Several of photographs in this gallery have already appeared in earlier publications.

Petrus Malesi: Peu Malesi

The first poet to come forward to record for my Uher tape recorder was Peu Malesi. His first recitation was an origin narrative—a version of the origin of fire and of cooking. Peu Malesi's recitation set in train an involved engagement that led to the gathering of most of the origin narratives of Termanu. His photograph is appropriately the first portrait for this gallery.

Peu Malesi was a frequent visitor to Ufa Len during my fieldwork in 1965–66 and again in 1972–73. He was the source of many recordings, most of which were mortuary rituals or 'life-course' compositions. Peu Malesi, who was a member of the commoner clan Dou Danga, always presented himself in a quiet manner. He rarely took part in the contentions and disputations that are a constant feature of Rotenese talk. Instead, he would wait to be called upon—as invariably, he was—and he would impart his comments in ritual language. One Rotenese called these interventions 'The Voice of Malesi', alluding to them like a radio broadcast heard on the Voice of Malaysia. This photograph is of Peu Malesi as he would often appear in Ufa Len in a traditional Rotenese hat and white shirt.

Stefanus Adulanu: 'Old Meno'

The second portrait for this gallery is that of Stefanus Adulanu: 'Old Meno' (*Meno Tua*) as he was known. Old Meno was the *Dae Langak* ('Head of the Earth') in clan Meno, a position that derived from the first ancestor of Termanu, Pada Lalais. He did not know exactly when he was born but he could remember as a teenager the ravages of what was the 'Spanish flu' which swept the island. He had attended three years of local school, learned high Malay and was, for a considerable period during Dutch times, the scribe (*juru tulis*) for Termanu's court. During my first visit, he continued to preside at Termanu's court sessions.

The *Manek* as the traditional 'Ruler' of Termanu designated Old Meno to assist me in gathering Termanu's oral history but Old Meno soon became my teacher in all matters Rotenese and my chief instructor in ritual language. He suffered a great deal from arthritis and generally kept close to his home, but he would also invite me to attend court sessions and when he was able, he attended ceremonies, mainly mortuary feasts, at which adjudication was often required to settle matters of inheritance. I particularly regret that I took only a few photos of Meno and none of these are in good quality. This is a photograph of Old Meno standing outside of his house in Ola Lain.

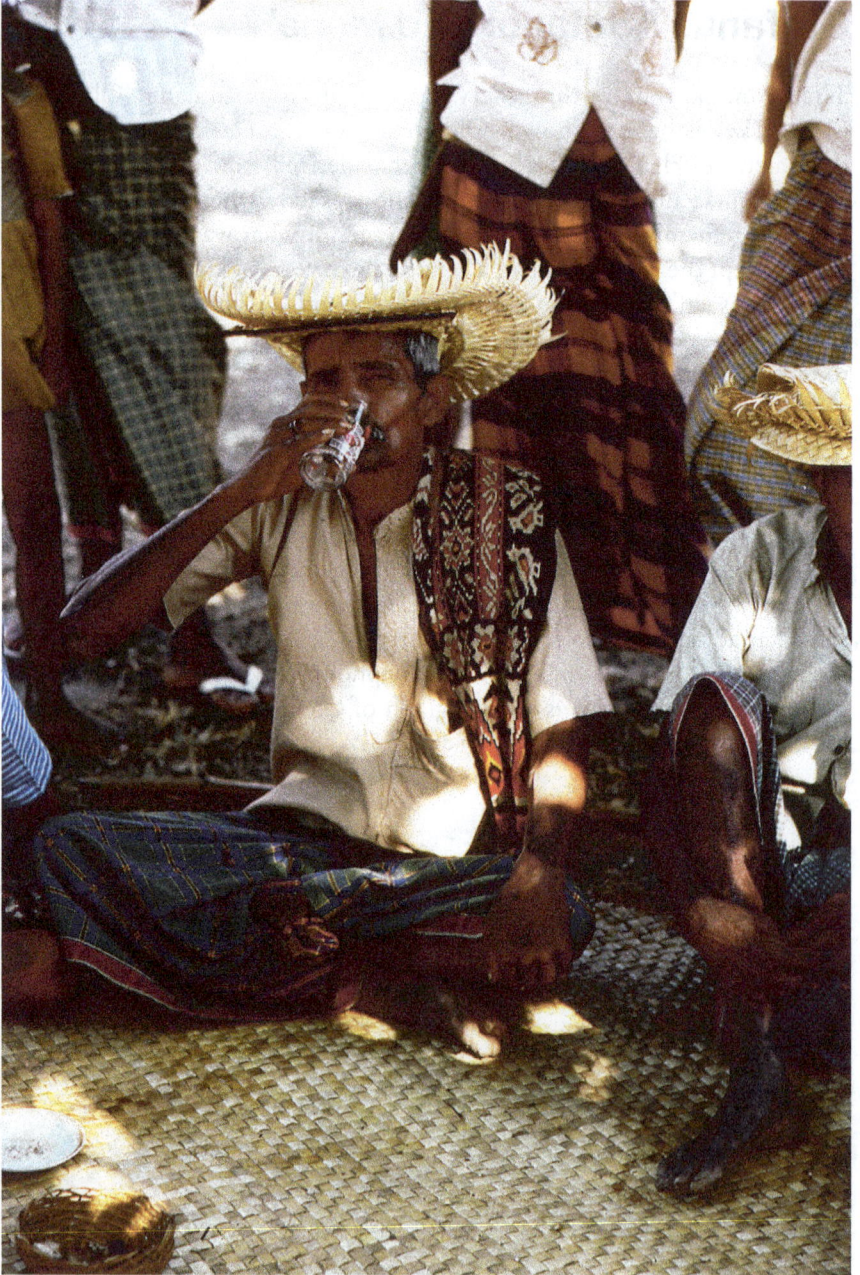

Eli Pellondou: Seu Ba'i

The third portrait is that of Eli Pellondou who was known as Seu Ba'i. Like Peu Malesi, Seu Ba'i was a member of clan Dou Danga but from a different branch. I first met him at Old Meno's house in Ola Lain. He lived in Namodale on Termanu's north coast and would come to Old Meno's to listen to the recordings I had made and Old Meno's recitations. Seu Ba'i was a recognised poet in his own right but was still learning from Old Meno.

Old Meno had died before I returned to Rote on my second field trip in 1972–73 and Seu Ba'i took over in trying to instruct me. He would give me his commentary on some of Old Meno's recitations which he knew that I had recorded. He also provided me with an expanded and significantly altered version of a mortuary composition that Old Meno had recited for me.

Seu Ba'i was particularly critical of the dual names given to some of the characters in the origin narratives by other poets. He could be counted on to dispute such names with Peu Malesi who never seemed perturbed by Seu Ba'i's judgments. In time, I learned that Seu Ba'i had brothers and cousins who were also noted poets and I was eventually able to record them as well. The photograph that I have used here is one of Seu Be'i seated on a mat and drinking lontar-gin, which the Rotenese call the 'water of words.'

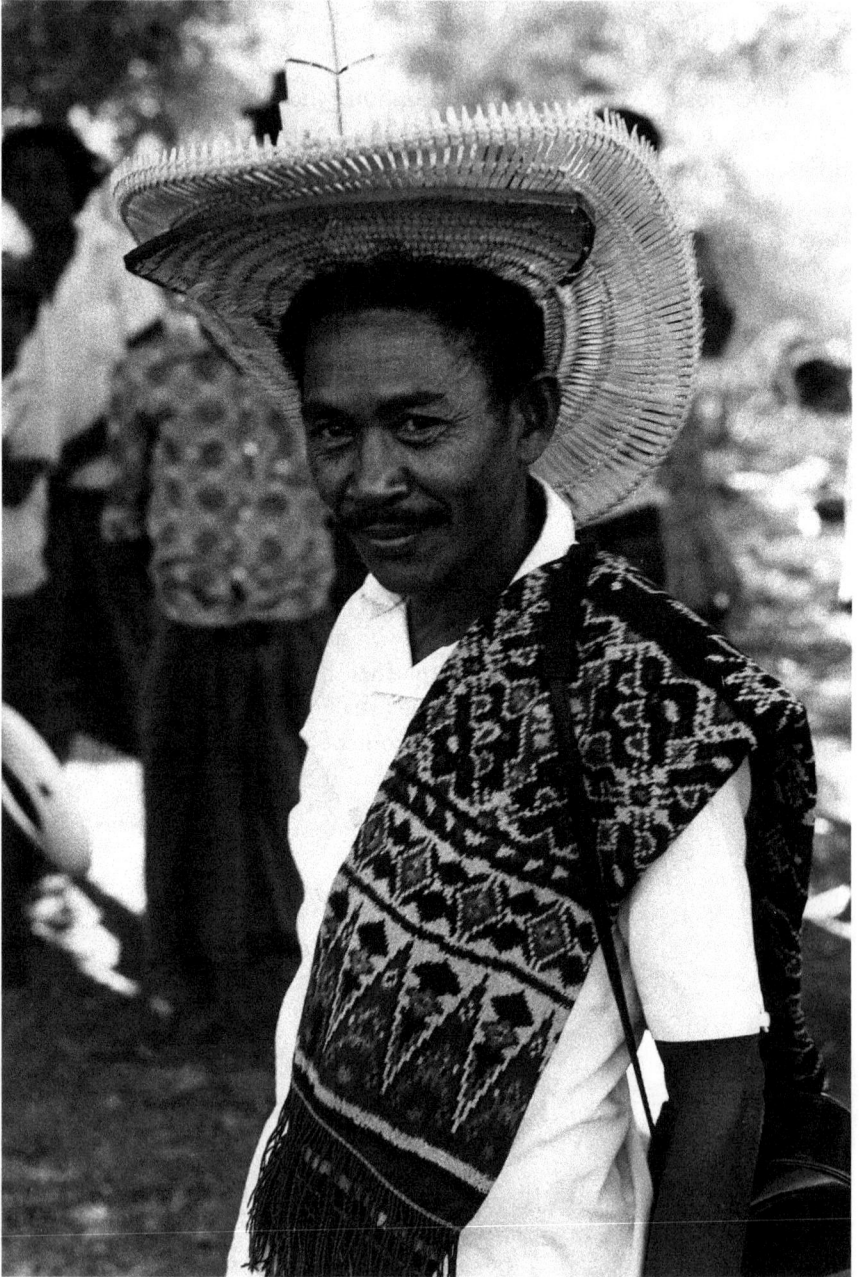

Esau Markus Pono: Pak Pono

The fourth photograph is of Esau Markus Pono who, in time, became my closest Rotenese friend and confidant. Our paths crossed briefly during my first field trip; so I only came to know him during my second period of fieldwork. Pak Pono lived in Hala, on the coast, and by the time we met, he had already gained a reputation as a noted preacher and an emerging poet. In planning the ritual to honour Old Meno, I visited Pak Pono in Hala and invited him to act as my ritual spokesman at the *Tutus*-ceremony[2]

From the late 1970s onwards, Esau Pono became my Rotenese 'elder brother.' He was involved in the filming I did on Rote with Tim Asch and visited Canberra in connection with that filming. He came to comprehend better than any Rotenese what I was trying to do in documenting Termanu's traditions and as he learned more of what I had already recorded, he became my closest advisor on Termanu's traditions.

When I began my 'Master Poet Project' in 2006 bringing poets to Bali to record their performances, Esau became a key member and continued to join each subsequent recording session until the ninth session in October 2014 when he was too ill to make the journey. We had collaborated for over 30 years, and we grew old together. I was able to compose a short chant that was read on my behalf at his funeral. Because a photograph of Pak Pono in his maturity is on the cover of this volume, I have chosen another photograph of him in his prime in 1973.

---

2   For a discussion of this ceremony, see Fox, J.J. 'To the Aroma of the Name: The Celebration of a Ritual of Rock and Tree' in *Explorations in Semantic Parallelism* 2014: 295–311. Some years later with Tim Asch, I also recorded one of Pak Pono's church services and analysed his sermon at that service: see Fox, J.J. 'The Rotenese sermon as a Linguistic Performance' in *Explorations in Semantic Parallelism*: 2014: 355–64.

N.D. Pah: Guru Pah

The fifth portrait is of N.D. Pah known as Guru Pah. I visited Guru Pah at his home in Thie on just two occasions: the first visit toward the end of my initial fieldwork in 1965–66 and again in the middle of my second field trip in 1972–73. Compared to my unplanned, occasional and somewhat disorganised catch-as-catch-can recordings in Termanu, my recording sessions with Guru Pah were intense and were concentrated on origin narratives. Both of my visits were for about a week each. I stayed at Guru Pah's house in Oe Handi sleeping each night on the resting platform under his roof. On each visit, there were ceremonies to attend—a funeral on the first visit and a wedding and a funeral on the second. On the first visit, all my recordings were from Guru Pah himself. On the second visit, Guru Pah invited his close colleague, Samuel Ndun, to join us and my recordings were from both men.

Guru Pah was slight and seemingly frail, but he had remarkable energy combined with enormous knowledge of the traditions of Thie. He was determined to impart to me as much as he could of that knowledge during my time with him. He was also a superb player of the *sesandu*—the traditional Rotenese bamboo zither with lontar leaf cover—and in the late afternoon and early evening, he would sit and play for himself. My photograph is of him on one of these occasions.

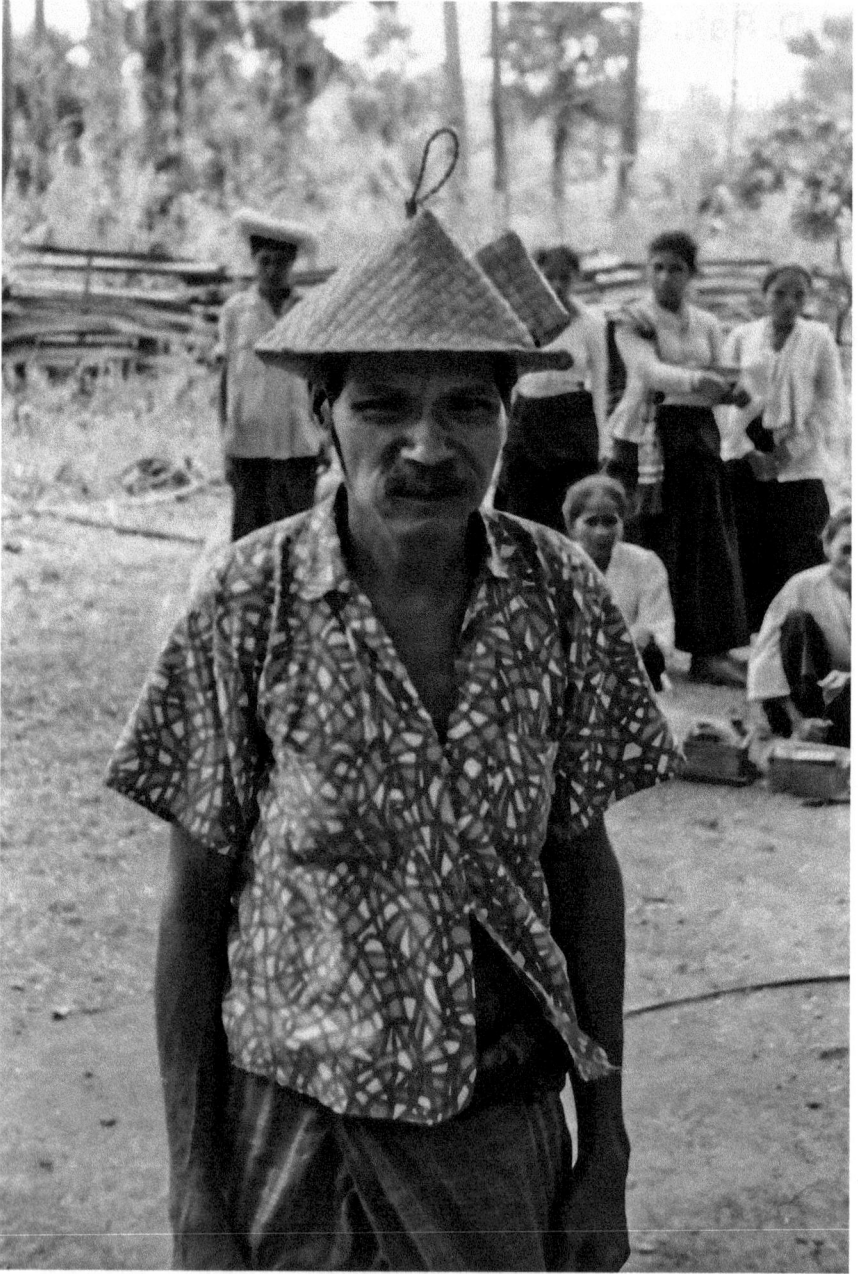

Samuel Ndun

The sixth portrait for this gallery is that of Samuel Ndun who joined Guru Pah during my second visit to Oe Handi in Thie. I know little of Samuel Ndun, other than what I learned in our brief time together. As a poet, his fluency was exceptional. Guru Pah's acknowledgement of his compositions was an endorsement of his depth of knowledge. As a pair, they would take turns reciting and commenting on each other. Like Guru Pah, Samuel Ndun was both a poet and a preacher. At the wedding I attended during my visit, I overheard him ask the parents of the bride and groom whether they would like a traditional ceremony or a Christian ceremony. He was prepared to do either. The parents opted for a Christian ceremony. This photograph is my only photo of Samuel Ndun.

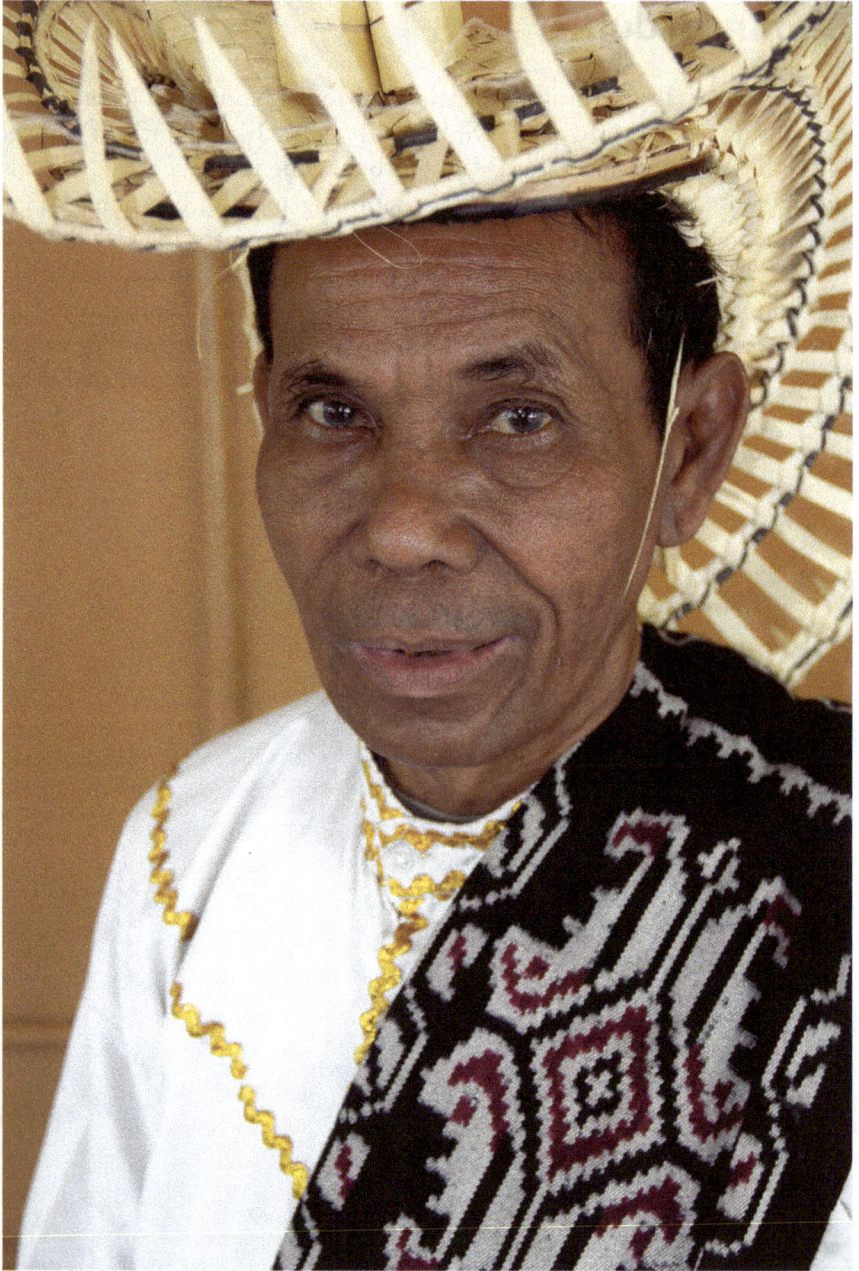

Jonas Mooy: Pak Jonas

The seventh portrait is that of Jonas Mooy from Thie. Jonas was a key participant in the 'Master Poets' sessions on Bali. He joined the fourth recording session in 2009 and then became a regular member for the 7th through the 11th sessions from 2011 and 2019. A schoolteacher, Pak Jonas was what might be considered a self-taught poet. He was constantly taking notes and was the only poet to do so in any sessions. He had excellent skills, but his recitations lacked the seemingly effortless fluency of some of the other poets. He reflected, however, on Rotenese traditions, saw connections between the traditions of the different domains and could, on several occasions, explain the meaning and implications of other poets' compositions better than they could themselves. It was only after he had recited his version of the origin of seeds that I showed him Guru Pah's version. He provided me with valuable exegesis on it clarifying it and making it more intelligible to me.

Yulius Iu: Pak Yulius

The eighth portrait is that of Yulius Iu from Landu. Pak Yulius was a participant at the 2nd and 7th sessions of the 'Master Poets Project'. Before I encountered him, I was unaware of how widespread the use of ritual language in semantic parallelism was in Christian ceremonies in parts of eastern Rote.

Pak Yulius was a fluent and talented poet who specialised in Christian compositions. He was able to take any passage in the Bible and transform it into parallel verse. His ability and his compositions came as a revelation to me. But I was not the only one to be impressed. Pak Jonas Mooy met Pak Yulius during the seventh session and heard him perform. Pak Jonas immediately set out to follow Pak Yulius' example and by the end of the week, with some preparation beforehand, Pak Jonas rendered his first Bible passage—the Judgement of Solomon—into traditional semantic parallelism. One of Pak Yulius's finest compositions was his rendering of Genesis as an origin narrative.

Anderias Ruy: Pak Ande

The appropriate ninth portrait in this gallery is of Anderias Ruy of Ringgou, a master poet who is widely acclaimed on Rote as one of the great performers of his time. When I began planning my 'Master Poet Project', I made a special trip to visit Pak Ande at his home and to invite him to join the initial session on Bali. He joined that session and continued thereafter as a participant at all recording sessions. He also took it upon himself to travel throughout Rote to identify other leading poets and to invite them to join particular sessions.

Pak Ande was both serious and intense: a poet with exceptional fluency and an immense repertoire combined with an extraordinary flair for performance. He would invariably come to Bali with a drum and would give a full recitation of certain compositions—mainly mortuary compositions—and then give the same recitation in a special initial-phrase-repeat style known as '*bapa*' to the beat of the drum. He would never perform any recitation without a drink of native gin and would work himself into tears to perform some mortuary recitations.

Pak Ande's compositions were dense and difficult to transcribe. My former PhD student, Dr Lintje Pellu, who would accompany the poets from Kupang, would work with him for hours struggling to get a proper transcription and some understanding of its meaning. For me, Pak Ande's dialect of Ringgou was difficult to understand and it would take many hours to begin to comprehend his compositions even after they had been transcribed.

Virtually the whole of Pak Ande's corpus of compositions remains to be translated into English.

Note: From left to right: Yulius Iu from Landu, Esau Pono from Termanu, Kornalius Medah from Bilba, Ande Ruy from Ringgou, Jonas Mooy from Thie, Mateos Poij from Oepao and Hendrik Foeh from Oenale.

The 'Master Poet Project' developed its own traditions and one of these traditions was a photography session on the final day before departure. Individual photographs and group photographs were taken in all sorts of combinations.

For a final photograph, I include a group photograph from the seventh 'Master Poets' session on the 29th of October 2011. This is a photograph of seven Rotenese master poets, each from a different domain on Rote.

Appendix II: The idea of topogeny and its use in the origin narratives of the Rotenese

A topogeny is like a genealogy. A genealogy consists of a successive recitation of names; a topogeny involves a successive recitation of places. Both are vehicles for the transmission of highly specific knowledge. As such, both genealogy and topogeny figure prominently as poetic devices in oral literature throughout the world. Both are a feature of the oral recitations of the Rotenese.

In my introduction to *The Poetic Power of Place*, 'Place and Landscape in Comparative Austronesian Perspective' (Fox 1997b: 8–12), I introduced the idea of a topogeny and illustrated its expression and function in Austronesian societies and, more widely, in a variety of other oral literary contexts.

Some of the most extensive Austronesian topogenies occur in the origin narratives of the Atoni Pah Meto of Timor. These recitations relate the successive exploits of named ancestors as they journey through a complex landscape of dual-named places, all in a form of parallel verse like that of the Rotenese:

> The fields of Oe Ana
> The hill of Oe Ana
> To stop there a while
> To rest there a while
> Then rising and going ...
> Coming directly to Oebaki
> By way of the rock Oehun

> Then coming and entering
> To the place of Ponain
> To the meeting spot of Fatu Mnanu.[1]

In many Timorese recitations, topogeny is so extensive and so interspersed with the continuing narrative that it carries the weight of the entire composition, conveying knowledge of a detailed landscape of ancestral actions.

A similar and more extensive use of topogeny occurs in the ritual recitations of the Sa'dan Toraja of Sulawesi. For the commemorative ceremony of buffalo sacrifice known as the *Merok*, the recitation by the poet–priests (*to mina*) is largely devoted to summoning gods and spirits in order of their rank and importance. This ritual recitation includes the principal gods, then the gods of the four directions as well as the gods of the nine levels of the firmament. When these gods have been summoned, the recitation calls forth the gods of all the local regions. This produces a stunning topogeny that runs for 81 coupled lines, with each couplet naming the invitee by title as 'God' and 'Lord' (*Deatal/Puangna*) and by dual-named location. This topogeny takes the following form:

> The God of the territory of the Leatung region
> The Lord of the district of Mangkaranga
> The God of the territory of the Patua' region
> The Lord of the district of Mila'
> The God of the territory of the Buntao' region
> The Lord of the district of Paniki.

(van der Veen 1965: 53)

In some Austronesian oral traditions, the versatility in the use of topogenies allows both the summoning of spirits and ancestors by location and the recounting of their journeys through a named landscape (see Lewis 1988b: 113).

---

1   This is an excerpt of a *nakanab* or *natoni* recitation that I recorded from the Meto chanters Nicodemus Sau and Nicolas Puay on a brief visit to Lasi in the mountains of West Timor. For a discussion of these origin narratives and their topogenies, see McWilliam (1997; 2002: 71–97).

The oldest recorded topogeny

Topogenies of varying sorts are found extensively in the world's oral traditions. One of the earliest recorded topogenies can be found in a cuneiform text of some 400 poetic lines of a harp lament for the destruction of the Sumerian capital of Ur that appears to have been used in a ritual for the restoration of Ur dating to about 1940 BCE.

The entire lament comprises 413 lines, almost all in strict canonical parallelism, and contains two separate topogenies. The first half of the poem is a lament by the god of Ur at the suffering endured when Ur was destroyed and has more than one topogeny. This first topogeny can be described as a recitation of abandonment. The invasion by the Elamites is likened to a storm in which a shepherd is forced to abandon his byre and sheepfold. The storm strikes one Sumerian city after another and destroys its temple, forcing the god or goddess of that city to abandon it. The topogeny is thus an ordered recitation of the cities of Sumer, the main temple in each city and the gods that held sway in those temples.

The topogeny begins with the following stanza:

> His byre he was abandoning,
> and his sheepfold, to the winds
> the herder was abandoning his byre
> and his sheepfold, to the winds,
> the lord of all lands was abandoning it
> and his sheepfold to the winds,
> at the temple close Enlil was abandoning Nippur
> and his sheepfold to the winds,
> his consort Ninlil was abandoning it
> and her sheepfold, to the winds
> at their dwelling house, Ninlil was abandoning Kiur
> and its sheepfold, to the winds.

These first lines establish the recurrent canonical formula that constitutes the topogeny. Examples of this formula are as follows:

> Isin's mistress was abandoning it
> and her sheepfold, to the winds
> at its temple close Nininsina was abandoning Kesh
> and her sheepfold to the winds.
> Uruk land's queen was abandoning it

and her sheepfold, to the winds
at its dwelling house Inanna was abandoning Uruk
and her sheepfold, to the winds.

This formula is then repeated to produce an ordered progress—
a procession—of gods and goddesses, each of whom abandons their city
and temple: 1) Enlil abandons Nippur, 2) Ninlil abandons Kiur, 3) Ninmah
abandons Kesh, 4) Nininsina abandons Egalmah, 5) Nanna abandons
Ekishnugal at Ur, 6) (his wife) Ningal abandons Agrunkug at Ur, 7) Enki
abandons Eridu, 8) Shara abandons Emma at Umma, 9) (his wife) abandons
Udsahara at Umma, 10) Baba abandons Urukug, 11) (her mother) Abbaba
abandons Gaguenna (at Urukug), 12) 'the cherub' abandons Etarsirsir
(at Urukug), 13) Gatumdug abandons Lagash, 14) Nanshe abandons
Siratr at Nina, 15) Dumuzi-Apsu abandons Kinirsha, and 16) Ninmara
abandons Guabba.[2]

This same cuneiform text contains a second topogeny, which continues the
lament of destruction, proceeding through the temples and cities of Sumer
with their gods and goddesses:

Brickwork of Ur, bitter is the wail
the wail is set up for you!
Ekishnugal, bitter is the wail,
the wail is set up for you!
Temple close Agrunkug, bitter is the wail
the wail is set up for you!
Brickwork of Ekur, bitter is the wail,
the wail is set up for you.

The 'catalogue of ships' in the 'Iliad'

Possibly the best-known topogeny in Classical literature is the so-called
catalogue of ships in the *Iliad*. This topogeny in Book II of the *Iliad* runs
for several hundred lines and identifies the ports, lands and islands with the
ships and the leaders of the Achaean forces that sailed to Troy:

Those of Boetia had as their commanders
Clonius, Leitus, Peneleus
Arceslaus and Prothoenor.

---

2   This lament is recorded in Jacobsen (1987: 447–74). I have written a yet unpublished paper on this
exemplary text (Fox n.d.).

They came from Graea, wide Mycalessus
Hryia, rocky Aulis, Schoenus, Scolus,
Thespia, Harma, hilly Eteonus
Eilesion, Erythrae, Eleon,
Hyle, Peteon, Ocalea, Copae,
Glisa, the citadel of Medeon.[3]

A similar, shorter topogeny lists the ships and origins of the Trojan forces, creating, as some have argued, a complex map of the ancient Aegean Sea.

Like Rotenese topogenies, all these very different topogenies link places with specific personages or groups in an ordered succession, generally by the use of recognisable formulae.

Rotenese topogenies from Termanu

There are two long topogenies in the oral narratives of Termanu: one in Recitation 7 and the other in Recitation 8 (Chapter 4, this volume). The accompanying exegeses to the recitations in this volume offer a step-by-step discussion of the meaning of the various passages that occur in these two topogenies, but such specific commentaries do not provide an adequate understanding of the structure of these compositions as a whole nor of their relationship to one another.

Both topogenies recount the female transmission of key cultural knowledge: Recitation 7 recounts the transmission from one woman to another of the knowledge of the planting of rice and millet and Recitation 8 recounts the transmission of the knowledge of tie-dyeing and weaving that is spread across the island of Rote. Crucial to these two recitations is the naming of places but also the naming of the women involved in this transmission process. Critically, the names of these women allude to the locations from which they come and are thus also markers of place. In both recitations, there is a similar litany of the principal ritual names of the domains of the island interspersed between names of additional places, particularly in the domain of Termanu.

---

3   These lines are taken from Emily Wilson's verse translation of the *Iliad* (Homer 2023: 42, lines 593 ff.).

The topogeny in Recitation 7

The topogeny in Recitation 7 is concerned with the spread of the planting of rice and millet.[4] It recounts in an ordered succession the field of local importance known for the production, particularly of rice, along with the names of the women who transfer the knowledge of planting from one locality to the next. In some instances, women are cited without reference to a specific area of planting. However, these women's names allude to their place of origin and thus continue to progress the topogeny in an ordered direction.

As an oral composition, this topogeny is variable in how it presents its corresponding knowledge. Women's names occur without placenames and placenames occur without women's names. Since both women's names and placenames are closely linked, the knowledge conveyed by this topogeny would be evident to its local audience.

As required in all parallel-language recitations, the names of places and of the women of these places are given in dual format. This schema identifies a confluence of women's names and ritual sites of plantation and the domains within these names are pertinent. The topogeny begins with the woman Masu Pasu//He Hai, who scoops up the sea creatures Doli Mo//Lutu Mala at the fish catch of *Tena Lai//Mae Oe*. The topogeny then shifts to planting sites on the island, proceeding westward along the northern coast of Rote before swinging around and moving eastward along the southern coast of the island, eventually arriving back at *Tena Lai//Mae Oe*.

In Chapter 2 of this volume, there is a list of the domains (*nusak*) of Rote identified by principal ritual names with a map of the location of these domains (Map 2.1). All the principal ritual names of the domains are cited in this topogeny but because domains have a variety of ritual names, this topogeny cites other domain names as well.

In what follows, I provide a schematic synopsis of this topogeny to compare it with the similar topogeny that occurs in Recitation 8.

---

4 I have already discussed aspects of this topogeny in Fox (1997c), tracing its progression around the island of Rote. This examination is intended to compare this topogeny specifically with that in Recitation 8, which moves in a different direction but also encompasses the entire island and its constituent domains.

Schematic synopsis of the topogeny in Recitation 7

Women's names	Ritual sites	Domain
Masu Pasu//He Hai	*Tunga Oli//Namo Ina*	Korbaffo
Fi Bau//Seda Kola	*Bau Peda Dele//Kola Sifi Ndai*	Termanu
Kada Ufa//Dila Latu	—	Termanu
Hau Hala//Kae Kopa	—	Termanu
Leli Onge//Fula Fopo	—	Termanu
Soe Leli//Pinga Pasa	—	Termanu
Fiti Nggoli//Lole Bako	*Bako Bau Dale//Nggoli Kai Tio*	Termanu
Dulu Kilik//Leo Lasuk	*Ki Lama//Le Ina*	Termanu
Pinga Peto//Lu'a Lela	*Peto Lesi-Ama//Lela Bala-Fia*	Termanu
	Pena Pua//Maka Lama	Ba'a
Loe Tesa//Dilu Tama	*Tanga Loi//Oe Mau*	Ba'a
Dae Mea Iko//Oe Ange Muli	*Dae Mea//Tete Lifu*	Dengka
Tete Kefa//Kali Solu	*Dela Muli//Ana Iko*	Delha
Meda Afe//Fai Nggengge	*Nale Dene//Nada Dona*	Oenale
Foi Lama//Teku Tada	*Tada Muli//Lene Kona*	Thie
	Tuda Meda//Do Lasi	Thie
	Teke Dua//Finga Telu	Loleh
Tui Beba//Oe Ange	*Ninga Ladi//Hengu Hena*	Loleh
Neu Lopo//Neu Nggele	*Tufa Laba//Ne'e Feo*	Keka
	Pila Sue//Nggeo Deta	Keka
	Longa Fa//Feo Ne	Talae
	Sosolo Lean Daen//Batu Tanga Lou	Talae [?]
Toin Dae//Le Kama	*Ko Solo//Nilu Foi*	Bokai
	Keko Nesu//Te Alu	Bokai
	Medi//Ndule	Bokai
Poko Tasi//Silu Meti	*Lenu Petu//Safe Solo*	Lelenuk
	Diu Dulu//Kana Langa	Diu
Leo Lata//Adu Pinga	*Pele Pou//Nggafu Lafa*	Diu
	Sapan Daen Oe Utuk//Seun Oen Fi Bolo	Diu [?]
Nggeo Lao//Pila Selu	*Pengo Dua//Hilu Telu*	Bilba
	Feni Fi//Tane Bau [D]	Bilba

Women's names	Ritual sites	Domain
Oko Beba//Tui Lele	*Londa Lusi//Batu Bela*	Ringgou
	Saba Lai//Dele Bui	Ringgou
	Tua Nae//Lele Beba	Ringgou
Meda Afe//Fai Nggengge	*Fai Fua//Ledo So'u*	Oepao
Kao Kai//Pena Ufa	*Lifa Lama//Lutu Oen*	Oepao
Liti Lifu//Henu Helok	*Soti Mori//Bola Tena*	Landu
	Tena Lai//Mae Oe	

The topogeny in Recitation 8

The topogeny in Recitation 8 recounts the spread of tie-dyeing and weaving and of the patterns that originate from the bodies of Shark and Crocodile, Pata Iuk and Dula Foek, who are killed and whose blood and insides are strewn across the tiny island of Ndao. On this island, *Folo Manu//Ndao Nusa*, off the western tip of Rote, the woman Haba Ndao//Lida Folo buys the shuttle and loom from the turtle and sea cow, *Kea Saik//Lui Liuk*, and proceeds to design patterns based on the remains of Pata Iuk and Dula Foek.

The topogeny in Recitation 8 describes by name the succession of women from neighbouring domains on Rote, each of whom, in turn, obtains the knowledge (and implements) of tie-dyeing and weaving and passes them on from one to another across the island.

The topogeny records the transfer of this knowledge from the island of Ndao to the western end of Rote and then proceeds through different clusters of domains, until all the domains have obtained these arts. The initial progress of this topogeny is eastward but, having reached domains in the east of the island, it swings back to include domains along part of the southern coast. This topogeny repeats the principal names of the domains of Rote, in some cases citing more than one ritual name for many of the domains.

While the ritual names of the domains are the same in both recitations, the names of the women in this topogeny (with one exception: Pinga Pasa//Soe Leli in Termanu) are different. Essentially, this topogeny relates a distinct succession of female transmission of knowledge from that in Recitation 7.

The topogeny ends with an invocation of the entire island of Rote by one of its most elaborate ritual names: *Lote Lolo Ei//Kale Ifa Lima* ('Lote of the Outstretched Legs and Kale of the Cradled Arms').

Schematic synopsis of the topogeny in Recitation 8

Women's names	Ritual sites	Domain
Haba Ndao//Lida Folo	*Folo Manu//Ndao Nusa*	Ndao
Sio Meko//Tesa Kola	*Dela Muli//Ana Iko*	Delha
Ango Beu//Baba Dela	*Tasi Puka//Li Sonu*	Oenale
Oe Ange Muli//Dae Mea Iko	*Lutu Mau//Holo Tula*	Dengka
Teo Tada//Leo Lene	*Lene Kona//Tada Muli*	Thie
Oe Ange//Dusi Beba	*Ninga Ladi//Hengu Hena*	Loleh
Nggede Ke//Dane Nane	*Tilo Nesi//Ose Mbok*	Lelain
Hulu Nggela//Seu Loko	*Tufa Laba//Ne'e Feo*	Keka
Loe Tesa//Dilu Tama	*Pena Pua//Maka Lama*	Ba'a
Lole Bako//Fiti Nggoli	*Boko Lino//Hoi Ledo*	Termanu
Soe Leli//Pinga Pasa	*Leli Papo Ama//Sani Solo Be*	Termanu
Tesa Nggusi//Tama Nggala	*Pinga Dale//Nggusi Bui*	Termanu
	Koli//Buna	Termanu
Lutu Namo//Heu Oli	*Asa Nao//Bole Sou*	Korbaffo
	Namo Ina//Tunga Oli	Korbaffo
Henu Helok//Liti Lifu	*Tena Lai//Mae Oe*	Landu
Tui Beba//Doko Meti	*Londa Lusi//Batu Bela*	Ringgou
Afe Ledo//Nggenge Fai	*Pao Kala//Pena Ufa*	Oepao
	Fai Fua//Ledo Sou	Oepao
Nggeo Lao//Pila Selu	*Tane Bau//Feni Fiu*	Bilba
	Hilu Telu//Pengo Du	Bilba
Leo Lata//Adu Pinga	*Pele Pou//Nggafu Lafa*	Diu
Poko Tasi//Solu Meti	*Lenu Petu//Safe Solo*	Lelenuk
	Kokote//Sonimanu	Lelenuk
Le Fango//Tui Daen	*Medi//Ndule*	Bokai
	Ko Sol//Nilu Foi	Bokai
Fula Seda//Sao Tangi	*Nggeo Deta//Pila Sue*	Talae
	Lona Fa//Feo Ue	Talae
	Lote Lolo Ei//Kale Ifa Lima	Rote

Topogenies in the recitations of Thie

In contrast with the topogenies in the recitations of Termanu, those in the recitations of Thie are relatively brief and seemingly focused on places within that domain. They are concerned mainly with the planting of the first seeds, particularly rice. In Thie, there are three recitations that relate the origins of planting: Recitations 4, 5 and 6 (Thie's Recitations 4 and 6 correspond to Termanu's Recitation 9, while Thie's Recitation 5 is similar to Termanu's Recitation 7).

In Recitation 4 (Chapter 6, this volume), there are eight lines (153–60) that list sites to which the woman Bui Len//Eno Lolo carries the shells Suti Solo//Bina Bane. These named places are: 1) *Deras//Le Lena*, 2) *Mundek// Na'u Dalek*, 3) *Rote//Kode Ana*, 4) *Oe Batu//Bau Foe*, 5) *Kone Ama//Sai Fua*, 6) *Nggonggoe//Lasi Lai*, and 7) *Liti//Sera Dale*. These are fields in Thie where the first planting occurs.

Recitation 6 also recounts the transfer of the shells Suti Solo//Bina Bane. In it, there occurs a minimal topogeny that cites two of the same places of planting mentioned in Recitation 4. Successful planting occurs first at *Fafa'e Tali Somba//Teke Me Re'ik Oen*, then at *Mundek//Na'u Dale* and then *Nggonggoer//Lasi Lain*. Two 'composite' names are cited to represent the whole island. The first, *Ledo So'u//Anda Iko* (literally, 'Sun's Rise and Land's Tail'), signifies the island from east to west while the second name, *Pena Pua//Rene Kona*—using the parts of the dual ritual names for Ba'a (*Pena Pua//Maka Lama*) and for Thie (*Rene Kona//Tada Muli*)—signifies the island from north to south.

Recitation 5 (lines 100–48) also contains a short topogeny. Ku Eo Iko//Tai Le Muri takes the crab Bole Sou and the sea snail Asa Nao, plants them and they sprout as rice and millet. These plants are harvested and then planted, first, at *Beu Bolu//Le'a So'o* and then, at *Landu Kona//Tena Serik* within Thie. This becomes an occasion for celebration, after which the seeds of these crops are transferred to the rest of Rote. Again, this transfer is represented by general ritual names for the east and west of the island and not by a systematic listing of the island's domains. The topogeny cites *Timu Dulu// Sepe Langga* ('Dawning East'//'Reddening Head'), *Dulu Oen//Langga Daen* ('Eastern Waters'//'Head Lands') and *Muri Loloe Olin//Iko Beku-te Tasin* ('West Descending to the Estuary'//'Tail Bending to the Sea').

Together, the short litanies of named places in Thie's Recitations 4, 5 and 6 are at best minor topogenies, hardly in the order of those in Recitations 7 and 8 from Termanu.

The topogeny of the planting of Christianity

The use of topogeny has been retained in the tradition of Christian oral narratives. At the jubilee ceremony in Thie in 1997, there was a special recitation of the narrative known as *Sanga Ndolu ma Tunga Lela*, which recounts the Rotenese quest for Christianity. Relying on a botanic idiom, Christianity is represented as the *Bau-Molek//Tui Sodak* ('The *Bau* Tree of Peace'//'The *Tui* Tree of Wellbeing') planted at *Dano Heo//Le Kosi* ('Lake Dano'//'River Kosi') in Thie. The spread of Christianity is then represented as the planting of these trees throughout the island. The accompanying topogeny is a well-recognised litany of the ritual names of all the domains of Rote and Ndao. The topogeny's listing of names moves eastward from Thie and then from Landu in the east shifting westward to encompass Termanu and the domains in western Rote. This topogeny, in Termanu dialect, demonstrates the continuation and recognition throughout the island of the principal ritual names that form the basis of Rote's most insistent topogenies.[5]

Ritual name	Domain
Tuda Meda//Do Lasi	Thie
Teke Dua//Finga Telu	Loleh
Tanga Loi//Oe Mau	Ba'a
Pila Sue//Nggeo Deta	Talae
Tufa Laba//Ne'e Feo	Keka
Meda//Ndule	Bokai
Lenu Petu//Safe Solo	Lelenuk
Diu Dulu//Kana Langa	Diu
Pengo Dua//Hilu Telu	Bilba
Londa Lusi//Batu Bela	Ringgou
Fai Fua//Ledo So'u	Oepao

---

5   There is also clear continuity at the level of individual poets. The poet chiefly responsible for this topogeny was Esau Pono, who was personally acquainted with the poet Peu Malesi, who often relied on topogeny in his recitations, as in the case of Recitation 7 from Termanu.

Ritual name	Domain
Soti Mori//Bola Tena	Landu
Tunga Oli//Namo Ina	Korbaffo
Koli do Buna	Termanu
Tefu Buna//Nggafu Huni	Lelain
Dae Mea//Tete Lifu	Dengka
Tasi Puka//Li Sonu	Oenale
Dela Muri//Anda Iko	Delha
Ndao Nusa//Folo Manu	Ndao

Bibliography

Arsip Nasional Republik Indonesia: "*Archief van de protestantse gemeenten in Batavia en van enige andere protestantse kerken buiten Batavia*", item no. 161: "*Timorse aankomende brieven van anno 1627 tot 1736 en Doopboek van anno 1669 tot 1737*".

Berlin, A. 2008 [1985]. *The Dynamics of Biblical Parallelism*. Revised and expanded edition. Grand Rapids: Wm B. Eerdmans Publishing Co.

Black, Jeremy. 1998. *Reading Sumerian Poetry*. London: Athlone Press.

Boodberg, P.A. 1954–55a. 'On Crypto-Parallelism in Chinese Poetry.' In *Cedules from a Berkeley Workshop in Asiatic Philology*, [#001–540701]. Berkeley.

Boodberg, P.A. 1954–55b. 'Syntactical Metaplasia in Stereoscopic Parallelism.' In *Cedules from a Berkeley Workshop in Asiatic Philology*, [#017–541210]. Berkeley.

Boodberg, P.A. 1954–55c. '"T"/"M" Parallelism Once More.' In *Cedules from a Berkeley Workshop in Asiatic Philology*, [#030–550420]. Berkeley.

Coe, M. 1992. *Breaking the Maya Code*. London: Penguin Books.

Dahl, Jacob (ed.). 1997–2006. *Electronic Text Corpus of Sumerian Literature*. [Online]. Digital Humanities @ Oxford. Oxford: University of Oxford. Available from: digital.humanities.ox.ac.uk/project/electronic-text-corpus-sumerian-literature.

Dahood, M. 1974. 'Chiasmus in Job: A Text-Critical and Philological Criterion.' In *A Light Unto My Path: Old Testament Studies in Honor of Jacob M. Myers*, edited by H.N. Bream, R.D. Heim, and C.A. Moore, 119–30. Philadelphia: Temple University Press.

Dahood, M. 1975. 'Ugaritic–Hebrew Parallel Pairs' and 'Ugaritic–Hebrew Parallel Pairs Supplement.' In *Ras Shamra Parallels: The Texts from Ugarit and the Hebrew Bible. Volume II*, edited by L.R. Fisher, 1–33, 34–39. Rome: Pontificium Institutum Biblicum.

Dahood, M. 1981. 'Ugaritic–Hebrew Parallel Pairs' and 'Ugaritic–Hebrew Parallel Pairs Supplement.' In *Ras Shamra Parallels: The Texts from Ugarit and the Hebrew Bible. Volume III*, edited by S. Rummel, 1–178, 179–206. Rome: Pontificium Institutum Biblicum.

Dahood, M., and T. Penar. 1972. 'Ugaritic–Hebrew Parallel Pairs.' In *Ras Shamra Parallels: The Texts from Ugarit and the Hebrew Bible. Volume I*, edited by L.R. Fisher, 71–95. Rome: Pontificium Institutum Biblicum.

Davis, J.F. 1830. 'XXI. On the Poetry of the Chinese.' *Transactions of the Royal Asiatic Society of Great Britain and Ireland* 2, no. 2: 393–461. doi.org/10.1017/S0950473700000525.

Edmonson, M.S. 1971. *The Book of Counsel: The Popol Vuh of the Quiche Maya of Guatemala*. Middle American Research Institute Publication 35. New Orleans: Tulane University Press.

Edmonson, M.S. 1973. 'Semantic Universals and Particulars in Quiche.' In *Meaning in Mayan Languages: Ethnolinguistic Studies*, edited by M.S. Edmonson, 235–46. The Hague: Mouton. doi.org/10.1515/9783110869675.

Edmonson, M.S. 2008. *Heaven Born Merida and its Destiny: The Book of Chilam Balam of Chumayel*. Austin: University of Texas.

Fanggidaej, J. 1895. *Manetualain Dede'a Manemi Soda-Molek-a Lukas (Het Evangelie van Lukas vertaald in het Rottineesch) [The Gospel of Luke Translated into Rotenese]*. Amsterdam: Nederlandsch Bijbelgenootschap.

Fox, J.J. n.d. 'The Oldest Topogeny: The Lament for Ur.' Unpublished manuscript.

Fox, J.J. 1971a. 'A Rotinese Dynastic Genealogy: Structure and Event.' In *The Translation of Culture*, edited by T.O. Beidelman, 37–77. London: Tavistock.

Fox, J.J. 1971b. 'Semantic Parallelism in Rotinese Ritual Language.' *Bijdragen tot de Taal-, Land- en Volkenkunde* 127: 215–55. [Reprinted in J.J. Fox, *Explorations in Semantic Parallelism*, Canberra: ANU Press, 2014, pp. 91–128.] doi.org/10.1163/22134379-90002782.

Fox, J.J. 1971c. 'Sister's Child as Plant: Metaphors in An Idiom of Consanguinity.' In *Rethinking Kinship and Marriage*, edited by R. Needham, 219–52. London: Tavistock.

Fox, J.J. 1974. '"Our Ancestors Spoke in Pairs": Rotinese Views of Language, Dialect and Code.' In *Explorations in the Ethnography of Speaking*, edited by R. Bauman and J. Sherzer, 65–85. Cambridge: Cambridge University Press. [Reprinted in J.J. Fox, *Explorations in Semantic Parallelism*, Canberra: ANU Press, 2014, pp. 129–48.] doi.org/10.1017/CBO9780511611810.007.

Fox, J.J. 1975. 'On Binary Categories and Primary Symbols: Some Rotinese Perspectives.' In *The Interpretation of Symbolism*, edited by R. Willis, 99–132. London: Malaby Press. [Reprinted in J.J. Fox, *Explorations in Semantic Parallelism*, Canberra: ANU Press, 2014, pp. 149–80.]

Fox, J.J. 1977a. *Harvest of the Palm: Ecological Change in Eastern Indonesia.* Cambridge: Harvard University Press. doi.org/10.4159/harvard.9780674331884.

Fox, J.J. 1977b. 'Roman Jakobson and the Comparative Study of Parallelism.' In *Roman Jakobson: Echoes of His Scholarship*, edited by C.H. van Schooneveld and D. Armstrong, 59–90. Lisse, Netherlands: Peter de Ridder Press. [Reprinted in J.J. Fox, *Explorations in Semantic Parallelism*, Canberra: ANU Press, 2014, pp. 19–40.] doi.org/10.1515/9783112329788-007.

Fox, J.J. 1979a. 'A Tale of Two States: Ecology and the Political Economy of Inequality on the Island of Roti.' In *Social and Ecological Systems*, edited by P. Burnham and R.F. Ellen, 19–42. ASA Monograph 18. London: Academic Press.

Fox, J.J. 1979b. 'Standing in Time and Place: The Structure of Rotinese Historical Narratives.' In *Perceptions of the Past in Southeast Asia. Number 4*, edited by A. Reid and D. Marr, 10–25. Kuala Lumpur: Heinemann Educational Books (Asia).

Fox, J.J. 1979c. 'The Ceremonial System of Savu.' In *The Imagination of Reality: Essays on Southeast Asian Coherence Systems*, edited by A. Becker and A.A. Yengoyan, 145–73. Norwood: Ablex Publishing Corporation.

Fox, J.J. 1980a. 'Figure Shark and Pattern Crocodile: The Foundations of the Textile Traditions of Roti and Ndao.' In *Indonesian Textiles*, edited by M. Gittinger, 39–55. Irene Emery Roundtable on Museum Textiles, 1979 Proceedings. Washington, DC: Textile Museum.

Fox, J.J. (ed.). 1980b. *The Flow of Life: Essays on Eastern Indonesia*. Cambridge: Harvard University Press. doi.org/10.4159/harvard.9780674331907.

Fox, J.J. 1980c. 'Obligation and Alliance: State Structure and Moiety Organization in Thie, Roti.' In *The Flow of Life: Essays on Eastern Indonesia*, edited by J.J. Fox, 98–133. Cambridge: Harvard University Press.

Fox, J.J. 1980d. 'Models and Metaphors: Comparative Research in Eastern Indonesia.' In *The Flow of Life: Essays on Eastern Indonesia*, edited by J.J. Fox, 327–33. Cambridge: Harvard University Press. doi.org/10.4159/harvard.978 0674331907.c18.

Fox, J.J. 1983a. 'Adam and Eve on the Island of Roti: A Conflation of Oral and Written Traditions.' *Indonesia* 36: 15–23. [Reprinted in J.J. Fox, *Explorations in Semantic Parallelism*, Canberra: ANU Press, 2014, pp. 343–54.] doi.org/10.2307/3351024.

Fox, J.J. 1983b. 'The Rotinese Chotbah as a Linguistic Performance.' In *Accent on Variety*, edited by A. Halim, L. Carrington, and S.A. Wurm, 311–18. Papers from the Third International Conference on Linguistics, Vol. 3. Canberra: Pacific Linguistics. [Reprinted in J.J. Fox, *Explorations in Semantic Parallelism*, Canberra: ANU Press, 2014, pp. 355–64.]

Fox, J.J. 1988a. '"Chicken Bones and Buffalo Sinews": Verbal Frames and the Organization of Rotinese Mortuary Performances.' In *Time Past, Time Present, Time Future: Essays in Honour of P.E. de Josselin de Jong*, edited by D.S. Moyer and H.J.M. Claessen, 178–94. KITLV, Verhandelingen No. 131. Dordrecht, Netherlands: Foris Publications.

Fox, J.J. 1988b. *To Speak in Pairs: Essays on the Ritual Languages of Eastern Indonesia*. Cambridge: Cambridge University Press. doi.org/10.1017/CBO9780511551369.

Fox, J.J. 1988c. 'Introduction.' In *To Speak in Pairs: Essays on the Ritual Languages of Eastern Indonesia*, edited by J.J. Fox, 1–28. Cambridge: Cambridge University Press. doi.org/10.1017/CBO9780511551369.001.

Fox, J.J. 1988d. '"Manu Kama's Road, Tepa Nilu's Path": Theme, Narrative, and Formula in Rotinese Ritual Language.' In *To Speak in Pairs: Essays on the Ritual Languages of Eastern Indonesia*, edited by J.J. Fox, 161–201. Cambridge: Cambridge University Press. [Reprinted in J.J. Fox, *Explorations in Semantic Parallelism*, Canberra: ANU Press, 2014, pp. 229–64.] doi.org/10.1017/CBO9780511551369.007.

Fox, J.J. 1989a. 'Category and Complement: Binary Ideologies and the Organization of Dualism in Eastern Indonesia.' In *The Attraction of Opposites: Thought and Society in a Dualistic Mode*, edited by D. Maybury-Lewis and U. Almagor, 33–56. Ann Arbor: University of Michigan Press. [Reprinted in J.J. Fox, *Explorations in Semantic Parallelism*, Canberra: ANU Press, 2014, pp. 181–200.]

Fox, J.J. 1989b. 'To the Aroma of the Name: The Celebration of a Rotinese Ritual of Rock and Tree.' *Bijdragen tot de Taal-, Land- en Volkenkunde* 145: 520–38. doi.org/10.1163/22134379-90003244.

Fox, J.J. 1993. 'Memories of Ridgepoles and Crossbeams: The Categorical Foundations of a Rotinese Cultural Design.' In *Inside Austronesian Houses: Perspectives on Domestic Designs for Living*, edited by J.J. Fox, 140–79. Canberra: Department of Anthropology, Research School of Pacific and Asian Studies, The Australian National University.

Fox, J.J. 1997a. 'Genealogies of the Sun and Moon: Interpreting the Canon of Rotinese Ritual Chants.' In *Koentjaraningrat dan Antropologi di Indonesia* [*Anthropological Studies in Indonesia*], edited by E.K.M. Masinambow, 321–30. Jakarta: Assosiasi Antropologi Indonesia/Yayasan Obor. [Reprinted in J.J. Fox, *Explorations in Semantic Parallelism*, Canberra: ANU Press, 2014, pp. 119–228.]

Fox, J.J. 1997b. 'Place and Landscape in Comparative Austronesian Perspective.' In *The Poetic Power of Place: Comparative Perspectives on Austronesian Ideas of Locality*, edited by J.J. Fox, 1–21. Canberra: Research School of Pacific and Asian Studies, The Australian National University.

Fox, J.J. 1997c. 'Genealogy and Topogeny: Toward an Ethnography of Rotinese Ritual Place Names.' In *The Poetic Power of Place: Comparative Perspectives on Austronesian Ideas of Locality*, edited by J.J. Fox, 91–102. Canberra: Research School of Pacific and Asian Studies, The Australian National University.

Fox, J.J. 2003. 'Admonitions of the Ancestors: Giving Voice to the Deceased in Rotinese Mortuary Rituals.' In *Framing Indonesian Realities*, edited by P.J.M. Nas, G. Persoon, and R. Jaffe, 87–109. Leiden, Netherlands: KITLV Press. [Reprinted in J.J. Fox, *Explorations in Semantic Parallelism*, Canberra: ANU Press, 2014, pp. 119–228.] doi.org/10.1163/9789004486829_003.

Fox, J.J. 2005. 'Ritual Languages, Special Registers and Speech Decorum in Austronesian Languages.' In *The Austronesian Languages of Asia and Madagascar*, edited by A. Adelaar and N. Himmelman, 87–109. London: Routledge Curzon Press.

Fox, J.J. 2008. 'Blutrote Hirse. Eine locale Ursprungserzählung von der Insel Roti [Blood Red Millet: A Local Origin Story from the Island of Roti].' In *Zwischen Aneignung und Verfremdung: Ethnologische Gratwanderung* [*Between Appropriation and Alienation: An Ethnological Tightrope Walk*], edited by V. Gottowik, H. Jebens, and E. Platte, 401–9. Frankfurt, Germany: Campus.

Fox, J.J. 2010. 'Exploring Oral Formulaic Language: A Five Poet Analysis.' In *A Journey through Austronesian and Papuan Linguistics and Cultural Space*, edited by J. Bowden and N.P. Himmelman, 573–87. Canberra: Pacific Linguistics. [Reprinted in J.J. Fox, *Explorations in Semantic Parallelism*, Canberra: ANU Press, 2014, pp. 201–15.]

Fox, J.J. 2014. *Explorations in Semantic Parallelism*. Canberra: ANU Press. doi.org/ 10.22459/ESP.07.2014.

Fox, J.J. 2016. *Master Poets, Ritual Masters: The Art of Oral Composition among the Rotenese of Eastern Indonesia*. Canberra: ANU Press. doi.org/10.22459/MPRM. 04.2016.

Fox, J.J. 2017. 'Remembering and Recreating Origins: The Transformation of a Tradition of Canonical Parallelism among the Rotenese of Eastern Indonesia.' *Oral Traditions* 31, no. 2: 233–58. doi.org/10.1353/ort.2017.0009.

Fox, J.J. 2021. 'Paths of Life and Death: Rotenese Life-Course Recitations and the Journey to the Afterworld.' In *Austronesian Paths and Journeys*, edited by J.J. Fox, 193–230. Canberra: ANU Press. doi.org/10.2307/j.ctv1prsr48.12.

Fox, J.J. 2023. 'Personal Encounters and Productive Engagement: A Vignette from the Continuing Effort at Understanding Rotenese Spiritual Representations.' In *In Tandem: Pathways towards a Postcolonial Anthropology*, edited by M. Lücking, A. Meiser, and I. Rohrer, 181–88. Wiesbaden, Germany: Springer VS. doi.org/ 10.1007/978-3-658-38673-3_10.

Freedman, D.N. 1972. 'Prolegomenon.' In *The Forms of Hebrew Poetry*, by G.B. Gray, vii–lvi. New York: KTAV Publishing House.

Garibay, A.M. 1953. *Historia de la Literatura Nahuatl* [*History of Nahuatl Literature*]. 2 vols. Mexico City: Editorial Porrúa.

Geller, S. 1979. *Parallelism in Early Hebrew Poetry*. Missoula: Scholars Press. doi.org/ 10.1163/9789004386815.

Gevirtz, S. 1963. *Patterns in the Early Poetry of Israel*. Studies in Ancient Oriental Civilization No. 32. Chicago: Chicago University Press.

Ginsberg, H.L. 1935. 'The Victory of the Land God over the Sea God.' *Journal of the Palestine Oriental Society* 15: 327.

Gossen, G.H. 1974a. *Chamulas in the World of the Sun*. Cambridge: Harvard University Press.

Gossen, G.H. 1974b. 'To Speak with a Heated Heart: Chamula Canons of Style and Good Performance.' In *Explorations in the Ethnography of Speaking*, edited by R. Bauman and J. Sherzer, 389–413. Cambridge: Cambridge University Press. doi.org/10.1017/CBO9780511611810.025.

Graafland, N. 1889. 'Het eiland Rote' and 'Eenige aantekeningen op ethnographisch gebied ten aanzien van het eiland Rote.' *Mededelingen van wege het Nederlandsche Zendinggenootschap*: 33:239–77 and 351–75.

Granet, M. 1932 [1919]. *Fêtes et Chansons Anciennes de la Chine* [*Festivals and Songs of Ancient China*]. English edn. Paris: Editions Ernest Leraux.

Gray, G.B. 1972 [1915]. *The Forms of Hebrew Poetry*. Reprint. New York: KTAV Publishing House.

Hägerdal, H. 2012. *Lords of the Land, Lords of the Sea: Conflict and Adaptation in Early Colonial Timor, 1600–1800*. Leiden, Netherlands: KITLV Press. doi.org/10.1163/9789004253506.

Hägerdal, H. 2013. 'The Native as Exemplum: Missionary Writings and Colonial Complexities in Eastern Indonesia.' *Itinerario* 37, no. 2: 73–99. doi.org/10.1017/S0165115313000478.

Heijmering, G. 1843–44. 'Zeden en Gewoonten op het Eiland Rottie [Manners and Customs on the Island of Rote].' *Tijdschrift voor Nederlandsche-Indië* [*Journal for the Dutch East Indies*] 5: 521–49, 623–39; 6: 81–98, 353–67.

Hightower, J.R. 1959. 'Some Characteristics of Parallel Prose.' In *Studia Serica Bernhard Karlgren*, 60–91. Copenhagen: Ejnar Munksgaard.

Holm, D. 2003. *Killing a Buffalo for the Ancestors: A Zhuang Cosmological Text from Southwest China*. DeKalb: Southeast Asia Publications, Center for Southeast Asian Studies, Northern Illinois University.

Holm, D. 2004. *Recalling Lost Souls: The Baeu Rodo Scriptures, Tai Cosmogonic Texts from Guangxi in South China*. Bangkok: White Lotus Co.

Holm, D. 2013. *Mapping the Old Zhuang Character Script: A Vernacular Writing System from Southern China*. Leiden, Netherlands: Brill. doi.org/10.1163/9789004242166.

Holm, D. 2015. 'Dialect Variation within Zhuang Traditional Manuscripts.' *The International Journal of Chinese Character Studies* 1, no. 2: 1–32. doi.org/10.18369/WACCS.2015.1.1.

Holm, D. 2017. 'Parallelism in the *Hanvueng*: A Zhuang Verse Epic from West-Central Guangxi in Southern China.' *Oral Tradition* 31, no. 2: 373–406. doi.org/10.1353/ort.2017.0015.

Holm, D., and Y. Meng (trans and eds). 2015. *Hanvueng: The Goose King and the Ancestral King—An Epic from Guangxi in Southern China*. Zhuang Traditional Texts Series, 1. Leiden, Netherlands: Brill. doi.org/10.1163/9789004290006_002.

Homer. 2023. *The Iliad*. Translated by Emily Wilson. New York: W.W. Norton & Company.

Hoskins, Janet. 1988. 'Etiquette in Kodi Spirit Communication: The Lips Told to Pronounce, the Mouths Told to Speak.' In *To Speak in Pairs: Essays on the Ritual Languages of Eastern Indonesia*, edited by J.J. Fox, 29–63. Cambridge: Cambridge University Press. doi.org/10.1017/CBO9780511551369.002.

Hull, K.M., and M.D. Carrasco (eds). 2012. *Parallel Worlds: Genre, Discourse, and Poetics in Contemporary, Colonial, and Classic Maya Literature*. Boulder: University of Colorado Press.

Jabłoński, W. 1935. 'Les "Siao-ha(i-eu)l-yu" de Pékin: un essai sur la poésie populaire en Chine [The "Siao-ha(i-eu)l-yu" of Beijing: An Essay on Popular Poetry in China].' Kraków: Polskiej Akademji Umiejętności [Polish Academy of Arts and Sciences].

Jacobsen, T. 1987. *The Harps That Once …: Sumerian Poetry in Translation*. New Haven: Yale University Press.

Jakobson, R. 1966. 'Grammatical Parallelism and its Russian Facet.' *Language* 42: 398–429. doi.org/10.2307/411699.

Jakobson, R. 1968. 'Poetry of Grammar and Grammar of Poetry.' *Lingua* 21: 597–609. doi.org/10.1016/0024-3841(68)90079-X.

Jakobson, R. 1969. 'The Modular Design of Chinese Regulated Verse.' In *Échanges et communications: Mélanges offerts à Claude Lévi-Strauss* [*Exchanges and Communications: Mixtures Offered to Claude Lévi Strauss*], edited by J. Pouillon and P. Maranda. The Hague: Mouton. doi.org/10.1515/9783111560168-044.

Jonker, J.C.G. 1905. Rottineesche Verhalen. *Bijdragen tot de Taal-, Land- en Volkenkunde* 58:369–464.

Jonker, J.C.G. 1908. *Rottineesch-Hollandsch Wordenboek*. Leiden: E. J. Brill.

Jonker, J.C.G. 1911. *Rottineesche Teksten met Vertaling*. Leiden: E. J. Brill.

Jonker, J.C.G. 1915. *Rottineeesche Spraakkunst*. Leiden: E. J. Brill.

Kramer, S.N. 1979. *From the Poetry of Sumer: Creation, Glorification, Adoration*. Berkeley: University of California Press.

Kugel, J. 1981. *The Idea of Biblical Poetry: Parallelism and Its History*. New Haven: Yale University Press.

Lau, D.C., and R.T. Ames. 1998. *Yuan Dao: Tracing Dao to its Source*. Classics of Ancient China. New York: Ballantine Books.

Le Grand, G.J.H. 1900. 'De zending op Roti [The Mission on Roti].' *Mededeelingen van wege het Nederlandsch Zendinggenootschap* [*Communications of the Dutch Missionary Society*] 44: 361–77.

Leon-Portilla, M. 1969. *Pre-Columbian Literature of Mexico*. Norman: University of Oklahoma Press.

Leon-Portilla, M., and E. Shorris. 2002. *In the Language of Kings: An Anthology of Mesoamerican Literature, Pre-Columbian to the Present*. New York: W.W. Norton & Company.

Lewis, E.D. 1988a. 'A Quest for the Source: The Ontogenesis of a Creation Myth of the Ata Tana 'Ai.' In *To Speak in Pairs: Essays on the Ritual Languages of Eastern Indonesia*, edited by J.J. Fox, 246–81. Cambridge: Cambridge University Press. doi.org/10.1017/CBO9780511551369.010.

Lewis, E.D. 1988b. *People of the Source*. Dordrecht, Netherlands: Foris Publications.

Liu, D.J. 1983. 'Parallel Structures in the Canon of Chinese Poetry: The Shih Ching.' *Poetics Today* 4, no. 4: 639–53. doi.org/10.2307/1772318.

Lounsbury, F.G. 1980. 'Some Problems in the Interpretation of the Mythological Portion of the Hieroglyphic Text on the Temple of the Cross at Palenque'. In *Third Palenque Round Table, 1978*, edited by Merle Greene Robertson, 99–115. Austin: University of Texas Press.

Lounsbury, F.G. 1989. 'The Ancient Writing of Middle America.' In *The Origins of Writing*, edited by W.N. Senner, 203–37. Lincoln: University of Nebraska Press.

Lowth, R. 1829 [1753]. *De Sacra Poesia Hebraeorum Praelectiones Academiae* [*Lectures on the Sacred History of the Hebrews*]. English edn. Boston.

Lowth, R. 1834 [1778]. *Isaiah X–XI*. English edn. Boston.

McWilliam, A. 1997. 'Mapping with Metaphor: Cultural Topographies in West Timor.' In *The Poetic Power of Place: Comparative Perspectives on Austronesian Ideas of Locality*, edited by J.J. Fox, 103–15. Canberra: Research School of Pacific and Asian Studies, The Australian National University.

McWilliam, A. 2002. *Paths of Origin, Gates of Life: A Study of Place and Precedence in Southwest Timor*. Leiden, Netherlands: KITLV Publications. doi.org/10.1163/9789004454408.

Meroekh, S.J. 1934. Sambungan dari hal pengembaran Injil di Pulau Rote [Continuation of the Spread of the Gospel on Rote Island]. Typescript.

Pardee, D. 2012. The Ugaritic Texts and the Origins of West-Semitic Literary Composition. Schweich Lectures on Biblical Archaeology. London: British Academy. doi.org/10.5871/bacad/9780197264928.001.0001.

Redfield, R., and A. Villa-Rojas. 1934. *Chan Kom: A Maya Village*. Washington, DC: Carnegie Institution of Washington.

Schlegel, G. 1896. *La loi du parallelisme en style chinois démonstrée par la preface du 'Si-yu-ki'* [*The Law of Parallelism in Chinese Style Demonstrated by the Preface to 'Si-yu-ki'*]. Leiden.

Tchang Tcheng-Ming, B.S.J. 1937. *Le Parallelisme dans le vers du Cheu King, Variétés Sinologiques No. 65* [*Parallelism in the Verse of Cheu King, Sinological Varieties No. 65*]. Paris: Paul Geuthner.

Tedlock, D. 1996 [1985]. *Popol Vuh: The Mayan Book of the Dawn of Life*. Revised and expanded edition. New York: Simon & Schuster.

Tedlock, D. 2003. *Rabinal Achi: A Mayan Drama of War and Sacrifice*. Oxford: Oxford University Press.

Terwiel, B.J., and R. Wichasin. 1992. *Tai Ahoms and the Stars: Three Ritual Texts to Ward Off Danger*. Ithaca: Southeast Asia Program, Cornell University. doi.org/10.7591/9781501719004.

Vandermeersch, L. 1989. 'Les origines divinatoires de la tradition chinoise du parallélisme littéraire [The Divinatory Origins of the Chinese Tradition of Literary Parallelism].' *Extrême-Orient, Extrême-Occident* 11: 11–33. doi.org/10.3406/oroc.1989.945.

van de Wetering, F.H. 1925. 'Het Huwelijk op Roti [Marriage on Roti].' *Tijdschrift voor Indische Taal-, Land- en Volkenkunde, uitgegeven door het Bataviaas Genootschap* [*Journal for Indies Language, Land and Ethnology, published by the Batavian Society*] 65: 1–36, 589–667.

Van der Veen, H. 1965. *The Merok Feast of the Sa'dan Toraja*. 's-Gravenhage, Netherlands: Martinus Nijhoff. doi.org/10.1007/978-94-017-4760-8.

Vogt, E.Z. 1969. *Zinacantan: A Maya Community in the Highlands of Chiapas*. Cambridge: Belknap Press of Harvard University. doi.org/10.4159/harvard.9780674436886.

Index

Page numbers in bold indicate images.

Adulanu, Stefanus ('Old Meno') 61,
  65, 66, 67, 68, 105–17, 119–67,
  178n.4, 255, 257, 266n.16, 293,
  297, **302**, 303
Adulilo, Lisabeth 66, 67, 86–94
adze and axe 31, 69, 82, 90, 103,
  113–17, 187
Akkadian 12
Amalo, Ayub 67, 117–19
Amalo, Stefanus 266n.16
Ambon 250
America 41n.10
  see also Mesoamerica
Americas 5
Asch, Tim 67, 307
Atapupu 41, 225
Austro-Asiatic 20
Austronesian 5, 20, 26, 46, 321, 322
axe and adze 31, 69, 82, 90, 103,
  113–17, 187
Aztec 5
  see also Mesoamerica

Ba'a 41, 126, 142, 174, 255, 261, 265,
  267, 327, 329
  ritual names for 39, 126, 330, 331
Bai, Se'u 257
Bali 41n.10, 178, 299, 307, 313, 315,
  317
base used for spinning cloth 3, 152,
  164, 167, 294
  see also spinning, of cloth

Batavia (Jakarta) 174, 261n.14, 262,
  264, 265
Bibi Manek 171, 172
Bibi Manu 225
Bible 4, 13, 48, 250, 269, 270, 315
Biblical 12n.6, 173, 209, 253, 270,
  281, 282
Bilba 39, 131, 148, 249, 263n.15,
  268, 327, 329
  ritual names for 39, 131, 331
Black Portuguese 39
Bokai 40, 129, 130n.2, 148, 149, 268,
  327, 329
  ritual names for 39, 40, 129,
  130n.2, 331
bore and chisel 31, 82, 83, 90, 91,
  103–4, 112, 187, 188, 197, 198,
  199
Brasseur de Bourbourg, Charles
  Étienne 15–16
British 250
Buddhist 20
Buddingh, S.N. 251

canonical pairing 11–13, 14, 23–4, 25
'canonical parallelism', *see*
  parallelism—'canonical'
Ceram (Seram) 41n.11
Ceylon 41n.11
China 18, 19, 20n.13
Chinese 5, 17–20, 41, 46, 225

chisel and bore, *see* bore and chisel

Christian God 42, 254, 257

Christianity 33n.4, 48, 54n.18, 173–4,
175, 176, 177, 189, 194, 247–96,
311, 315, 331
and ritual language 252, 253–6,
262, 270, 274, 282, 288, 315
Holy Spirit 176, 193, 194, 254,
263, 264
in Landu 267, 268, 270, 281, 331
in Loleh 174, 249, 265, 267
in Termanu 249–50, 251, 252
in Thie 173–4, 175, 176, 177, 189,
249–50, 251, 263, 267, 331
in Timor 249n.2, 250, 254, 263,
270
see also Evangelical Church

cloth patterning, *see* patterning of cloth

Concordia 248

cooking
fire for 31, 58, 75, 87, 94, 106,
107, 185–6
knowledge of 31, 189
of rice and millet 45, 108
origins in Termanu 75–168, 172,
299
origins in Thie 172, 181–87, 189
origins of 3, 58, 76–85, 86–96,
97–104, 105–12, 259
Sea as source of 31, 80, 88, 100,
101, 106, 108, 109, 184, 186
tools for 23, 31, 82, 83, 90, 91,
103, 113, 188–9, 259, 281

cuneiform 7, 12, 323, 324

Davis, John Francis 17

Delha 40, 126, 127, 139, 140, 211,
229, 269, 327, 329
ritual names for 39, 40, 332

Dengka 40, 64, 126, 140, 261, 269,
327, 329
ritual names for 39, 40, 126, 332

Desa Oebo 225

designs, *see* patterning of cloth

Diu 39, 40, 131, 148, 149, 268, 327,
329
ritual names for 39–40, 331

drill and plumbline marker 82–3, 90,
91, 112, 197, 198, 199

Dutch 33n.5, 41n.10, 61, 64, 250, 251
and religion 247, 250–1
in Termanu 64, 249n.2, 261n.14,
303
intermarriage with Rotenese 248,
249
records 1n.1, 65, 170, 173, 248,
250
resistance to 64, 148, 261n.14
see also Netherlands

Dutch East India Company 39, 47,
61, 63, 248, 250, 262
and religion 247, 248, 262
in Termanu 64, 170, 249, 261, 262
in Thie 1n.1, 170, 173, 249n.2,
261–2
in Timor 39, 64, 248, 249n.2
intermarriage with Rotenese 248,
249
recognition of domains 1n.1, 37,
64, 170, 269

Dutch East Indies Government 2

dyeing
container for indigo dye 3, 76,
152–67, 294
knowledge of 32, 38, 71, 139–40,
142, 144, 146, 148–9, 151,
165, 325, 328
origin of 3, 32, 58, 71, 75, 133,
134–52, 170
see also patterning of cloth

dyeing and weaving 26, 33, 47, 72, 76,
164–5, 237
and Christian metaphors 254
in Landu 146
in Loleh 142
see also patterning of cloth; weaving

European 247

Evangelical Church 263, 270
  see also Christianity

Fanggidaej, J. 252, 254, 260, 261n.13,
  261n.14
Feo Soru 171
fire
  knowledge of 31
  origins of in Termanu 76–83,
    86–96, 97–104, 105–11, 172,
    299
  origins of in Thie 181–245
  Sea as source of 31
  use for cooking 31, 58, 75, 87, 94,
    106, 107, 185–6
fire tools 75, 82–3, 90, 103, 107,
  185–6, 187, 259
  firestick and flintstone 82, 107
  flintstone and fire-drill 90, 103,
    185, 186, 187
Flores 21, 22, 248
Foe Mbura/Benjamin Mesak 173, 250
Foeh, G.A. 174
Foeh, Hendrik **318**
Fola-Teik 64, 65
food, *see* cooking; millet; rice
Fort Henricus 248

genealogical names, *see* names—
  genealogical
Gilgamesh 6
Graafland, N. 251–2
Guru Pah, *see* Pah, N.D.

Hebrew 4, 6, 11–12, 13
Heijmering, G. 251, 254n.10
Helong 41
Henu Lai 171
Holi ceremony 215–16, 225, 226–7,
  231
Holm, David 18, 19–20
Holy Spirit, *see* Christianity—Holy
  Spirit

house, of Sun and Moon 56, 84, 92,
  118, 173, 186, 190–202
house-building 69, 71, 84, 103, 173,
  175–6
  and Christianity 176, 194, 259,
    290, 293, 294
  origin of tools for 31, 58, 75, 82,
    90, 112, 187, 196, 259
  rituals for in Termanu 26, 72
  rituals for in Thie 199, 207
houses 21, 32, 43, 92
  and cosmic order 32, 34
  and familial relations 42–3, 50
  and rituals 48, 156, 199
  origins 3, 56, 58, 69, 290, 293,
    294
  origins in Termanu 75–167, 169,
    172, 293
  origins in Thie 169, 172, 175–6,
    178, 190–202
  ritual language 43
  Sea as origin of 31, 79, 87, 196, 294

implements for living 75, 76–85,
  90–4, 103–4, 107, 112, 172, 259
  see also tools
Inca 5
indigo, container for 3, 76, 152–67,
  294
  see also dyeing, patterning of cloth
Iu, Yulius (Pak Yulius) 270, 271–82,
  292, **314**, 315, **318**

Jakarta 174, 248n.1
  see also Batavia
Joko Widodo 281
Jonker, J.C.G. 37n.7, 260–1, 295n.23

Kana Ketu 171, 172
Keka 129, 142, 252, 268, 327, 329
  ritual names for 39, 331
Keka Dulu 171, 172
Kola 122
Kolek 171

Kona 171, 172
Korbaffo 40, 121, 122, 146, 248, 249,
    268, 327, 329
    ritual names for 39, 40, 146, 332
Kota Deak 64
Kota Leleuk 64, 261n.14, 262
Kuli 40
Kupang 41, 64, 248, 249, 250, 251,
    261, 263n.15, 278, 317

Landu 155, 171, 249n.2, 254, 281,
    299, 315, 328, 329
    and Christianity 267, 268, 270,
        281, 331
    arrival of rice and millet 120, 133,
        215, 330
    knowledge of dyeing and weaving
        146
    ritual names for 39, 332
Landu Kona 176, 195, 214, 215, 330
Langga Ledo 171
Le Bruijn, Dr R. 251
Le Grand, G.J.H. 252, 253, 255
Le'e 171, 172
Lelain 142, 269, 329
    ritual names for 39, 332
Lelenuk 129, 148, 149, 268, 327, 329
    ritual names for 39, 129, 331
Limba ceremony 172, 179, 215–16,
    223–4, 225, 226–7, 231, 238
Loleh 40, 71, 135, 136, 249n.2, 261,
    262, 327, 329
    and Christianity 174, 249, 265, 267
    arrival of rice and millet 128–9
    dyeing and weaving 142
    ritual names for 39, 40, 128, 331
loom
    origin of 71, 75
    ritual language 47
    transfer of knowledge of 71, 133,
        134, 138, 140, 146, 328
    see also shuttle, weaving
Lowth, Robert 4, 5n.2, 6, 12, 17

Ma Bulan 63
Makassar 261
Malay 64, 250–2, 253, 255, 261n.14,
    303
Malesi, Petrus (Peu) 41n.10, 66, 67,
    68, 76–85, 119–33, 256–7, 259,
    260, 272, 274, 299, **300**, 301,
    305, 331n.5
Man'Dato 171
Manu'ain, Lazaar Tioek 255, 256
Masa-Huk 64, 65, 73
Maya 5, 13–16, 23
    see also Mesoamerica; Quiché
Mbura Lai 171, 172, 249n.2, 250n.3
Mbura Mesa, see Poura Messa
Meo Leok 171, 172
Meo Umbuk 171
Mesa Feo 171
Mesoamerica 13–14
    see also Aztec; Maya; Nahuatl;
        Quiché
Mesopotamia 6–7, 13
Messa Poura (Mesa Mbura) 173
Messakh 173
Messakh, Jeremias 249n.2
Middle East 5, 11
    see also Sumer; Syro-Palestinian
millet 31, 46, 54, 120, 208, 325
    as pair with maize 46, 119, 160–1
    as pair with sorghum 46
    cooking of 45, 94, 95, 100, 108
    cultivation of 45, 77, 81
    eating of 94, 95, 100, 108, 222,
        223, 239
    importance as food 45, 46, 58
    origin narratives 45, 46, 58, 75,
        119–33, 169–70, 172, 177,
        178, 179, 210–24
    origin of red millet 117–19, 170
    origins of in Termanu 3, 46,
        117–19, 124–6, 169–70, 172,
        178, 294
    origins of in Thie 169–70, 172, 177,
        178, 179, 210–24, 267, 294

paired with pork and civet 94, 95,
100, 108
planting narratives 26, 72, 146,
169–70, 177, 179, 223, 267,
294, 325, 326, 330
preparation of 80, 100, 112
ritual importance 46, 58
rituals for 72, 156, 223, 226, 231
tools for preparation of 82, 90
topogeny 169–70, 326, 330
see also rice
Moka Leok 171
Moluccas 41n.11
Mongolian 5
Mooy, Jonas 178, 179, 216–24, **312**,
313, 315, **318**
mortar and pestle 23, 31, 82, 83, 90,
91, 113, 188–9, 281
Musu Hu 171, 172

Nahuatl 5n.2, 13
see also Mesoamerica
name-giving 48, 49, 257, 322
names 11, 261, 262, 272
as subject of contention 10, 36, 37,
68–9, 157, 305
Christian 48, 173, 248, 249, 254,
257
dual 8–10, 36–7, 68–9, 153, 193,
257, 305, 321, 322, 326
for Diu 131
for Thie 1n.1
genealogical 9, 38, 48, 49, 68,
152, 158, 173, 193, 196, 203,
250n.3
interpretation of 36–41, 89, 120
of clans 64, 65
significance of 36–7, 68–70, 325
see also personal names,
placenames, ritual names
Nate Feo 171, 172
Ndana Feo 171

Ndao 37, 41, 71–2, 135–40, 170, 225,
227, 228, 233, 234–7, 267, 269,
328, 329
ritual names for 39, 41, 225, 331,
332
Ndaomanu Sinlae, 249
Ndun, Samuel 177–8, 181–9,
194–210, 309, **310**, 311
Netherlands 253, 261n.13
see also Dutch
Netherlands Mission Society
(Nederlandsche Zending
Genootschap) 250, 252n.6
Nggau Pandi 171, 172

Oenale 39, 40, 126, 127–8, 140, 269,
295n.23, 327, 329
ritual names for 39, 40, 127, 332
Oepao 131–2, 146, 268, 328, 329
ritual names for 39, 146, 331
'Old Meno' (Stefanus Adulanu), see
Adulanu, Stefanus ('Old Meno')
Old Testament 4
see also Bible
oral scripture 2, 3–5, 11, 19
origins
of cloth patterning 3, 32, 58, 75,
170, 294
of cooking 3, 58, 76–85, 86–96,
97–104, 105–12, 259
of cooking in Termanu 75–168,
172, 299
of cooking in Thie 172, 181–87,
189
of dyeing 3, 32, 58, 71, 75, 133,
134–52, 170
of fire 31, 58
of fire in Termanu 76–83, 86–96,
97–104, 105–11, 172, 299
of fire in Thie 181–245
of fire use for cooking 31, 87, 94,
106, 107, 185–6

of house-building tools 31, 58, 75,
    82, 90, 103, 112, 113, 114,
    187, 196, 259
of houses 3, 56, 58, 69, 290, 293,
    294
of loom 71, 75
of shuttle 71
of spindle 76, 152–67, 294
of tools for creation of fire 75,
    82–3, 90, 103, 107, 185–6,
    187, 259
of weaving 3, 26, 32, 47, 58, 71–2,
    134–52, 165, 170
origin narratives
    millet 45, 46, 58, 75, 119–33,
        169–70, 172, 177, 178, 179,
        210–24
    ice 45, 46, 75, 119–33, 172, 177,
        178, 179, 210–24, 267

Pacific 20
Pada Lalais 63, 64, 65, 303
Pah, N.D. (Guru Pah) 177, 178,
    181–216, 225–45, 255, **308**, 309,
    313
Pak Ande, see Ruy, Anderias
Pak Pono, see Pono, Esau
Pak Yulius, see Iu, Yulius
parallelism 4–8, 11, 12, 13–16, 17–27,
    29, 256, 263, 270, 294, 298, 299,
    315, 321, 323, 326
    'canonical' 2, 4, 5, 13, 29, 294,
        323
    'semantic' 4–5, 7, 17n.11, 22, 297,
        315
patterning of cloth 71, 270
    origins of 3, 32, 58, 75, 170, 294
    transfer of knowledge 71–2, 133,
        134–52, 328
    shark and crocodile 32, 71, 72,
        134–52, 328
    see also dyeing
Pello, Jon 66

Pellondou, Eli (Seu Ba'i) 67, 68, 94–6,
    304, 305
personal names 8, 36
    and status 42, 254, 289
    Christian 48, 173, 248, 249, 254,
        257
    genealogical 9, 38, 48, 49, 68,
        152, 158, 173, 193, 196, 203,
        250n.3
    insults to one's name 48
    see also names
pestle and mortar, see mortar and pestle
placenames 8, 34, 36, 38, 40–1, 68,
    126, 144, 148, 211, 222
    as topogeny 38, 70, 122, 169–70,
        209, 267, 321–32
plumbline marker and drill 82–3, 90,
    91, 112, 197, 198, 199
Pono, Esau (Pak Pono) iv, 41n.10, 67,
    68, 97–104, 263n.15, 266n.16,
    306, 307, **318**, 331n.5
Popol Vuh 13n.7, 15, 16
Poura Messa (Mbura Mesa) 173, 249,
    250

Quiché (K'iche') 13n.7, 15, 16
    see also Maya; Mesoamerica

Rabinal Achí 13n.7, 15, 16
rice 19, 21, 46, 50, 54, 59, 160, 283,
    284
rice and millet
    arrival in Landu 120, 133, 215,
        330
    arrival in Loleh 128–9
    cooking of 45, 94, 95, 100, 108
    cultivation of 45, 64, 77, 81, 124,
        125, 208, 222, 224, 261, 285
    eating of 94, 95, 100, 208, 222, 223
    importance as food 45, 46, 58
    knowledge of 31, 325, 326
    origin narratives 45, 46, 75,
        119–33, 172, 177, 178, 179,
        210–24, 267

origins in Termanu 3, 45, 169–70, 172, 294
origins in Thie 169–70, 172, 177, 178, 179, 210–24, 267, 294
paired with pork and civet 94, 95, 100, 108
planting narratives 26, 72, 146, 169, 223, 267, 294, 325, 326, 330
preparation 80, 100, 108, 112, 281
ritual importance 46
ritual names for 45, 120, 121, 122, 221
rituals for 72, 156, 158, 226, 231
tools for preparation of 82, 90
topogeny 169, 325, 326, 330
see also millet
Ringgou 131–2, 146, 254, 268, 270, 281, 285, 286, 299, 317, 328, 329
ritual names for 39, 131, 331
ritual language 23–6, 27, 29, 32–6, 42, 43, 44–7, 51, 57–8, 61, 63, 66, 68, 156, 174, 177, 253, 285, 286, 298, 299, 301, 303
and Christianity 252, 253–6, 262, 270, 274, 282, 288, 315
and dialects 24, 25, 178, 252, 254, 270, 281, 298, 299, 331
canonical pairs in 11, 23, 24, 25
dyadic sets in 24, 38, 40n.9, 41, 42, 44, 48–9, 55n.19, 57–8, 73n.4, 285, 289
interpretation of 36, 37, 39, 40, 120n.1, 270, 282
significance of names in 36, 37
Termanu 24, 42, 48, 55, 57, 66, 68–9, 73, 225, 285
Thie 24, 73n.4, 225
traditions of 36, 174, 178, 253, 257n.12, 270, 285
ritual names 36, 41, 42, 289
for Ba'a 39, 126, 330, 331
for Bilba 39, 131, 331
for Bokai 39, 40, 129, 130n.2, 331

for Delha 39, 40, 332
for Dengka 39, 40, 126, 332
for Diu 39–40, 331
for Keka 39, 331
for Kola 122
for Korbaffo 39, 40, 146, 332
for Landu 39, 332
for Lelain 39, 332
for Lelenuk 39, 129, 331
for Loleh 39, 40, 128, 331
for Ndao 39, 41, 225, 331, 332
for Oenale 39, 40, 127, 332
for Oepao 39, 146, 331
for rice and millet 45, 120, 121, 122, 221
for Ringgou 39, 131, 331
for Rote 32–3, 38, 222, 263, 328–31
for Rote's domains 36, 37–41, 122, 325, 326, 328, 331, 332
for Talae 39, 40, 129, 331
for Termanu 39, 45, 63, 65, 122, 126, 130n.2, 144, 325, 332
for Thie 39, 40, 327, 329, 330, 331
for Timor 41
rituals
for house-building in Termanu 26, 72
for house-building in Thie 199, 207
for houses 48, 156, 199
for millet 72, 156, 223, 226, 231
for rice 72, 156, 158, 226, 231
Termanu 26, 73–74, 172, 225
Thie 26, 54n.18, 74, 170–3, 178, 179, 207, 223, 225
see also Holi ceremony; *Limba* ceremony
Rote, ritual names for 32–3, 38, 222, 263, 328, 330, 331
Ruy, Anderias (Pak Ande) 270, 281, 282–91, 292, 293, 295, **316**, 317, **318**

Saba Lai 131, 132, 171, 328
Sabarai 171, 172, 176, 193, 194
Sandi 171
Savu 41, 237
scriptural
    text 11
    traditions 12
    voice 3–5, 12, 13, 17–18, 21, 22,
        25, 252–6, 263, 269–70
scripture 2, 17, 19, 20n.13
    Christian 247, 252–6, 263,
        269–70
    oral 2, 3–5, 11, 19
'semantic parallelism', see parallelism—
    'semantic'
semantics 8n.4, 11, 14n.9, 24n.14,
    25n.15, 36n.6, 57n.20, 247, 270,
    293
Semau 41
Seu Ba'i, see Pellondou, Eli
shuttle
    origin of 71
    ritual language 47
    transfer of knowledge of 71, 134,
        138, 140, 146, 328
    see also loom; weaving
Sino-Tibetan 20
Solor 248
Soru Umbuk 171
South-East Asia 5, 20–2, 296
spindle 47
    origin of 76, 152–67, 294
    see also weaving
spinning, of cloth 3, 47, 152, 164,
    167, 294
    see also weaving
Sua 171, 172
Sulawesi 21, 322
Sumba 21
Sumer 2, 5, 6, 7, 11, 323, 324
    see also Middle East
Syro-Palestinian 12, 23

Tai-Kadai 20
Talae 40, 129–31, 148, 149, 252, 268,
    327, 329
    ritual names for 39, 40, 129, 331
Taoist 20
Taratu 171, 172, 176, 193, 194
Teachers' Training School (School tot
    Opleiding van Indische Leraren, or
    STOVIL) 253, 255, 263n.15
ter Linden, J.K. 251
Termanu 1, 63–74, 75–167, 169–70,
    172, 177, 178, 179, 256, 261,
    266n.16, 268, 285, 293, 294, 295,
    298, 299, 303, 305, 307, 309
    and Christianity 249–50, 251, 252
    and Dutch East India Company
        64, 170, 249, 261, 262
    clans 64, 65, 67, 68, 73
    dialect 24–5, 36n.6, 203n.1, 252,
        261, 263n.15, 298
    Dutch education 250, 251
    Dutch in 64, 249n.2, 261n.14,
        303
    dyadic sets 24–5, 36n.6, 48, 55,
        57, 203n.1
    dynastic rule 42, 63–5, 170, 172,
        249–50, 251, 261–2, 303
    Lord of 63, 64
    origins of cloth patterning 3, 170
    origins of cooking 75–168, 172,
        299
    origins of dyeing 3, 170
    origins of fire 76–83, 86–96,
        97–104, 105–11, 172, 299
    origins of house 75–167, 169, 172,
        293
    origins of indigo container 3
    origins of rice and millet 3, 45, 46,
        170
    origins of spindle 3
    origins of weaving 3, 170
    ritual language 24, 42, 48, 55, 57,
        66, 68–9, 73, 225, 285

ritual names for 39, 45, 63, 65, 122, 126, 130n.2, 144, 325, 332
rituals 26, 73–74, 172, 225
topogeny 170, 325–31
Therik, Tom 263n.15
Thie 1, 169–79, 249–50, 266n.16, 309, 311, 313
and Dutch 64, 251, 262
and Dutch East India Company 1n.1, 170, 173, 249n.2, 261–2
Christianity 173–4, 175, 176, 177, 189, 249–50, 251, 263, 267, 331
clans 171–3, 193
dialect 24–25, 250n.3
moieties 171–2, 177, 193, 261,
origin narratives 3, 24, 26, 45n.16, 71, 169–79, 181–245, 261–2, 267, 294, 295n.24, 298, 299
origins of cooking 172, 181–87, 189
origins of fire 181–245
origins of house 169, 172, 175–6, 178, 190–202
origins of millet 169–70, 172, 177, 178, 179, 210–24, 267, 294
origins of rice 169–70, 172, 177, 178, 179, 210–24, 267, 294
ritual language 24, 73n.4, 225
ritual names for 39, 40, 327, 329–31
rituals 26, 54n.18, 74, 170–3, 178, 179, 207, 223, 225
ruling lineages 173–4, 176, 193, 219, 249, 250, 251, 261–2
Timor 21, 32, 39, 41, 64, 225, 250, 263, 321, 322n.1
and Dutch 64
and Dutch East India Company 39, 64, 248, 249n.2
Christianity in 249n.2, 250, 254, 263n.15
Evangelical Church of 263, 270

language 23, 254
names for 41
topogeny 322
Tode Feo 171
tools
axe and adze 31, 69, 82, 90, 103, 113–17, 187
base for spinning cloth 3, 152, 164, 167, 294
bore and chisel 31, 82, 83, 90, 91, 103–4, 112, 187, 188, 197, 198, 199
container for indigo dye 3, 76, 152–67, 294
firestick and flintstone 82, 107
flintstone and fire-drill 90, 103, 185, 186, 187
for agriculture 90, 112–13, 116, 187
for cooking 23, 31, 82, 83, 90, 91, 103, 113, 188–9, 259, 281
for creation of fire 75, 82–3, 90, 103, 107, 185–6, 187, 259
for gardening 75, 90
for house-building 31, 58, 75, 82, 90, 103, 112, 113, 114, 187, 196, 259
for preparation of millet 82, 90
for preparation of rice 82, 90
for weaving 32, 47, 71, 75, 133, 134, 138, 140, 146, 328
loom 47, 71, 75, 133, 134, 138, 140, 146, 328
mortar and pestle 23, 31, 82, 83, 90, 91, 113, 188–9, 281
plumbline marker and drill 82–3, 90, 91, 112, 197, 198, 199
shuttle 47, 71, 134, 138, 140, 146, 328
spindle 47, 76, 152–67, 294
see also implements for living
topogeny 38, 70, 122, 139, 169–70, 267, 321–32
of millet 169–70, 326, 330

of rice 169, 325, 326, 330
placenames as 38, 70, 122,
169–70, 209, 267, 321–32
Termanu 170, 325–31

Ur 323, 324
Uralic 5

Vietnam 18
Visscher, Gerhard Bernard 249

weaving 46–7, 72, 164–5
origin of 3, 26, 32, 47, 58, 71–2,
134–52, 165, 170
Sea as source of 31–2
tools for 32, 47, 71, 75, 133, 134,
138, 140, 146, 328
transfer of knowledge of 38, 71–2,
133, 134–52, 170, 325, 328
see also dyeing; indigo, container
for; loom; spinning, of cloth

Yucatecan 15

Zhuang 17, 18, 19–20

www.ingramcontent.com/pod-product-compliance
Lightning Source LLC
Chambersburg PA
CBHW070245290326
41929CB00047B/2598